A UNIVERSITY
GRAMMAR OF ENGLISH

A UNIVERSITY GRAMMAR OF ENGLISH

RANDOLPH QUIRK *University of London*
SIDNEY GREENBAUM *University of Wisconsin*

Based on *A Grammar of Contemporary English*
by Randolph Quirk, Sidney Greenbaum,
Geoffrey Leech, Jan Svartvik

LONGMAN

LONGMAN GROUP LIMITED
Longman House, Burnt Mill, Harlow,
Essex CM20, 2JE, England
and Associated Companies throughout the world

First published 1973
Thirteenth impression 1984
ISBN 0 582 55207 9

Printed in Hong Kong by
Commonwealth Printing Press Ltd

PREFACE

In preparing this shorter version of *A Grammar of Contemporary English*, our aim has been to satisfy the needs of university students who require the comprehensiveness of the original work but not its detail or extensive theoretical discussion or wealth of exemplification. But, insofar as it has been compatible with so curtailed a treatment, we have been careful to preserve the structure of the parent book so that reference to the fuller study can be easy and direct, chapter by chapter, as required.

In order to accommodate actual student needs in our treatment, we consulted a number of friends and colleagues all over the world: scholars with rich and varied experience of teaching English at institutions with widely different traditions; scholars whose opinion we valued on the kind of abridged *Grammar* that would best suit their students' needs. We are happy to acknowledge our gratitude to John Algeo (Georgia), M. A. G. Cerrudo (Buenos Aires), Rudolf Filipović (Zagreb), Jan Firbas (Brno), Denis Girard (Paris), Harold V. King (Michigan), Gerhard Nickel (Stuttgart), Wulf Praeger (Lörrach), Andrew Rogers (Texas), Alfred Schopf (Freiburg), and Takashi Shimaoka (Tokyo), all of whom studied *A Grammar of Contemporary English* in proof, with abridgment for student use in mind. Above all, we have benefited from the skilled and detailed guidance generously provided by R. A. Close (London) from his fund of university teaching experience in Japan, China, Czechoslovakia, Chile, Greece, and elsewhere.

Awareness of the correspondence with the parent book is taken for granted throughout the present treatment, and no reference is made to it in the bibliographical notes with which we conclude chapters. Nor do we refer in these chapter notes to other major descriptions of English (by Jespersen, Kruisinga, etc), though they are of course listed in the Bibliography, *pp* 462–4, in acknowledgment of their permanent relevance to grammatical studies and their contribution to our own research. For all grammarians draw freely on the work of their predecessors and at the same time use their new vantage point to see where fresh headway can be made. We have indeed precisely this double relation with *A Grammar of Contemporary English:* as well as producing an epitome of the larger work, we have taken the opportunity to improve the description in numerous respects. In this way, we have made the labour of the present enterprise as fruitful and stimulating to ourselves as we hope it will be rewarding to our students.

RQ SG

June 1973

PREFACE TO FIFTH IMPRESSION

For the hundreds of improvements incorporated since the first impression, we are in large measure indebted to colleagues all over the world who have presented us with detailed comments, whether in published reviews or in private communications. In particular, we should like to express our gratitude to Broder Carstensen, D. Crystal, R. Dirven, V. Fried, G. Guntram, R. R. K. Hartmann, R. A. Hudson, Y. Ikegami, R. Ilson, S. Jacobson, H. V. King, R. B. Long, André Moulin, Y. Murata, N. E. Osselton, M. Rensky, M. L. Samuels, Irène Simon, B. M. H. Strang, Gabriele Stein, M. Swan, J. Taglicht, and R. W. Zandvoort.

January 1976

CONTENTS

Six
Prepositions and prepositional phrases   143
*Place relations 146; Time relations 154; Other relations chiefly as
adjunct 157, as disjunct 162, as complementation of verb or adjective 163*

Seven
The simple sentence   166
*Clause patterns 166; Elements and their meanings 171; Concord 176;
Negation 183; Questions 191; Commands 200*

Eight
Adjuncts, disjuncts, conjuncts   207
*Limiter and additive adjuncts 211; Intensifiers 214; Adjuncts of manner,
means, and instrument 220, of place 224, of time 229; Style and
attitudinal disjuncts 242; Conjuncts 246*

Nine
Coordination and apposition   251
*Ellipsis 251; Coordination of clauses 254; Coordination of phrases 267;
Apposition 276; Non-restrictive apposition 278; Restrictive
apposition 282*

Ten
Sentence connection   284
*Time relaters 285; Logical connecters 287; Substitution 294;
Discourse reference 302; Ellipsis in dialogue 305*

Eleven
The complex sentence   309
*Finite, non-finite, and verbless clauses 310; Subordinators and
subordination 313; Nominal clauses 316; Adverbial clauses 322;
Comparative sentences 330; The verb phrase in dependent clauses 337;
Direct and indirect speech 341*

Twelve
The verb and its complementation   347
*Phrasal and prepositional verbs 347; Complementation of adjective
phrase 354; Units as direct object 358; Complex transitive
complementation 363; Ditransitive complementation 370*

SYMBOLS AND TECHNICAL CONVENTIONS

Since our use of symbols, abbreviations, and the like follows standard practice, all that we need here is a visual summary of the main conventions, with a brief explanation or a reference to where fuller information is given.

4.37; App I.12:
: *Cross-references are given by chapter (or appendix) and section number.*

AmE, BrE:
: *American English, British English (cf 1.6).*

S, V, O, C, A, O_1, etc.:
: *See 2.5 ff; when italicized, strings of these symbols refer to the clause types explained in 7.2.*

a ˈbetter GRÀMMar|:
: *Capitals in examples indicate nuclear syllables, accents indicate the intonation, raised verticals indicate stress, and long verticals tone unit boundaries: see App II.2 ff, 7 ff.*

*a more better one:
: *A preceding asterisk indicates an unacceptable structure.*

?they seem fools:
: *A preceding question mark indicates doubtful acceptability; combined with an asterisk it suggests virtual unacceptability.*

Help me (to) write:
: *Parentheses indicate optional items.*

Bolinger (1971):
: *References at the end of a chapter are expanded in the Bibliography, pp 462 ff.*

He came $\begin{Bmatrix} \text{to} \\ \text{from} \end{Bmatrix} \begin{Bmatrix} \text{London} \\ \text{New York} \end{Bmatrix}$
: *Curved braces indicate free alternatives*

$\begin{bmatrix} \text{He} \\ \text{She} \end{bmatrix}$ does $\begin{bmatrix} \text{his} \\ \text{her} \end{bmatrix}$ best:

Square brackets indicate contingent alternatives: eg selection of the top one in the first pair entails selection of the top one in the second also.

{His [expensive (house insurance)]}:

Contrasts in bracketing give a linear indication of hierarchical structure.

/ɪz/, /z/, /s/:

Slants enclose phonemic transcriptions, usually of inflections. The symbols have widely familiar values: /ɪ/ *as in* bid, /i/ *as in* beat, /z/ *as in* zip, /ə/ *as in the first syllable of* alone, *etc.*

ONE
VARIETIES OF ENGLISH

1.1
Variety classes

There are numerous varieties of the English language, and what we ordinarily mean by 'English' is a common core or nucleus which is realized only in the different forms of the language that we actually hear or read. We can distinguish six kinds of varieties ranged as below and interrelated in ways we shall attempt to explain.

THE COMMON CORE OF ENGLISH

VARIETY CLASSES	VARIETIES WITHIN EACH CLASS
Region:	$R_1, R_2, R_3, R_4, \ldots$
Education and social standing:	$E_1, E_2, E_3, E_4, \ldots$
Subject matter:	$S_1, S_2, S_3, S_4, \ldots$
Medium:	$M_1, M_2, \ldots$
Attitude:	$A_1, A_2, A_3, A_4, \ldots$
Interference:	$I_1, I_2, I_3, I_4, \ldots$

The fact that in this figure the 'common core' dominates all the varieties means that, however esoteric or remote a variety may be, it has running through it a set of grammatical and other characteristics that are common to all. From this initial point onwards, it is claimed by the sets of braces that each variety class is related equally and at all points to each of the other variety classes. We shall however return and make qualifications to this claim. The classes themselves are arranged in a meaningful order and the justification will become clear in what follows.

Regional variation
1.2
Varieties according to region have a well-established label both in popular and technical use: 'dialects'. Geographical dispersion is in fact the classic basis for linguistic variation, and in the course of time, with poor communications and relative remoteness, such dispersion results in dialects becoming so distinct that we regard them as different languages. This latter stage was long ago reached with the Germanic dialects that are now Dutch, English, German, Swedish, etc, but it has not been reached (and may not necessarily ever be reached, given the modern ease of communication) with the dialects of English that have resulted from the regional separation of English-speaking communities both within the British Isles and throughout the world.

Regional variation seems to be realized predominantly in phonology. That is, we generally recognize a different dialect from a speaker's pronunciation before we notice that his vocabulary (or lexicon) is also distinctive. Grammatical variation tends to be less extensive and certainly less obtrusive. But all types of linguistic organization can readily enough be involved.

1.3
It is pointless to ask how many dialects of English there are: there are indefinitely many, depending solely on how detailed we wish to be in our observations. But they are of course more obviously numerous in the long-settled Britain than in the more recently settled North America or in the still more recently settled Australia and New Zealand. The degree of generality in our observation depends crucially upon our standpoint as well as upon our experience. An Englishman will hear an American Southerner primarily as an American and only as a Southerner in addition if further subclassification is called for and if his experience of American English dialects enables him to make it. To an American the same speaker will be heard first as a Southerner and then (subject to similar conditions) as, say, a Virginian, and then perhaps as a Piedmont Virginian. One might suggest some broad dialectal divisions which are rather generally recognized. Within North America, most people would be able to distinguish Canadian, New England, Midland, and Southern varieties of English. Within the British Isles, Irish, Scots, Northern, Midland,

Welsh, South-western, and London varieties would be recognized with similar generality. Some of these – Irish and Scots for example – would be recognized as such by many Americans and Australians too, while in Britain many people could make subdivisions: Ulster and Southern might be distinguished within Irish, for example, and Yorkshire picked out as a subdivision of northern speech. British people can also, of course, distinguish North Americans from all others (though not usually Canadians from Americans), South Africans from Australians and New Zealanders (though mistakes are frequent), but not usually Australians from New Zealanders.

1.4
Education and social standing
Within each of the dialect areas, there is considerable variation in speech according to education and social standing. There is an important polarity of uneducated and educated speech in which the former can be identified with the regional dialect most completely and the latter moves away from dialectal usage to a form of English that cuts across dialectal boundaries. On the other hand, there is no simple equation of dialectal and uneducated English. Just as educated English cuts across dialectal boundaries, so do many features of uneducated use: a prominent example is the double negative as in *I don't want no cake*, which has been outlawed from all educated English by the prescriptive grammar tradition for hundreds of years but which continues to thrive in uneducated speech wherever English is spoken.

Educated speech – by definition the language of education – naturally tends to be given the additional prestige of government agencies, the learned professions, the political parties, the press, the law court and the pulpit – any institution which must attempt to address itself to a public beyond the smallest dialectal community. The general acceptance of 'BBC English' for this purpose over almost half a century is paralleled by a similar designation for general educated idiom in the United States, 'network English'. By reason of the fact that educated English is thus accorded implicit social and political sanction, it comes to be referred to as Standard English, and provided we remember that this does not mean an English that has been formally standardized by official action, as weights and measures are standardized, the term is useful and appropriate. In contrast with Standard English, forms that are especially associated with uneducated (rather than dialectal) use are often called 'substandard'.

1.5
Standard English
The degree of acceptance of a single standard of English throughout the

world, across a multiplicity of political and social systems, is a truly remarkable phenomenon: the more so since the extent of the uniformity
involved has, if anything, increased in the present century. Uniformity is
greatest in what is from most viewpoints the relatively unimportant
matter of spelling. Although printing houses in all English-speaking
countries retain a tiny area of individual decision (some preferring -*ise*
and others -*ize* in words like *realise*; some preferring *judgment* and
others *judgement*; etc), there is basically a single system, with two minor
subsystems. The one is the subsystem with British orientation (used in
all English-speaking countries except the United States) with distinctive
forms in only a small class of words, *colour, centre, levelled*, etc. The
other is the American subsystem: *color, center, leveled*, etc. In Canada,
the British subsystem is used for the most part, but some publishers
(especially of popular material) follow the American subsystem and
some a mixture (*color* but *centre*). In the American Mid-West, some
newspaper publishers (but not book publishers) use a few additional
separate spellings such as *thru* for *through*.

In grammar and vocabulary, Standard English presents somewhat less
of a monolithic character, but even so the world-wide agreement is extraordinary and – as has been suggested earlier – seems actually to be increasing under the impact of closer world communication and the spread
of identical culture, both material and non-material. The uniformity is
especially close in neutral or formal styles (1.12) of written English (1.11)
on subject matter (1.10) not of obviously localized interest: in such
circumstances one can frequently go on for page after page without
encountering a feature which would identify the English as belonging to
one of the *national standards*.

National standards of English
1.6
British and American English
There are two national standards that are overwhelmingly predominant
both in the number of distinctive usages and in the degree to which these
distinctions are 'institutionalized': American English and British
English. Grammatical differences are few and the most conspicuous are
widely known; the fact that AmE has two past participles for *get* and BrE
only one (3.14), for example, and that in BrE the indefinite pronoun
one is repeated in co-reference where AmE uses *he* as in

One cannot succeed at this unless $\begin{Bmatrix} \text{one} \\ \text{he} \end{Bmatrix}$ tries hard

Lexical examples are far more numerous, but many of these are familiar
to users of both standards: for example, *railway* (BrE), *railroad* (AmE);

tap (BrE), *faucet* (AmE); *autumn* (BrE), *fall* (AmE). More recent lexical innovations in either area tend to spread rapidly to the other. Thus while radio sets have had *valves* in BrE but *tubes* in AmE, television sets have cathode ray *tubes* in both, and *transistors* are likewise used in both standards.

1.7
Scotland, Ireland, Canada
Scots, with ancient national and educational institutions, is perhaps nearest to the self-confident independence of BrE and AmE, though the differences in grammar and vocabulary are rather few. Irish (or Hiberno-) English should also be regarded as a national standard, for though we lack descriptions of this long-standing variety of English it is consciously and explicitly regarded as independent of BrE by educational and broadcasting services. The proximity of Britain, the easy movement of population, and like factors mean however that there is little room for the assertion and development of separate grammar and vocabulary.

Canadian English is in a similar position in relation to AmE. Close economic, social, and intellectual links along a 4000-mile frontier have naturally caused the larger community to have an enormous influence on the smaller, not least in language. Though in many respects Canadian English follows British rather than United States practice, in many other respects it has approximated to AmE and seems likely to continue in this direction.

1.8
South Africa, Australia, New Zealand
South Africa, Australia and New Zealand are in a very different position, remote from the direct day-to-day impact of either BrE or AmE. While in orthography and grammar the South African English in educated use is virtually identical with BrE, rather considerable differences in vocabulary have developed.

New Zealand English is more like BrE than any other non-European variety, though it now feels the powerful influence of Australia and – to no small degree – of the United States.

Australian English is undoubtedly the dominant form of English in the Antipodes, and it is even exerting an influence in the northern hemisphere, particularly in Britain, though much of what is distinctive in Australian English is confined to familiar use.

1.9
Pronunciation and Standard English
This list does not exhaust the regional or national variants that approximate to the status of a standard (the Caribbean might be mentioned, for

example), but the important point to stress is that all of them are remarkable primarily in the trivial extent to which even the most firmly established, BrE and AmE, differ from each other in vocabulary, grammar, and spelling. We have been careful, however, not to mention pronunciation in this connection. Pronunciation distinguishes one national standard from another most immediately and completely, and links in a most obvious way the national standards to the regional varieties.

In BrE, one type of pronunciation comes close to enjoying the status of 'standard': 'Received Pronunciation' or 'RP'. Because this has been largely associated with a private education system based upon boarding schools insulated from the locality in which they happen to have been situated, it is significantly non-regional and of considerable prestige. But RP no longer has the unique authority it had in the first half of the twentieth century.

1.10
Varieties according to subject matter

Varieties according to the subject matter involved in a discourse are sometimes referred to as 'registers'. While one does not exclude the possibility that a given speaker may choose to speak in a national standard at one moment and in a regional dialect the next – and possibly even switch from one national standard to another – the presumption has been that an individual adopts one of the varieties so far discussed as his permanent form of English. With varieties according to subject matter, on the other hand, the presumption is rather that the same speaker has a repertoire of varieties and habitually switches to the appropriate one as occasion arises. Most typically, perhaps, the switch involves nothing more than turning to the particular set of lexical items habitually used for handling the subject in question: law, cookery, engineering, football.

Although in principle the type of language required by a particular subject matter would be roughly constant against the variables already discussed (dialect, national standard), the use of a specific variety of one class frequently presupposes the use of a specific variety of another. A well-formed *legal* sentence, for example, presupposes an *educated* variety of English.

1.11
Varieties according to medium

The only varieties according to medium that we need to consider are those conditioned by *speaking* and *writing* respectively. Most of the differences involved arise from two sources. One is situational: the use of a written medium normally presumes the absence of the person(s) to whom the piece of language is addressed. This imposes the necessity of a far greater explicitness: the careful and precise completion of a sentence, rather than the odd word, supported by gesture, and terminating when the speaker is assured by word or look that his hearer has understood.

The second source of difference is that many of the devices we use to transmit language by speech (stress, rhythm, intonation, tempo, for example) are impossible to represent with the crudely simple repertoire of conventional orthography. They are difficult enough to represent even with a special prosodic notation: *cf* App II. This means that the writer has often to reformulate his sentences if he is to convey fully and successfully what he wants to express within the orthographic system.

1.12
Varieties according to attitude

Varieties according to attitude are often called 'stylistic', but 'style' like 'register' is a term which is used with several different meanings. We are here concerned with the choice of linguistic form that proceeds from our attitude to the hearer (or reader), to the subject matter, or to the purpose of our communication. And we postulate that the essential aspect of the non-linguistic component (that is, the attitude) is the gradient between stiff, formal, cold, impersonal on the one hand and relaxed, informal, warm, friendly on the other. It is useful to pursue the notion of the 'common core' (1.1) here, so that we can acknowledge a neutral or unmarked variety of English, bearing no obvious colouring that has been induced by attitude. On each side of this, we can then distinguish sentences containing features that are markedly formal or informal. In this book, we shall for the most part confine ourselves to this three-term distinction, leaving the middle one unlabelled and specifying only usages that are relatively formal or informal:

(rigid ~) FORMAL ~ (neutral) ~ INFORMAL (~ familiar)

1.13
Varieties according to interference

Varieties according to interference should be seen as being on a very different basis from the other types of variety discussed. In this case, we refer to the trace left by someone's native language upon the foreign language he has acquired. Thus, the Frenchman who says 'I am here since Thursday' is imposing a French grammatical usage on English; the Russian who says 'There are four assistants in our chair of mathematics' is imposing a Russian lexico-semantic usage on the English word 'chair'. But there are interference varieties that are so widespread

in a community and of such long standing that they may be thought
stable and adequate enough to be regarded as varieties of English in their
own right rather than stages on the way to a more native-like English.
There is active debate on these issues in India, Pakistan and several
African countries, where efficient and fairly stable varieties of English
are prominent in educated use at the highest political and professional
level.

1.14
Relationship between variety classes

In presenting the table of varieties in a schematic relationship (1.1),
reference was made to each stratum of varieties being equally related to
all others. But, as we have seen, there are limitations to this. Since writing is an educated art, we shall not expect to find other than educated
English of one or other national standard in this medium. Indeed, when
we try on occasion to represent regional or uneducated English in
writing, we realize how narrowly geared to Standard English are our
graphic conventions. For the same reason there are some subjects that
can scarcely be handled in writing and others (*eg* legal statutes) that
can scarcely be handled in speech.

Attitudinal varieties have a great deal of independence in relation to
other varieties: it is possible to be formal or informal on biochemistry or
politics in AmE or BrE, for example. But informal or casual language
across an 'authority gap' or 'seniority gap' (a student talking to an arch-
bishop) presents difficulties, and on certain topics (funerals) it would be
unthinkably distasteful. An attempt at formal or rigid language when
the subject is courtship or football would seem comic at best.

Our approach in this book is to keep our sights firmly fixed on the
COMMON CORE which constitutes the major part of any variety of
English, however specialized, and without which fluency in any variety
at a higher than parrot level is impossible. Only at points where a
grammatical form is being discussed which is associated with a specific
variety will mention be made of the fact that the form is no longer of the
common core. The varieties chiefly involved on such occasions will be
AmE and BrE; speech and writing; formal and informal.

1.15
Varieties within a variety

Two final points need to be made. First, the various conditioning factors
(region, medium, attitude, for example) have no *absolute* effect: one
should not expect a consistent all-or-nothing response to the demands of
informality or whatever the factor may be. The conditioning is real but
relative and variable. Secondly, when we have done all we can to account

for the choice of one rather than another linguistic form, we are still left
with a margin of variation that cannot with certainty be explained in
terms of the parameters set forth in 1.1 and discussed in subsequent
paragraphs.

For example, we can say (or write)

He stayed a week	*or*	He stayed for a week
Two fishes	*or*	Two fish
Had I known	*or*	If I had known

without either member of such pairs being necessarily linked to any of
the varieties that we have specified. We may sometimes have a clear impression that one member seems rarer than another, or relatively old-
fashioned, but although a rare or archaic form is likelier in relatively
formal rather than in relatively informal English, we cannot always make
such an identification. All societies are constantly changing their languages with the result that there are always coexistent forms, the one
relatively new, the other relatively old; and some members of a society
will be temperamentally disposed to use the new (perhaps by their youth)
while others are comparably inclined to the old (perhaps by their age).
But many of us will not be consistent either in our choice or in our tem-
peramental disposition. Perhaps English may give rise to such fluctua-
tion more than some other languages because of its patently mixed
nature: a basic Germanic wordstock, stress pattern, word-formation,
inflection and syntax overlaid with a classical and Romance wordstock,
stress pattern, word-formation – and even inflection and syntax. The extent to which even highly educated people will treat the Latin and Greek
plurals in *data* and *criteria* as singulars or will use *different to* and *averse
to* rather than *different from* and *averse from* – and face objections from
other native speakers of English – testifies to the variable acknowledgment that classical patterns of inflection and syntax (Latin *differre ab*, 'to
differ *from*'; *aversus ab*, 'averse *from*') apply within English grammar.
It is one of the senses in which English is to be regarded as the most
international of languages and it adds noticeably to the variation in
English usage with which a grammar must come to terms.

Bibliographical Note
On varieties of English, see Crystal and Davy (1969); McDavid-Mencken (1963);
Quirk (1972); Turner (1973).

TWO
ELEMENTS OF GRAMMAR

2.1

The purpose of this chapter is to explore certain outstanding features of English structure in such a way as to provide, as it were, a small-scale map of areas that will be viewed in much greater detail in later chapters. As with any small-scale map, a great many features will be ignored and complicated contours will be smoothed out. The reader's attention will not be distracted even by forward references to the parts of the book in which the focus will allow such complication to become visible. But to compensate for the disadvantages in this degree of oversimplification, we have hoped to achieve the advantages of the geographical analogue as well. In other words, we have tried to provide enough broad information to enable the reader to understand – and place in a wider context – the more detailed discussion that subsequent chapters involve.

Parts of a sentence
2.2
Subject and predicate

In order to state general rules about the construction of sentences, it is constantly necessary to refer to smaller units than the sentence itself. Our first task must therefore be to explain what these smaller units are that we need to distinguish, confining our attention for the present to a few sentences which, though showing considerable variety, are all of fairly elementary structure.

Traditionally, there is a primary distinction between SUBJECT and PREDICATE:

John	carefully searched the room	[1]
The girl	is now a student at a large university	[2]
His brother	grew happier gradually	[3]
It	rained steadily all day	[4]
He	had given the girl an apple	[5]
They	make him the chairman every year	[6]

Although such a division obviously results in parts which are (in these examples) very unequal in size and dissimilar in content, it is of course by no means arbitrary. The subject of the sentence has a close general relation to 'what is being discussed', the 'theme' of the sentence, with the normal implication that something new (the predicate) is being said about a 'subject' that has already been introduced in an earlier sentence. This is of course a general characteristic and not a defining feature: it is patently absurd in relation to sentence [4], for example. Another point is that the subject determines concord. That is, with those parts of the verb that permit a distinction between singular and plural, the form selected depends on whether the subject is singular as in [2], *the girl is*, or plural as in [6], *they make*.

Furthermore, the subject is the part of the sentence that changes its position as we go from statement to question:

Had *he* given the girl an apple? [5q]

2.3
Operator, auxiliary, and predication
In contrast with the subject, there are few generalizations that we can usefully make about the predicate since – as our examples have illustrated – it tends to be a more complex and heterogeneous unit. We need to subdivide it into its elements or constituents. One division has already been suggested; this distinguishes AUXILIARY as OPERATOR (as in [5q]) from what we may call the PREDICATION. The distinctions may be illustrated as follows:

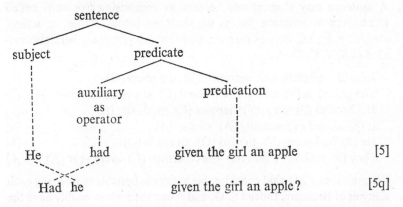

This particular division of the sentence helps us to understand, for example, how interrogative and negative sentences are formed, how certain adjuncts are positioned, and how certain types of emphasis are achieved.

2.4
Range of operators
The verb expression may have several auxiliaries; *eg*

He *should have been questioned* by the police

In such cases, it is the first auxiliary that acts as operator:

Should he have been questioned by the police?
No, he *shouldn't* have been questioned by the police
Yes, he *should*

Where the verb expression has no auxiliary in the positive declarative sentence, *do* is introduced when an operator is required:

It *rained* steadily all day
Did it rain steadily all day?
No, it *didn't*

The verb *be* can act as operator whether it is an auxiliary, as in

John *is* searching the room ~ *Is* John searching . . . ?

or not, as in

The girl *is* now a student ~ *Is* the girl now . . . ?

The same is true to some extent (especially in BrE) for *have:*

He *has* a degree ~ *Has* he a degree?

2.5
Sentence elements
A sentence may alternatively be seen as comprising five units called ELEMENTS of sentence (or, as we shall see below, clause) structure: SUBJECT, VERB, COMPLEMENT, OBJECT, ADVERBIAL, here abbreviated as S, V, C, O, A:

John (S) carefully (A) searched (V) the room (O)   [1]
The girl (S) is (V) now (A) a student (C) at a large university (A) [2]
His brother (S) grew (V) happier (C) gradually (A)   [3]
It (S) rained (V) steadily (A) all day (A)   [4]
He (S) had given (V) the girl (O) an apple (O)   [5]
They (S) make (V) him (O) the chairman (C) every year (A)   [6]

We shall see in 2.11 that considerable variety is possible in realizing each element of structure. Indeed S, O, and A can themselves readily have the internal constituents of sentences:

She (S) saw (V) that [*it* (S) *rained* (V) *all day* (A)] (O)   [7]
His brother (S) grew (V) happier (C) when [*his friend* (S)
     arrived (V)](A)   [8]

That [*she* (S) *answered* (V) *the question* (O) *correctly* (A)] (S)
pleased (V) him (O) enormously (A)   [9]

The italicizing is intended to emphasize the similarity between subordinate (or dependent) clauses and independent sentences. At the same
time this and the bracketing can interestingly suggest that *when* in [8]
and *that* in [7] and [9] operate as A, O, and S respectively (though this is
only partly true) while more importantly being themselves 'expanded'
by the dependent clauses.

2.6
Complements and objects

The relation between *the room* in illustration [1] and the other elements
in that sentence is very different from the relation between *the girl* in [5]
and its fellow elements, though both are labelled 'object'. Even more
obviously, perhaps, the two elements labelled 'object' in [5] play
sharply distinct roles in this sentence. We need in fact to distinguish two
types of object and two types of complement in the sentences so far
illustrated:

object $\begin{cases} \text{direct object } (O_d) \\ \text{indirect object } (O_i) \end{cases}$

complement $\begin{cases} \text{subject complement } (C_s) \\ \text{object complement } (C_o) \end{cases}$

The direct object is illustrated in

John carefully searched *the room* (O_d)   [1]
He had given the girl *an apple* (O_d)   [5]

The direct object is by far the more frequent kind of object, and (with
certain outstanding exceptions) it must always be present if there is an
indirect object in the sentence:

He had given *the girl* (O_i) an apple   [5]

As here, the indirect object almost always precedes the direct object; it is
characteristically (though by no means always) a noun referring to a
person, and the semantic relationship is often such that it is appropriate
to use the term 'recipient'. Loosely, one might say in most cases that
something (the direct object) tends to be done for (or received by) the
indirect object.

Turning to complements, we may illustrate first the subject complement:

The girl is now *a student* (C_s) at a large university   [2]
His brother grew *happier* (C_s) gradually   [3]

Here the complements have a straightforward relation to the subjects of
their respective sentences such that the subject of [2] is understood as
being a 'girl student' and the subject of [3] a 'happier brother'. The
'object complement' can be explained as having a similar relation to a
direct object (which it follows) as the subject complement has to a subject:

They make him *the chairman* (C_o) every year   [6]

That is to say, the direct object and object complement in this example,
'him the chairman', correspond to the subject and subject complement in

He is *the chairman* (C_s)

Categories of verb
2.7
There are different types of verb corresponding closely to the different
types of object and complement. Sentences such as [2] and [3], which
have subject complements, have INTENSIVE verbs and all other sentences have EXTENSIVE verbs. The latter are INTRANSITIVE if as in

It rained steadily all day   [4]

they do not permit any of the four object and complement types so far
distinguished. Extensive verbs are otherwise TRANSITIVE. All transitive
verbs take a direct object; some, like *give* in [5], permit an indirect
object, and these will be distinguished as DITRANSITIVE. A few verbs,
like *make* in [6], take an object complement and these are among the
verbs referred to as COMPLEX TRANSITIVE. The rest are MONO-
TRANSITIVE.

2.8
But distinctions between verbs need to be drawn not only in relation to
object- and complement-types but also in relation to whether they themselves admit the aspectual contrast of 'progressive' and 'non-progressive'. Thus it is possible to say

John carefully *searched* the room   [1]
or   John *was* carefully *searching* the room

It *rained* steadily all day   [4]
or   It was *raining* steadily all day

But it is not possible to use the progressive in

The girl *is* now a student at a large university   [2]
    *The girl *is* now *being* a student ...
John *knew* the answer   [10]
    *John *was knowing* the answer

When verbs (either habitually or in certain uses) will not admit the progressive, as in [2] and [10], they are called STATIVE. When they will admit it, as in [1] and [4], they are called DYNAMIC. It is normal for verbs to be dynamic and even the minority that are almost always stative can usually be given a dynamic use on occasion. See further, 2.16.

2.9
Categories of adverbial

Next we may take a preliminary look at adverbials, concerning ourselves only with such distinctions as are necessary to explain some of the chief restrictions in constructing the simplest sentences. We may begin by looking again at a sentence with two adverbials:

The girl is *now* a student *at a large university*

This might have had fewer elements:

The girl is a student *at a large university*
The girl is a student
The girl is *now* a student
The girl is *at a large university*

but the sentence could not have been formed initially as:

*The girl is *now*

On this evidence we may say that the adverbials *now* and *at a large university* belong to different classes and it seems natural to label them 'time' and 'place' respectively.

Consider now the fact that the adverbial *carefully* in illustration [1] could be replaced by many others, making acceptable sentences in each case:

John searched the room $\begin{cases} \text{carefully} \\ \text{slowly} \\ \text{noisily} \\ \text{sternly} \\ \text{without delay} \end{cases}$

But if these same adverbials were inserted in sentences which had stative verbs, the sentences would become unacceptable:

$\left.\begin{array}{l} \text{The girl is now a student} \ldots \\ \text{John knew the answer} \ldots \end{array}\right\} \begin{cases} \text{*carefully} \\ \text{*slowly} \\ \text{*noisily} \\ \text{*sternly} \\ \text{*without delay} \end{cases}$

It is clear that we again have a subclass of adverbials. Because the verbs
with which they can occur allow the progressive, the aspect of on-going
activity, it is appropriate to refer to these adverbials as 'process'.

2.10
Types of sentence structure

Bringing together the distinctions so far made, we can present some
basic sentence-structure rules diagrammatically. Each line constitutes a
pattern which is illustrated by means of a correspondingly numbered
example having just those obligatory and optional (parenthesized)
elements that are specified in the formula. The order in which the elements appear is common but by no means fixed. It is a principle of
sentence organization that what is contextually familiar or 'given' comes
relatively early, while the part which needs to be stressed or which seems
to convey the greatest information is given the special prominence of
'end-focus'.

$$
S \begin{cases}
V\ stat \begin{cases}
intens \begin{cases} A\ place & [1] \\ C_s & [2] \end{cases} \\
ext\ \&\ trans: O_d & [3]
\end{cases} \\
V\ dyn \begin{cases}
intens: C_s & [4] \\
ext \begin{cases} trans \begin{cases} mono: O_d & [5] \\ di: (O_i)\ O_d & [6] \\ complex: O_d\ C_o & [7] \end{cases} \\ intransitive & [8] \end{cases}
\end{cases}
\end{cases}
\begin{matrix} \\ (A \\ process) \end{matrix}
\begin{matrix} \\ (A \\ place) \end{matrix}
\begin{matrix} (A \\ time) \end{matrix}
$$

She is in London (now)	[1]
She is a student (in London) (now)	[2]
John heard the explosion (from his office) (when he was locking the door)	[3]
Universities (gradually) became famous (in Europe) (during the Middle Ages)	[4]
They ate the meat (hungrily) (in their hut) (that night)	[5]
He offered (her) some chocolates (politely) (outside the hall) (before the concert)	[6]
They elected him chairman (without argument) (in Washington) (this morning)	[7]
The train had arrived (quietly) (at the station) (before we noticed it)	[8]

2.11
Element realization types

Sentence elements can be realized by linguistic structures of very different form. The verb element is always a *verb phrase*. This may, as in all the examples used so far, be 'finite' (showing tense, mood, aspect, and voice) or 'non-finite' (not showing tense or mood but still capable of indicating aspect and voice). Consider the three types of *non-finite verb phrase* functioning as the V element in the italicized *non-finite clauses:*

Mary wanted [*to be* (V) *a student* (C$_s$) *at that university* (A)] (O$_d$)
[*Carefully* (A) *searching* (V) *the room* (O$_d$)] (A), John found a ring
[*Made* (V) *the chairman* (C$_o$) *every year* (A)] (A), he was very busy

Whether finite or non-finite, the verb phrase can consist of one word, as in most illustrative sentences so far, or of more than one word, in which case the phrase consists of a 'head verb' preceded by one or more 'auxiliary verbs' as with the verb phrases in the following (the first three finite, the fourth non-finite):

He *had given* the girl an apple
He *may be growing* happier
He *had been challenged* rudely, and *having been challenged* he was
    angry

The subject of a sentence may be a 'clause' as in

That she answered the question correctly pleased him

but it is usually a 'noun phrase', at its simplest a pronoun such as *They* or a proper noun such as *John*. But a noun phrase may be an indeterminately long and complex structure having a noun as head, preceded by other words such as an article, an adjective, or another noun, and followed by a prepositional phrase or by a relative clause; it is by no means uncommon to find all such items present in a noun phrase:

The new gas stove in the kitchen which I bought last month has a very
    efficient oven

Subject complements, direct objects, and object complements may be realized by the same range of structures as subjects: *He was the chairman; She saw the chairman; They made him the chairman.* But subject and object complements have the additional possibility of being realized by adjective phrases (having an adjective as head), as in

She made him $\begin{cases} happy \\ very\ much\ happier \end{cases}$

Indirect objects, on the other hand, have fewer possibilities than subjects, and their realizations are chiefly noun phrases, as in

He had given *the girl* an apple

Unlike direct objects and subjects, they cannot be realized by *that*-clauses.

Finally, adverbials can be realized (a) by adverb phrases, having an adverb as head; (b) by noun phrases; (c) by prepositional phrases – that is, structures consisting of a noun phrase dominated by a preposition; and (d) by clauses, finite or non-finite:

(a) John *very carefully* searched the room
(b) They make him the chairman *every year*
(c) She studied *at a large university*
(d) He grew happier *when his friend arrived*
    Seeing the large crowd, John stopped his car.

Parts of speech
2.12

The structures realizing sentence elements are composed of units which can be referred to as *parts of speech*. These can be exemplified for English as follows:

(a) *noun* – John, room, answer, play
    adjective – happy, steady, new, large, round
    adverb – steadily, completely, really, very, then
    verb – search, grow, play, be, have, do
(b) *article* – the, a(n)
    demonstrative – that, this
    pronoun – he, they, anybody, one, which
    preposition – of, at, in, without, in spite of
    conjunction – and, that, when, although
    interjection – oh, ah, ugh, phew

We should notice that the examples are listed as *words* in their 'dictionary form' and not as they often appear in sentences when they function as constituents of phrases: thus the singular *room* and not the plural *rooms*, the simple *happy* and not the comparative *happier*, the infinitive (or uninflected) *grow* and not the past *grew*, the subject form *he* and not the object form *him*.

Note
From even the few examples given, it can be seen that a part-of-speech item may consist of more than a single word. This is especially common in the case of complex prepositions (6.4), such as *in spite of*, *out of*.

2.13

Some of the examples in 2.12 appear as more than one part of speech (*play* as noun and verb, *that* as demonstrative and conjunction) and more of them could have been given additional entries in this way (*round* can be noun, verb, adjective, adverb, and preposition). Similarly, we should notice a direct correspondence between most adjectives and adverbs, the latter usually consisting of the former plus -*ly*. Less obviously, there is an important correspondence between all words beginning /ð/ (*the*, *that*, *then*, for example) and many of those beginning *wh*- (*which*, *when*, for example): basically the former are relater or indicator words and the latter interrogative words.

2.14
Closed-system items

The parts of speech in 2.12 are listed in two groups, (a) and (b), and this introduces a distinction of very great significance. Set (b) comprises what are called 'closed-system' items. That is, the sets of items are *closed* in the sense that they cannot normally be extended by the creation of additional members: a moment's reflection is enough for us to realize how rarely in a language we invent or adopt a new or additional pronoun. It requires no great effort to list all the members in a closed system, and to be reasonably sure that one has in fact made an exhaustive inventory (especially, of course, where the membership is so extremely small as in the case of the *article*).

The items are said to constitute a *system* in being (i) reciprocally exclusive: the decision to use one item in a given structure excludes the possibility of using any other (thus one can have *the book* or *a book* but not **a the book*); and (ii) reciprocally defining: it is less easy to state the meaning of any individual item than to define it in relation to the rest of the system. This may be clearer with a non-linguistic analogy. If we are told that a student came *third* in an examination, the 'meaning' that we attach to 'third' will depend on knowing how many candidates took the examination: 'third' in a set of four has a very different meaning from 'third' in a set of thirty.

2.15
Open-class items

By contrast, set (a) comprises 'open classes'. Items belong to a class in that they have the same grammatical properties and structural possibilities as other members of the class (that is, as other nouns or verbs or adjectives or adverbs respectively), but the class is 'open' in the sense that it is indefinitely extendable. New items are constantly being created and no one could make an inventory of all the nouns in English (for example) and be confident that it was complete. This inevitably affects the way in which we attempt to define any item in an open class: while it would obviously be valuable to relate the meaning of *room* to other nouns with which it has semantic affinity (*chamber, hall, house, . . .*) one could not

define it as 'not *house*, not *box*, not *plate*, not *indignation*, . . .', as one
might define a closed-system item like *this* as 'not *that*'.

Of course, in any one phrase or sentence the decision to select a particular word at one place in the structure obviously imposes great constraints on what can be selected at another. But it is essential to see
that in an arrangement like the following there is in principle a sharp difference between the number of possibilities in columns *i*, *iii*, and *iv*
('closed') and the number in *ii* and *v* ('open'):

		ii	*iii*	*iv*	*v*
(John)	may	sit	by	this	fountain
	will	stare	at	that	tree
	must	read	from		window
	⋮	hurry	along		blackboard
		⋮	on		girl
			⋮		path
					⋮

The distinction between 'open' and 'closed' parts of speech must be
treated cautiously, however. On the one hand, we must not exaggerate
the ease with which we create new words: we certainly do not make up
new nouns as a necessary part of speaking in the way that making up
new sentences is necessary. On the other hand, we must not exaggerate
the extent to which parts of speech in set (b) of 2.12 are 'closed': new
prepositions (usually of the form 'prep+noun+prep' like *by way of*)
are by no means impossible.

Although they have deceptively specific labels, the parts of speech tend
in fact to be rather heterogeneous. The adverb and the verb are perhaps
especially mixed classes, each having small and fairly well-defined groups
of closed-system items alongside the indefinitely large open-class items.
So far as the verb is concerned, the closed-system subgroup is known by
the well-established term 'auxiliary'. With the adverb, one may draw
the distinction broadly between those in *-ly* that correspond to adjectives
(*complete-ly*) and those that do not (*now*, *there*, *forward*, *very*, for
example).

2.16
Stative and dynamic

The open classes have some notable general characteristics. We have
just seen that adverbs of the productive class are in a one-to-one relation
with adjectives. There are regular word-formation processes giving a
comparable one-for-one relation between nouns and adjectives, and
between nouns and verbs. For the rest, it is useful to see nouns, adjectives,

and verbs in connection with the opposition of stative and dynamic introduced in 2.8. Broadly speaking, nouns and adjectives can be characterized naturally as 'stative'; thus, nouns refer to entities that are regarded as stable, whether these are concrete (physical) like *house*, *table*, *paper*, or abstract (of the mind) like *hope*, *botany*, *length*. On the other hand, verbs and adverbs can be equally naturally characterized as 'dynamic': most obviously, verbs, which are fitted (by their capacity to show tense and aspect, for example) to indicate action, activity, and temporary or changing conditions. These relations between the open classes can be summarized thus:

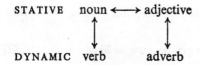

STATIVE   noun ←——→ adjective

DYNAMIC   verb   adverb

But we saw in 2.8 that there were some verbs such as *know* which could not normally be used with the progressive (*he is knowing): that is, which could not be seen as referring to something that was in progress. Verbs so used we called 'stative', and they should be seen as exceptions within the class of verbs. There are exceptions in the other direction among the nouns, not all of which need be stative. For example, a child may be well-behaved one minute and *a nuisance* the next. The situation is similar when we turn to the remaining open word-class, adjectives. Although they are predominantly stative (*tall*, *red*, *old*), some adjectives can resemble verbs in referring on occasion to transitory conditions of behaviour or activity such as *naughty* or *insolent*. And since *be* must be used to make predications having any noun or adjective as complement, we must qualify the statement made in 2.8 that this is a stative verb: it can also be used dynamically, in the progressive, when the complement is dynamic:

He is being $\begin{Bmatrix} \text{a nuisance} \\ \text{naughty} \end{Bmatrix}$ again

Indeed, it is essential to realize that these primary distinctions are in the nature of general characteristics rather than immutable truths. No small part of language's value lies in its flexibility. Thus we can take a normally dynamic item (say the verb in 'He *wrote* the book') and 'nominalize' it ('The *writing* of the book'), pretending – as it were – to see the action as a static 'thing'. So also the verb *tax* beside the noun *taxation*. Again, the name 'participle' reflects the fact that such a form participates in the features both of the *verb* ('The girl is sitting there') and of the *adjective* ('The sitting girl').

2.17
Pro-forms

The names of the parts of speech are traditional, however, and neither
in themselves nor in relation to each other do these names give a safe
guide to their meaning, which instead is best understood in terms of
their grammatical properties. 'Adverb' is a classic instance. We have
seen some justification in the previous section for 'participle', and of
course the 'pronoun' is an even clearer exception in correctly suggesting
that it can serve as a replacement for a noun:

John searched the big *room* and the small *one*   [1]

More usually, however, pronouns replace noun phrases rather than
nouns:

The man invited *the little Swedish girl* because *he* liked *her*   [2]

There are pro-forms also for place, time, and other adverbials under
certain circumstances:

Mary is *in London* and John is *there* too   [3]
Mary arrived *on Tuesday* and John arrived *then* too   [4]
John searched the big room very *carefully* and the small one
less *so*   [5]

But *so* has a more important pro-function, namely, to replace – along
with the 'pro-verb' *do* – a predication (*cf* 2.3):

She hoped that he would *search the room carefully before her
arrival* but he didn't *do so*   [6]

Here *do so* replaces all the italicized portion, the head verb *search* and
the rest of the predication, as is shown below:

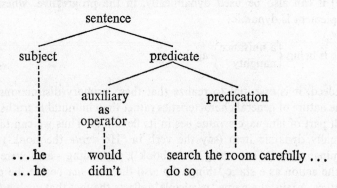

Frequently, however, the pro-predication is achieved by the operator
alone:

A: He didn't *give her an apple*. B: Yes, he *did*.   [7]
They suspected that he had *given her an apple* and he *had*   [8]

Finally, it may be briefly observed that the use of the pro-forms greatly facilitates sentence connection as in [7], the conjoining of sentences to form 'compound sentences' as in [3] or [8], and the subordination of one sentence within another to form 'complex sentences' as in [2].

Question and negation
2.18
Wh-questions
The pro-forms we have been considering may be regarded as having the general meaning 'We know what this item refers to, so I need not state it in full'. In 2.13 attention was drawn to correspondences of the *then-when* type, and we may now consider the *wh*-words of English as a special set of pro-forms diametrically opposed to the others in having the general meaning 'It has not been known what this item refers to and so it needs to be stated in full'. This informal statement will account for the use of *wh*-forms in questions:

Mary is *in London*
Mary is *there*
Where is Mary?

By such means, we can ask for the identification of the subject, object, complement or an adverbial of a sentence:

They (i) make him (ii) the chairman (iii) every year (iv)
Who makes him the chairman every year?   [i]
Whom do they make the chairman every year?   [ii]
What do they make him every year?   [iii]
When do they make him the chairman?   [iv]

It will be noticed that in each case the *wh*-form is placed in first position and that unless this is questioning the subject, as in [i], when the verb follows in its normal second position (2.5), the *wh*-form is followed by the operator (2.3) which in turn is followed by the subject and predication.

Note
The *wh*-forms include not only *which, when, why, where*, etc but also, less obviously, a few items pronounced with initial /h/, some having *wh*- in spelling (*who, whose, whom*), and one not (*how*).

2.19
Yes-no questions
Besides *wh*-questions, which elicit information on particular parts of a

sentence, there are questions which seek a *yes* or *no* response in relation to the validity of (normally) an entire predication:

Is the girl now a student?
Did John search the room?
Had he given the girl an apple?

Such questions normally open with an operator which is then followed by the subject and the predication (2.3).

2.20
Negation and non-assertion
While a *yes-no* question normally challenges the validity of a predication as a whole, negation rejects it. And like *yes-no* questions, negative sentences involve the operator, requiring the insertion of *not* (or the affixal contraction *-n't*) between the operator and the predication:

The girl isn't a student
John did not search the room
He hadn't given the girl an apple

We need to see a further similarity between questions and negations. Let us call a sentence such as

He offered her some chocolates   [1]

an *assertion*. Now, a sentence can be *non-assertive* in one of two ways: by being negative or by being a question. We do not therefore have two independent systems

positive : negative
declarative : interrogative

but rather an interrelated system in which *assertion* involves both 'positive' and 'declarative' while *non-assertion* has a subsystem either 'negative' or 'interrogative'. The relationship may be diagrammed thus:

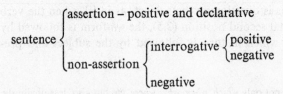

While it is right to show 'interrogative' as lying between the upper extreme 'positive and declarative' and the lower extreme 'negative', it is important to recognize that 'interrogative' has a closer relationship to 'negative' in springing like it from the 'non-assertion' node. Evidence for this is not difficult to find. As compared with the *some* of the positive-declarative [1], we find *any* in the corresponding question and negation:

Did he offer her any chocolates ? [1q]

He didn't offer her any chocolates [1n]

Bibliographical note

On parts of speech, see Lyons (1968), Ch 4; on stativeness, see Schopf (1969), Ch 3. Guidance on further reading is otherwise reserved for those chapters where specific topics here sketched are discussed in more detail. For general bibliography, see Scheurweghs (1963–68).

THREE
VERBS AND THE VERB PHRASE

3.1
Types of verb

There are various ways in which it will be necessary to classify verbs in this chapter. We begin with a classification relating to the function of items in the verb phrase. This distinguishes *lexical* verbs from the closed system (2.14) of *auxiliary* verbs, and subdivides the latter into *primary* and *modal* auxiliaries.

LEXICAL		*walk, write, play, beautify,* etc.
AUXILIARY	Primary	*do, have, be*
	Modal	*can, may, shall, will, could, might, should, would, must, ought to, used to, need, dare*

Note
As we shall see (3.22), some of the modals listed differ in their inflectional and syntactic behaviour from others and will be referred to as 'marginal'. On the other hand, further items like *had better* or *tend to* could be added to the list since they have a similar semantic relation in the verb phrase to the modals; these other expressions are often called 'semi-auxiliaries'.

3.2
Verbal forms and the verb phrase

Many English verbs have five forms: the BASE, the *-S* FORM, the PAST, the *-ING* PARTICIPLE, and the *-ED* PARTICIPLE. Examples of these forms and an indication of their functions are given in the table below. Regular lexical verbs have the same *-ed* inflection for both the past tense and the *-ed* participle (*called*, see 3.4). Irregular lexical verb forms vary from three (*eg: put, puts, putting,* see 3.10 *ff*) to eight (*be, am, is, are, was, were, being, been,* see 3.20). The modal auxiliaries are defective in not having infinitive (**to may*), *-ing* participle (**maying*), *-ed* participle (**mayed*), or imperative (**may!*). See further 3.21.

FORM	SYMBOL	EXAMPLE	FUNCTIONS
(1) base	V	*call* *drink* *put*	(a) all the present tense except 3rd person singular: I/you/we/they *call* every day (b) imperative: *Call* at once! (c) subjunctive: He demanded that she *call* and see him (d) the bare infinitive: He may *call*; and the *to*-infinitive: He wants her *to call*
(2) -*s* form (3rd person singular present)	V-*s*	*calls* *drinks* *puts*	3rd person singular present tense: He/she/it *calls* every day
(3) past	V-*ed₁*	*called* *drank* *put*	past tense: He *called* yesterday
(4) -*ing* participle (present participle)	V-*ing*	*calling* *drinking* *putting*	(a) progressive aspect (*be* + V-*ing*): He's *calling* in a moment (b) in -*ing* participle clauses: *Calling* early, I found her at home
(5) -*ed* participle (past participle)	V-*ed₂*	*called* *drunk* *put*	(a) perfective aspect (*have* + V-*ed₂*): He has *drunk* the water (b) passive voice (*be* + V-*ed₂*): He is *called* Jack (c) in -*ed* participle clauses: *Called* early, he had a quick breakfast

The abbreviation V-*ed* will be used where V-*ed₁* has the same form as V-*ed₂*.

The morphology of lexical verbs
3.3
We will consider lexical verbs under two heads: regular (such as *call*) and irregular (such as *drink*). In all of them, the *-s* form and *-ing* participle are predictable from the base form. They differ in that the *-ed*₁ and *-ed*₂ forms in irregular verbs cannot be predicted from the base.

Regular lexical verbs
3.4
Regular lexical verbs have the following forms:

V	BASE	call	like	try
V-*ing*	-*ING* PARTICIPLE	calling	liking	trying
V-*s*	-*S* FORM	calls	likes	tries
V-*ed*	PAST/-*ED* PARTICIPLE	called	liked	tried

These are regular in that we can predict the other forms if we know the base of such a verb. This is a very powerful rule, since the base is the form listed in dictionaries and the vast majority of English verbs belong to this regular class. Furthermore, all new verbs that are coined or borrowed from other languages adopt this pattern.

3.5
The -*ing* and -*s* forms
The *-ing* form is a straightforward addition to the base:

push ~ pushing   *sleep ~ sleeping*

Syllabic /l/ ceases to be syllabic before the inflection (as in *wriggle, wriggling*), and whether or not speakers pronounce final *r* (as in *pour*), the *r* is pronounced before the inflection.

The *-s* form is also predictable from the base. It has three spoken realizations: /ɪz/, /z/, and /s/, and two spellings, *-s* and *-es*.

(1) Pronounced /ɪz/ after bases ending in voiced or voiceless sibilants and spelled *-es* unless the base already ends in *-e*, eg

pass ~ passes	*budge ~ budges*
buzz ~ buzzes	*push ~ pushes*
catch ~ catches	*camouflage ~ camouflages*

(2) Pronounced /z/ and spelled *-s* after bases ending in other voiced sounds, *eg*

call ~ calls   *rob ~ robs*   *flow ~ flows*

Note: *do ~ does*   *go ~ goes*
      say ~ says   *have ~ has*

(3) Pronounced /s/ and spelled *-s* after bases ending in other voiceless sounds, *eg*

> *cut ~ cuts   lock ~ locks   sap ~ saps*

3.6
The past and the *-ed* participle

The past (V-*ed*$_1$) and the *-ed* participle (V-*ed*$_2$) of regular verbs (spelled *-ed* unless the base ends in *-e*) have three spoken realizations:

> /ɪd/ after bases ending in /d/ and /t/, *eg*
> > *pad ~ padded*   *pat ~ patted*
>
> /d/ after bases ending in voiced sounds other than /d/, *eg*
> > *mow ~ mowed*   *budge ~ budged*
>
> /t/ after bases ending in voiceless sounds other than /t/, *eg*
> > *pass ~ passed*   *pack ~ packed*

Further inflectional spelling rules
3.7
Doubling of consonant

Final base consonants (except *x*) are doubled before inflections beginning with a vowel letter when the preceding vowel is stressed and spelled with a single letter:

> *bar*   *barring*   *barred*
> *permit*   *permitting*   *permitted*

There is no doubling when the vowel is unstressed or written with two letters:

> *enter*   *entering*   *entered*
> *dread*   *dreading*   *dreaded*

EXCEPTIONS:

(a) Bases ending in certain consonants are doubled also after single unstressed vowels: *-g* → *-gg-*, *-c* → *-ck-:*

> *humbug*   *humbugging*   *humbugged*
> *traffic*   *trafficking*   *trafficked*

(b) BrE, as distinct from AmE, breaks the rule with respect to certain other consonants also: *-l* → *-ll-*, *-m* → *-mm-*, *-p* → *-pp-:*

> *signal*   *signalling*   *signalled*   (BrE)
> *signal*   *signaling*   *signaled*   (AmE)
> *travel*   *travelling*   *travelled*   (BrE)
> *travel*   *traveling*   *traveled*   (AmE)

program(me)	programming	programmed (BrE) ⎱
program	programing	programed (AmE) ⎰
worship	worshipping	worshipped (BrE) ⎱
worship	worshiping	worshiped (AmE) ⎰

Most verbs ending in *-p*, however, have the regular spellings in both BrE and AmE, *eg: develop, envelop, gallop, gossip.*

.3.8
Treatment of -y

(a) In bases ending in a consonant+*y*, the following changes occur before inflections that do not begin with *i:*

> *carry ~ carries*   *carry ~ carried*   but *carry ~ carrying*

The past of the following two verbs has a change *y → i* also after a vowel:

> *lay ~ laid*   *pay ~ paid*

Say ~ said has the same change of spelling but, in addition, a change of vowel; see also 3.5.

(b) In bases ending in *-ie*, the *ie* is replaced by *y* before the *-ing* inflection:

> *die ~ dying*   *lie ~ lying*

3.9
Deletion of -e

Final *-e* is regularly dropped before the *-ing* and *-ed* inflections:

> *shave   shaving   shaved*

Verbs with bases in *-ee*, *-ye*, *-oe*, and often *-ge* are exceptions to this rule in that they do not drop the *-e* before *-ing*; but they do drop it before *-ed*, as do also forms in *-ie* (*tie ~ tied*):

-ee:	*agree*	*agreeing*	*agreed*
-ye:	*dye*	*dyeing*	*dyed*
-oe:	*hoe*	*hoeing*	*hoed*
-ge:	*singe*	*singeing*	*singed*

Irregular lexical verbs
3.10

Irregular lexical verbs differ from regular verbs in the following ways:

(a) Irregular verbs either do not have a /d/ or /t/ inflection (*drink ~ drank ~ drunk*) or break the rule in 3.6 for a voiced inflection (*eg: burn ~ burnt* /t/, beside the regular *burned* /d/).

(b) Irregular verbs typically, but not necessarily, have variation in their base vowel:

find ~ found ~ found   *write ~ wrote ~ written*

(c) Irregular verbs have a varying number of distinct forms. Since the -*s* and -*ing* forms are predictable for regular and irregular verbs alike, the only forms that need be listed for irregular verbs are the base (V), the past (V-*ed*$_1$), and the past participle (V-*ed*$_2$). Most irregular verbs have, like regular verbs, only one common form for the past and the -*ed* participle, but there is considerable variation in this respect, as the table shows:

	BASE	V-*ed*$_1$	V-*ed*$_2$
all alike	*cut*	*cut*	*cut*
V-*ed*$_1$ = V-*ed*$_2$	*meet*	*met*	*met*
V = V-*ed*$_2$	*come*	*came*	*come*
all different	*speak*	*spoke*	*spoken*

These characteristics form the basis of the classification that follows. In many cases, there are prefixed verbs having the same inflections, *eg: outdo* beside *do*. 'R' denotes that the item occurs also with regular inflections.

3.11

CLASS 1: V-*ed*$_1$ is identical with V-*ed*$_2$
Suffixation is used but voicing is variable
Vowel identity in all the parts

	V	V-*ed*		V	V-*ed*
1a	*burn*	*burnt* (R)	1b	*bend*	*bent*
	dwell	*dwelt* (R)		*build*	*built*
	learn	*learnt* (R)		*lend*	*lent*
	smell	*smelt* (R)		*rend*	*rent*
	spell	*spelt* (R)		*send*	*sent*
	spill	*spilt* (R)		*spend*	*spent*
	spoil	*spoilt* (R)	1c	*have*	*had*
				make	*made*

Note

For Class 1a verbs, the regular /d/ form is especially AmE and the /t/ form especially BrE.

3.12

CLASS 2: V-ed_1 is identical with V-ed_2
        Suffixation is used but voicing is variable
        Change of base vowel

	V	V-*ed*		V	V-*ed*
2a	*bereave*	*bereft* (R)	2b	*beseech*	*besought*
	cleave	*cleft*		*bring*	*brought*
	creep	*crept*		*buy*	*bought*
	deal	*dealt*		*catch*	*caught*
	dream	*dreamt* (R)		*seek*	*sought*
	feel	*felt*		*teach*	*taught*
	flee	*fled*		*think*	*thought*
	keep	*kept*			
	kneel	*knelt* (R)	2c	*lose*	*lost*
	lean	*leant* (R)		*sell*	*sold*
	leap	*leapt* (R)		*tell*	*told*
	leave	*left*		*hear*	*heard*
	mean	*meant*		*say*	*said*
	sleep	*slept*		*shoe*	(*shod*) (R)
	sweep	*swept*			
	weep	*wept*			

Note
Where there are regular variants, these are usually preferred in AmE.

3.13

CLASS 3: All three parts V, V-ed_1, and V-ed_2 are identical
        No suffix or change of the base vowel

V and V-*ed*	V and V-*ed*	V and V-*ed*
bet (R)	*knit* (R)	*shut*
bid 'make a bid' (R)	*let*	*slit*
burst	*put*	*split*
cast	*quit* (R)	*spread*
cost	*rid* (R)	*sweat* (R)
cut	*set*	*thrust*
hit	*shed*	*wed* (R)
hurt	*shit*	*wet* (R)

Note
The transitive *cost* 'estimate the cost of' and *shed* 'put in a shed' are R.

3.14

CLASS 4: V-ed_1 is identical with V-ed_2
　　　　　No suffixation
　　　　　Change of base vowel

V	V-ed		V	V-ed
4a	*bleed*	*bled*	4c	*bind*	*bound*
	breed	*bred*		*find*	*found*
	feed	*fed*		*grind*	*ground*
	hold	*held*		*wind*	*wound*
	lead	*led*	4d	*light*	*lit* (R)
	meet	*met*		*slide*	*slid*
	read	*read*			
	speed	*sped* (R)	4e	*sit*	*sat*
4b	*cling*	*clung*		*spit*	$\begin{cases} spat \\ (spit) \\ \quad (\text{esp AmE}) \end{cases}$
	dig	*dug*			
	fling	*flung*	4f	*get*	$\begin{cases} got \\ gotten \ (\text{AmE}) \end{cases}$
	hang	*hung*			
	sling	*slung*		*shine*	*shone*
	slink	*slunk*		*shoot*	*shot*
	spin	*spun*	4g	*fight*	*fought*
	stick	*stuck*			
	sting	*stung*	4h	*stand*	*stood*
	strike	*struck*	4i	*stride*	*strode*
	string	*strung*			
	swing	*swung*			
	win	*won*			
	wring	*wrung*			

Note

[a] When *hang* means 'execute', it is usually R.
[b] The metaphorical *strike* is in Class 6c.
[c] AmE *gotten* is used in the sense 'acquired', 'caused', 'come'.
[d] The transitive *shine* 'polish' can be R, esp in AmE.

3.15

CLASS 5: V-ed_1 is regular; V-ed_2 has two forms, one regular, the other
　　　　　nasal.

V	V-ed_1	V-ed_2	V	V-ed_1	V-ed_2
hew	*hewed*	*hewn* (R)	*shear*	*sheared*	*shorn* (R)
mow	*mowed*	*mown* (R)	*show*	*showed*	*shown* (R)
saw	*sawed*	*sawn* (R)	*sow*	*sowed*	*sown* (R)
sew	*sewed*	*sewn* (R)	*strew*	*strewed*	*strewn* (R)
			swell	*swelled*	*swollen* (R)

3.16

CLASS 6: V-*ed*$_1$ and V-*ed*$_2$ are irregular, the latter always suffixed and
usually with -(*e*)*n*. There are subclasses as follows:

A: V-*ed*$_1$ and V-*ed*$_2$ have the same vowel
B: V and V-*ed*$_2$ have the same vowel
C: all three parts have different vowels
D: all three parts have the same vowel
E: V-*ed*$_1$ and V-*ed*$_2$ have different vowels

	V	V-*ed*$_1$	V-*ed*$_2$		V	V-*ed*$_1$	V-*ed*$_2$
6Aa	*break*	*broke*	*broken*	6Bc	*(for)bid*	*(for)- bad(e)*	*(for)bidden*
	choose	*chose*	*chosen*		*give*	*gave*	*given*
	freeze	*froze*	*frozen*	6Bd	*draw*	*drew*	*drawn*
	speak	*spoke*	*spoken*				
	steal	*stole*	*stolen*	6Be	*fall*	*fell*	*fallen*
	(a)wake	*(a)woke*	*(a)woken* (R)	6Bf	*eat*	*ate*	*eaten*
	weave	*wove*	*woven*	6Bg	*see*	*saw*	*seen*
6Ab	*bear*	*bore*	*borne*	6Bh	*slay*	*slew*	*slain*
	swear	*swore*	*sworn*	6Ca	*drive*	*drove*	*driven*
	tear	*tore*	*torn*		*ride*	*rode*	*ridden*
	wear	*wore*	*worn*		*rise*	*rose*	*risen*
6Ac	*bite*	*bit*	*bitten*		*strike*	*struck*	*stricken (meta- phorical)*
	hide	*hid*	{*hidden* (*hid*)		*strive*	*strove*	*striven* (R)
6Ad	*forget*	*forgot*	*forgotten*		*write*	*wrote*	*written*
	tread	*trod*	*trodden*	6Cb	*fly*	*flew*	*flown*
6Ae	*lie*	*lay*	*lain*	6Cc	*do*	*did*	*done*
6Ba	*blow*	*blew*	*blown*		*go*	*went*	*gone*
	grow	*grew*	*grown*	6D	*beat*	*beat*	*beaten*
	know	*knew*	*known*	6E	*dive*	*dove (AmE)*	*dived* (R)
	throw	*threw*	*thrown*		*thrive*	*throve* (R)	*thrived* (R)
6Bb	*forsake*	*forsook*	*forsaken*				
	shake	*shook*	*shaken*				
	take	*took*	*taken*				

Note
'She has *borne* six children and the youngest was *born* a month ago.'

3.17

CLASS 7: V-*ed*$_1$ and V-*ed*$_2$ are irregular; there is no suffixation but
there is always some vowel change.

	V	V-*ed*$_1$	V-*ed*$_2$
7a	*begin*	*began*	*begun*
	drink	*drank*	*drunk*
	ring	*rang*	*rung*

	shrink	$\begin{cases} shrank \\ shrunk \end{cases}$	shrunk
	sing	sang	sung
	sink	sank	sunk
	spring	sprang	sprung
	stink	stank	stunk
	swim	swam	swum
7b	come	came	come
	run	ran	run

The auxiliaries *do, have, be*
3.18
Do
The auxiliary *do* has the following forms:

	NON-NEGATIVE	UNCONTRACTED NEGATIVE	CONTRACTED NEGATIVE
present	$\begin{cases} do \\ does \end{cases}$	do not / does not	don't / doesn't
past	did	did not	didn't

Do as lexical verb ('perform', etc) and as pro-verb has the full range of forms, including the present participle *doing* and the past participle *done* (see 3.16):

> What have you been *doing* today?
> A: You said you would finish it.   B: I have *done* so.

3.19
Have
Have has the following forms:

	NON-NEGATIVE	UNCONTRACTED NEGATIVE	CONTRACTED NEGATIVE
base	have, 've	have not, 've not	haven't
-s form	has, 's	has not, 's not	hasn't
past	had, 'd	had not, 'd not	hadn't
-ing form	having	not having	
-ed participle	had (only as lexical verb)		

Note
In the stative sense (3.35) of possession, *have* is often (especially in BrE) constructed as an auxiliary. AmE prefers the *do*-construction:

I $\begin{cases} haven't \\ don't\ have \end{cases}$ any books

In dynamic senses (*receive, take, experience*, etc), lexical *have* in both AmE and BrE normally has the *do*-construction:

> *Does* he *have* coffee with his breakfast?
> *Did* you *have* any difficulty getting here?

The *do*-construction is required in such expressions as

> *Did* you *have* a good time?

There is also the informal *have got*, where *have* is constructed as an auxiliary, which is frequently preferred (especially in BrE) as an alternative to *have*. It is particularly common in negative and interrogative sentences. As a further alternative for expressing negation, we have the negative determiner *no:*

> I *haven't got* any books   I *have no* books

3.20
Be

The lexical and auxiliary verb *be* is unique among English verbs in having eight different forms:

		NON-NEGATIVE	UNCONTRACTED NEGATIVE	CONTRACTED NEGATIVE
base		*be*		
present	1st person singular	*am, 'm*	*am not, 'm not*	*(aren't, ain't)*
	3rd person singular	*is, 's*	*is not, 's not*	*isn't*
	2nd person, 1st and 3rd person plural	*are, 're*	*are not, 're not*	*aren't*
past	1st and 3rd person singular	*was*	*was not*	*wasn't*
	2nd person, 1st and 3rd person plural	*were*	*were not*	*weren't*
-ing form		*being*	*not being*	
-ed participle		*been*		

Note

[a] *Aren't I* is widely used in BrE, but there is no generally acceptable contracted form for *am not* in declarative sentences. *Ain't* is substandard in BrE and is so considered by many in AmE; as well as serving as a contracted *am not*, it is used also for *isn't, aren't, hasn't,* and *haven't.*

[*b*] The lexical verb *be* may have the *do*-construction in persuasive imperative sentences and regularly has it with negative imperatives:

Do be quiet!   Don't be silly!

The modal auxiliaries
3.21
The modal auxiliaries are the following:

NON-NEGATIVE	UNCONTRACTED NEGATIVE	CONTRACTED NEGATIVE
{ *can*	*cannot, can not*	*can't*
{ *could*	*could not*	*couldn't*
{ *may*	*may not*	*mayn't*
{ *might*	*might not*	*mightn't*
{ *shall*	*shall not*	*shan't*
{ *should*	*should not*	*shouldn't*
{ *will, 'll*	*will not, 'll not*	*won't*
{ *would, 'd*	*would not, 'd not*	*wouldn't*
must	*must not*	*mustn't*
ought to	*ought not to*	*oughtn't to*
used to	*used not to*	*usedn't to*
		didn't use to
need	*need not*	*needn't*
dare	*dare not*	*daren't*

Note

[*a*] *Mayn't* is restricted to BrE, where it is rare.

[*b*] *Shan't* is rare in AmE.

[*c*] *Ought* regularly has the *to*-infinitive, but AmE occasionally has the bare infinitive in negative sentences and in questions (although *should* is commoner in both cases): *You oughtn't smoke so much*; *Ought you smoke so much?*

3.22
Marginal modal auxiliaries
Used always takes the *to*-infinitive and occurs only in the past tense. It may take the *do*-construction, in which case the spellings *didn't used to* and *didn't use to* both occur. The interrogative construction *used he to* is especially BrE; *did he used to* is preferred in both AmE and BrE.

Dare and *need* can be constructed either as modal auxiliaries (with bare infinitive and with no inflected *-s* form) or as lexical verbs (with *to*-infinitive and with inflected *-s* form). The modal verb construction is restricted to non-assertive contexts (see 2.20), *ie* mainly negative and interrogative sentences, whereas the lexical verb construction can always be used and is in fact the more common. *Dare* and *need* as auxiliaries are probably rarer in AmE than in BrE.

	MODAL AUXILIARY CONSTRUCTION	LEXICAL VERB CONSTRUCTION
positive		He *needs to* go now
negative	He *needn't* go now	He *doesn't need to* go now
interrogative	*Need* he go now?	*Does* he *need to* go now?
negative- interrogative	*Needn't* he go now?	*Doesn't* he *need to* go now?

Note

[a] Non-assertive forms are not confined to overtly negative and/or interrogative sentences but can also be present in adverbials, *eg: He need do it only under these circumstances, He need do it but once;* in determiners, *eg: He need have no fear, No soldier dare disobey;* in pronouns, *eg: No one dare predict . . .;* or even implicitly, *eg: All you need do is, . . .* ('You need do no more than . . .').

[b] Blends of the two constructions are widely acceptable in the case of *dare: We do not dare speak.*

Finite and non-finite verb phrases
3.23

The verb forms operate in finite and non-finite verb phrases, which are distinguished as follows:

(1) Finite verb phrases have tense distinction (see 3.26 *ff*):

$$He \begin{Bmatrix} studies \\ studied \end{Bmatrix} English$$

(2) Finite verb phrases occur as the verb element of a clause. There is person and number concord between the subject and the finite verb (*cf* 7.18 and 7.26). Concord is particularly overt with *be* (*cf* 3.20):

   I + *am*   You/we/they + *are*   He/she/it + *is*

With most lexical verbs, concord is restricted to a contrast between 3rd and non-3rd person singular present:

   He *reads* } the paper every morning
   They *read* }

With the modal auxiliaries there is, however, no concord:

   I/you/he/we/they *can* play the cello

(3) Finite verb phrases have mood (3.45). In contrast to the 'unmarked' INDICATIVE mood, we distinguish the 'marked' moods IMPERATIVE (see 7.58 *ff*), and SUBJUNCTIVE (see 3.46).

(4) The non-finite forms of the verb are the infinitive (*(to) call*), the *-ing* participle (*calling*), and the *-ed* participle (*called*). Non-finite verb phrases consist of one or more such items. Compare:

FINITE VERB PHRASES	NON-FINITE VERB PHRASES
He *smokes* heavily	*To smoke* like that must be dangerous
He *is working*	I found him *working*
He *had been offended* before	*Having been offended* before, he was sensitive

3.24

The modal, perfective, progressive and passive auxiliaries follow a strict order in the complex verb phrase:

[I] MODAL, always followed by an infinitive, as in

He would visit

[II] PERFECTIVE, always followed by an *-ed* form, as in

He had visited
He would have visited

[III] PROGRESSIVE, always followed by an *-ing* form, as in

He was visiting
He would have been visiting

[IV] PASSIVE, always followed by an *-ed* form, as in

He was visited
He would have been being visited

The last example is added for completeness but the full range of auxiliaries is rarely found simultaneously in this way (though less rarely with the *get* passive: 7.5). Rather, it should be noted that, while the above order is strictly followed, gaps are perfectly normal. For example:

I+III: He may be visiting
II+IV: He has been visited

3.25

Contrasts expressed in the verb phrase

In addition to the contrasts of tense, aspect, and mood (which are dealt with in the present chapter, 3.26–55), it may be convenient to list here the other major constructions which affect the verb phrase or in which verb-phrase contrasts play an important part.

(a) *Voice*, involving the active-passive relation, as in

> A doctor *will examine* the applicants
> ~ The applicants *will be examined* by a doctor

will be discussed in 7.5 and 12.14–32.

(b) *Questions* requiring subject movement involve the use of an auxiliary as operator:

> John *will sing* ~ *Will* John *sing*?
> John *sang*   ~ *Did* John *sing*?

This topic is dealt with in 7.44–57.

(c) *Negation* makes analogous use of operators, as in

> John *will sing* ~ John *won't sing*
> John *sang*   ~ John *didn't sing*

and will be handled in 7.33–42.

(d) *Emphasis*, which is frequently carried by the operator as in

> John WÌLL sing!
> John DÌD sing!

is treated in 14.35.

(e) *Imperatives*, as in *Go home, John; You go home, John; Don't (you) go yet; Let's go home*, are discussed in 7.58–62.

Tense, aspect, and mood
3.26
Time is a universal, non-linguistic concept with three divisions: past, present, and future; by *tense* we understand the correspondence between the form of the verb and our concept of time. *Aspect* concerns the manner in which the verbal action is experienced or regarded (for example as completed or in progress), while *mood* relates the verbal action to such conditions as certainty, obligation, necessity, possibility. In fact, however, to a great extent these three categories impinge on each other: in particular, the expression of time present and past cannot be considered separately from aspect, and the expression of the future is closely bound up with mood.

Tense and aspect
3.27
We here consider the *present* and *past* tenses in relation to the *progressive* and *perfective* aspects. The range can be seen in the sentence frame

'I ————— with a special pen', filling the blank with a phrase having the verb base *write:*

	SIMPLE	COMPLEX	
		progressive	
present	write	am writing	*present*
		was writing	*past*
		perfective	
past	wrote	have written	*(present) perfect*
		had written	*past (or plu-) perfect*
		perfect progressive	
		have been writing	*(present) perfect*
		had been writing	*past (or plu-) perfect*

3.28
Present

We need to distinguish three basic types of present:

(a) *Timeless*, expressed with the simple present form:

> I (always) *write* with a special pen (when I sign my name)

As well as expressing habitual action as here, the timeless present is used for universal statements such as

> The sun *sets* in the west
> Spiders *have* eight legs

(b) *Limited*, expressed with the present progressive:

> I *am writing* (on this occasion) with a special pen (since I have mislaid my ordinary one)
> Normally he *lives* in London but at present he *is living* in Boston

In indicating that the action is viewed as in process and of limited duration, the progressive can express incompleteness even with a verb like *stop* whose action cannot in reality have duration; thus *the bus is stopping* means that it is slowing down but has not yet stopped. The progressive (usually with an adverb of high frequency) can also be used of habitual action, conveying an emotional colouring such as irritation:

> He's always *writing* with a special pen – just because he likes to be different

(c) *Instantaneous*, expressed with either the simple (especially in a series) or the progressive form:

Watch carefully now: first, I *write* with my ordinary pen; now,
 I *write* with a special pen
As you see, I *am dropping* the stone into the water

The simple present is, however, usual in radio commentary on
sport ('Moore passes to Charlton'), and in certain performative
declarations ('I name this ship *Snaefell*') it is obligatory.

Note
The verbs *keep (on), go on* have a similar function to the normal progressive auxiliary
be:

John $\begin{Bmatrix} keeps \\ goes\ on \end{Bmatrix}$ asking silly questions

Past
3.29
An action in the past may be seen

(1) as having taken place at a particular point of time; or
(2) over a period; if the latter, the period may be seen as

   (a) extending up to the present, or
   (b) relating only to the past; if the latter, it may be viewed as

      (i) having been completed, or as
      (ii) not having been completed

	Past	Present	Future
(1)	×	v	
(2a)	▨▨▨▨▨▨▨▨▨	v	
(2bi)	▨▨▨▨	v	
(2bii)	┄▨▨▨┄	v	

Typical examples will be seen to involve the perfective and progressive
aspects as well as the simple past:

(1)   I *wrote* my letter of 16 June 1972 with a special pen
(2a) I *have written* with a special pen since 1972
(2bi) I *wrote* with a special pen from 1969 to 1972
(2bii) I *was writing* poetry with a special pen

Habitual activity can also be expressed with the simple past ('He always
wrote with a special pen'), but since – unlike the simple present – this is

not implied without a suitable adverb, *used to* or (less commonly) *would* may be needed to bring out this sense:

$$\text{He} \left\{ \begin{array}{l} \textit{used to} \\ \textit{would} \end{array} \right\} \textit{write} \text{ with a special pen}$$

Note

Past time can be expressed with present tense forms. The 'historic present' is fairly common in vivid narrative:

> At that moment, in *comes* a policeman

but has no such journalistic overtones with verbs of communicating:

> John *tells* me that there was a car accident last night

On the other hand, past tense forms need not refer to past time. 'Did you want to see me?' is little more than a slightly politer version of 'Do you...?' For the 'modal past', see 3.47 and 11.48; for the past by 'back-shift' in indirect speech, see 11.53.

3.30
The past and the perfective

In relation to (2a), it is not the time specified in the sentence but the period relevant to the time specified that must extend to the present. Contrast

> John *lived* in Paris for ten years

(which entails that the period of residence has come to an end and which admits the possibility that John is dead) with

> John *has lived* in Paris for ten years

which entails that John is still alive but permits the residence in Paris to extend either to the present (the usual interpretation) or to some unspecified date in the past. Compare also:

> For generations, Nepal *has produced* brilliant mountaineers
>
> For generations, Sparta $\left\{ \begin{array}{l} \textit{produced} \\ \textit{was producing} \end{array} \right\}$ fearless warriors

The first claims that Nepal is still in a position to produce more mountaineers, even if a long time may have elapsed since the last was produced. The second sentence, on the other hand, is uncommitted as to whether any further warriors can be produced by Sparta.

The choice of perfective aspect is associated with time-orientation and consequently also with various time-indicators (*lately, since, so far*, etc). It is therefore helpful to consider these two together. Here are some examples:

ADVERBIALS	ADVERBIALS
WITH SIMPLE PAST	WITH PRESENT PERFECT
(refer to a period now past)	(refer to a period beginning in the past and stretching up to the present)

$$I \text{ worked} \begin{cases} \text{yesterday (evening)} \\ \text{throughout January} \\ \text{on Tuesday} \end{cases} \qquad I \text{ have worked} \begin{cases} \text{since last January} \\ \text{up to now} \\ \text{lately} \\ \text{already} \end{cases}$$

ADVERBIALS WITH EITHER
SIMPLE PAST OR PRESENT PERFECT

$$I \begin{cases} \text{worked} \\ \text{have worked} \end{cases} \begin{cases} \text{today} \\ \text{this month} \\ \text{for an hour} \end{cases}$$

Note
There is some tendency (especially in AmE) to use the past informally in place of the perfective, as in *I saw it already* (='I have already seen it').

3.31
Indefinite and definite
Through its ability to involve a span of time from earliest memory to the present, the perfective has an indefiniteness which makes it an appropriate verbal expression for introducing a topic of discourse. As the topic is narrowed down, the emerging definiteness is marked by the simple past as well as in the noun phrases (*cf* 4.20). For example:

> He says that he *has seen* a meteor at some time (between earliest memory and the present)

as compared with

> He says that he *saw* the meteor last night that everyone is so excited about

Compare also:

> Did you know that John *has painted* a portrait of Mary?
> Did you know that John *painted* this portrait of Mary?

3.32
Past perfect
What was said of the perfect in 3.29*f* – applies to the past perfect, with the complication that the point of current relevance to which the past perfect extends is a point in the past:

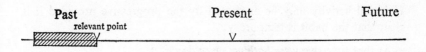

Past   Present   Future
  relevant point

Thus:

   (I say now [*present*] that) When I met him [*relevant point in the past*]
     John had lived in Paris for ten years

In some contexts, the simple past and the past perfect are interchangeable; *eg:*

I ate my lunch after my wife $\left\{\begin{matrix} came \\ had\ come \end{matrix}\right\}$ home from her shopping

Here the conjunction *after* is sufficient specification to indicate that the arrival from the shopping expedition had taken place before the eating, so that the extra time indication by means of the past perfect becomes redundant.

Note

There is no interchangeability when the past perfect is the past of the perfect:

   John tells me that he *hasn't seen* Mary since Monday
   John told me that he *hadn't seen* Mary since Monday
   *John told me that he *didn't see* Mary since Monday

3.33
The past and the progressive

As with the present (3.28), the progressive when used with the past specifies the limited duration of an action:

   I *was writing* with a special pen for a period last night but my hand
     grew tired

In consequence, it is a convenient device to indicate a time span within which another event (indicated by the simple past) can be seen as taking place:

   While I *was writing*, the phone *rang*

The ability to express incomplete action with the progressive is illustrated by the contrasting pair:

   He *read* a book that evening (implies that he finished it)
   He *was reading* a book that evening (implies that he did not finish it)

and more strikingly by:

   The girl *was drowning* in the lake (will permit 'but someone dived in
     and rescued her')
   The girl *drowned* in the lake

Habitual activity may be expressed by the progressive provided it is clear that the habit is temporary:

At that time, we *were bathing* every day

and not merely sporadic:

*We were sometimes walking to the office

But general habits may be pejoratively referred to (*cf* 3.28):

My brother *was* always *losing* his keys

3.34
The perfect progressive
Limited duration (or incompleteness) and current relevance can be jointly expressed with the perfect progressive. Compare:

He *has eaten* my chocolates (they are all gone)
He *was eating* my chocolates (but I stopped him)
He *has been eating* my chocolates (but there are some left)

Frequently the perfect progressive implies an especially recent activity, the effects of which are obvious, and the adverb *just* commonly accompanies this usage:

It *has rained* a great deal since you were here
Oh look! It *has* just *been raining*

3.35
Verbal meaning and the progressive
As pointed out in 2.8, the progressive occurs only with dynamic verbs (or more accurately, with verbs in dynamic use). These verbs [A] fall into five classes while the stative verbs [B], which disallow the progressive, can be seen as belonging to one of two classes.

[A] DYNAMIC
    (1) Activity verbs: *abandon, ask, beg, call, drink, eat, help, learn, listen, look at, play, rain, read, say, slice, throw, whisper, work, write*, etc.
    (2) Process verbs: *change, deteriorate, grow, mature, slow down, widen*, etc. Both activity and process verbs are frequently used in progressive aspect to indicate incomplete events in progress.
    (3) Verbs of bodily sensation (*ache, feel, hurt, itch*, etc) can have either simple or progressive aspect with little difference in meaning.
    (4) Transitional event verbs (*arrive, die, fall, land, leave, lose*, etc)

occur in the progressive but with a change of meaning compared with simple aspect. The progressive implies inception, *ie* only the approach to the transition.

(5) Momentary verbs (*hit, jump, kick, knock, nod, tap,* etc) have little duration, and thus the progressive aspect powerfully suggests repetition.

[B] STATIVE

(1) Verbs of inert perception and cognition: *abhor, adore, astonish, believe, desire, detest, dislike, doubt, feel, forgive, guess, hate, hear, imagine, impress, intend, know, like, love, mean, mind, perceive, please, prefer, presuppose, realize, recall, recognize, regard, remember, satisfy, see, smell, suppose, taste, think, understand, want, wish,* etc. Some of these verbs may take other than a recipient subject (7.11), in which case they belong with the A1 class. Compare:

> I *think* you are right [B1]
> I *am thinking* of you all the time [A1]

(2) Relational verbs: *apply to* (everyone), *be, belong to, concern, consist of, contain, cost, depend on, deserve, equal, fit, have, include, involve, lack, matter, need, owe, own, possess, remain* (a bachelor), *require, resemble, seem, sound, suffice, tend,* etc.

The future
3.36
There is no obvious future tense in English corresponding to the time/tense relation for present and past. Instead there are several possibilities for denoting future time. Futurity, modality, and aspect are closely related, and future time is rendered by means of modal auxiliaries or semi-auxiliaries, or by simple present forms or progressive forms.

3.37
Will and *shall*

> *will* or *'ll*+infinitive in all persons
> *shall*+infinitive (in 1st person only; chiefly BrE)

> I *will/shall arrive* tomorrow
> He*'ll be* here in half an hour

The future and modal functions of these auxiliaries can hardly be separated (*cf* 3.50*f*), but *shall* and, particularly, *will* are the closest approximation to a colourless, neutral future. *Will* for future can be used in all persons throughout the English-speaking world, whereas *shall* (for 1st person) is largely restricted in this usage to southern BrE.

The auxiliary construction is also used to refer to a statement seen in the past from a point of orientation in the future:

They *will have finished* their book by next year

Note
Other modal auxiliaries can have future reference also: 'He *may leave* tomorrow'= 'He *will* possibly *leave* . . .'

3.38
Be going to + infinitive
This construction denotes 'future fulfilment of the present'. Looked at more carefully, *be going to* has two more specific meanings, of which one, 'future of present intention', is used chiefly with personal subjects:

When *are* you *going to get married?*

The other meaning is 'future of present cause', which is found with both personal and non-personal subjects:

She'*s going to have* a baby
It'*s going to rain*

Both of these suggest that the event is already 'on the way'. *Be going to* is not generally used in the main clause of conditional sentences, *will/'ll* or *shall* being preferred instead:

If you leave now, you'*ll* never *regret* it

3.39
Present progressive
The present progressive refers to a future happening anticipated in the present. Its basic meaning is 'fixed arrangement, plan, or programme':

He'*s moving* to London

Since the progressive is used to denote present as well as future, a time adverbial is often used to clarify in which meaning the verb is being used:

They *are washing* the dishes $\begin{cases} now \\ later \end{cases}$

The present progressive is especially frequent with dynamic transitional verbs like *arrive, come, go, land, start, stop,* etc, which refer to a transition between two states or positions:

The plane *is taking off* at 5.20
The President *is coming* to the UN this week

3.40
Simple present
The simple present is regularly used in subordinate clauses that are conditional (introduced by *if*, *unless*, etc) or temporal (introduced by *as soon as*, *before*, *when*, etc; see 11.47):

> What will you say if I *marry* my boss?
> The guests will be drunk before they *leave*

The use of the simple present in main clauses may be said to represent a marked future aspect of unusual certainty, in that it attributes to the future something of the positiveness one normally associates with present and past events. It is used for statements about the calendar:

> Yesterday was Monday, today is Tuesday, and tomorrow *is*
> Wednesday

and to describe immutable events or 'fixtures':

> When *is* high tide?
> What time *is* the football match?

Both the simple present and the progressive (3.28) are often used with dynamic transitional verbs: *arrive*, *come*, *leave*, etc, both having the meaning of 'plan' or 'programme':

> The train $\begin{Bmatrix} leaves \\ is\ leaving \end{Bmatrix}$ tonight from Chicago

3.41
Will/shall + progressive
The auxiliary verb construction (3.37) can be used together with the progressive infinitive to denote a 'future-as-a-matter-of-course': *will/shall* + *be* + V-*ing*. The use of this combination avoids the interpretation (to which *will*, *shall*, and *be going to* are liable) of volition, insistence, etc:

> He'*ll do* his best (future or volitional interpretation possible)
> He'*ll be doing* his best (future interpretation only)

This complex construction can be used to convey greater tact and consideration than the simple auxiliary construction does:

> When *will* you $\begin{Bmatrix} put\ on \\ be\ putting\ on \end{Bmatrix}$ another performance?

> When *will* you $\begin{Bmatrix} come? \\ be\ coming? \end{Bmatrix}$

3.42
Be to + infinitive
This expresses (a) arrangement, (b) command, or (c) contingent future:

(a) We *are to be married* soon
There'*s to be* an investigation
(b) You *are to be* back by 10 o'clock
(c) If he *is to* succeed, he must work harder

3.43
Be about to + infinitive
This construction expresses near future, *ie* imminent fulfilment:

The taxi is here and we *are about to* leave

Be . . . to may enclose other items such as *shortly* or *soon* to provide a means of future expression; with other items again (*bound, liable, certain, (un)likely*), future expression is overlaid with modal meaning:

He *is certain to* address the meeting (= *It is certain* that
he *will* address . . .)

3.44
Future time in the past
Some of the future constructions just discussed can be used in the past tense to express time which is in the future when seen from a viewpoint in the past.

(1) AUXILIARY VERB CONSTRUCTION with *would* (rare; literary narrative style)

The time was not far off when he *would regret* this decision

(2) *be going to* + INFINITIVE (often with the sense of 'unfulfilled intention')

You *were going to give* me your address

(3) PAST PROGRESSIVE

I *was meeting* him in Bordeaux the next day

(4) *be to* + INFINITIVE (formal = 'was destined', 'was arranged')

He *was* later *to regret* his decision
The meeting *was to be held* the following week

(5) *be about to* ('on the point of'); *cf* 3.43

He *was about to hit* me

Mood
3.45
Mood is expressed in English to a very minor extent by the subjunctive,
as in

So *be* it then!

to a much greater extent by past tense forms, as in

If you *taught* me, I would learn quickly

but above all, by means of the modal auxiliaries, as in

It is strange that he *should* have left so early

3.46
The subjunctive
Three categories of subjunctive may be distinguished:

(a) The MANDATIVE SUBJUNCTIVE in *that*-clauses has only one
form, the base (V); this means there is lack of the regular indicative concord between subject and finite verb in the 3rd person
singular present, and the present and past tenses are indistinguishable. This subjunctive can be used with any verb in subordinate
that-clauses when the main clause contains an expression of recom-
mendation, resolution, demand, and so on (*We demand, require,
move, insist, suggest, ask*, etc *that* . . .). The use of this subjunctive
occurs chiefly in formal style (and especially in AmE) where in less
formal contexts one would rather make use of other devices, such
as *to*-infinitive or *should*+infinitive:

It is/was necessary that every member *inform* himself of these
rules
It is necessary that every member *should inform* himself of these
rules
It is necessary for every member *to inform* himself of these rules

(b) The FORMULAIC SUBJUNCTIVE also consists of the base (V) but
is only used in clauses in certain set expressions which have to be
learned as wholes (see 7.64):

Come what may, we will go ahead
God *save* the Queen!
Suffice it to say that . . .
Be that as it may . . .
Heaven *forbid* that . . .

(c) The SUBJUNCTIVE *were* is hypothetical in meaning and is used in
conditional and concessive clauses and in subordinate clauses after

optative verbs like *wish* (see 11.48). It occurs as the 1st and 3rd person singular past of the verb *be*, matching the indicative *was*, which is the more common in less formal style:

If she $\begin{Bmatrix} were \\ was \end{Bmatrix}$ to do something like that, ...

He spoke to me as if I $\begin{Bmatrix} were \\ was \end{Bmatrix}$ deaf

I wish I $\begin{Bmatrix} were \\ was \end{Bmatrix}$ dead

Note

Only *were* is acceptable in 'As it were' (=so to speak); *were* is usual in 'If I were you'.

3.47
Modal past

Just as *was* could replace *were* in 'If I were rich', so in closed or unreal conditions involving all other verbs than *be*, it is the past tense that conveys the impossibility. See further, 11.48. Other modal or quasi-modal uses of the past are illustrated by

   I *wondered* if you'd like a drink

which involves an attitudinal rather than a time distinction from 'I *wonder* if you'd like a drink', and

   We *were catching* the 8 o'clock train and it is nearly 8 o'clock already

which seems to depend on a covert subordinating clause such as 'We agreed that . . .' in which the past tense is purely temporal.

The uses of the modal auxiliaries
3.48
CAN/COULD
can

(1) Ability
  = *be able to,*
   be capable of,
   know how to
	He can speak English but he can't write it very well ('He is able to speak/ capable of speaking ...')

(2) Permission
  = *be allowed to,*
   be permitted to
  (*Can* is less formal than *may* in this sense)
	Can
	May $\Big\}$ I smoke in here?
	
	('Am I allowed to smoke in here?')

| (3) Theoretical possibility (Contrast *may* = factual possibility) | Anybody can make mistakes
The road can be blocked ('It is possible to block the road') |

could

(1) Past ability	I never could play the banjo
(2) Present or future permission	Could I smoke in here?
(3) Present possibility (theoretical or factual)	We could go to the concert The road could be blocked
(4) Contingent possibility or ability in unreal conditions	If we had more money, we could buy a car

Note

[*a*] Ability can bring in the implication of willingness (especially in spoken English):

Can
Could } you do me a favour?

[*b*] Past permission is sometimes expressed by *could*:

This used to be the children's room but they couldn't make a noise there because of the neighbours

More generally, the past *can/could* for permission and possibility is *could have* + *V-ed*:

Tonight you can dance if you wish but you could have danced last night equally

[*c*] With some perception verbs (3.35), *can V* corresponds to the progressive aspect *be V-ing* with dynamic verbs:

I *can hear* footsteps; who's coming?

3.49

MAY/MIGHT

may

(1) Permission = *be allowed to* (In this sense *may* is more formal than *can*. Instead of *may not* or rare *mayn't*, the stronger *mustn't* is often used in the negative to express prohibition.)	You may borrow my car if you like You { mustn't / are not allowed to / may not } borrow my car
(2) Possibility (usually factual)	The road may be blocked ('It is possible that the road is blocked'; less probably: 'It is possible to block the road')

might

(1) Permission (rare)	Might I smoke in here?
(2) Possibility (theoretical or factual)	We might go to the concert What you say might be true

Note

[a] *May* and *might* are among the modal auxiliaries which involve differences of meaning in passing from declarative to interrogative or negative; see 7.42, 7.51.

[b] There is a rare use of *may* as a 'quasi-subjunctive' auxiliary, *eg* to express wish, normally in positive sentences (*cf* 7.64):

    May he never set foot in this house again!

3.50

SHALL/SHOULD

shall (volitional use; *cf* 3.37)

(1) Willingness on the part of the speaker in 2nd and 3rd person. Restricted use	He shall get his money You shall do exactly as you wish
(2) Intention on the part of the speaker, only in 1st person	I shan't be long We shall let you know our decision We shall overcome
(3) *a* Insistence. Restricted use	You shall do as I say He shall be punished
b Legal and quasi-legal injunction	The vendor shall maintain the equipment in good repair

Of these three meanings it is only the one of intention that is widely used today. *Shall* is, on the whole and especially outside BrE, an infrequent auxiliary with restricted use compared with *should, will,* and *would*; *will* is generally preferred, except in 1st person questions:

    Shall/*Will I come at once?

In the first person plural, *eg*

    What shall/will we drink?

shall asks for instructions, and *will* is non-volitional future (especially in AmE). *Will I/we* has become increasingly common not only in contexts of non-volitional futurity (*Will I see you later?*), but also in sentences expressing helplessness, perplexity, etc:

    How will I get there?   What will I do?   Which will I take?

This usage is predominantly AmE (though *should* is commonly preferred) but examples may be found in BrE too. A similar meaning is also conveyed by *be going to*:

    What are we going to do?

should

(1) Obligation and logical necessity (=*ought to*)	You should do as he says They should be home by now
(2) 'Putative' use after certain expressions, *eg: it is a pity that, I am surprised that* (see 11.51, 12.12, 12.17)	It is odd that you should say this to me I am sorry that this should have happened
(3) Contingent use (1st person only and especially BrE) in the main clause (=*would*)	We $\begin{Bmatrix} \text{should} \\ \text{would} \end{Bmatrix}$ love to go abroad (if we had the chance)
(4) In rather formal real conditions	If you should change your mind, please let us know

3.51
WILL/WOULD
will (*cf* 3.37)

(1) Willingness. Used in polite requests	He'll help you if you ask him Will you have another cup of coffee? Will you (please, kindly, etc) open the window?
(2) Intention. Usually contracted *'ll*; mainly 1st person	I'll write as soon as I can We won't stay longer than two hours
(3) Insistence. Stressed, hence no *'ll* contraction	He ˈwill do it, whatever you say ('He insists on doing it . . .') (*Cf* He ˈshall do it, whatever you say = 'I insist on his doing it . . .') He ˈwill keep interrupting me
(4) Prediction *Cf* the similar meanings of other expressions for logical necessity and habitual present. The contracted form *'ll* is common.	(a) Specific prediction: The game $\begin{Bmatrix} \text{will} \\ \text{must} \\ \text{should} \end{Bmatrix}$ be finished by now (b) Timeless prediction: Oil $\begin{Bmatrix} \text{will float} \\ \text{floats} \end{Bmatrix}$ on water (c) Habitual prediction: He'll (always) talk for hours if you give him the chance

would

(1) Willingness	Would you excuse me?
(2) Insistence	It's your own fault; you ˈwould take the baby with you
(3) Characteristic activity in the past (often aspectual in effect: 3.26 *ff*)	Every morning he would go for a long walk (*ie* 'it was customary') John ˈwould make a mess of it (informal = 'it was typical')
(4) Contingent use in the main clause of a conditional sentence	He would smoke too much if I didn't stop him
(5) Probability	That would be his mother

Note

Volition with preference is expressed with *would rather/sooner:*

> A: Would you like tea or would you rather have coffee?
> B: I think I'd rather have tea.

The expression with *sooner* is informal.

3.52
MUST

(1) Obligation or compulsion in the present tense (=*be obliged to, have* (*got*) *to*); except in reported speech, only *had to* (not *must*) is used in the past. There are two negatives: (1) = 'not be obliged to': *needn't, don't have to*; (2)='be obliged not to': *mustn't*. See 3.22, 3.49, 7.42.	You must be back by 10 o'clock Yesterday you had to be back by 10 o'clock Yesterday you said you $\begin{Bmatrix} \text{had to} \\ \text{must} \end{Bmatrix}$ be back by 10 o'clock You $\begin{Bmatrix} \text{needn't} \\ \text{don't have to} \\ \text{are not obliged to} \end{Bmatrix}$ be back by 10 o'clock
(2) (Logical) necessity *Must* is not used in sentences with negative or interrogative meanings, *can* being used instead. *Must* can occur in superficially interrogative but answer-assuming sentences.	There must be a mistake *but:* There cannot be a mistake Mustn't there be another reason for his behaviour?

3.53
OUGHT TO

Obligation; logical necessity or expectation	You ought to start at once They ought to be here by now

Note

Ought to and *should* both denote obligation and logical necessity, but are less categorical than *must* and *have to*. *Ought to* is often felt to be awkward in questions involving inversion, and *should* is preferred. Still less categorical than *ought* is *had/'d better/best* (plus bare infinitive):

A: Must you go?
B: Well, I don't have to, but I think I'd better (go).

3.54
The tense of modals
Only some of the modals have corresponding present and past forms:

PRESENT	PAST
can	*could*
may	*could* (*might*)
shall	*should*
will/'ll	*would/'d*
must	(*had to*)
—	*used to*
ought to	—
need	—
dare	*dared*

He can speak English now	He couldn't come yesterday
He'll do anything for money	He wouldn't come when I asked him yesterday

The usual past tense of *may* denoting permission is *could*:

Today, we $\begin{Bmatrix} can \\ may \end{Bmatrix}$ stay the whole afternoon

Yesterday, we could only stay for a few minutes

The following modals are not used in the past tense except in reported speech: *must*, *ought to*, and *need* (but *cf* 3.22). *Had to* serves as the past of both *must* and *have to*:

He $\begin{Bmatrix} must \\ has\ to \end{Bmatrix}$ leave now

He $\begin{Bmatrix} *must \\ had\ to \end{Bmatrix}$ leave in a hurry yesterday

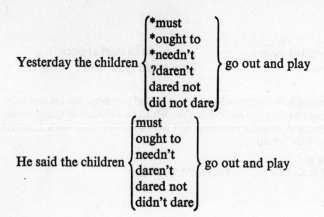

$$
\text{Yesterday the children}
\begin{cases}
\text{*must} \\
\text{*ought to} \\
\text{*needn't} \\
\text{?daren't} \\
\text{dared not} \\
\text{did not dare}
\end{cases}
\text{go out and play}
$$

$$
\text{He said the children}
\begin{cases}
\text{must} \\
\text{ought to} \\
\text{needn't} \\
\text{daren't} \\
\text{dared not} \\
\text{didn't dare}
\end{cases}
\text{go out and play}
$$

3.55
The modals and aspect

The perfective and progressive aspects are normally excluded when the modal expresses 'ability' or 'permission', and also when *shall* or *will* express 'volition'. These aspects are freely used, however, with other modal meanings; *eg*

'possibility'
{
He may have missed the train
He may have been visiting his mother
He can't be swimming all day
He can't have been working
}

'necessity'
{
He must have left his umbrella on the bus
I must be dreaming
You must have been sitting in the sun
}

'prediction'
{
The guests will have arrived by now
John will still be reading his paper
}

Bibliographical note

On tense and aspect, see Allen (1966); Palmer (1974); Schopf (1969); on the meanings of the modal auxiliaries, see Halliday (1970); Leech (1971); Lyons (1977).

FOUR
NOUNS, PRONOUNS, AND THE
BASIC NOUN PHRASE

4.1
The basic noun phrase

The noun phrase typically functions as subject, object, complement of sentences, and as complement in prepositional phrases. Consider the different subjects in the following:

(a) *The girl*
(b) *The pretty girl*
(c) *The pretty girl in the corner* } is Mary Smith
(d) *The pretty girl who became angry*
(e) *She*

Since noun phrases of the types illustrated in (b–d) include elements that will be dealt with in later chapters (adjectives, prepositional phrases, etc), it will be convenient to postpone the treatment of the noun phrase incorporating such items. We shall deal here with the elements found in those noun phrases that consist of pronouns and numerals, and of nouns with articles or other closed-system items that can occur before the noun head, such as predeterminers like *all*.

Noun classes
4.2

It is necessary, both for grammatical and semantic reasons, to see nouns as falling into different subclasses. This is easily demonstrated by taking the four nouns *John, bottle, furniture* and *cake* and considering the extent to which it is possible for each to appear as head of the noun phrase operating as object in the following sentence (*some* in the fourth line is the unstressed determiner: 4.5):

	(1)	(2)	(3)	(4)
	John	*bottle	furniture	cake
	*the John	the bottle	the furniture	the cake
I saw	*a John	a bottle	*a furniture	a cake
	*some John	*some bottle	some furniture	some cake
	*Johns	bottles	*furnitures	cakes

The difference between column 1 (with its four impossible usages) and column 4 (with none) indicates the degree of variation between classes. Nouns that behave like *John* in column 1 (*Paris, Mississippi, Gandhi, . . .*) are PROPER NOUNS, further discussed in 4.23. The nouns in columns 2, 3 and 4 are all COMMON NOUNS, but there are important differences within this class. Nouns which behave like *bottle* in column 2 (*chair, word, finger, remark, . . .*), which must be seen as individual countable entities and cannot be viewed as an undifferentiated mass, are called COUNT NOUNS. Those conforming like *furniture* to the pattern of column 3 (*grass, warmth, humour, . . .*) must by contrast be seen as an undifferentiated mass or continuum, and we call them NON-COUNT NOUNS. Finally in column 4 we have nouns which combine the characteristics of count and non-count nouns (*cake, paper, stone, . . .*); that is, we can view *stone* as the non-count material (as in column 3) constituting the entity *a stone* (as in column 2) which can be picked up from a pile of stones and individually thrown.

4.3

It will be noticed that the categorization count and non-count cuts across the traditional distinction between 'abstract' (broadly, immaterial) nouns like *warmth*, and 'concrete' (broadly, tangible) nouns like *bottle*. But while abstract nouns may be count like *remark* or non-count like *warmth*, there is a considerable degree of overlap between abstract and non-count. This does not proceed from nature but is language-specific, and we list some examples which are non-count in English but count nouns in some other languages:

anger, applause, behaviour, chaos, chess, conduct, courage, dancing, education, harm, homework, hospitality, leisure, melancholy, moonlight, parking, photography, poetry, progress, publicity, research (*as in* do some research), resistance, safety, shopping, smoking, sunshine, violence, weather

Note
Another categorization that cuts across the count and non-count distinction will identify a small class of nouns that behave like most adjectives in being gradable. Though such degree nouns are chiefly non-count ('His acts of *great foolishness*'='His acts

were *very* foolish'), they can also be count nouns: 'The children are such thieves!' See further 5.27.

4.4

Nevertheless, when we turn to the large class of nouns which can be both count and non-count, we see that there is often considerable difference in meaning involved and that this corresponds broadly to concreteness or particularization in the count usage and abstractness or generalization in the non-count usage. For example:

COUNT	NON-COUNT
I've had many *difficulties*	He's not had much *difficulty*
He's had many odd *experiences*	This job requires *experience*
Buy an evening *paper*	Wrap the parcel in brown *paper*
She was a *beauty* in her youth	She had *beauty* in her youth
The *talks* will take place in Paris	I dislike idle *talk*
There were bright *lights* and harsh *sounds*	*Light* travels faster than *sound*
The *lambs* were eating quietly	There is *lamb* on the menu

In many cases the type of distinction between *lamb* count and *lamb* non-count is achieved by separate lexical items: (*a*) *sheep* ~ (*some*) *mutton;* (*a*) *calf* ~ (*some*) *veal;* (*a*) *pig* ~ (*some*) *pork;* (*a*) *loaf* ~ (*some*) *bread;* (*a*) *table* ~ (*some*) *furniture*.

Note

Virtually all non-count nouns can be treated as count nouns when used in classificatory senses:

There are several French *wines* available (=kinds of wine)
This is *a bread* I greatly enjoy (=kind of bread)

4.5
Determiners

There are six classes of determiners with respect to their co-occurrence with the noun classes singular count (such as *bottle*), plural count (such as *bottles*), and non-count nouns (such as *furniture*). The check marks in the figures that follow indicate which noun classes will co-occur with members of the determiner class concerned.

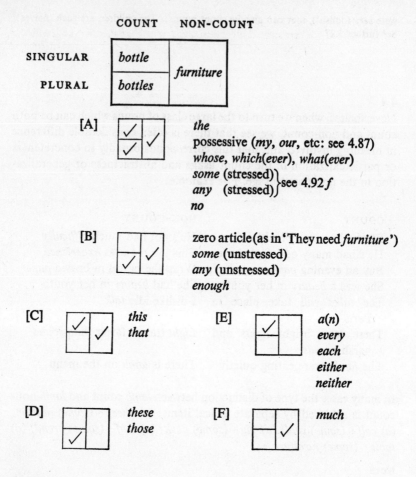

Note

[a] Many of the determiners can be pronominal (4.78):

> *Either* book ∼ *Either* of the books ∼ You can have *either*

[b] *Every* can co-occur with possessives: *his every word* (=‘each of his words’).

4.6
Closed-system premodifiers

In addition to determiners, there is a large number of other closed-system items that occur before the head of the noun phrase. These form three classes (predeterminers, ordinals, and quantifiers) which have been set up on the basis of the possible positions that they can have in relation to determiners and to each other. Within each of the three classes, we will make distinctions according to their patterning with the classes of singular count, plural count, and non-count nouns.

Note
We will also include here some open-class premodifiers that commute to a significant extent with closed-system items, *eg: three times* (*cf: once, twice*), *a large quantity of* (*cf: much*).

Predeterminers
4.7
All, both, half

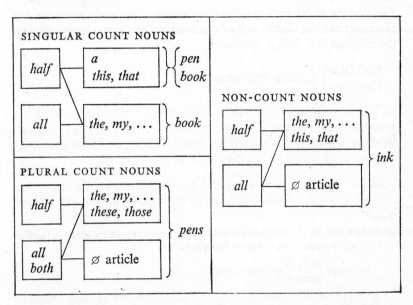

These predeterminers can occur only before articles or demonstratives but, since they are themselves quantifiers, they do not occur with the following 'quantitative' determiners: *every, (n)either, each, some, any, no, enough.*

All, both, and *half* have *of*-constructions, which are optional with nouns and obligatory with personal pronouns:

all (of) the meat   all of it
both (of) the students   both of them
half (of) the time   half of it

With a quantifier following, the *of*-construction is preferred (especially in AmE):

all of the many boys

All three can be used pronominally:

All/both/half passed their exams

All and *both* (but not *half*) can occur after the head, either immediately or within the predication:

The students⎫ ⎧all ⎫
They   ⎬ ⎨both ⎬ passed their exams
            ⎭ ⎩   ⎭

The students were all hungry
They may have all finished

The predeterminer *both* and the determiners *either* and *neither* are not plural proper but 'dual', *ie* they can refer only to two. Compared with the numeral *two*, *both* is emphatic:

Both (the)⎫
The two   ⎬ students were excellent
           ⎭

All is rare with singular concrete count nouns (*?I haven't used all the pencil*) though it is less rare with contrastive stress: *I haven't read ALL the book*, where *book* is treated as a kind of divisible mass. The normal constructions would be *all of the book* or *the whole book*.

Before certain singular temporal nouns, and especially in adjunct phrases, *all* is often used with the zero article: *I haven't seen him all day*.

Note

[a] There is also an adverbial *half* (as in *half wine, half water*) which occurs in familiar emphatic negation and can precede *enough*:

He hasn't ⎧half ⎫ enough money!
          ⎩nearly⎭

Added to numbers from *one* upwards, *a half* co-occurs with plural nouns: *one and a half days*. A preceding determiner or numeral is common with *of*- construction (*my half of the room, one half of her time*), but infrequent otherwise.

[b] The postposed *all* in 'They were all hungry' must not be confused with its use as an informal intensifying adverb in 'He is all upset' (5.23 Note *b*).

[c] The items *such* (*a*), *what* (*a*) as predeterminers are discussed in 5.27.

4.8

Double, twice, three/four . . . times

The second type of predeterminer includes *double, twice, three times*, etc, which occur with non-count and plural count nouns, and with singular count nouns denoting number, amount, etc.:

double their salaries
twice his strength
three times this amount

Three, four, etc *times* as well as *once* can co-occur with the determiners *a, every, each,* and (less commonly) *per* to form 'distributive' expressions with a temporal noun as head:

$$
\left.\begin{array}{l} \text{once} \\ \text{twice} \\ \text{three} \\ \text{four} \\ \ldots \end{array}\right\} \text{times}
\left\{\begin{array}{l} \text{a} \\ \text{every} \\ \text{each} \\ \text{(per)} \end{array}\right\}
\left\{\begin{array}{l} \text{day} \\ \text{week} \\ \text{month} \\ \text{year} \\ \text{decade} \\ \ldots \end{array}\right.
$$

4.9
One-third, two-fifths, etc
The fractions *one-third, two-fifths, three-quarters*, etc, used with non-count and with singular and plural count nouns, can also be followed by determiners, and have the alternative *of*-construction:

> He did it in one-third (of) the time it took me

Postdeterminers
4.10
Items which must follow determiners but precede adjectives in the pre-modification structure include numerals (ordinal and cardinal) and quantifiers. The numerals are listed in 4.97.

4.11
Cardinal numerals
Apart from *one*, which can co-occur only with singular count nouns, all cardinal numerals (*two*, *three*, ...) co-occur only with plural count nouns:

> He has one sister and three brothers
> The two blue cars belong to me

Note
One may be regarded as a stressed form of the indefinite article: 'I would like *a/one* large cigar'. In consequence, although the definite article may precede any cardinal, the indefinite can not.

4.12
Ordinal numerals and general ordinals
In addition to the ordinals which have a one-for-one relation with the cardinals (*fourth ~ four; twentieth ~ twenty*), we consider here items like *next, last, (an)other, additional*, which resemble them grammatically and semantically. Ordinal numerals, except *first*, co-occur only with count nouns. All ordinals usually precede any cardinal numbers in the noun phrase:

> The first three planes were American

The general ordinals, however, may be used freely before or after cardinals, according to the meaning required:

His $\begin{Bmatrix} \text{last two} \\ \text{two last} \end{Bmatrix}$ books were novels

Note

Another has two functions. It can be the unstressed form of *one other* (*cf* 4.11 Note) or it can have the same meaning as 'second' with indefinite article:

I don't like this house: I'd prefer another one

$\begin{Bmatrix} \text{Another} \\ \text{A second} \end{Bmatrix} \begin{Bmatrix} \text{blue car} \\ \text{two volumes of poetry} \end{Bmatrix}$

Quantifiers
4.13

There are two small groups of closed-system quantifiers:

(1) *many*, (*a*) *few*, and *several* co-occur only with plural count nouns:

The few words he spoke were well chosen

(2) *much* and (*a*) *little* co-occur only with non-count nouns:

There hasn't been much good weather recently

Several is rarely (and *much* virtually never) preceded by a determiner, and in the case of *few* and *little* there is a positive/negative contrast according as the indefinite article is or is not used:

He took $\begin{Bmatrix} \text{a few biscuits} & (= \text{several}) \\ \text{few biscuits} & (= \text{not many}) \\ \text{a little butter} & (= \text{some}) \\ \text{little butter} & (= \text{not much}) \end{Bmatrix}$

Since the first of these has a plural count noun and the third a non-count noun, neither of which (4.5) co-occurs with the indefinite article, it will be clear that in these instances *a* belongs to the quantifier alone.

Note

[a] The quantifier (*a*) *little* must be distinguished from the homonymous adjective as in *A little bird was singing*.

[b] *Many* and *few* can be used predicatively in formal style (*His faults were many*), and *many* has the additional potentiality of functioning as a predeterminer with singular count nouns preceded by *a(n)*:

Many an ambitious student (= Many ambitious students)

[c] The quantifier *enough* is used with both count and non-count nouns:

There are (not) *enough* chairs
There is (not) *enough* furniture

Occasionally it follows the noun (especially non-count) but this strikes many people as archaic or dialectal.

4.14

There is also a large open class of phrasal quantifiers. Some can co-occur equally with non-count and plural count nouns:

$$\text{The room contained} \left\{ \begin{matrix} \text{plenty of} \\ \text{a lot of} \\ \text{lots of} \end{matrix} \right\} \left\{ \begin{matrix} \text{students} \\ \text{furniture} \end{matrix} \right.$$

These (especially *lots*) are chiefly used informally, though *plenty of* is stylistically neutral in the sense 'sufficient'. Others are restricted to occurring with non-count nouns:

$$\text{The room contained} \left\{ \begin{matrix} a \left\{ \begin{matrix} \text{great} \\ \text{good} \end{matrix} \right\} \text{deal of} \\ a \left\{ \begin{matrix} \text{(large)} \\ \text{(small)} \end{matrix} \right\} \left\{ \begin{matrix} \text{quantity} \\ \text{amount} \end{matrix} \right\} \text{of} \end{matrix} \right\} \text{money}$$

or to plural count nouns:

$$\text{The room contained a} \left\{ \begin{matrix} \text{(great)} \\ \text{(large)} \\ \text{(good)} \end{matrix} \right\} \text{number of students}$$

As these examples suggest, it is usual to find the indefinite article and a quantifying adjective, the latter being obligatory in Standard English with *deal*.

4.15

The phrasal quantifiers provide a means of imposing countability on non-count nouns as the following partitive expressions illustrate:

$$\text{GENERAL PARTITIVES} \left\{ \begin{matrix} \text{two pieces} \\ \text{a bit} \\ \text{an item} \end{matrix} \right\} \text{of} \left\{ \begin{matrix} \text{news} \\ \text{information} \\ \text{furniture} \end{matrix} \right.$$

$$\text{TYPICAL PARTITIVES} \left\{ \begin{matrix} \text{a slice of cake} \\ \text{a roast of meat} \\ \text{a few loaves of bread} \\ \text{a bowl of soup} \\ \text{a bottle of wine} \end{matrix} \right.$$

$$\text{MEASURES} \left\{ \begin{matrix} \text{a pint of beer} \\ \text{a spoonful of medicine} \\ \text{a pound of butter} \end{matrix} \right.$$

Reference and the articles
4.16
Specific/generic reference
In discussing the use of the articles, it is essential to make a distinction between specific and generic reference. If we say

A lion and two tigers are sleeping in the cage

the reference is specific, since we have in mind specific specimens of the class 'tiger'. If, on the other hand, we say

Tigers are dangerous animals

the reference is generic, since we are thinking of the class 'tiger' without special reference to specific tigers.

The distinctions that are important for count nouns with specific reference disappear with generic reference. This is so because generic reference is used to denote what is normal or typical for members of a class. Consequently, the distinctions of number and definiteness are neutralized since they are no longer relevant for the generic concept. Singular or plural, definite or indefinite can sometimes be used without change in the generic meaning, though plural definite occurs chiefly with nationality names (*cf* 4.18):

The German⎫
A German ⎬ is a good musician

The Germans⎫
Germans   ⎬ are good musicians

At least the following three forms can be used generically with a count noun:

The tiger⎫
A tiger ⎬ is a dangerous animal

Tigers are dangerous animals

But with non-count nouns, only the zero article is possible:

Music can be soothing

Note

There is considerable (though by no means complete) interdependence between the dynamic/stative dichotomy in the verb phrase and the specific/generic dichotomy in the noun phrase, as appears in the following examples:

generic reference/simple aspect		*The tiger lives* in the jungle
specific reference	simple aspect	*The tiger* at this circus *performs* twice a day
	progressive aspect	*The tiger is sleeping* in the cage
generic reference/simple aspect		*The English drink* beer in pubs
specific reference	simple aspect	*The Englishmen* (who live here) *drink* beer every day
	progressive aspect	*The Englishmen are* just now *drinking* beer in the garden

4.17
Systems of article usage

We can thus set up two different systems of article use depending on the type of reference:

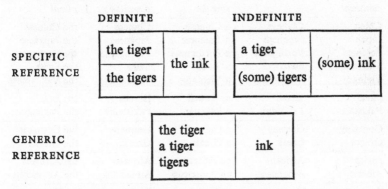

With definite specific reference, the definite article is used for all noun classes:

Where is the pen
Where are the pens ⎫ I bought?
Where is the ink ⎭

With indefinite specific reference, singular count nouns take the indefinite article *a(n)*, while non-count and plural count nouns take zero article or unstressed *some* (*any* in non-assertive contexts, 4.93):

I want a pen/some pens/some ink
I don't want a pen/any pens/any ink

Generic reference
4.18
Nationality words and adjectives as head

There are two kinds of adjectives that can act as noun-phrase head with generic reference (*cf* 5.6 *ff*):

(a) PLURAL PERSONAL (for example: *the French = the French nation; the rich = those who are rich*)

(b) SINGULAR NON-PERSONAL ABSTRACT (for example: *the evil = that which is evil*)

The lexical variation in a number of nationality words, as between *an Englishman/several Englishmen/the English*, depending on type of reference, appears from the following table.

Where nationality words have no double form (like *English, Englishman*), *the* + plural can be both generic and specific:

The Greeks are musical [generic]
The Greeks that I know are musical [specific]

name of country or continent	adjective	specific reference		generic reference
		singular	plural(two,...)	plural
China	Chinese	a Chinese	Chinese	the Chinese
Japan	Japanese	a Japanese	Japanese	the Japanese
Portugal	Portuguese	a Portuguese	Portuguese	the Portuguese
Switzerland	Swiss	a Swiss	Swiss	the Swiss
Vietnam	Vietnamese	a Vietnamese	Vietnamese	the Vietnamese
Israel	Israeli	an Israeli	Israelis	the Israelis
Pakistan	Pakistani	a Pakistani	Pakistanis	the Pakistanis
Germany	German	a German	Germans	the Germans
Greece	Greek	a Greek	Greeks	the Greeks
Africa	African	an African	Africans	the Africans
America	American	an American	Americans	the Americans
Europe	European	a European	Europeans	the Europeans
Asia	Asian	an Asian	Asians	the Asians
Australia	Australian	an Australian	Australians	the Australians
Italy	Italian	an Italian	Italians	the Italians
Russia	Russian	a Russian	Russians	the Russians
Belgium	Belgian	a Belgian	Belgians	the Belgians
Brazil	Brazilian	a Brazilian	Brazilians	the Brazilians
Hungary	Hungarian	a Hungarian	Hungarians	the Hungarians
Norway	Norwegian	a Norwegian	Norwegians	the Norwegians
Denmark	Danish	a Dane	Danes	the Danes
Finland	Finnish	a Finn	Finns	the Finns
Poland	Polish	a Pole	Poles	the Poles
Spain	Spanish	a Spaniard	Spaniards	the Spaniards
Sweden	Swedish	a Swede	Swedes	the Swedes
Arabia	Arabic	an Arab	Arabs	the Arabs
England	English	an Englishman	Englishmen	{ Englishmen / the English
France	French	a Frenchman	Frenchmen	{ Frenchmen / the French
Holland, the Netherlands }	Dutch	a Dutchman	Dutchmen	{ Dutchmen / the Dutch
Ireland	Irish	an Irishman	Irishmen	{ Irishmen / the Irish
Wales	Welsh	a Welshman	Welshmen	{ Welshmen / the Welsh
Britain	British	(a Briton)	(Britons)	{ the British / (Britons)
Scotland	{ Scots / Scottish / (Scotch)	a Scotsman / a Scot / (a Scotchman)	Scotsmen / Scots / (Scotchmen)	Scotsmen / the Scots / (Scotchmen, the Scotch)

Note

[a] The adjective *Grecian* refers chiefly to ancient Greece: *a Grecian urn*.

[b] *Arabic* is used in *Arabic numerals* (as opposed to *Roman numerals*) and in *the Arabic language; he speaks Arabic fluently*. But *an Arabian camel*.

[c] *A Britisher* is colloquial (esp AmE).

[d] The inhabitants themselves prefer *Scots* and *Scottish* to *Scotch*, which however is commonly used in such phrases as *Scotch terrier, Scotch whisky*; contrast *the Scottish universities, the Scottish Highlands, a Scottish accent*, etc, denoting nationality rather than type.

[e] Nationality nouns tend to be used only of men: *He is a Spaniard but she is Swedish.*

4.19

Non-count and plural count nouns

When they have generic reference, both concrete and abstract non-count nouns, and usually also plural count nouns, are used with the zero article:

He likes $\begin{cases} \text{wine, wood, cream cheese, ...} \\ \text{music, chess, literature, history, skiing, ...} \\ \text{lakes, games, long walks, ...} \end{cases}$

Postmodification by an *of*-phrase usually requires the definite article with a head noun, which thus has limited generic (partitive) reference:

He likes $\begin{cases} \text{the wine(s)} \\ \text{the music} \\ \text{the countryside} \\ \text{the lakes} \end{cases}$ of France

Similarly, *the wines of this shop* is an instance of limited generic reference, in the sense that it does not refer to any particular wines at any one time. Postmodification with other prepositions is less dependent on a preceding definite article:

Mrs Nelson adores $\begin{cases} \text{Venetian glass} \\ \text{the glass of Venice} \\ \text{*glass of Venice} \\ \text{the glass from Venice} \\ \text{glass from Venice} \end{cases}$

This type of postmodification structure should be compared to the frequent alternative with an adjectival premodification. In comparison with some other languages English tends to make a liberal interpretation of the concept 'generic' in such cases, so that the zero article is used also where the reference of the noun head is restricted by premodification.

NON-COUNT NOUNS	Canadian paper	{the paper of Canada {paper from Canada
	Chinese history	the history of China
	Trotskyite politics	the politics of Trotsky
	American literature	the literature of America
	Restoration comedy	the comedy of the Restoration
PLURAL COUNT NOUNS	Japanese cameras	cameras from Japan
	Oriental women	the women of the Orient

The zero article is also used with other plural nouns that are not unambiguously generic:

> Appearances can be deceptive
> Things aren't what they used to be

Note

Just as non-count nouns can be used as count (4.4 Note), so count nouns can be used as non-count in a generic sense:

> This bread tastes of *onion;* has it been alongside *onions?*

Specific reference
4.20
Indefinite and definite

Just as we have seen in 4.16 a correspondence between aspect and reference in respect of generic and specific, so we have seen in 3.31 a correspondence between the simple and perfective in respect of what must be regarded as the basic article contrast:

> *An* intruder has stolen *a* vase;
> *the* intruder stole *the* vase from *a* locked cupboard;
> *the* cupboard was smashed open.

As we see in this (unusually explicit) example, the definite article presupposes an earlier mention of the item so determined. But in actual usage the relation between presupposition and the definite article may be much less overt. For example, a conversation may begin:

> *The* house on the corner is for sale

and the postmodification passes for some such unspoken preamble as

> There is, as you know, *a* house on the corner

Compare also *What is the climate like?* – that is, the climate of the area being discussed. Even more covert are the presuppositions which permit the definite article in examples like the following:

John asked his wife to put on *the* kettle while he looked in *the*
paper to see what was on *the* radio

No prior mention of *a kettle, a paper, a radio* is needed, since these things
are part of the cultural situation.

On a broader plane, we talk of *the sun, the moon, the stars, the sky* as aspects of experience common to mankind as a whole. These seem to require no earlier indefinite reference because each term is so specific as to
be in fact unique for practical human purposes. This gives them something approaching the status of those proper names which are based on
common count nouns: *the Bible, the United States,* for example (*cf* 4.24 *ff*).

Note

[a] The indefinite article used with a proper name means 'a certain', 'one giving his
name as':

A Mr Johnson wants to speak to you

[b] The definite article given heavy stress is used (especially informally) to indicate
superlative quality:

Chelsea is THE place for young people
Are you THE Mr Johnson (=the famous)?

4.21
Common nouns with zero article

There are a number of count nouns that take the zero article in abstract
or rather specialized use, chiefly in certain idiomatic expressions (with
verbs like *be* and *go* and with prepositions):

go by car	*but*	sit in/look at, ... the car
be in bed		make/sit on, ... the bed
go to school		go into/take a look at, ... the school
(an institution)		(a building)

The following list gives a number of common expressions with zero
article; for comparison, usage with the definite article is also illustrated.

SEASONS: spring, summer, autumn (BrE), fall (AmE), winter
Eg In winter, we go skiing. After the winter is over, the swallows will return.

'INSTITUTIONS' (often with *at, in, to,* etc)

be in / go to		
	bed	lie down on the bed
	church	admire the church
	prison	walk round the prison
	hospital (esp BrE)	redecorate the hospital
	class (esp AmE)	

be at	school	drive past the school
go to	college	
	sea	look out towards the sea
	university	be at/go to/study at the university (esp AmE)

be at/go home
be in/leave town   approach the town

MEANS OF TRANSPORT (with *by*)

travel		bicycle	sit on the bicycle
leave	by	bus	be on the bus
come		car	sleep in the car
		boat	sit in the boat
		train	take the/a train
		plane	be on the plane

TIMES OF THE DAY AND NIGHT (particularly with *at, by, after, before*)

at dawn/daybreak, when day breaks	during the day
at sunrise/sunset	admire the sunrise/sunset
at/around noon/midnight	in the afternoon
at dusk/twilight	see nothing in the dusk
at/by night	wake up in the night
(by) day and night	in the daytime
before morning came (rather	in/during the morning
evening came on formal	in the evening
after night fell style)	in the night

MEALS

have	breakfast	the breakfast was good
before	brunch (esp AmE)	
at	lunch	he enjoyed the lunch
after	tea (esp BrE)	
stay for	cocktails (esp AmE)	
	dinner	prepare (the) dinner
	supper	

dinner will be served soon   the dinner was well cooked

ILLNESSES

appendicitis	the plague
anaemia	(the) flu
diabetes	(the) measles
influenza	(the) mumps

PARALLEL STRUCTURES

arm in arm	he took her by the arm
hand in hand	a paper in his hand
day by day	
teaspoonful by teaspoonful	
he's neither man nor boy	
husband and wife	
man to man	
face to face	
from dawn to dusk	
from beginning to end	from the beginning of the day to the end of it
from right to left	keep to the right
from west to north	he lives in the north

Note

Compare also familiar or peremptory vocatives: *That's right, girl! Come here, man!*
Vocatives take neither definite nor indefinite article in English.

4.22
Article usage with common nouns in intensive relation
Unlike many other languages, English requires the definite or indefinite article with the count noun complement in an intensive relation (7.6).

With indefinite reference, the indefinite article is used:

(i) intensive complementation	John became a businessman
(ii) complex transitive complementation (active verb)	Mary considered John a genius
(iii) complex transitive complementation (passive verb)	John was taken for a linguist

The complement of *turn* and *go*, however, has zero article (12.9 Note *a*):

John started out a music student before he turned linguist

Definite reference requires the definite article:

(i) John became
(ii) Mary considered John } the genius of the family
(iii) John was taken for

However, the zero article may be used with the noun complement after copulas and 'naming verbs', such as *appoint*, *declare*, *elect*, when the noun designates a unique office or task:

(i) John is (the) captain of the team
(ii) They elected him⎫
(iii) He was elected   ⎬ (the) President of the United States

Unique reference
Proper nouns
4.23
Proper nouns are names of specific people (*Shakespeare*), places (*Milwaukee*), countries (*Australia*), months (*September*), days (*Thursday*), holidays (*Christmas*), magazines (*Vogue*), and so forth. Names have 'unique' reference, and (as we have seen in 4.2) do not share such characteristics of common nouns as article contrast. But when the names have restrictive modification to give a partitive meaning to the name (*cf* 4.19), proper nouns take the (cataphoric) definite article.

UNIQUE MEANING	PARTITIVE MEANING
during Easter	during the Easter of that year
in England	in the England of Queen Elizabeth
in Denmark	in the Denmark of today
Chicago	the Chicago I like (='the aspect of Chicago')
Shakespeare	the young Shakespeare

Proper names can be converted into common nouns (App I.29):

Shakespeare (the author) ⎧ a Shakespeare ('an author like S.')
⎨ Shakespeares ('authors like S.' or
⎩ 'copies of the works of S.')

Note
Proper nouns are written with initial capital letters. So also, frequently, are a number of common nouns with unique reference, which are therefore close to proper nouns, *eg: fate, fortune, heaven, hell, nature, paradise.*

4.24
The following list exemplifies the main classes of proper nouns:

Personal names (with or without titles; 4.25)
Calendar items (4.26):
  (a) Festivals
  (b) Months and days of the week

Geographical names (4.27):
  (a) Continents
  (b) Countries, counties, states, etc
  (c) Cities, towns, etc
  (d) Lakes
  (e) Mountains
Name+common noun (4.28).

4.25
Personal names
Personal names with or without appositive titles:

Dr Watson	Lady Churchill
President Pompidou	Cardinal Spellman
Mr and Mrs Johnson	Judge Darling (mainly AmE)

Note the following exceptions:

the Emperor (Napoleon)	the Lord (God)
(but: Emperor Haile Selassie)	(the) Czar (Alexander)
the Duke (of Wellington)	

The article may also precede some other titles, including *Lord* and *Lady* in formal use. Family relations with unique reference behave like proper nouns:

Father (Daddy, Dad, *familiar*) is here
Mother (Mummy, Mum, *familiar*) is out
Uncle will come on Saturday

Compare:

The father was the tallest in the family

4.26
Calendar items
  (a) Names of festivals:

Christmas (Day)	Independence Day
Easter (Sunday)	Whit(sun) (mainly BrE)
Good Friday	Passover

  (b) Names of the months and the days of the week:

January, February, ...	Monday, Tuesday, ...

Note
Many such items can readily be used as count nouns:

I hate Mondays
There was an April in my childhood I well remember

4.27
Geographical names
(a) Names of continents:

(North) America   (Medieval) Europe
(Central) Australia   (East) Africa

Note *Antarctica* but *the Antarctic,* like *the Arctic.*

(b) Names of countries, counties, states, etc (normally no article with premodifying adjective):

(modern) Brazil   (industrial) Staffordshire
(west) Scotland   (northern) Arkansas

Note *Argentina* but *the Argentine, the Ruhr, the Saar, the Sahara, the Ukraine, the Crimea, (the) Lebanon, the Midwest; the Everglades* (and other plural names, see 4.30).

(c) Cities and towns (normally no article with premodifying word):

(downtown) Boston   (ancient) Rome   (suburban) London

Note *The Hague; the Bronx; the City, the West End, the East End (of London).*

(d) Lakes:

Lake Windermere   Silver Lake

(e) Mountains:

Mount Everest   Vesuvius

Note *the Mount of Olives (cf* 4.19).

4.28
Name + common noun
Name + common noun denoting buildings, streets, bridges, etc. There is a regular accentuation pattern as in *Hampstead* HEATH, except that names ending in *Street* have the converse: LAMB *Street.*

Madison Avenue	Westminster Bridge	Kennedy Airport
Park Lane	Westminster Abbey	Oxford Street
Portland Place	Greenwich Village	

Note *the Albert Hall, the Mansion House; the Haymarket, the Strand, the Mall* (street names in London); *the Merrit Parkway, the Pennsylvania Turnpike; (the) London Road* as a proper name but only *the London road* to denote 'the road leading to London'.

Note
Names of universities where the first part is a place-name can usually have two forms: *the University of London* (which is the official name) and *London University*. Universities named after a person have only the latter form: *eg: Yale University, Brown University*.

4.29
Proper nouns with definite article
The difference between an ordinary common noun and a common noun turned name is that the unique reference of the name has been institutionalized, as is made overt in writing by the use of initial capitals. The following structural classification illustrates the use of such proper nouns which retain the phrasal definite article:

WITHOUT MODIFICATION
   The Guardian   *The Times*

WITH PREMODIFICATION
   the Suez Canal   *The Washington Post*
   the Ford Foundation   the British Broadcasting Corporation (the BBC)

WITH POSTMODIFICATION
   the House of Commons   the Cambridge College of Arts
   the Institute of Psychiatry   and Technology
   the Bay of Biscay   the District of Columbia

ELLIPTED ELEMENTS
The original structure of a proper noun is sometimes unclear when one element has been dropped and the elliptic form has become institutionalized as the full name:

   the Tate (Gallery)   the Mermaid (Theatre)
   the Atlantic (Ocean)   the (River) Thames

Note
When the ellipted item is a plural or a collective implying plurality, the truncated name is pluralized:

the Canary Islands ~ the Canaries
the Pennine Range (*or* Chain) ~ the Pennines

4.30

The following classes of proper nouns are used with the definite article:

(a) Plural names

the Netherlands
the Midlands
the Hebrides, the Shetlands, the Bahamas
the Himalayas, the Alps, the Rockies, the Pyrenees

So also, more generally, the names of woods, families, etc: *the Wilsons* (=the Wilson family).

(b) Geographical names

Rivers: the Avon, the Danube, the Euphrates
Seas: the Pacific (Ocean), the Baltic, the Mediterranean
Canals: the Panama (Canal), the Erie Canal

(c) Public institutions, facilities, etc

Hotels and restaurants: the Grand (Hotel), the Savoy, the Hilton
Theatres, cinemas, clubs, etc: the Globe, the Athenaeum
Museums, libraries, etc: the Tate, the British Museum, the Huntingdon

Note *Drury Lane, Covent Garden.*

(d) Newspapers: *the Economist, the New York Times, the Observer*

After genitives and possessives the article is dropped: *today's New York Times.*

Note that magazines and periodicals normally have the zero article: *Language, Life, Time, Punch, New Scientist.*

Number
Invariable nouns
4.31

The English number system comprises SINGULAR, which denotes 'one', and PLURAL, which denotes 'more than one'. The singular category includes common non-count nouns and proper nouns. Count nouns are VARIABLE, occurring with either singular or plural number (*boy ~ boys*), or have INVARIABLE plural (*cattle*). *Fig* 4:1 provides a summary, with relevant section references.

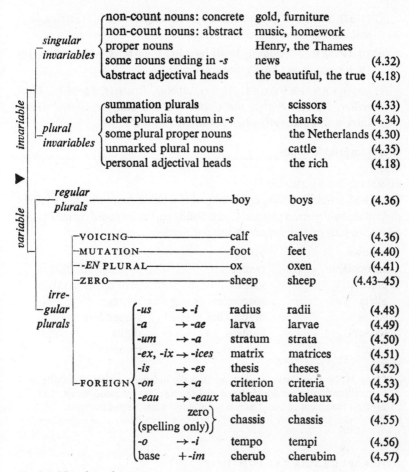

Fig 4:1 Number classes

Note
In addition to singular and plural number, we may distinguish dual number in the case of *both*, *either*, and *neither* (4.5, 4.7, 4.94) since they can only be used with reference to two. On reference to three or more, see 4.91.

4.32
Invariable nouns ending in -*s*
Note the following classes which take a singular verb, except where otherwise mentioned:

(a) *news:* The news is bad today

(b) SOME DISEASES: *measles, German measles, mumps, rickets, shingles.* Some speakers also accept a plural verb.

(c) SUBJECT NAMES IN -*ICS* (usually with singular verb): *classics, linguistics, mathematics, phonetics*, etc

(d) SOME GAMES: *billiards, bowls* (esp BrE), *darts, dominoes, draughts* (BrE), *checkers* (AmE), *fives, ninepins*

(e) SOME PROPER NOUNS: *Algiers, Athens, Brussels, Flanders, Marseilles, Naples, Wales; the United Nations* and *the United States* have a singular verb when considered as units.

Plural invariable nouns
4.33
SUMMATION PLURALS

Tools and articles of dress consisting of two equal parts which are joined constitute summation plurals. Countability can be imposed by means of *a pair of: a pair of scissors, three pairs of trousers.*

bellows	tongs	pants
binoculars	tweezers	pyjamas (BrE),
pincers	glasses	pajamas (AmE)
pliers	spectacles	shorts
scales	braces (BrE)	suspenders
scissors	flannels	tights
shears	knickers	trousers

Note

[a] Many of the summation plurals can take the indefinite article, especially with premodification: *a garden shears, a curling-tongs*, etc (*cf* zero plurals, 4.43 *ff*); obvious treatment as count nouns is not infrequent: *several tweezers*.

[b] Plural nouns commonly lose the inflection in premodification: *a suspender belt*.

4.34
OTHER 'PLURALIA TANTUM' IN -*S*

Among other 'pluralia tantum' (*ie* nouns that only occur in the plural), the following nouns end in -*s*. In many cases, however, there are forms without -*s*, sometimes with difference of meaning.

the Middle Ages

amends (make every/all possible amends)

annals

the Antipodes

archives

arms ('weapons', an arms depot)

arrears

ashes (*but* tobacco ash)

auspices

banns (of marriage)

bowels

brain(s) ('intellect', he's got good brains, *beside* a good brain)

clothes (*cf* cloths, /s/, *plural of* cloth)

the Commons (the House of Commons)

contents (*but* the silver content of the coin)

customs (customs duty)

dregs (coffee dregs)
earnings
entrails
fireworks (*but* he let off a fire-
 work)
funds ('money'; *but* a fund, 'a
 source of money')
goods (a goods train)
greens
guts ('bowels'; *but* cat-gut)
heads (heads or tails?)
holidays (summer holidays, BrE,
 but he's on holiday, he's
 taking a holiday in Spain)
letters (a man of letters)
lodgings
looks (he has good looks)
the Lords (the House of Lords)
manners
means (a man of means)
oats
odds (in betting)
outskirts

pains (take pains)
particulars (note the particulars)
premises ('building')
quarters, headquarters (*but* the
 Latin quarter)
regards (*but* win his regard)
remains
riches
savings (a savings bank)
spirits ('mood'; *but* he has a
 kindly spirit)
spirits ('alcohol'; *but* alcohol is a
 spirit)
stairs (a flight of stairs)
suds
surroundings
thanks
troops (*but* a troop of scouts)
tropics (*but* the Tropic of Cancer)
valuables
wages (*but* he earns a good wage)
wits (she has her wits about her;
 but he has a keen wit)

Note
Cf also *pence* in 'a few pence', 'tenpence', beside the regular *penny ~ pennies.*

4.35

UNMARKED PLURALS

cattle
clergy (*but also singular*)
folk (*but also informal* folks)
gentry

people (*but regular when* =
 'nation')
police
vermin
youth (*but regular when* =
 'young man')

Variable nouns
4.36
Regular plurals
Variable nouns have two forms, singular and plural, the singular being
the form listed in dictionaries. The vast majority of nouns are variable in
this way and normally the plural (-*s* suffix) is fully predictable both in
sound and spelling by the same rules as for the -*s* inflection of verbs (3.5).
Spelling creates numerous exceptions, however.

(a) Treatment of -*y*:

Beside the regular *spy*~*spies*, there are nouns in -*y* to which *s* is added:

with proper nouns: *the Kennedys, the two Germanys*
after a vowel (except the *u* of -*quy*): *days, boys, journeys*
in a few other words such as *stand-bys*

(b) Nouns of unusual form sometimes pluralize in '*s*:

letter names: *dot your i's*
numerals: *in the 1890's* (or, increasingly, *1890s*)
abbreviations: *two MP's* (or, increasingly, *MPs*)

(c) Nouns in -*o* have plural in -*os*, with some exceptions having either optional or obligatory -*oes*¹

Plurals in -*os* and -*oes*:

archipelago, banjo, buffalo, cargo, commando, flamingo, halo, motto, tornado, volcano

Plurals only in -*oes*:

echo, embargo, hero, Negro, potato, tomato, torpedo, veto

4.37
Compounds

Compounds form the plural in different ways, but (c) below is the most usual.

(a) PLURAL IN FIRST ELEMENT

attorney general	attorneys general, but more usually as (c)
notary public	notaries public
passer-by	passers-by
mother-in-law	mothers-in-law, but also as (c) informally
grant-in-aid	grants-in-aid
man-of-war	men-of-war
coat of mail	coats of mail
mouthful	mouthsful ⎫ but also as (c)
spoonful	spoonsful ⎭

(b) PLURAL IN BOTH FIRST AND LAST ELEMENT

gentleman farmer	gentlemen farmers
manservant	menservants
woman doctor	women doctors

(c) PLURAL IN LAST ELEMENT (*ie* normal)
    assistant director   assistant directors
    So also: boy friend, fountain pen, woman-hater, breakdown, grown-up, sit-in, stand-by, take-off, forget-me-not, etc

Irregular plurals
4.38
Irregular plurals are by definition unpredictable and have to be learned as individual items. In many cases where foreign words are involved, it is of course helpful to know about pluralization in the relevant languages particularly Latin and Greek. Thus, on the pattern of

    analysis → analyses

we can infer the correct plurals:

    axis → axes   basis → bases   crisis → crises, etc

But we cannot rely on etymological criteria: plurals like *areas* and *villas*, for example, do not conform to the Latin pattern (*areae, villae*).

4.39
VOICING+-*S* PLURAL
Some nouns which in the singular end in the voiceless fricatives spelled -*th* and -*f* have voiced fricatives in the plural, followed by /z/. In one case the voiceless fricative is /s/ and the plural has /zɪz/: *house ~ houses*.

(a) Nouns in -*th*
    There is no change in spelling.
    With a consonant before the -*th*, the plural is regular: *berth, birth, length*, etc.
    With a vowel before the -*th*, the plural is again often regular, as with *cloth, death, faith, moth*, but in a few cases the plural has voicing (*mouth, path*), and in several cases there are both regular and voiced plurals: *bath, oath, sheath, truth, wreath, youth*.

(b) Nouns in -*f(e)*
    Plurals with voicing are spelled -*ves*.
    Regular plural only: *belief, chief, cliff, proof, roof, safe*.
    Voiced plural only: *calf, elf, half, knife, leaf, life, loaf, self, sheaf, shelf, thief, wife, wolf*.
    Both regular and voiced plurals: *dwarf, handkerchief, hoof, scarf, wharf*.

Note
The painting term *still life* has a regular plural: *still lifes*.

4.40
MUTATION

Mutation involves a change of vowel in the following seven nouns:

foot ~ feet   man ~ men   woman ~ women
tooth ~ teeth   louse ~ lice   /ʊ/   /ɪ/
goose ~ geese   mouse ~ mice

Note

With *woman/women*, the pronunciation differs in the first syllable only, while *postman/postmen*, *Englishman/-men*, etc have no difference in pronunciation at all between singular and plural.

4.41
THE -*EN* PLURAL

This occurs in three nouns:

brother   brethren   *brethren* (with mutation) = 'fellow members of
                       a religious society'; otherwise regular *brothers*
child   children   (with vowel change /aɪ/ → /ɪ/)
ox   oxen

ZERO PLURAL
4.42

Some nouns have the same spoken and written form in both singular and plural. Note the difference here between, on the one hand, invariable nouns, which are either singular (*This music is too loud*) or plural (*All the cattle are grazing in the field*), and, on the other, zero plural nouns, which can be both singular and plural (*This sheep looks small; All those sheep are mine*).

4.43
Animal names

Animal names often have zero plurals. They tend to be used partly by people who are especially concerned with animals, partly when the animals are referred to as game. Where there are two plurals, the zero plural is the more common in contexts of hunting, etc, *eg: We caught only a few fish*, whereas the regular plural is used to denote different individuals or species: *the fishes of the Mediterranean*.

4.44

The degree of variability with animal names is shown by the following lists:

Regular plural: *bird, cow, eagle, hen, rabbit*, etc
Usually regular: *elk, crab, duck* (zero only with the wild bird)

Both plurals: *antelope, reindeer, fish, flounder, herring*
Usually zero: *pike, trout, carp, deer, moose*
Only zero: *grouse, sheep, plaice, salmon*

4.45
Quantitative nouns

The numeral nouns *hundred, thousand,* and usually *million* have zero plurals except when unpremodified; so too *dozen, brace, head* (of cattle), *yoke* (rare), *gross, stone* (BrE weight).

> He always wanted to have *hundreds/thousands* of books and he has recently bought *four hundred/thousand*

Other quantitative and partitive nouns can be treated similarly, though the zero plurals are commoner in informal or technical usage:

> Dozens of glasses; tons of coal
> He is six foot/feet (tall)
> He bought eight ton(s) of coal

Note
Plural measure expressions are normally singularized when they premodify (4.33 Note b): *a five-pound note, a ten-second pause.*

4.46
Nouns in -*(e)s*

A few nouns in -*(e)s* can be treated as singular or plural:

> He gave *one series/two series* of lectures

So too *species*. With certain other nouns such as *barracks, gallows, headquarters, means, (steel) works,* usage varies; they are sometimes treated as variable nouns with zero plurals, sometimes as 'pluralia tantum' (4.34).

FOREIGN PLURALS
4.47

Foreign plurals often occur along with regular plurals. They are commoner in technical usage, whereas the -*s* plural is more natural in everyday language; thus *formulas* (general) ~ *formulae* (in mathematics), *antennas* (general and in electronics) ~ *antennae* (in biology).

Our aim here will be to survey systematically the main types of foreign plurals that are used in present-day English and to consider the extent to which a particular plural form is obligatory or optional. Most (but by no means all) words having a particular foreign plural originated in the language mentioned in the heading.

4.48
Nouns in *-us* (Latin)
The foreign plural is *-i*, as in *stimulus ~ stimuli.*

> Only regular plural (*-uses*): *bonus, campus, chorus, circus, virus*, etc
> Both plurals: *cactus, focus, fungus, nucleus, radius, terminus, syllabus*
> Only foreign plural: *alumnus, bacillus, locus, stimulus*

Note
The usual plurals of *corpus* and *genus* are *corpora, genera.*

4.49
Nouns in *-a* (Latin)
The foreign plural is *-ae*, as in *alumna ~ alumnae.*

> Only regular plural (*-as*): *area, arena, dilemma, diploma, drama*, etc
> Both plurals: *antenna, formula, nebula, vertebra*
> Only foreign plural: *alga, alumna, larva*

4.50
Nouns In *-um* (Latin)
The foreign plural is *-a*, as in *curriculum ~ curricula.*

> Only regular plural: *album, chrysanthemum, museum*, etc
> Usually regular: *forum, stadium, ultimatum*
> Both plurals: *aquarium, medium, memorandum, symposium*
> Usually foreign plural: *curriculum*
> Only foreign plural: *addendum, bacterium, corrigendum, desideratum,*
> *erratum, ovum, stratum*

Note
Media with reference to press and radio and *strata* with reference to society are sometimes used informally as singular. In the case of *data*, reclassification as a singular non-count noun is widespread, and the technical singular *datum* is rather rare.

4.51
Nouns in *-ex, -ix* (Latin)
The foreign plural is *-ices*, as in *index ~ indices.*

> Both regular and foreign plurals: *apex, index, vortex, appendix, matrix*
> Only foreign plural: *codex*

4.52
Nouns in *-is* (Greek)
The foreign plural is *-es*, as in *basis ~ bases.*

> Regular plural (*-ises*): *metropolis*
> Foreign plural: *analysis, axis, basis, crisis, diagnosis, ellipsis, hypo-*
> *thesis, oasis, parenthesis, synopsis, thesis*

4.53
Nouns in -*on* (Greek)
The foreign plural is -*a*, as in *criterion* ~ *criteria*.

> Only regular plurals: *demon, electron, neutron, proton*
> Chiefly regular: *ganglion*
> Both plurals: *automaton*
> Only foreign plural: *criterion, phenomenon*

Note
Informally, *criteria* and *phenomena* are sometimes used as singulars.

4.54
French nouns
A few nouns in -*e(a)u* retain the French -*x* as the spelling of the plural, beside the commoner -*s*, but the plurals are almost always pronounced as regular, /z/, irrespective of spelling, *eg: adieu, bureau, tableau, plateau.*

4.55
Some French nouns in -*s* or -*x* are pronounced with a final vowel in the singular and with a regular /z/ in the plural, with no spelling change: *chamois, chassis, corps, faux pas, patois.*

4.56
Nouns in -*o* (Italian)
The foreign plural is -*i* as in *tempo* ~ *tempi.*

> Only regular plural: *soprano*
> Usually regular plural: *virtuoso, libretto, solo, tempo*

Note
Graffiti is usually a 'pluralia tantum' (4.34), *confetti, spaghetti* non-count singular.

4.57
Hebrew nouns
The foreign plural is -*im*, as in *kibbutz* ~ *kibbutzim.*

> Usually regular: *cherub, seraph*
> Only foreign plural: *kibbutz*

Gender
4.58
English makes very few gender distinctions. Where they are made, the connection between the biological category 'sex' and the grammatical category 'gender' is very close, insofar as natural sex distinctions determine English gender distinctions.

It is further typical of English that special suffixes are not generally used to mark gender distinctions. Nor are gender distinctions made in the article. Some pronouns are gender-sensitive (the personal *he, she, it,* and the relative *who, which*), but others are not (*they, some, these,* etc). The patterns of pronoun substitutions for singular nouns give us a set of ten gender classes as illustrated in *Fig* 4:2.

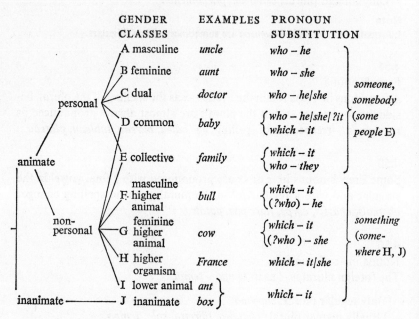

Fig 4:2 Gender classes

4.59
[A/B] Personal masculine/feminine nouns
These nouns are of two types. Type (i) has no overt marking that suggests morphological correspondence between masculine and feminine, whereas in Type (ii) the two gender forms have a derivational relationship (*cf* App I.14).

(i)

morphologically	bachelor	spinster	king	queen
unmarked for	brother	sister	man	woman
gender	father	mother	monk	nun
	gentleman	lady	uncle	aunt

(ii)

morphologically	bridegroom	bride	host	hostess
marked for	duke	duchess	steward	stewardess
gender	emperor	empress	waiter	waitress
	god	goddess	widower	widow
	hero	heroine	usher	usherette

Some masculine/feminine pairs denoting kinship have common (dual) generic terms, for example, *parent* for *father/mother*, and *child* for *son/daughter* as well as for *boy/girl*. Some optional feminine forms (*poetess, authoress,* etc) are now rare, being replaced by the dual gender forms (*poet, author,* etc).

4.60
[C] Personal dual gender
This is a large class including, for example, the following:

artist	fool	musician	servant
chairman	foreigner	neighbour	speaker
cook	friend	novelist	student
criminal	guest	parent	teacher
doctor	inhabitant	person	writer
enemy	librarian	professor	

For clarity, it is sometimes necessary to use a 'gender marker':

boy friend	girl friend
man student	woman student

The dual class is on the increase, but the expectation that a given activity is largely male or female dictates the frequent use of sex markers: thus *a nurse,* but *a male nurse; an engineer* but *a woman engineer.*

Note
Where such nouns are used generically, neither gender is relevant though a masculine reference pronoun may be used (*cf* 7.30):

> If *any student* calls, tell *him* I'll be back soon

When they are used with specific reference, they must of course be either masculine or feminine and the context may clearly imply the gender in a given case:

> I met a (*handsome*) student (and *he* . . .)
> I met a (*beautiful*) student (and *she* . . .).

4.61
[D] Common gender
Common gender nouns are intermediate between personal and non-personal. The wide selection of pronouns (*who, he/she/it*) should not be

understood to mean that all these are possible for all nouns in all contexts. A mother is not likely to refer to her baby as *it*, but it would be quite possible for somebody who is not emotionally concerned with the child or is ignorant of or indifferent to its sex. *Cf* 4.63.

4.62
[E] Collective nouns
These differ from other nouns in taking as pronoun substitutes either singular (*it*) or plural (*they*) without change of number in the noun (*the army* ~ *it/they; cf: the armies* ~ *they*): *cf* 7.20. Consequently, the verb may be in the plural after a singular noun (though less commonly in AmE than in BrE):

$$\text{The committee} \begin{bmatrix} \text{has} \\ \text{have} \end{bmatrix} \text{met and} \begin{bmatrix} \text{it has} \\ \text{they have} \end{bmatrix} \text{rejected the proposal}$$

The difference reflects a difference in attitude: the singular stresses the non-personal collectivity of the group and the plural the personal individuality within the group.

We may distinguish three subclasses of collective nouns:

(a) SPECIFIC: army, clan, class, club, committee, crew, crowd, family, flock, gang, government, group, herd, jury, majority, minority

(b) GENERIC: the aristocracy, the bourgeoisie, the clergy, the élite, the gentry, the intelligentsia, the laity, the proletariat, the public

(c) UNIQUE: the Arab League, (the) Congress, the Kremlin, the Papacy, Parliament, the United Nations, the United States, the Vatican

4.63
[F/G] Higher animals
Gender in higher animals is chiefly observed by people with a special concern (*eg* with pets).

buck	doe	gander	goose
bull	cow	lion	lioness
cock	hen	stallion	mare
dog	bitch	tiger	tigress

A further class might be set up, 'common higher animals', patterning with *which* – *it*, (*?who*) – *he/she*, to account for *horse, cat, tiger*, etc, when no sex distinction is made or known. In such cases, *he* is more usual than *she*.

4.64
[H] Higher organisms

Names of countries have different gender depending on their use. (i) As geographical units they are treated as [J], inanimate: 'Looking at the map we see France here. *It is* one of the largest countries of Europe.' (ii) As political/economic units the names of countries are often feminine, [B] or [G]: 'France *has* been able to increase *her* exports by 10 per cent over the last six months.' 'England *is* proud of *her* poets.' (iii) Esp. in BrE, sports teams representing countries can be referred to as personal collective nouns, [E]: 'France *have* improved *their* chance of winning the cup.'

The gender class [H] is set up to embrace these characteristics, and in it we may place ships and other entities towards which an affectionate attitude is expressed by a personal substitute:

What a lovely ship. What is *she* called?

The proud owner of a sports car may refer to it as *she* (or perhaps as *he* if the owner is female).

4.65
[I/J] Lower animals and inanimate nouns

Lower animals do not differ from inanimate nouns in terms of our present linguistic criteria; *ie* both *snake* and *box* have *which* and *it* as pronouns. Sex differences can, however, be indicated by a range of gender markers for any animate noun when they are felt to be relevant: *eg: she-goat, he-goat, male frog, hen-pheasant.*

Case
4.66
Common/genitive case

As distinct from personal pronouns (4.79), English nouns have a two-case system: the unmarked COMMON CASE (*boy*) and the marked GENITIVE CASE (*boy's*). Since the functions of the common case can be seen only in the syntactic relations of the noun phrase (subject, object, etc), it is the functions of the genitive that need separate scrutiny.

The forms of the genitive inflection
4.67

The *-s* genitive of regular nouns is realized in speech only in the singular, where it takes one of the forms /ɪz/, /z/, /s/, following the rules for *s* inflection (3.5). In writing, the inflection of regular nouns is realized in the singular by *-'s* and in the plural by putting an apostrophe after the plural *s*.

As a result, the spoken form /spaɪz/ may be related to the noun *spy* as follows:

The *spies* were arrested
The *spy's* companion was a woman
The *spies'* companions were women in each case

(It could of course also be the *s* form of the verb as in 'He *spies* on behalf of an industrial firm'.) By contrast, an irregular noun like *man* preserves a number distinction independently of genitive singular and genitive plural distinctions: *man, men, man's, men's*.

Note
In postmodified noun phrases, there can be a difference between the genitive and plural because of the different location of the inflection (4.74):

The palace was the King of Denmark's
They praised the Kings of Denmark

4.68
In addition to its use with regular plurals, the 'zero' genitive occurs

(a) with Greek names of more than one syllable, as in *Euripides'* /-diz/ *plays*₁

(b) with many other names ending in /z/ where, in speech, zero is a variant of the regular /ɪz/ genitive. There is vacillation both in the pronunciation and spelling of these names, but most commonly the pronunciation is the /ɪz/ form and the spelling an apostrophe only. Thus *Burns'* (or, less commonly, *Burns's*), is pronounced, irrespective of the spelling, /zɪz/ (or /z/);

(c) with fixed expressions of the form *for . . . sake* as in *for goodness' sake* /s/, *for conscience' sake* /s/.

4.69
Two genitives
In many instances there is a functional similarity (indeed, semantic identity) between a noun in the genitive case and the same noun as head of a prepositional phrase with *of*. We refer to the *-s* GENITIVE for the inflection and to the *OF-*GENITIVE for the prepositional form. For example:

What is *the ship's* name?
What is the name *of the ship*?

Although as we shall see (4.71 *f*) there are usually compelling reasons for preferring one or other construction in a given case, and numerous environments in which only one construction is grammatically acceptable, the degree of similarity and overlap has led grammarians to regard the two constructions as variant forms of the genitive.

4.70
Genitive meanings
The meanings of the genitive can best be shown by sentential or phrasal analogues such as we present below. For comparison, a corresponding use of the *of*-genitive is given where this is possible.

GENITIVES	ANALOGUES
(a) *possessive genitive*	
my son's wife	my son has a wife
Mrs Johnson's passport	Mrs Johnson has a passport
cf the gravity of the earth	the earth has gravity
(b) *subjective genitive*	
the boy's application	the boy applied
his parents' consent	his parents consented
cf the rise of the sun	the sun rose
(c) *objective genitive*	
the family's support	(. . .) supports the family
the boy's release	(. . .) released the boy
cf a statement of the facts	(. . .) stated the facts
(d) *genitive of origin*	
the girl's story	the girl told a story
the general's letter	the general wrote a letter
cf the wines of France	France produced the wines
(e) *descriptive genitive*	
a women's college	a college for women
a summer's day	a summer day/a day in the summer
a doctor's degree ⎫	
cf the degree of doctor ⎭	a doctoral degree/a doctorate
(f) *genitive of measure and*	
partitive genitive	
ten days' absence ⎫	
an absence of ten days ⎭	the absence lasted ten days
the height of the tower	the tower is (of) a certain height
part of the problem	the problem is divisible into parts
(g) *appositive genitive*	
the city of York	York is a city
the pleasure of meeting you	meeting you is a pleasure

Note
Except for temporal measure, the *-s* genitive is now only rarely found with meanings (f) and (g), but *cf: the earth's circumference, journey's end, Dublin's fair city.*

4.71
The choice of genitives

The semantic classification in 4.70 is in part arbitrary. For example, we could claim that *cow's milk* is not a genitive of origin but a descriptive genitive ('the kind of milk obtained from a cow') or even a subjective genitive ('the cow provided the milk'). For this reason, meanings and sentential analogues can provide only inconclusive help in choosing between *-s* and *of*-genitive use.

The choice can be more securely related to the gender classes represented by the noun which is to be genitive. Generally speaking, the *-s* genitive is favoured by the classes that are highest on the gender scale (see *Fig* 4:2), *ie* animate nouns, in particular persons and animals with personal gender characteristics. Although we can say either *the youngest children's toys* or *the toys of the youngest children*, the two forms of the genitive are not normally in free variation. We cannot say, for example, **the door's knob* or **the hat of John*.

Relating this fact to 4.70, we may infer that the possessive use is especially associated with the *-s* genitive and that this is because we think of 'possession' chiefly in terms of our own species. It is possible to see the partitive genitive at the opposite pole on comparable grounds: the disallowance of the *-s* genitive matches the irrelevance of the gender of a noun which is merely being measured or dissected.

A further factor influencing the choice of genitive is information focus, the *-s* genitive enabling us to give end-focus to one noun, the *of*-genitive to another (*cf.* 14.2). Compare the following:

(a) The explosion damaged *the ship's funnel*
(b) Having looked at all the funnels, he considered that the most handsome was *the funnel of the Orion*

This principle is congruent again with the preference for the *of*-genitive with partitives and appositives where an *-s* genitive would result in undesirable or absurd final prominence: **the problem's part*.

Note
The relevance of gender is shown also in the fact that the indefinite pronouns with personal reference (4.58) admit the *-s* genitive while those with non-personal reference do not: *someone's shadow, *something's shadow*.

4.72
Choice of -s genitive

The following four animate noun classes normally take the *-s* genitive:

(a) PERSONAL NAMES: Segovia's pupil
                         George Washington's statue

(b) PERSONAL NOUNS: the boy's new shirt
                       my sister-in-law's pencil

(c) COLLECTIVE NOUNS : the government's conviction
                       the nation's social security

(d) HIGHER ANIMALS: the horse's tail
                       the lion's hunger

The inflected genitive is also used with certain kinds of inanimate nouns:

(e) GEOGRAPHICAL and INSTITUTIONAL NAMES:
    Europe's future   the school's history
    Maryland's Democratic   London's water supply
      Senator

(f) TEMPORAL NOUNS
    a moment's thought   a week's holiday
    the theatre season's first big today's business
      event

(g) NOUNS OF SPECIAL INTEREST TO HUMAN ACTIVITY
    the brain's total solid weight the game's history
    the mind's general develop-   science's influence
      ment

4.73
Choice of the *of*-genitive
The *of*-genitive is chiefly used with nouns that belong to the bottom part of the gender scale (4.58), that is, especially with inanimate nouns: *the title of the book, the interior of the room*. In these two examples, an *-s* genitive would be fully acceptable, but in many instances this is not so: *the hub of the wheel, the windows of the houses*. Related no doubt to the point made about information focus (4.71), however, the corresponding personal pronouns would normally have the inflected genitive: *its hub, their windows*.

In measure, partitive, and appositive expressions, the *of*-genitive is the usual form except for temporal measure (*a month's rest*) and in idioms such as *his money's worth, at arm's length. Cf* 4.70 Note.

Again, where the *of*-genitive would normally be used, instances are found with the inflected form in newspaper headlines, perhaps for reasons of space economy:

FIRE AT UCLA: INSTITUTE'S ROOF DAMAGED

where the subsequent news item might begin: 'The roof of a science institute on the campus was damaged last night as fire swept through . . .'

Note

On the other hand, beside the regular *-s* genitive in *John's life, the child's life*, the idiom *for the life of me/him* requires both the *of*-genitive and a pronoun.

4.74
The group genitive

In some postmodified noun phrases it is possible to use an *-s* genitive by affixing the inflection to the final part of the postmodification rather than to the head noun itself. Thus:

>the *teacher's* room
>the *teacher of music's* room

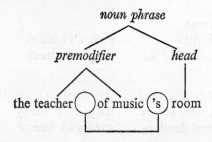

This 'group genitive' is regularly used with such postmodifications as in *someone else's house, the heir apparent's name*, as well as prepositional phrases. Other examples involve coordinations: *an hour and a half's discussion, a week or so's sunshine*. The group genitive is not normally acceptable following a clause, though in colloquial use one sometimes hears examples like:

>*Old man what-do-you-call-him's* house has been painted
>?*A man I know's* son has just been arrested

In normal use, especially in writing, such *-s* genitives would be replaced by *of*-genitives:

>The son of a man I know has just been arrested

The genitive with ellipsis
4.75

The noun modified by the *-s* genitive may be omitted if the context makes its identity clear:

>My car is faster than John's (*ie: than John's car*)
>His memory is like an elephant's
>John's is a nice car, too

With the *of*-genitive in comparable environments, a pronoun is normally necessary:

The population of New York is greater than *that* of Chicago

4.76
Ellipsis is especially noteworthy in expressions relating to premises or establishments:

I shall be at *Bill's*

Here *Bill's* would normally mean 'where Bill lives', even though the hearer might not know whether the appropriate head would be *house*, *apartment, flat, digs* (BrE); 'lives' is important, however, and *hotel room* (where Bill could only be 'staying') would be excluded. By contrast

I shall be at *the dentist's*

would refer to the dentist's professional establishment and the same applies to proper names where these refer to commercial firms. It would not be absurd to write:

I shall be at Harrod's/Foyle's/Macy's

This usage is normal also in relation to small 'one-man' businesses: *I buy my meat at Johnson's.*
   With large businesses, however, their complexity and in some sense 'plurality' cause interpretation of the *-s* ending as the plural inflection, and the genitive meaning – if it survives – is expressed in writing by moving the apostrophe (*at Macys'*). On the other hand, conflict between plurality and the idea of a business as a collective unity results in vacillation in concord:

Harrods is/are very good for clothes

4.77
Double genitive
An *of*-genitive can be combined with an *-s* genitive in a construction called the 'double genitive'. The noun with the *-s* genitive inflection must be both definite and personal:

An opera of Verdi's   An opera of my friend's

but not:

*A sonata of a violinist's   *A funnel of the ship's

There are conditions which also affect the noun preceding the *of*-phrase. This cannot be a proper noun; thus while we have:

Mrs Brown's Mary

we cannot have:

*Mary of Mrs Brown   *Mary of Mrs Brown's

Further, this noun must have indefinite reference: that is, it must be seen as one of an unspecified number of items attributed to the postmodifier:

A friend of the doctor's has arrived
*The daughter of Mrs Brown's has arrived
A daughter of Mrs Brown's has arrived
Any daughter of Mrs Brown's is welcome
*The *War Requiem* of Britten's

The double genitive thus involves a partitive (4.70) as one of its components: 'one of the doctor's friends' (he has more than one) and hence not '*one of Britten's *War Requiem*'. Yet we are able, in apparent defiance of this statement, to use demonstratives as follows:

That wife of mine   This *War Requiem* of Britten's

In these instances, which always presuppose familiarity, the demonstratives are not being used in a directly defining role; rather, one might think of them as having an ellipted generic which allows us to see *wife* and *War Requiem* appositively as members of a class of objects: 'This instance of Britten's works, namely, *War Requiem*'.

Note
So too when 'A daughter of Mrs Brown's' is already established in the linguistic context, we could refer to 'The/That daughter of Mrs Brown's (that I mentioned)'.

Pronouns
4.78
Pronouns constitute a heterogeneous class of items (see *Fig* 4:3) with numerous subclasses. Despite their variety, there are several features that pronouns (or major subclasses of pronouns) have in common, which distinguish them from nouns:

(1) They do not admit determiners (but *cf* 4.96);
(2) They often have an objective case: 4.79;
(3) They often have person distinction: 4.80;
(4) They often have overt gender contrast: 4.81;
(5) Singular and plural forms are often not morphologically related.

We can broadly distinguish between items with *specific* reference (4.83–90) and those with more *indefinite* reference (4.91–97).

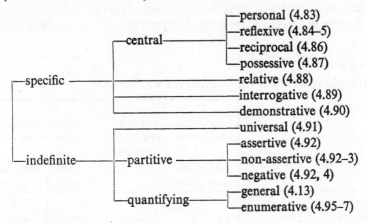

Fig 4:3 Pronouns

Note
Many of the items dealt with here have an alternative (*this, which*) or exclusive (*my, her*) determiner function. The interrelations make it convenient, however, to bring them together.

4.79
Case
Like nouns, most pronouns in English have only two cases: COMMON (*somebody*) and GENITIVE (*somebody's*). But six pronouns have an objective case, thus presenting a three-case system, where common case is replaced by SUBJECTIVE and OBJECTIVE. There is identity between genitive and objective *her*, and partial overlap between subjective *who* and objective *who* (see 4.88). The genitives of personal pronouns are, in accordance with grammatical tradition and a primary meaning (4.70), called 'possessive pronouns'.

subjective	*I*	*we*	*he*	*she*	*they*	*who*
objective	*me*	*us*	*him*	*her*	*them*	*who(m)*
genitive	*my*	*our*	*his*	*her*	*their*	*whose*

There is no inflected or -s genitive with the demonstratives or with the indefinites except those in *-one, -body*.

4.80
Person
Personal, possessive, and reflexive pronouns (*Table* 4:1) have distinctions of person:

1st person refers to the speaker (*I*), or to the speaker and one or more others (*we*);

2nd person refers to the person(s) addressed (*you*);

3rd person refers to one or more other persons or things (*he/she/it, they*).

Table 4:1

PERSONAL, REFLEXIVE, POSSESSIVE PRONOUNS

			PERSONAL PRONOUNS		REFLEX-IVE PRO-NOUNS	POSSESSIVE PRONOUNS	
			subj case	obj case		determiner function	nominal function
1st pers		sing	*I*	*me*	*myself*	*my*	*mine*
		pl	*we*	*us*	*ourselves*	*our*	*ours*
2nd pers		sing	*you*		*yourself*	*your*	*yours*
		pl			*yourselves*		
3rd pers	sing	masc	*he*	*him*	*himself*	*his*	
		fem	*she*	*her*	*herself*	*her*	*hers*
		non-personal	*it*		*itself*	*its*	
	pl		*they*	*them*	*themselves*	*their*	*theirs*

Note

Both 2nd person *you* and 3rd person *they* have an indefinite usage: 4.96 and Note.

4.81
Gender

In 3rd person singular, the personal, reflexive, and possessive pronouns distinguish in gender between masculine (*he/him/himself/his*), feminine (*she/her/herself/hers*), and non-personal (*it/itself/its*). Relative and inter-·rogative pronouns and determiners distinguish between personal and non-personal gender: see 4.89.

4.82
Number

The 2nd person uses a common form for singular and plural in the personal and possessive series but has a separate plural in the reflexive (*yourself, yourselves*). *We*, the 1st person plural pronoun, does not denote 'more than I' (*cf: the boy ~ the boys*) but 'I plus one or more others'. There is thus an interrelation between number and person. *We* may exclude the person(s) addressed:

Are we [John and I] late, Mary?   (*ie* 3rd + 1st)
 ('Yes, *you* are')

or it may be inclusive:

Are we [you and I] late, Mary?   (*ie* 2nd + 1st)
 ('Yes, *we* are')

Are we [you, John, and I] late, Mary?   (*ie* 2nd + 3rd + 1st)

See further 4.84.

Note
In several dialects, and fairly generally in familiar AmE, there are devices for indicating plural *you: you all* (Sthn AmE), *you guys*, etc.

4.83
Personal pronouns
The relation of personal to reflexive and possessive pronouns is shown in
Table 4:1. Personal pronouns function as replacements for co-referential
noun phrases in neighbouring (usually preceding) clauses:

John waited a while but eventually *he* went home
John told *Mary* that *she* should wait for *him*
When *John* arrived, *he* went straight to the bank

When a subordinate clause precedes the main as in this last example, the
pronoun may anticipate its determining co-referent:

When *he* arrived, *John* went straight to the bank

The personal pronouns have two sets of case-forms. The subjective
forms are used as subjects of finite verbs and often as subject complement:

He hoped the passenger would be Mary and indeed it was *she*

The objective forms are used as objects, and as prepositional complements. Especially in informal usage, they also occur as subject complements and as the subject (chiefly 1st person) of sentences whose predicates
have been ellipted:

I saw *her* with *them*; at least, I thought it was *her*
A: Who broke the vase? B: *Me.*

Reflexive pronouns
4.84
Reflexive pronouns replace a co-referential noun phrase, normally within
the same finite verb clause:

John has hurt *himself*
Mary intended to remind *herself*
The rabbit tore *itself* free

Mary told *John* that *she* would look after $\begin{cases} \textit{herself} \\ \textit{him} \\ \textit{*himself} \end{cases}$

When a mixture of persons is involved, the reflexive conforms to a 1st person or, if there is no 1st person, to a 2nd person:

> *You, John and I* mustn't deceive *ourselves*
> *You and John* mustn't deceive *yourselves*

The indefinite *one* (4.96) has its own reflexive as in '*One* mustn't fool *oneself*', but other indefinites use *himself* or *themselves:*

> *No one* must fool *himself*

4.85

In prepositional phrases expressing spatial relationship, usually between concretes, the personal pronouns are used despite co-reference with the subject:

> He looked about *him*
> Have you any money on *you*?
> She had her fiancé beside *her*
> They placed their papers in front of *them*

But reflexive pronouns are often preferred when the reference is metaphorical and emotive; in the following example, the reflexive is obligatory:

> She was beside *herself* with rage

There are however non-metaphorical examples in which there is considerable vacillation:

> She felt within *her(self)* the stirring limbs of the unborn child
> Holding a yellow bathrobe around *her(self)*, she walked up to him

In variation with personal pronouns, reflexives often occur after *as, like, but, except*, and in coordinated phrases:

For somebody like $\begin{Bmatrix} \text{me} \\ \text{myself} \end{Bmatrix}$ this is a big surprise

My brother and $\begin{Bmatrix} \text{I} \\ \text{myself} \end{Bmatrix}$ went sailing yesterday

In a related but emphatic usage, reflexives occur in apposition, with positional mobility:

> I've never been there *myself*
> I *myself* have never been there
> I have never *myself* been there

4.86
Reciprocal pronouns
We can bring together two sentences such as

John likes Mary   Mary likes John

with a reciprocal structure somewhat similar to a reflexive:

John and Mary like $\begin{cases} each\ other \\ one\ another \end{cases}$

In this example, with two antecedents, *each other* would be commoner,
but where more than two are involved, *one another* is often preferred:

The four children are fond of *one another*
He put all the books beside *one another*

The reciprocal pronouns can be freely used in the genitive:

The students borrowed *each other's* notes

4.87
Possessive pronouns
The possessive pronouns combine genitive functions (as described for
nouns with the -*s* genitive, 4.70 *ff*) with pronominal functions. In the latter respect, the co-referential item they replace may be in the same clause
(as with reflexives) or a neighbouring one (as with the personal pronouns):

John has cut *his* finger; apparently there was a broken glass on *his*
   desk

The possessives belong to two series: the attributives (*my, your*, etc,
which are syntactically determiners: 4.5) and the nominals (*mine, yours*
etc, which are used like the genitive with ellipsis: 4.75). Compare

$\left. \begin{matrix} \text{Mary's} \\ Her \end{matrix} \right\}$ book   The book is $\begin{cases} \text{Mary's} \\ hers \end{cases}$

Unlike many other languages, English uses possessives with reference to
parts of the body and personal belongings, as well as in several other expressions:

He stood at the door with *his* hat in *his* hand
Mary has broken *her* leg
Don't lose *your* balance!
They have changed *their* minds again!

The definite article is, however, usual in prepositional phrases related to
the object, or, in passive constructions, the subject:

She took me by *the* hand
Somebody must have hit me on *the* head with a hammer
I must have been hit on *the* head with a hammer

4.88
Relative pronouns

The functions and interrelations of the relative pronouns are best handled in connection with relative clauses (13.8 *f*) and nominal relative clauses (11.16). Here we need only tabulate an inventory of the items, none of which shows number distinction.

(a) The *wh-* series reflects the gender (personal/non-personal) of the antecedent:

> personal: *who, whom, whose*
> non-personal: *which, whose*

> There is an inflected genitive (used as a relative determiner: 'the man *whose* daughter') for both *who* and *which*, but there is a preference for the *of*-genitive (*of which*) with non-personal antecedents. The personal objective *whom* is often replaced by *who* but never when preceded by a preposition. For nominal relative clauses, there is the personal *whoever* and the non-personal pronoun and determiner *which(ever)*; in addition there is a nominal relative pronoun and determiner *what(ever)*: '*What(ever)* (money) I have you can borrow'.

(b) *That* is a general purpose relative pronoun, used irrespective of gender or case except that the genitive must involve postposed *of:* 'the knife *that* I broke the blade *of*' (informal).

(c) Zero is used identically to *that* except that it is unacceptable where the relative pronoun is subject in its clause:

> The pen *I want* is missing
> *The pen *writes best* is missing

4.89
Interrogative pronouns

The interrogatives are identical in form and in case relations with the relative pronouns, but in addition to the basic difference between interrogative and relative there are functional differences in detail.

(a) *Interrogative determiners*
> personal: *whose*
> personal or non-personal: *which, what*

(b) *Interrogative pronouns*
> personal: *who, whom, whose*
> non-personal: *what*
> personal or non-personal: *which*

Whether as pronouns or determiners, *which* and *what* have a constant relationship to each other with respect to definiteness (4.20); *what* has indefinite reference and *which* has definite reference:

$$\left.\begin{array}{l}\text{Which}\\\text{What}\end{array}\right\}\left\{\begin{array}{l}\text{girls}\\\text{books}\end{array}\right\}\text{ do you like best?}$$

Which here implies that the choice is made from a limited number of known girls or books, whereas *what* implies a choice from an indefinite number of girls or books, not previously specified. Moreover, the answer to a *which*-question would probably be more specific than the answer to a *what*-question. Like many other determiners (*eg: both* and *all*), *which* has an alternative *of*-phrase construction:

$$\text{Which (of the) }\left\{\begin{array}{l}\text{girls}\\\text{books}\end{array}\right\}\text{ do you like best?}$$

4.90
Demonstrative pronouns

The demonstratives have number contrast and can function both as determiners and pronouns. The general meanings of the two sets can be stated as 'near' and 'distant' reference:

	singular	plural
'near' reference:	*this*	*these*
'distant' reference:	*that*	*those*

In this respect, they match the pairs *here/there*, *now/then*, and, as with these, the relative immediacy and relative remoteness operates both literally and metaphorically:

I like *these* (pictures, which are near me) better than *those*
    (pictures, over there on the far side)
I like *this* (idea that you've just mentioned) better than *that*
    (other one that you wrote to me about last year)
I will tell you *this* secret [forward or cataphoric reference] because
    you kept *that* other one [back or anaphoric reference] so faithfully

By further metaphorical extension, we have *this/these* used to connote interest and familiarity in informal style ('Then I saw, away in the distance, *this* lovely girl, and . . .'). There can be a corresponding emotive rejection implied in *that/those* ('Here is *that* awful Jones and *those* children of his').

As subject, pronouns may have personal or non-personal reference:

$$\left.\begin{array}{l}\text{This/That girl}\\\text{This/That}\end{array}\right\}\text{ is Mary}\qquad\left.\begin{array}{l}\text{This/That pen}\\\text{This/That}\end{array}\right\}\text{ is mine}$$

In other than subject function, pronoun reference is non-personal:

$$\text{He is going to marry }\left\{\begin{array}{l}\text{this girl}\\\text{*this}\end{array}\right.\qquad\text{I bought }\left\{\begin{array}{l}\text{this picture}\\\text{this}\end{array}\right.$$

As relative antecedent, *that/those* can appear in formal use but there is no contrast with *this/these*, and only *those* can have personal reference:

He admired $\begin{cases} \text{that which was expensive (rare)} \\ \text{*that who danced well} \\ \text{those which were expensive} \\ \text{those who danced well} \end{cases}$

4.91
Universal pronouns and determiners

The universal pronouns and determiners comprise *each, all, every*, and the *every* compounds. Two have *-s* genitives: *everyone's, everybody's*. Despite their singular form, the compounds have collective reference, and along with *every* they entail reference to a number of three or (usually) more. *Each* entails reference to two or more, and has individual reference. Thus:

There were two boys who called and I gave an apple to $\begin{cases} \text{each} \\ \text{*everybody} \end{cases}$

There were seven boys who called and I gave an apple to $\begin{cases} \text{each} \\ \text{everybody} \end{cases}$

There is, however, a meaning difference between *each* and *everybody*. *Each* refers to individuals already specified, whereas *everybody* does not:

I walked into the room and gave an apple to $\begin{cases} \text{*each} \\ \text{everybody} \end{cases}$

Every one, each (one), and *all* have *of*-constructions; and except *all*, these pronouns can have a singular or plural pronoun for co-reference:

$\left. \begin{array}{l} \text{Every one} \\ \text{Each} \\ \text{Each one} \end{array} \right\}$ of the students should have $\begin{Bmatrix} \text{their} \\ \text{his} \end{Bmatrix}$ own books

Every can also be used with plural expressions such as *every two weeks, every few months*, and there is a universal place compound *everywhere* as in *Everywhere looks beautiful in the spring*.

Note
It all can also be used in reference to non-personal divisible count nouns:
    I have started *the book* but I haven't read *it all*

4.92
Partitive pronouns

Parallel to the universal pronouns, we have three sets of partitive pronouns with associated determiners: see *Table* 4:2. Their use can be illustrated as follows:

He saw *something/some* material
Did he see *anything/any* material?
He saw *nothing/no* material

As well as their use with plurals and non-count nouns (4.5), the determiners *some* and *any* can be used with singular count nouns when they are stressed. *Some* is frequently followed by *or other*:

ÀNY apology will satisfy them

There was ˈsome ˈBÒOK (or other) published on the subject last year

Note

[*a*] In familiar style, the stressed *some* means 'extraordinary':

That's ˈsome PÈN you have there!

[*b*] We should note the partitive place compounds as in *He went somewhere, Did he go anywhere?, He went nowhere.*

Table 4:2

UNIVERSAL AND PARTITIVE PRONOUNS AND DETERMINERS

| | | | COUNT | | NON-COUNT |
			Personal	Non-Personal	
UNIVERSAL	singular	pronoun	everyone everybody each	everything each (*place:* every-where)	it (. . .) all
		determiner		every each	
	plural	pronoun	(they (. . .)) all/both (them) all/both		all
		predeter-miner	all/both		
PARTITIVE Assertive	singular	pronoun	someone somebody	something (*place:* some-where)	some
		determiner	a(n)		
	plural	pronoun and determiner	some		
Non-Assertive	singular	pronoun	anyone anybody	anything (*place:* anywhere)	any
		determiner	either any		
	plural	pronoun and determiner	any		
Negative	singular	pronoun	no one nobody	nothing (*place:* nowhere)	none
			none		
		pronoun and determiner	neither		
	plural	pronoun	none		
	determiner		no		

4.93
Non-assertive usage
The contexts which require the *any* series or 'non-assertive' forms (*cf* 7.35) chiefly involve

(a) the negatives *not, never, no, neither, nor;*
(b) the 'incomplete negatives' *hardly, little, few, least, seldom,* etc;
(c) the 'implied negatives' *before; fail, prevent; reluctant, hard, difficult,* etc; and comparisons with *too;*
(d) questions and conditions.

Although the main markers of non-assertion are negative, interrogative, and conditional clauses, it is the basic meaning of the whole sentence which ultimately determines the choice of the *some* or the *any* series. For example, in the sentence

Freud contributed more than anyone to the understanding of dreams

the use of the non-assertive *anyone* is related to the fact that the basic meaning is negative, as appears in the paraphrase

Nobody contributed more to the understanding of dreams than Freud

Conversely, *some* is often used in negative, interrogative, or conditional sentences, when the basic meaning is assertive ('positive orientation', see 7.46):

Did $\begin{Bmatrix} \text{somebody} \\ \text{anybody} \end{Bmatrix}$ telephone last night?

The difference between these last two can be explained in terms of different presuppositions: *somebody* suggests that the speaker expected a telephone call, whereas *anybody* does not. In making an invitation or an offer, it is for the same reason polite to presuppose an acceptance:

Would you like some wine?

Note
The following examples further illustrate the use of the *some* series in superficially non-assertive contexts:

If someone were to drop a match here, the house would be on fire in two minutes
But what if somebody decides to break the rules?
Will somebody please open the door?
Why don't you do something else?

Conversely, the *any* series is used with stress (*cf* 4.92) in superficially assertive sentences with the special meaning of 'no matter who, no matter what':

He will eat anything

Anyone interested in addressing the meeting should let us know
Any offer would be better than this
You must marry sŏMEONE – and you mustn't marry just ĀNyone

4.94
Either, neither, and the negatives

Among the partitive pronouns, the relationship between *either*, *neither*, and *none* is similar to that between *each*, *every*, and *none* among the universal pronouns. Both as pronouns and as determiners, *either* and *neither* have in fact a strictly dual reference. Compare:

$$\left.\begin{array}{l}\text{None (of the }\left\{\begin{array}{l}\text{many}\\\text{thirty}\end{array}\right\}\text{ students)}\\\text{Neither (of the [two])}\\\text{Neither (student)}\end{array}\right\}\text{ failed the exam}$$

$$\text{Either}\left\{\begin{array}{l}\text{(of the [two] students)}\\\text{(student)}\end{array}\right\}\text{ may fail the exam}$$

4.95
Quantifiers

The general quantifiers used pronominally are (a) the 'multal' *many* and *much*, (b) the 'paucal' *few* and *little*, and (c) *several* and *enough*. Their use in respect to count and non-count reference matches the position outlined in connection with their determiner function: 4.13.

Numerals
4.96
The uses of one

(a) NUMERICAL *ONE* when used with animate and inanimate singular count nouns is a stressed variant of the indefinite article *a(n)*. It is in contrast with the dual *two* and *both* and the plural numerals *three*, *four*, etc; *several*, and indefinite *some*. It has similar contrasts when used pronominally:

$$\text{I need}\left\{\begin{array}{l}\text{a nail}\\\text{one}\end{array}\right.\sim\text{ I need}\left\{\begin{array}{l}\text{some nails}\\\text{some}\end{array}\right.$$

$$\left.\begin{array}{l}\text{(The) one}\\\quad\quad\text{A}\end{array}\right\}\text{ boy/pen}\sim\text{ One of the boys/pens}$$

(The) one is also in contrast with *the other* in the correlative construction:

One went this way, the other that way

Note that there is a somewhat formal or old-fashioned use of *one* meaning 'a certain' before personal proper names:

I remember one Charlie Brown at school

(b) REPLACIVE *ONE* is used as an anaphoric substitute for a singular or plural count noun. It has the singular form *one* and the plural *ones*. Replacive *one* can take determiners and modifiers (though not usually possessives or plural demonstratives):

> A: I am looking for a particular book on syntax.
> B: Is this *the one you mean?* (=Is this it?)
> A: Yes, I'd like a drink, but just *a small one*.
> B: I thought you preferred *large ones*.

It is modified by the -*s* genitive in preference to the *of*-genitive, in sharp contrast to the demonstratives which can take only the *of*-genitive; compare:

$$\text{I prefer John's car to} \begin{cases} \text{his employer's one} \\ \text{that of his employer} \end{cases}$$

(c) INDEFINITE *ONE* means 'people in general', implying inclusion of the speaker. This use of *one* is chiefly formal and is often replaced by the more informal *you:*

$$\begin{rcases} \text{One would} \\ \text{You'd} \end{rcases} \text{think they would run a later bus than that!}$$

Indefinite *one* has the genitive *one's* and the reflexive *oneself*. In AmE, repetition of co-referential *one* is characteristically formal, *he* or (informally) *you* being preferred instead:

$$\text{One can't be too careful, can} \begin{cases} \text{one?} \\ \text{you?} \end{cases}$$

Note

The corresponding indefinite which implies exclusion of the speaker is *they:* 'They say (=it is said that) they (=some relevant unspecified people) are going to dig up our street next month.'

4.97
Cardinals and ordinals

The system of cardinal (*one, two,* etc) and ordinal (*first, second,* etc) numerals will be clear from the following list. Both types can function pronominally or as premodifiers, except that *nought* occurs chiefly as the name of the numeral, being replaced by the determiner *no* or the pronoun *none* in general use. With *hundred, thousand, million,* the indefinite article often replaces *one*. Pronominally, the ordinals are preceded by an article (*Today is the fourth of July*) and resemble superlatives with elliptical heads: *cf* 5.8.

0	nought, zero		
1	one	1st	first
2	two	2nd	second
3	three	3rd	third
4	four	4th	fourth
5	five	5th	fifth
6	six	6th	sixth
7	seven	7th	seventh
8	eight	8th	eighth
9	nine	9th	ninth
10	ten	10th	tenth
11	eleven	11th	eleventh
12	twelve	12th	twelfth
13	thirteen	13th	thirteenth
14	fourteen	14th	fourteenth
15	fifteen	15th	fifteenth
16	sixteen	16th	sixteenth
17	seventeen	17th	seventeenth
18	eighteen	18th	eighteenth
19	nineteen	19th	nineteenth
20	twenty	20th	twentieth
21	twenty-one, etc	21st	twenty-first, etc
30	thirty	30th	thirtieth
40	forty	40th	fortieth
50	fifty	50th	fiftieth
60	sixty	60th	sixtieth
70	seventy	70th	seventieth
80	eighty	80th	eightieth
90	ninety	90th	ninetieth
100	one hundred	100th	(one) hundredth
101	one hundred and one, etc	101st	(one) hundred and first, etc
1,000	one thousand	1,000th	(one) thousandth
100,000	one hundred thousand	100,000th	(one) hundred thousandth
1,000,000	one million	1,000,000th	(one) millionth

Bibliographical note

For theoretical discussion of nouns and noun phrases, see Sørensen (1958); Bach (1968). On reference and the articles, see Christophersen (1939); Robbins (1968). On relevant transformational studies, see Stockwell *et al* (1973), Ch 3, 4, 11.

FIVE
ADJECTIVES AND ADVERBS

Characteristics of the adjective
5.1

We cannot tell whether a word is an adjective by looking at it in isolation: the form does not necessarily indicate its syntactic function. Some suffixes are indeed found only with adjectives, *eg: -ous* (App I.20), but many common adjectives have no identifying shape, *eg: good, hot, little, young, fat*. Nor can we identify a word as an adjective merely by considering what inflections or affixes it will allow. It is true that many adjectives inflect for the comparative and superlative, *eg: great, greater, greatest*. But many do not allow inflected forms, *eg: disastrous, *disastrouser, *disastrousest* (5.36). Moreover, a few adverbs can be similarly inflected, *eg: (He worked) hard, harder, hardest* (5.38). It is also true that many adjectives provide the base from which adverbs are derived by means of an *-ly* suffix, *eg:* adjective *happy*, adverb *happily* (App I.22). Nevertheless, some do not allow this derivational process; for example, there is no adverb **oldly* derived from the adjective *old*. And there are a few adjectives that are themselves derived from an adjective base in this way, *eg: kindly*, an item functioning also as an adverb.

5.2

Most adjectives can be both attributive and predicative (5.3), but some are either attributive only (5.13*ff*) or predicative only (5.18).

Two other features usually apply to adjectives:

(1) Most can be premodified by the intensifier *very*, *eg: The children are very happy*.

(2) Most can take comparative and superlative forms. The comparison may be by means of inflections, *eg: The children are happier now, They are the happiest people I know*, or by the addition of the premodifiers *more* and *most* (periphrastic comparison) *eg: These students are more intelligent, They are the most beautiful paintings I have ever seen*.

An ADJECTIVE PHRASE is a phrase with an adjective as head, as in (*He was*) *so very happy*, or as sole realization, as in (*He was*) *happy*. Adjectives function syntactically only in adjective phrases, but since it is the adjective that generally determines the function of the adjective phrase, we have often found it convenient to use adjectives alone to illustrate the functions of adjective phrases and we have often referred to adjectives as a shorter way of referring to adjective phrases.

Syntactic functions of adjectives
5.3
Attributive and predicative

The major syntactic functions of adjectives are attributive and predicative.

Adjectives are attributive when they premodify nouns, *ie:* appear between the determiner (4.5) and the head of the noun phrase:

the *beautiful* painting
his *main* argument

Predicative adjectives can be

(a) subject complement:

Your daughter is *pretty*

(b) object complement:

He made his wife *happy*

They can be complement to a subject which is a finite clause (11.3):

Whether he will resign is *uncertain*

or a non-finite clause (11.3):

Driving a bus isn't *easy*

Similarly, adjectives can be object complement to clauses:

I consider $\left\{ \begin{array}{l} \text{what he did} \\ \text{playing so hard} \end{array} \right\}$ *foolish*

The adjective functioning as object complement often expresses the result of the process denoted by the verb (7.9):

He pulled his belt *tight* (As a result, his belt was then tight)
He pushed the window *open* (As a result, the window was then open)

Postpositive
5.4
Adjectives can sometimes be postpositive, *ie* they can sometimes follow the item they modify. A postposed adjective (together with any complementation it may have) can usually be regarded as a reduced relative clause.

Indefinite pronouns ending in *-body, -one, -thing, -where* can be modified only postpositively:

I want to try on something larger (*ie* 'which is larger')

Postposition is obligatory for a few adjectives, which have a different sense when they occur attributively or predicatively. The most common are probably *elect* ('soon to take office') and *proper* ('as strictly defined'), as in

the president *elect*   the City of London *proper*

In several compounds (mostly legal or quasi-legal) the adjective is postposed, the most common being: *attorney general, body politic, court martial, heir apparent, notary public* (AmE), *postmaster general*.

Postposition (in preference to attributive position) is usual for a few *a*-adjectives (5.42) and for *absent, present*, and (esp BrE) *concerned, involved*, which normally do not occur attributively in the relevant sense:

The house *ablaze* is next door to mine
The people *involved* were not found

Some postposed adjectives, especially those ending in *-able* or *-ible*, retain the basic meaning they have in attributive position but convey the implication that what they are denoting has only a temporary application (13.4). Thus, *the stars visible* refers to stars that are visible at a time specified or implied, while *the visible stars* refers to a category of stars that can (at appropriate times) be seen.

5.5
If an adjective is alone or premodified merely by an intensifier, postposition is normally not allowed:

The (*rather*) *timid* soldiers ⎱
*The soldiers (*rather*) *timid* ⎰ approached their officer

However, if the noun phrase is generic and indefinite, coordinated adjectives or adjectives with a clause element added can be postposed, though such constructions are not very frequent:

Soldiers *timid or cowardly* don't fight well
A man *usually honest* will sometimes cheat

More commonly, we find

Timid or cowardly soldiers
Soldiers *who are timid or cowardly* $\Big\}$ don't fight well

A man *who is usually honest* will sometimes cheat

It is unacceptable to prepose the whole of an adjective phrase in which there is complementation of the adjective:

*The *easiest to teach* boys were in my class

Postposition is normally possible:

The boys *easiest to teach* were in my class
They have a house *much larger than yours*
Students *brave enough to attempt the course* deserve to pass

though it is more usual to prepose the adjective (and its premodifiers, if any) and postpose the complementation:

The *easiest* boys *to teach* were in my class
They have a *much larger* house *than yours*

But if the adjective is modified by *enough, too,* or *so,* the modified adjective normally cannot be separated from its complementation:

*Brave enough students *to attempt the course* deserve to pass
*A *brave enough* student *to attempt the course* deserves to pass
**Too/So easy* boys *to teach* were in my class
*A *too/so easy* boy *to teach* was in my class

Note

[a] An adjective modified by *enough, too,* or *so* can be separated from its complementation if the modified adjective is positioned before the indefinite article of the noun phrase:

He is (*not*) *brave enough* a student *to attempt the course*
He thought him *too difficult* a boy *to teach*

But with *enough* and *too,* this construction seems to be possible only if the adjective phrase is part of the subject complement or object complement, and with *enough* it is more common if the adjective is premodified by *not.* With *so,* the construction is also possible if the adjective phrase is part of the subject or object:

So easy a boy *to teach* deserves to pass
I have never met *so difficult* a man *to please*

[b] *Aplenty* (AmE) and *galore* (both informal) are postposed obligatorily, *eg: There were presents galore.*

Head of a noun phrase
5.6

Adjectives can often function as heads of noun phrases. As such, they do not inflect for number or for the genitive case and must take a definite determiner. Most commonly, such adjectives have personal reference:

The extremely old need a great deal of attention
We will nurse *your sick* and feed *your hungry*
The young in spirit enjoy life
The rich will help only *the humble poor*
The wise look to *the wiser* for advice
The old who resist change can expect violence

These adjectives have generic and plural reference. It is often possible to add a general word for human beings such as *people* and retain the generic reference (in which case the definite determiner is normally omitted) but the use of the adjective as head of the noun phrase is probably more common. The adjective can itself be modified, usually by restrictive modification (13.3).

Note
Although adjectives functioning as noun-phrase heads generally require a definite determiner, they can be without a determiner if they are conjoined (*cf* 'Parallel Structures', 4.21):

He is acceptable to *both old and young*.

5.7
Some adjectives denoting nationalities can be noun-phrase heads:

You British and *you French* ought to be allies
The industrious Dutch are admired by their neighbours

The adjectives in question are virtually restricted to words ending in -(*i*)*sh* (*eg: British, Spanish*), -*ch* (*Dutch, French*) and -*ese* (*eg: Chinese, Japanese*), and the adjective *Swiss*. As with the previous type, these noun phrases have generic reference and take plural concord, but they cannot be modified by adverbs. They can be modified by adjectives, which are normally non-restrictive, *ie: the industrious Dutch* is interpreted as 'the Dutch, who are industrious,...' (13.3).

Note
[*a*] Postmodifying prepositional phrases and relative clauses can be either restrictive or non-restrictive:

The Irish (*who live*) *in America* retain sentimental links with Ireland
The Polish, who are very rebellious, resisted strongly

[*b*] These adjectives are sometimes used not to refer to the nation as a whole but to some part of it; for example, troops:

The British have control of the bridge

5.8
Some adjectives can function as noun-phrase heads when they have abstract reference. These take singular concord. A few are modifiable by adverbs. They include, in particular, superlatives:

The latest (*ie* 'the latest news, thing') is that he is going to run for
   election
The very best (*ie* 'the very best part, thing') is yet to come
He ventured into *the unknown*
He went from *the sublime* to *the extremely ridiculous*

Note

There are a number of set phrases in which such an adjective is complement of a preposition, *eg: (He left) for good, (He enjoyed it) to the full, in short.*

Verbless adjective clause
5.9

An adjective (alone or as head of an adjective phrase) can function as a
verbless clause. The clause is mobile, though it usually precedes or follows
the subject of the superordinate clause:

   (*By then*) *nervous*, the man opened the letter
   The man, (*by then*) *nervous*, opened the letter
   The man opened the letter, (*by then*) *nervous*

The implied subject is usually the subject of the sentence. Thus, while we
have

   The man restrained the woman, *who was aggressive*

we do not have as its equivalent

   *The man restrained the woman, *aggressive*

However, if the clause contains additional clause constituents, its implied
subject can be other than the subject of the sentence:

   She glanced with disgust at the cat, *quiet* (*now*) *in her daughter's lap*

Other examples of verbless adjective clauses:

   Long and untidy, his hair played in the breeze
   Anxious for a quick decision, the chairman called for a vote

The implied subject of the adjective clause can be the whole of the
superordinate clause. For example,

   Strange, it was she who initiated divorce proceedings

is semantically equivalent to: *That it was she who initiated divorce proceedings is strange.*

   An adverb may sometimes replace, with little difference in meaning, an
adjective functioning as a verbless clause:

   Nervously, ⎫
   Nervous,   ⎬ the man opened the letter
            ⎭

The adjective refers to the subject without explicit reference to the action, and unless otherwise stated, the characterization is only temporary in its application. But if an explicit time indicator is introduced, the application of the adjective is extended in time. For example, when we insert *always*, the man's nervousness becomes a permanent characteristic, and is not specifically connected with the action:

> *Always nervous*, the man opened the letter

Note
When the implied subject is the whole clause, a corresponding adverb can replace the adjective with little or no difference in meaning, as with *strangely* for *strange:*

> *Strangely*, it was she who initiated divorce proceedings

The adjective, unlike the adverb, allows a *that-* or *how-* clause to follow:

> *Strange* $\begin{cases} \text{that it turned out that way} \\ \text{how she still likes him} \end{cases}$

In such cases, *It's* is ellipted (9.6) and the adjective is not separated from the clause by a comma.

5.10
CONTINGENT ADJECTIVE CLAUSE
A contingent adjective clause expresses the circumstance or condition under which what is said in the superordinate clause applies. A subordinator is often present but can be omitted.

> *Enthusiastic*, they make good students (= When enthusiastic, . . .)
> *Whether right or wrong*, he always comes off worst in an argument because of his inability to speak coherently
> *When ripe*, these apples are sweet

The implied subject of the contingent adjective clause is normally the subject of the superordinate clause, but it can also be the object:

> We can drink it *hot*
> You must eat it *when fresh*

The adjective then usually comes finally and could be regarded as a complement (*cf* 12.26*f*).
   The implied subject can be the whole of the superordinate clause:

> *If* (it is) *possible*, the dog should be washed every day

5.11
Exclamatory adjective sentence
An adjective as head of an adjective phrase or as its sole realization can be an exclamation:

> How good of you! How wonderful! Excellent!

Syntactic subclassification of adjectives
5.12
Adjectives can be subclassified according to whether they can function as:

(1) both attributive and predicative, *eg:* a *hungry* man~the man is *hungry;* these are the majority and constitute the central adjectives
(2) attributive only, *eg:* an *utter* fool ~ *the fool is *utter*
(3) predicative only, *eg:* *a *loath* woman ~ the woman is *loath* to admit it

The restrictions of adjectives to attributive or predicative use are not always absolute, and sometimes vary with individual speakers.

Attributive only
5.13
In general, adjectives that are restricted to attributive position or that occur predominantly in attributive position do not characterize the referent of the noun directly. For example, *an old friend* ('one who has been a friend for a long period of time') does not necessarily imply that the person is old, so that we cannot relate *my old friend* to *my friend is old*. *Old* refers to the friendship and does not characterize the person. In that use, *old* is attributive only. On the other hand, in *that old man, old* is a central adjective (the opposite of *young*) and we can relate *that old man* to *that man is old*.

Adjectives that characterize the referent of the noun directly are termed INHERENT, those that do not are termed NON-INHERENT.

Some non-inherent adjectives occur also predicatively. For example, both *a new student* and *a new friend* are non-inherent, though the former can be used predicatively:

That student is new
*My friend is new

Note
A few words with strongly emotive value are restricted to attributive position, *eg: you poor man, my dear lady, that wretched woman.*

5.14
INTENSIFYING ADJECTIVES
Some adjectives have a heightening or lowering effect on the noun they modify. Two semantic subclasses of intensifying adjectives can be distinguished for our present purpose (*cf* 8.12*ff*): emphasizers and amplifiers. Emphasizers have a general heightening effect: amplifiers scale upwards from an assumed norm, denoting the upper extreme of the scale or a high point on the scale.

Emphasizers are attributive only. Examples include:

a certain ('sure') winner pure ('sheer') fabrication
an outright lie   a real ('undoubted') hero

Amplifiers are central adjectives when they are inherent:

a complete victory ~ the victory was complete
their extreme condemnation ~ their condemnation was extreme
his great folly ~ his folly was great

But when they are non-inherent, they are attributive only:

a complete fool ~ *the fool is complete
a perfect idiot ~ *the idiot is perfect

Other examples of amplifiers that are attributive only:

a close friend utter folly a strong opponent
his entire salary the very end a great supporter

Several intensifiers have homonyms that are central adjectives, *eg:*

Those are real flowers ~ Those flowers are real ('not artificial')

Note
[a] Certain intensifying adjectives are always attributive only, in particular *mere, sheer, utter.*
[b] Many adjectives can be used as intensifiers, usually with restrictions on the nouns they modify, *eg: a great/big fool* ('very foolish'), *a great/big baby* ('very babyish'), *a great friend,* but not **a big friend* ('very friendly'). These are also restricted to attributive position.

5.15
LIMITER ADJECTIVES
Limiter adjectives particularize the reference of the noun (*cf* 8.8). Examples include:

the main reason the precise reason
the only occasion the same student

Some of these have homonyms. For example, *certain* in *a certain person* is a limiter ('a particular person'), while in *a certain winner* it is an intensifier ('a sure winner'). In *John is certain that he will win,* it is semantically related to the intensifier, but it is equivalent to *sure* in the sense of 'confident' and is limited to predicative position.

Note
Notice the use of *very* as a limiter adjective in *You are the very man I want.*

5.16
RELATED TO ADVERBIALS

Other adjectives that are attributive only can be related to adverbials. These non-inherent adjectives include:

my *former* friend ~ formerly my friend
an *occasional* visitor ~ occasionally a visitor

Some require implications additional to the adverbial:

the *late* president ~ till lately the president (now dead)

If the adjectives premodify agentive nouns, the latter suggest as well a relationship to the verb base:

a *hard* worker ~ a worker who works hard
a *big* eater ~ someone who eats a great deal

There are also instances where the noun normally lacks a corresponding verb but where the adjective (not always attributive) refers to the process part of the noun's meaning:

an *excellent* pianist ~ a pianist who plays the piano excellently

The implied process can be associated with an inanimate object:

a *fast* car ~ a car that one drives fast
a *fast* road ~ a road on which one can drive fast

Some of these adjectives have a temporal meaning. We might include with them *acting* ('for the time being') as in *the acting chairman*.

5.17
DENOMINAL ADJECTIVES

Some adjectives derived from nouns (5.20 (h)) are attributive only, *eg:*

criminal law ~ law concerning crime
an *atomic* scientist ~ a scientist specializing in atomic science
a *medical* school ~ a school for students of medicine

Note

The same item may also be a central adjective. For example, *a criminal law* can be a law which seems criminal, in which case *criminal* is a central adjective. For positional differences between these two in the adjective phrase, see 13.40 *f*. With particular noun phrase heads, an attributive noun may be an alternative to the denominal adjective, *eg: criminal detection/crime detection*, or may be used exclusively, *eg: law school*, not **legal school; cf* the converse in *medical school*, not **medicine school*.

5.18
Predicative only

Adjectives that are restricted or virtually restricted to predicative position are most like verbs and adverbs. They tend to refer to a (possibly temporary: 13.4) condition rather than to characterize. Perhaps the most common are those referring to health or lack of health: *faint, ill* (esp BrE), *well, unwell*. However, some people use *ill* and (to a lesser extent) *unwell* as attributives too.

A larger group comprises adjectives that can or must take complementation (12.11), *eg: afraid* (*that, of, about*), *conscious* (*that, of*), *fond* (*of*), *loath* (*to*).

Many closely resemble verbs semantically:

He is *afraid* to do it ~ He *fears* to do it
They are *fond* of her ~ They *like* her

Some have homonyms that can occur both predicatively and attributively, *eg: the conscious patient* ~ *the patient is conscious*.

Note
Sick (esp AmE) is the exception among these 'health' adjectives in that its attributive use is very common:

The sick woman ~ The woman is sick

Semantic sub-classification of adjectives
5.19
[A] Stative/dynamic
Adjectives are characteristically stative, but many can be seen as dynamic (2.16). In particular, most adjectives that are susceptible to subjective measurement (5.20) are capable of being dynamic. Stative and dynamic adjectives differ in a number of ways. For example, a stative adjective such as *tall* cannot be used with the progressive aspect or with the imperative: **He's being tall*, *Be tall. In contrast, we can use *careful* as a dynamic adjective: *He's being careful, Be careful*.

Adjectives that can be used dynamically include: *awkward, brave, calm, careless, cruel, extravagant, foolish, funny, good, greedy, impudent, irritable, jealous, naughty, noisy, rude, timid*.

[B] Gradable/non-gradable
Most adjectives are gradable, that is to say, can be modified by adverbs which convey the degree of intensity of the adjective. Gradability (5.33) includes comparison:

tall   taller   tallest
beautiful   more beautiful   most beautiful

and other forms of intensification:

very young   *so* plain   *extremely* useful

All dynamic adjectives are gradable. Most stative adjectives (*tall, old*) are gradable; some are non-gradable, principally 'technical adjectives'

like *atomic* (*scientist*) and *hydrochloric* (*acid*) and adjectives denoting
provenance, *eg: British* (*cf.* 5.20).

[C] Inherent/non-inherent
Most adjectives are inherent (5.13), and it is especially uncommon for
dynamic adjectives to be other than inherent; an exception is *wooden* in
The actor is being wooden, which is both dynamic and non-inherent.

Note
Whether or not an adjective is inherent or non-inherent, it may involve relation to an
implicit or explicit standard. *Big* is inherent in *a big mouse*, the standard being the relative size of mice; contrast *a little mouse*. *Big* is non-inherent in *a big fool*, the standard
being degrees of foolishness; contrast *a bit of a fool*. The relative standard is to be distinguished from gradability as well as from the inherent/non-inherent contrast. For
example, *perfect* and *good* are non-inherent in *a perfect mother* and *a good mother*, the
standard being motherhood, but only *good* is gradable (*a very good mother*, **a very perfect mother*). Similarly, though the inherent *big* in *a big elephant* is gradable (*a very big
elephant*), the inherent adjective in *an enormous N* is not gradable (**a very enormous
N*).

5.20
Semantic sets and adjectival order
Semantic sets have been proposed to account for the usual order of adjec-
tives and for their co-occurrence (13.40 *f*):

(a) intensifying adjectives (5.14), *eg: a real hero, a perfect idiot*
(b) postdeterminers (4.10), and limiter adjectives (5.15), *eg: the fourth
    student, the only occasion*
(c) general adjectives susceptible to subjective measure, *eg: careful,
    naughty, lovely*
(d) general adjectives susceptible to objective measure, including those
    denoting size or shape, *eg: wealthy, large, square*
(e) adjectives denoting age, *eg: young, old, new*
(f) adjectives denoting colour, *eg: red, black*
(g) denominal adjectives denoting material, *eg: a woollen scarf, a metal-
    lic substance*, and denoting resemblance to a material, *eg: metallic
    voice, silken hair, cat-like stealth*
(h) denominal adjectives denoting provenance or style, *eg: a British
    ship, a Parisian dress*

Characteristics of the adverb
5.21
The most common characteristic of the adverb is morphological: the
majority of adverbs have the derivational suffix *-ly*.
    There are two types of syntactic function that characterize adverbs, but
an adverb need have only one of these:

(1) adverbial
(2) modifier of adjective and adverb.

In both cases the adverb functions directly in an ADVERB PHRASE of which it is head or sole realization. Thus, in the adjective phrase *far more easily intelligible*, *intelligible* is modified by the adverb phrase *far more easily*, *easily* is modified by the adverb phrase *far more*, and *more* is modified by the adverb phrase *far*, in this last case an adverb phrase with an adverb as sole realization. In this chapter we have often found it convenient to refer to the syntactic functions of a particular adverb or type of adverb, since it is generally the adverb that dictates the syntactic functions of an adverb phrase (*cf* 5.2).

5.22
Adverb as adverbial

An adverb may function as adverbial, a constituent distinct from subject, verb, object, and complement (2.5).

Three classes of adverbials are established and discussed in Chapter 8: adjuncts, disjuncts, conjuncts.

ADJUNCTS are integrated within the structure of the clause to at least some extent. *Eg:*

They are waiting *outside*
I can *now* understand it
He spoke to me about it *briefly*

DISJUNCTS and CONJUNCTS, on the other hand, are not integrated within the clause. Semantically, DISJUNCTS express an evaluation of what is being said either with respect to the form of the communication or to its content. *Eg:*

Frankly, I am tired
Fortunately, no one complained
They are *probably* at home

Semantically, CONJUNCTS have a connective function. They indicate the connection between what is being said and what was said before. *Eg:*

We have complained several times about the noise, and *yet* he does
    nothing about it
I have not looked into his qualifications. He seems very intelligent,
    though
If they open all the windows, *then* I'm leaving

Adverb as modifier
5.23
Modifier of adjective

An adverb may premodify an adjective:

That was a *VERY funny* film
It is *EXTREMELY good* of you
She has a *REALLY beautiful* face

One adverb – *enough* – postmodifies adjectives, as in *high enough*.

Most commonly, the modifying adverb is an intensifier (*cf* 5.14). The most frequently used intensifier is *very*. Other intensifiers include *so/ pretty/rather/unusually/quite/unbelievably* (*tall*). Many are restricted to a small set of lexical items, *eg: deeply* (*anxious*), *highly* (*intelligent*), *strikingly* (*handsome*), *sharply* (*critical*). Many intensifiers can modify adjectives, adverbs, and verbs alike.

Adverbs as premodifiers of adjectives may also be 'viewpoint' (*cf* 8.7), as in *politically expedient* ('expedient from a political point of view'), *technically possible, theoretically sound*.

Note

[*a*] Viewpoint adjuncts that appear after the noun phrase are related to the premodifying adjective within the phrase:

A *good* paper *EDITORIALLY* can also be a *good* paper *COMMERCIALLY*

more usually,

An *EDITORIALLY good* paper can also be a *COMMERCIALLY* good paper

[*b*] *All*, as an informal synonym of *completely*, premodifies certain adjectives, mostly having an unfavourable sense: *He is all upset, Your brother is all wrong.*

5.24
Modifier of adverb

An adverb may premodify another adverb, and function as intensifier:

They are smoking *VERY heavily*
They didn't injure him *THAT severely* (informal)
I have seen *SO very* many letters like that one

As with adjectives, the only postmodifier is *enough*, as in *cleverly enough*.

A few intensifying adverbs, particularly *right* and *well*, premodify particles in phrasal verbs:

He knocked the man *RIGHT out*
They left him *WELL behind*

5.25
Modifier of prepositional phrase

The few adverbs that premodify particles in phrasal verbs also premodify prepositions or (perhaps rather) prepositional phrases:

The nail went *RIGHT through* the wall
His parents are *DEAD against* the trip

5.26
Modifier of determiner, predeterminer, postdeterminer
Intensifying adverbs can premodify indefinite pronouns, predeterminers, and cardinal numerals:

> *NEARLY everybody* came to our party
> *OVER two hundred* deaths were reported
> I paid *MORE THAN ten* pounds for it

The indefinite article can be intensified when it is equivalent to the un-stressed cardinal *one:*

> They will stay *ABOUT a* week

With ordinals and superlatives, a definite determiner is obligatory:

> She gave me *ALMOST the largest* piece of cake

Modifier of noun phrase
5.27
A few intensifiers may premodify noun phrases: *quite, rather* (esp BrE), and the predeterminers *such* and exclamatory *what*. The noun phrase is normally indefinite, and the intensifiers precede any determiners. *Rather* requires the head to be a singular count noun and gradable (4.3 Note):

> He told SUCH $\begin{cases} a\ (funny)\ story \\ (funny)\ stories \end{cases}$
> I have never heard *SUCH wickedness*
> It was *RATHER a mess*
> He was *QUITE some player*
> *WHAT a (big) fool* he is!

So and interrogative and exclamatory *how* also precede the indefinite article, but they require the noun phrase to contain a gradable adjective and the head of the noun phrase to be a singular countable noun. In this use, they cause the adjective to move in front of the article:

> I didn't realize that he was *SO big a fool*

> *HOW tall a man* is he?   *HOW tall a man* he is!

Note
[a] In superficially similar noun phrases, *rather* may be intensifying the adjective, in which case it may precede or follow the determiner:
> *It is rather a table
> It is rather a big table
> It is a rather big table

[b] *Kind of* and *sort of* (both informal) usually follow the determiner:
> He gave a SORT OF *laugh*

but may sometimes precede it: *That was sort of a joke.*

Other *of* phrases precede a determiner:

I had A BIT OF *a shock*

[c] In informal or familiar style, *wh*-interrogatives can be intensified by *ever* and by certain set phrases, *eg:*

Where *ever* did I leave my keys?
Who *on earth* opened my letter?
What *in heaven's name* are you doing? (familiar)
Who *the hell* are you? (familiar)

Those intensified by *ever* are to be distinguished from *wh*-subordinators (11.6 *ff*), which are written as one word with *ever:*

Wherever I park my car, I get fined

[d] For anaphoric *such* ('like that'), see 10.39.

5.28

Some adverbs signifying place or time postmodify noun phrases (13.24):

PLACE: *the way ahead, the neighbour upstairs, the sentence below*
TIME: *the meeting yesterday, the day before*

Note
Indefinite pronouns, *wh*-pronouns, and *wh*-adverbs are postmodified by *else: someone else('s), all else, who else, what else. Else* also postmodifies compounds with *where: somewhere, anywhere, everywhere, nowhere.*

5.29

In some of the phrases in 5.28 the adverb can also be used as a premodifier: *his home journey, the above photo, the upstairs neighbour.*

A few other adverbs are also used as premodifiers: *the away games, the then president, in after years. Then* and *above* are probably the most common.

5.30

Adverb as complement of preposition
Some place and time adverbs function as complement of a preposition. Of the place adverbs, *here* and *there* take the most prepositions: *along, around, down, from, in, near, on, out (of), over, round, through, under, up. Home* can be the complement of the prepositions *at, from, near, toward(s).* Others are restricted to the preposition *from:*

above, abroad, below, downstairs, indoors, inside, outdoors, outside, upstairs, within, without

Time adverbs most commonly functioning as complement of prepositions are shown in the diagram.

PREPOSITIONS   ADVERBS

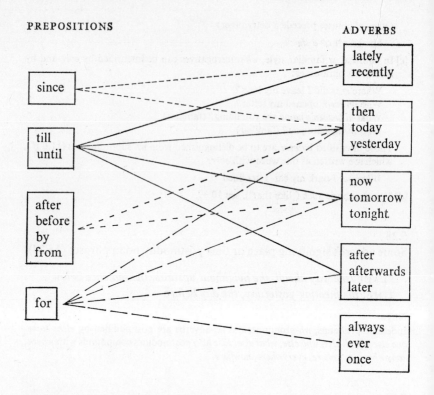

Comparison and intensification
5.31
There are three degrees of comparison:

> ABSOLUTE: *young/easily*
>
> COMPARATIVE: *younger/more easily*
>
> SUPERLATIVE: *youngest/most easily*

The comparative is used for a comparison between two, and the superlative where more than two are involved. The superlative is sometimes used for a comparison between two, 'He is the youngest (of the two brothers)', but this is considered loose and informal by many.

Comparison (*cf* 11.37 *ff*) is expressed by

(1) the inflected forms in *-er* and *-est*,
(2) their periphrastic equivalents in *more* and *most*,
(3) the forms for equational, lesser and least degrees of comparison, notably *as, less, least.*

Too in the sense 'more than enough' might also be mentioned here, *eg: It's too long* ('longer than it should be').

Note

[a] *More* and *most* have other uses in which they are not equivalent to the comparison inflections, as the paraphrases of the following sentences show:

He is more than happy about it (= He is happy about it to a degree that is not adequately expressed by the word *happy*)

He is more good than bad (= It is more accurate to say that he is good than that he is bad)

In BrE, the sentence *She is most beautiful* can mean only that she is extremely beautiful and not that she is more beautiful than all others. This absolute sense of *most* is common in AmE too.

[b] *Too* is also commonly used (esp in AmE) as a synonym of *very* in negative sentences, as in *I don't feel too good*.

5.32

Basis of comparison

We can make the basis of comparison explicit. The most common ways of doing so include correlative constructions introduced by *than* (correlative to *more, less*) and by *as* (correlative to *as*), and prepositional phrases with *of*:

John is *more/less* stupid *than Bob* (*is*)	[1]
John behaves *more/less* politely *than Bob* (*does*)	[2]
John is as stupid *as Bob* (*is*)	[3]
John behaves as politely *as Bob* (*does*)	[4]
John is the stupider *of the* (*two*) boys	[5]
Of the (*two*) *boys*, John behaves the more politely	[6]
John is the most stupid *of the* (*three*) boys	[7]
Of the (*three*) *boys*, John behaves the most politely	[8]

The basis of comparison can also be shown by the noun which the adjective premodifies:

John is the more stupid *boy* (formal; more commonly 'John is more stupid than the other boy')

John is the most stupid *boy*

Note

[a] The prepositional phrases in [5–8] can be either initial or final. Final position is more frequent, especially when the comparison involves an adjective rather than an adverb.

[b] A basis of comparison may be implicit in the use of the absolute form, and in such cases the basis of comparison can also be made explicit (6.44):

He is stupid *for a child of his age*

5.33

Gradability

Amplifiers and comparatives can modify gradable adjectives and adverbs. The range for emphasizers and those downtoners not expressing degree (*eg: virtually*) is much wider, as we can see from their co-occurrence with a non-gradable adjective such as *non-Christian:*

He is definitely/virtually/*more/*very non-Christian

cf He is very unchristian.

There are also restrictions on the use of particular intensifiers, and these can sometimes be stated in semantic terms:

most $\begin{cases} \text{happy ('subjective', } cf \text{ 5.20)} \\ \text{*tall ('objective', } cf \text{ 5.20)} \end{cases}$

utterly $\begin{cases} \text{wrong ('negative')} \\ \text{*right ('positive')} \end{cases}$

Amplifiers and comparatives are available for adjectives that refer to a quality that is thought of as having values on a scale, and for adverbs that refer to a manner or to a time that is thought of in terms of a scale. Thus, in *John is English* the adjective *English* does not allow amplifiers or comparatives if it refers to John's nationality, but admits them if it refers to his behaviour:

John is $\begin{cases} \text{very English} \\ \text{more English than the English} \end{cases}$

We can also achieve an intensifying effect by repeating attributive adjectives or degree intensifiers:

an old, old man ('a very old man')
very, very good ('extremely good')

Note
There are exceptions to the co-occurrence of a particular intensifier with a semantic class of adjectives. For example, though *utterly* tends to co-occur with 'negative' adjectives, *utterly reliable* and *utterly delightful* are common. People vary in the exceptions they allow.

5.34
Unmarked term in 'How' questions and measure phrases
How is used as a pro-form for degree intensifiers of the adjective or adverb in questions and exclamations:

How *efficient* is he?   How *efficiently* does he work?
How *beautiful* she is!   How *beautifully* she dances!

'Measure' adjectives that cover a scale of measurement and have a term for each end of the scale use the upper extreme as the 'unmarked' term in *How* questions and with the measurements:

A: How old is your son?   B: He's three months (old)

How old is he? is equivalent to *What is his age?*, and *He's three months old* is equivalent to *His age is three months.*

Adjectives that are used as the unmarked term in *How* questions and with measurements are listed, with the marked term given in parenthesis:

deep (shallow)	old (young)	thick (thin)
high (low)	tall (short)	wide (narrow)
long (short)		

Other adjectives are used as the unmarked term for premodification by interrogative *How* (*How heavy is it?*) but are not used with measurements (**It is two pounds heavy*). They include:

big (small)	fat (thin)	large (little)
bright (dim)	heavy (light)	strong (weak)

Some adverbs also use an unmarked term in *How* questions, *eg:*

How *much/often/quickly* did they complain?

Note
If we use the marked term, as in *How young is John?* we are asking a question that presupposes that John is young, whereas the unmarked term in *How old is John?* does not presuppose that John is old. Notice that neither term is neutral in exclamations:

How young he is! ('He is extremely young')
How old he is! ('He is extremely old')

Inflection of adjectives for comparison
5.35
The inflectional suffixes are *-er* for the comparative and *-est* for the superlative: *young ~ younger ~ youngest.* A small group of highly frequent adjectives have their corresponding comparatives and superlatives formed from different stems:

good ~ better ~ best   bad ~ worse ~ worst
far ~ further/farther ~ furthest/farthest

Old is regularly inflected as *older, oldest,* but in a specialized use, restricted to human beings in family relationships, the irregular forms *elder, eldest* are normally substituted, but only attributively or as noun phrase head:

My *elder/eldest brother* is an artist   John is *the elder*
*My brother is *elder* than I am

The regular inflections sometimes involve changes in spelling or pronunciation.

CHANGES IN SPELLING

(1) Final base consonants are doubled when the preceding vowel is
stressed and spelled with a single letter (*cf* 3.7):

   big ~ bigger ~ biggest

(2) In bases ending in a consonant + *y*, final *y* is changed to *i* (3.8):

   early ~ earlier ~ earliest

(3) Final -*e* is dropped before the inflections (3.9):

   brave ~ braver ~ bravest   *free ~ freer ~ freest*

CHANGES IN PRONUNCIATION

(1) Syllabic /l/, as in *simple*, ceases to be syllabic before inflections.

(2) Whether or not speakers pronounce final *r*, as in *poor*, the *r* is of
course pronounced before the inflections.

Note

Well ('in good health') and *ill* ('in bad health', esp BrE) are inflected like *good* and *bad*
respectively for the comparative:

He feels better/worse

5.36

Monosyllabic adjectives can normally form their comparison by inflection. Many disyllabic adjectives can also do so, though like most monosyllabic adjectives they have the alternative of the periphrastic forms:

My jokes are $\begin{cases} \text{funnier/funniest} \\ \text{more funny/most funny} \end{cases}$

Common disyllabic adjectives that can take inflected forms are those
ending in an unstressed vowel, syllabic /l/, or /ə(r)/:

(1) -*y*: *funny, noisy, wealthy, friendly*
(2) -*ow*: *hollow, narrow, shallow*
(3) -*le*: *gentle, feeble, noble*
(4) -*er, -ure*: *clever, mature, obscure*

Common adjectives outside these four categories that can take inflectional forms include *common, handsome, polite, quiet, wicked*.

Other adjectives can take only periphrastic forms:

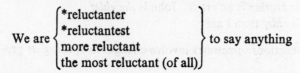

We are $\begin{cases} \text{*reluctanter} \\ \text{*reluctantest} \\ \text{more reluctant} \\ \text{the most reluctant (of all)} \end{cases}$ to say anything

Note
Adjectives of participle form do not take inflections:

   *tiringer, *woundeder

5.37
Most adjectives inflected for comparison seem to be able to take periphrastic forms more easily when they are predicative and are followed by the basis of comparison:

   He is *more* wealthy than I thought

Periphrastic forms are, however, abnormal with a number of monosyllabic adjectives, including those listed in 5.35 as forming their comparison irregularly.

5.38
Inflection of adverbs for comparison
For a small number of adverbs, the inflected forms used for comparison are the same as those for adjectives. As with adjectives, there is a small group with comparatives and superlatives formed from different stems:

   well ~ better ~ best   badly ~ worse ~ worst
   little ~ less ~ least   much ~ more ~ most
   far ~ further/farther ~ furthest/farthest

Adverbs that are identical in form with adjectives take inflections, following the same spelling and phonetic rules as for adjectives, *eg: early, late, hard, slow, fast, quick, long. Soon*, which has no corresponding adjective, is frequently used in the comparative (*sooner*), but is not common in the superlative (*soonest*).

5.39
Modification of comparatives and superlatives
The comparatives of both adjectives and adverbs can themselves be premodified by amplifying intensifiers – certain noun phrases (most of them informal) and adverbs. In the following examples we parenthesize intensifiers of these intensifiers:

$$
\left.\begin{array}{r}
\left.\begin{array}{r}\text{(that)}\\ \text{(so) (very)}\end{array}\right\}\text{much}\\
\text{(all) the}\\
\text{far}\\
\text{a good bit/a lot}\\
\text{a good deal/a great deal}\\
\text{lots}
\end{array}\right\}
\begin{array}{l}
\text{better}\\
\text{sooner}\\
\left.\begin{array}{l}\text{more}\\ \text{less}\end{array}\right\}\begin{array}{l}\text{careful}\\ \text{carefully}\end{array}
\end{array}
$$

Similarly, many downtoners may premodify the comparatives:

rather }	better	
somewhat }	sooner	
a little }	more }	careful
a (little) bit }	less }	carefully

The inflectional superlative may be premodified by *very: the very best.* If *very* premodifies the superlative, a determiner is obligatory, as in *She put on her very best dress.* Comparatives and superlatives can also be postmodified by intensifying phrases, the most common of which is *by far*, eg: *He is funnier/funniest by far.*

Correspondence between adjective and adverb
5.40
Adverbs are regularly, though not invariably, derived from adjectives by suffixation (App I.22). In addition, a correspondence often exists between constructions containing adjectives and those containing the corresponding adverbs. The simplest illustration is with adverbs equivalent to prepositional phrases containing a noun phrase with the corresponding adjective:

He liked Mary *considerably*
He liked Mary *to a considerable extent*
He spoke to John *sharply*
He spoke to John *in a sharp manner*
Politically, it is a bad decision
From the political point of view, it is a bad decision

Sometimes, either the adjective or the adverb forms may appear, with little or no semantic difference (5.9, 5.43). But normally, the adjective and its corresponding adverb appear in different environments:

her *incredible* beauty: her beauty is *incredible* ~ she is *incredibly*
beautiful

5.41
There are many cases where a construction with the adverb form seems basic to an understanding of the corresponding construction with the adjective form.

(1) There are regular correspondences between sentences with an adverb and noun phrases with an adjective:

He loved her *deeply* ~ his *deep* love for her
He writes *legibly* ~ his *legible* writing

(2) The adjective-noun sequence may imply a process or a time relationship, with a corresponding noun phrase containing an adverb
(5.16). For example, in the second of the following two interpretations of *a beautiful dancer*, the adjective refers to the process part of
the agentive noun:

    (a) a dancer who is beautiful
    (b) a person who dances beautifully

(3) Most intensifying adjectives (5.14) can be seen as related to adverbs:

    a real idiot ~ he is really an idiot

(4) Many limiter adjectives (*cf* 5.15) can be seen as related to adverbs:

    the main reason ~ it was mainly the reason

The adjective and other word-classes
Adjective and adverb
5.42

Certain words beginning with *a-* have a predominantly predicative use.
With respect to their ability to be used predicatively with both *be* and
another intensive verb such as *seem*, we can contrast an *a-* adjective such
as *asleep* with an *a-* adverb such as *abroad:*

The patient was $\begin{cases} asleep \\ abroad \end{cases}$ The patient seemed $\begin{cases} asleep \\ *abroad \end{cases}$

A- adjectives are unacceptable as part of the predication after verbs of
motion. *A-* adverbs, however, are acceptable and denote direction after
such verbs. Notice the contrast between the *a-* adverbs in *He went aboard/
abroad/around/away* and the *a-* adjectives in **He went afraid/alert/
asleep/awake.*

Common *a-* adjectives are: *ablaze, afloat, afraid, aghast, alert, alike,
alive, alone, aloof, ashamed, asleep, averse, awake, aware.*

Note

[a] *Alert* and *aloof* are freely used attributively. Some of the other *a-* adjectives occasionally function attributively, though normally only when they are modified: *the
half-asleep children, a somewhat afraid soldier, a really alive student* ('lively'), *a very
ashamed girl.*

[b] Some *a-* adjectives freely take comparison and premodification by *very, eg: afraid,
alert, alike, aloof, ashamed, averse.* Others do so marginally, *eg: asleep* and *awake.
Alive to* in the sense 'aware of' can be premodified by *very* and compared. Some
of the *a*-adjectives, like many verbs, can also be premodified by *very much* (particularly *afraid, alike, ashamed, aware*), and *aware* can be premodified by (*very*) *well*
too.

5.43
Certain items that function as adjectives are also used to define in some
way the process denoted by the verb; this is a typical use of adverbs, *eg:*
loud and *clear* in *He spoke loud and clear.* If in its adverbial use the item is
not restricted to a position after the verb or (if present) the object, it
undoubtedly belongs to both the adjective and adverb classes. For
example, *long* and *still*, which commonly function as adjectives, are adverbs in pre-verb position in the following sentences:

> Such animals have *long* had to defend themselves
> They *still* can't make up their minds whether to go or not

Furthermore, the item clearly represents two different words if there is a
semantic difference in the two uses, as with *long* and *still*.

In some cases, the adjective form and a corresponding *-ly* adverb can
be used interchangeably, with little or no semantic difference, except that
many people find the adjective form objectionable:

> He spoke *loud* and *clear*/*loudly* and *clearly*
> Drive *slow* (esp AmE)/*slowly*
> She buys her clothes *cheap*/*cheaply* (*cf* 12.26 *f*)

In other cases, there is no corresponding adverb form of the same lexical
item, so that only the adjective form is available:

> We returned *early*/*fast*/*late* today

Only a limited number of adjectives have adverbial uses: **We returned
rapid today*.
The principal syntactic difference between the use of the adjective and
adverb forms is that the adjective form, if admissible at all, is restricted
to a position after the verb or (if present) the object:

> He *slowly* drove the car into the garage
> He drove the car *slowly* into the garage
> *He *slow* drove the car into the garage
> (?)He drove the car *slow* into the garage

Note
For adverbs as postmodifiers and as premodifiers in noun phrases, see 5.27 *ff*.

Adjective and noun
5.44
Some items can be both adjectives and nouns (*cf* also 5.6 *ff*). For example,
criminal is an adjective in that it can be used both attributively (*a criminal
attack*) and predicatively (*The attack seemed criminal to us*).
But *criminal* also has all the characteristics of a noun; for example, in

having number contrast and the capacity to be subject of a clause, as in *The criminals pleaded guilty to all charges.*

   Criminal is therefore both an adjective and a noun, and the relationship between the adjective *criminal* and the noun *criminal* is that of conversion (App I.25). Examples of other converted nouns:

> There was only one *black* in my class
> He is investigating the *ancients'* conception of the universe
> The king greeted his *nobles*

5.45

Nouns commonly function as premodifiers of other nouns (13.34 *f*):

the city council	a love poem
a stone wall	August weather

In this function, the attributive nouns resemble adjectives. However, the basically nominal character of these premodifiers is shown by their correspondence to prepositional phrases with the noun as complement:

the council of the city	a poem about love
a wall (made) of stone	weather (usual) in August

Such a correspondence is not available for attributive adjectives:

the urban council	a long poem
a thick wall	hot weather

though we can sometimes use a postmodifying prepositional phrase with a related noun as complement, *eg: a long poem ~ a poem of considerable length.*

   Some nouns can even function both attributively and predicatively. Moreover, these nouns are like adjectives in that they do not take number variation. The nouns denote material from which things are made or refer to style (*cf* the corresponding classes of adjective, 5.20):

> that concrete floor ~ that floor is concrete (= is of concrete)
> Worcester porcelain ~ this porcelain is Worcester

   Some nouns can appear in predicative noun phrases after *seem*. In this, they resemble adjectives:

> He seems a fool
> His friend seems very much an Englishman
> Your remark seems nonsense to me

These are indeed very close semantically to adjectives (*foolish, English, nonsensical*). The closeness is of course greatest for non-count nouns such as *nonsense* and *fun*, since, like adjectives, they do not have number variation and can appear without an overt determiner. But, unlike adjectives functioning as heads of noun phrases (5.6 *ff*), these non-count nouns take the zero article when they function (say) as direct object:

I like *nonsense*   He experienced *bliss*

Adjective and participle
5.46
There are many adjectives that have the same form as participles (*cf* 13.29 *ff*):

His views were very *surprising*   The man seemed very *offended*

These adjectives can also be attributive: *his surprising views, the offended man, the downhearted children.*

The *-ed* participle of intransitive verbs can also be used attributively: *the escaped prisoner* ('the prisoner who has escaped'), *a grown boy* ('a boy who has grown (up)'). Only with some of these is the predicative use allowed:

*The prisoner is *escaped*
Her son is *grown* (dubious in BrE, but *full-grown* or *grown-up* is fully acceptable)

As with *downhearted*, there may be no corresponding verb, and sometimes a corresponding verb has a different meaning. We can therefore have ambiguous sentences where the ambiguity depends on whether we have a participle or an adjective:

They were (very) *relieved* (to find her at home) – adjective
They were *relieved* (by the next group of sentries) – participle

5.47
Often the difference between the adjective and the participle is not clear-cut, and lies in the verbal force retained by the latter. The verbal force is explicit for the *-ing* form when a direct object is present. Hence, in *His views were alarming his audience*, the *-ing* form is a participle. Similarly, the verbal force is explicit for the *-ed* form when a *by* agentive phrase with a personal agent is present, indicating the correspondence to the active form of the sentence, as in *The man was offended by the policeman*.

For both participle forms, modification by the intensifier *very* is an explicit indication that the forms have adjective status:

His views were very *alarming*   The man was very *offended*

We might therefore expect that the presence of *very* together with an explicit indicator of verbal force would produce an unacceptable sentence. This is certainly so for the *-ing* participle form:

*His views were very *alarming* his audience

However, with the *-ed* participle form, there appears to be divided usage, with increasing acceptance of the co-occurrence of *very* with a *by* agentive phrase containing a personal agent:

?The man was very *offended* by the policeman

And there is certainly no problem of co-occurrence if the agent is non-personal:

I'm very *disturbed* by your attitude

Note

[a] A participle is sometimes made fully adjectival by being compounded with another element:

He is *looking* (at a painting)	He is (very) *good-looking*
It is *breaking* (his heart)	It is (very) *heart-breaking*

[b] It is not only participles allowing the intensifier *very* that can be attributive (13.29): *the winning team, his published work, the captured prisoner*.

[c] A few adjectives are differentiated from participles by taking the *-en* suffix where participles with the same base have the *-ed* suffix (*shaved*) or are without a suffix (*drunk, shrunk*): *shaven, drunken, shrunken*. For a few others, there is no difference between adjective and participle in spelling, but there is in pronunciation. Whereas the vowel of the participle suffix *-ed* is not pronounced, the suffix is treated in the adjective as a separate syllable pronounced /ɪd/: *blessed, crooked, dogged, learned, ragged.* The adjective *aged* is disyllabic when it is a synonym of *elderly* (*my aged father*), but is monosyllabic in such a sentence as *My father is aged seventy.*

The adverb and other word-classes
5.48
Conjunct and conjunction

A few conjuncts, *eg: so, yet*, resemble coordinators both in being connectives and in having certain syntactic features (*cf* 9.10 *ff*). In particular, unlike clauses introduced by subordinators, those introduced by conjuncts cannot be moved in front of the preceding clause. Thus, the order of the following two clauses (with the conjunct *so* in the second clause) is fixed:

We paid him a very large sum. *So* he kept quiet about what he saw.

If we change the order of the clauses, the relationship is changed and *so* must now refer to some preceding clause. However, the conjuncts differ from coordinators in that they can be preceded by a coordinator:

We paid him a very large sum, *and so* he kept quiet about what he saw.

5.49
Reaction signal and initiator

Certain other items must be positioned initially. They are important be-

cause of their high frequency in spoken English and some are restricted
to the spoken language.

(1) *reaction* signals, *eg: no, yes, hm*
(2) *initiators, eg: well, oh, ah*

Reaction signals normally serve only as response utterances. Initiators
can serve both as response utterances and as initiators of conversations.

Bibliographical note

On adjectives in general, see Vendler (1968). On the position of adjectives, see particularly Bolinger (1967b); on stative and dynamic adjectives, see Schopf (1969); on
the intensification of adjectives and adverbs, see Bolinger (1972); on adverbs in general, see Chapter 8 below.

SIX
PREPOSITIONS AND PREPOSITIONAL PHRASES

6.1

In the most general terms, a preposition expresses a relation between two entities, one being that represented by the prepositional complement. Of the various types of relational meaning, those of PLACE and TIME are the most prominent and easy to identify. Other relationships such as INSTRUMENT and CAUSE may also be recognized, although it is difficult to describe prepositional meanings systematically in terms of such labels. Some prepositional uses may be best elucidated by seeing a preposition as related to a clause; *eg: The man with the red beard ~ The man who has the red beard; my knowledge of Hindi ~ I know Hindi* (4.70, 6.37).

6.2
The prepositional phrase
A prepositional phrase consists of a preposition followed by a prepositional complement, which is characteristically a noun phrase or a *wh-*clause or V-*ing* clause:

PREPOSITION	PREPOSITIONAL COMPLEMENT
at	the bus-stop
from	what he said
by	signing a peace treaty

That-clauses and infinitive clauses, although they frequently have a nominal function in other respects, do not occur as prepositional complements. Alternations between the presence and absence of a preposition are observed in cases like:

He was surprised at {her remark / her saying this / what she said}
He was surprised that she said this

Further examples of verbs and adjectives which can have either prepositional complements or *that*-clauses are:

decide (on), inform (of), insist (on), afraid (of), aware (of), sorry (about),
sure (of): see 12.11 *f.*

Note

[*a*] Exceptionally (mainly in idioms), an adverb (5.30) or an adjective may function as
prepositional complement: *at once, before long, in there, until now, since when, at
least, at worst, in brief.* Prepositional phrases can themselves be prepositional complements: 'He crawled from *under the table.*'

[*b*] *That*-clauses can often become in effect prepositional complements through the
use of the appositive construction *the fact that:*

> She became aware of *the fact that* I had deceived her

6.3
Postposed prepositions

Normally a preposition must be followed by its complement; but there
are some circumstances in which this does not happen, either because
the complement has to take first position in the clause, or because it is
absent:

WH-QUESTIONS: Which house did you leave it *at?* (7.52 *f*)
> *At* which house is he staying? (formal)

RELATIVE CLAUSES: The old house which I was telling you *about* is
empty (13.6 *ff*) (*about* which I was telling you: formal)

WH-CLAUSES: What I'm convinced *of* is that the world's population
will grow to an unforeseen extent (11.16)

EXCLAMATIONS: What a mess he's got *into!* (7.63).

PASSIVES: She was sought *after* by all the leading impresarios of the
day (14.8)

INFINITIVE CLAUSES: He's impossible to work *with* (12.13)

A prejudice against such postposed prepositions remains in formal
English, which offers (for relative clauses and for direct or indirect
questions) the alternative of an initial preposition:

> It was a situation *from which* no escape was possible

This construction is often felt, however, to be stilted and awkward in
informal English, especially in speech, and indeed in some cases (7.53
Note *a*) the postposed preposition has no preposed alternative.

Note

In formal style, *notwithstanding* is sometimes postposed:

> His intelligence *notwithstanding*, he was not successful in the examination

In addition there are several idiomatic usages such as *all the world over, all the year
round, search the house through* (*cf: search through it*).

6.4
Simple and complex prepositions

Most of the common English prepositions, such as *at, in,* and *for,* are

SIMPLE, *ie* consist of one word. Other prepositions, consisting of more than one word, are called COMPLEX. Most of these are in one of the following categories:

[A] ADVERB or PREP+PREP: *along with, as for, away from, out of, up to,* etc

[B] VERB/ADJECTIVE/CONJUNCTION/etc+PREP: *owing to, due to, because of,* etc

[C] PREP+NOUN+PREP: *by means of, in comparison with, in front of,* etc

In [C], which is by far the most numerous category, the noun in some complex prepositions is preceded by a definite or indefinite article:

in *the* light of; as *a* result of

Note

Monosyllabic simple prepositions are normally unstressed; polysyllabic prepositions (whether simple or complex) are normally stressed. In complex prepositions, the stress falls on the word (adverb, noun, etc) preceding the final preposition.

6.5
Prepositions and prepositional adverbs

A prepositional adverb is a particle which behaves like a preposition with ellipted complement:

A car drove past the door (*past* is a preposition)

A car drove past (*past* is a prepositional adverb; *ie: past* something or someone identified in the context)

In the examples below, the adverb is respectively (a) an adjunct, (b) a postmodifier:

(a) Despite the fine weather, we stayed *in* all day (place adjunct)
He hasn't been here *since* (time adjunct)

(b) The day *before*, I had spoken to him in the street (postmodifier)

Note

Prepositions normally unstressed are accented when they are prepositional adverbs:

He 'stayed in the 'house
He 'stayed 'in

6.6
Syntactic functions of prepositional phrases

Prepositional phrases may function as:

(*a*) *Adjunct* (8.2):
The people were singing *on the bus*

(*b*) *Disjunct* (8.2):
To my surprise, the doctor phoned

(c) *Conjunct* (8.2):
> *On the other hand,* he made no attempt to help the victim or
> apprehend her attacker

(d) *Postmodifier in a noun phrase* (13.19 *ff*):
> The people *on the bus* were singing

(e) *Complementation of a verb* (12.10, 12.29):
> We depend *on you*

(f) *Complementation of an adjective* (12.11):
> I am sorry *for his parents*

Note

[a] Prepositional phrases may occasionally have a nominal function, *eg* as subject of a clause:

> *Between six and seven* will suit me

[b] In (e) and (f) the preposition is closely related to and is determined by the preceding verb or adjective.

| | POSITIVE | | NEGATIVE | |
	direction	position	direction	position
DIMENSION-TYPE 0 (point)	*to* ⟶X	*at* ●X	*(away) from* X⟶	*away from* X ●
DIMENSION-TYPE 1/2 (line or surface)	*on(to)*	*on*	*off*	*off*
DIMENSION-TYPE 2/3 (area or volume)	*in(to)*	*in*	*out of*	*out of*

Fig 6:1 Place and dimension

Prepositional Meanings: Place
6.7
Dimension

When we use a preposition to indicate place, we do so in relation to the dimensional properties, whether subjectively or objectively conceived, of the location concerned. Consider the following examples:

My car is *at* the cottage
There is a new roof *on* the cottage
There are two beds *in* the cottage

The use of *at* makes *cottage* a dimensionless location, a mere point in relation to which the car's position can be indicated. With *on*, the cottage becomes a two-dimensional area, covered by a roof, though *on* is also capable of use with a one-dimensional object, as in 'Put your signature on this line'. With *in*, the cottage becomes the three-dimensional object which in reality it is, though *in* is capable of being used with objects which are essentially two-dimensional, as in 'The cow is in the field', where *field* is conceived of as an enclosed space (contrast 'We walked on the beach'). *Fig* 6:1 sets out the dimensional orientation of the chief prepositions of place.

Note
Some of the prepositions in *Fig* 6:1 can be replaced by other prepositions with the same meaning: *upon* is a formal equivalent of *on; inside* and *within* can substitute for *in*, and *outside* for *out of*.

6.8
Positive position and direction: *at, to,* etc
Between the notions of simple position (or static location) and direction (movement with respect to a destination) a cause-and-effect relationship obtains:

DIRECTION	POSITION
Tom went *to* the door	*as a result:* Tom was *at* the door
Tom fell *on(to)* the floor	*as a result:* Tom was *on* the floor
Tom dived *in(to)* the water	*as a result:* Tom was *in* the water

A prepositional phrase of 'position' can accompany any verb, although the meaning of 'direction' generally (but by no means always – see 6.16) requires a dynamic verb (3.35) of 'motional' meaning, such as *go, move, fly*, etc.

The contrast between *on* (='surface') and *in* (='area') has various implications according to context, as these examples show:

on the window: The frost made patterns on the window
                                       (window = glass surface)
in the window/mirror: A face appeared in the window/mirror
                                       (window, mirror = framed area)

on the island: Robinson Crusoe was marooned on an
                                    uninhabited island
in the island: He was born in Long Island
                                    (the island has an institutional identity)

The opposition between *at* (dimension-type 0) and *in* (dimension-type 2/3) can also cause difficulty. *In* is used for continents, countries, provinces, and sizeable territories of any kind; but for towns, villages, etc, either *at* or *in* is appropriate, according to point of view: *at/in Stratford-upon-Avon*. A very large city, such as New York, London, or Tokyo, is generally treated as an area: *He works in London, but lives in the country*. But one could treat it as a point on the map if global distances were in mind: *Our plane refuelled at London on its way from New York to Moscow*.

With buildings, also, both *at* and *in* can be used. The difference here is that *at* refers to a building in its institutional or functional aspect, whereas *in* refers to it as a three-dimensional structure:

$$\text{He's} \begin{cases} \text{at school (BrE)} \\ \text{in school (AmE)} \end{cases} (=\text{'He attends/is attending school'})$$

He's in school (= (in BrE) 'He's actually inside the building – not, *eg* on the playing fields')

So too, *at/in Oxford.*

Note

[a] In many cases (especially in colloquial English), *on* and *in* may be used for both position and destination: *He dived in the water; He fell on the floor*.

[b] In addition to the prepositions mentioned, *against*, *about*, and *around* are commonly used as prepositions of simple position or destination: *against* in the sense 'touching the side surface of' (*He's leaning against the wall*); *about* and *around* in the sense of 'in the vicinity of' (*He's been snooping about/around the place all day*).

[c] Two additional meanings of *on* as a preposition of position are 'attached to':

the apples *on* the tree

and 'on top of'

Humpty Dumpty sat *on* the wall

6.9

Negative position and direction: *away from, off*, etc

There is a parallel cause and effect relation with the negative prepositions *away from, off, off of* (informal AmE), *out of*:

DIRECTION	POSITION
Tom went *away from* the door	Tom was *away from* the door
	(= Tom was *not at* the door)

The negative character of these prepositions is shown by the parenthesized paraphrase. *Cf: off*='not on', *out of*='not in'.

6.10

Relative position: *by, over, under*, etc

Apart from simple position, prepositions may express the RELATIVE POSITION of two objects or groups of objects:

He was standing *by* his brother (= 'at the side of')
I left the keys *with* my wallet (= 'in the same place as')

Above, over, on top of, under, underneath, beneath, below express relative position vertically whereas *before, in front of, behind, after* represent it horizontally. The diagram depicts the relations expressed by 'A *is above* X', 'D *is behind* X', etc. The antonyms *above* and *below, over*

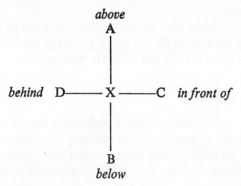

above
A

behind   D————X————C   *in front of*

B
below

and *under, in front of* and *behind* are not positive and negative, but converse opposites:

The picture is *above* the mantelpiece = The mantelpiece is *below* the
    picture
The bus is *in front of* the car = The car is *behind* the bus

Over and *under* as place prepositions are roughly synonymous with *above* and *below* respectively. The main differences are that *over* and *under* tend to indicate a direct vertical relationship and/or spatial proximity, while *above* and *below* may indicate simply 'on a higher/lower level than':

The castle stands on a hill above (*rather than* over) the valley
The doctor and the policeman were leaning over (*rather than* above)
    the body when we arrived

Underneath and *beneath* are less common substitutes for *under; beneath* is formal in style. *Underneath,* like *on top of,* generally indicates a contiguous relation.

Note
Other prepositions of relative position are *beside, near (to), between, amid(st)* (formal), *among, amongst* (esp BrE).

6.11
Relative destination: *by, over, under,* etc
As well as relative position, the prepositions listed in 6.10 (but not, generally, *above* and *below*) can express RELATIVE DESTINATION:

The bush was the only conceivable hiding-place, so I dashed *behind* it

When it started to rain, we all went *underneath* the trees

This use is distinct from that denoting passage behind, under, etc (6.12).

6.12
Passage: *by, over, under,* etc

With verbs of motion, prepositions may express the idea of PASSAGE (*ie* movement towards and then away from a place) as well as destination. With the prepositions listed in 6.10, this occurs in sentences like:

He jumped *over* a ditch

Someone ran *behind* the goal-posts

In sentences like the last, or like *The ball rolled underneath the table*, there is an ambiguity: we can supply either the meaning of 'passage' (='the ball passed under the table on the way to some other destination') or the meaning of 'destination' (='the ball rolled under the table and stayed there').

Note

A triple ambiguity may in fact arise with the above sentences, or more clearly with *A mouse scuttled behind the curtain*, which may be interpreted not only in the senses of 'passage' and 'destination', but also in a positional sense, implying that the mouse stayed (scuttling back and forth) behind the curtain all the time.

6.13
Passage: *across, through, past*

The sense of 'passage' is the primary locative meaning attached to *across* (dimension-type 1/2), *through* (dimension-type 2/3) and *past* (the 'passage' equivalent of *by* which may also, however, be substituted for *past* in a 'passage' sense). Note the parallel between *across* and *on*, *through* and *in* in the diagram:

DIMENSION-
TYPE 1/2   ●   on the grass   ⟶ across the grass

DIMENSION-
TYPE 2/3   ⊥⊥⊥⊥●⊥⊥⊥ in the grass   ⊥⊥⊥⊥⊥⊥⊥⟶ through the grass

The upper pair treat the grass as a surface, and therefore suggest short grass; the lower pair, by treating the grass as a volume, suggest that it has height as well as length and breadth – that is, that the grass is long. There is a meaning of *over* corresponding to *across* in this sense: *The ball rolled over/across the lawn.*

6.14
Direction: *up, down, along,* etc
Up, down, along, across (in a slightly different sense from that of 6.13), and *(a)round,* with verbs of motion, make up a group of prepositions expressing movement with reference to an axis or directional path. *Up* and *down* contrast in terms of vertical direction, while *along* (='from one end towards the other') contrasts with *across* (='from one side to another') in terms of a horizontal axis.

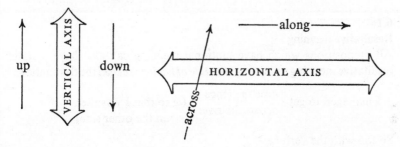

But *up* and *down* are also used idiomatically in reference to a horizontal axis:

    I walked up and down the platform

Up and *down* here express the notion of 'along', and need not have any vertical implications.

    With *(a)round,* the directional path is an angle or a curve:

    We ran up the hill
    We ran (a)round the corner

Toward(s) is in a category of its own, having the meaning 'in the direction of'.

6.15
Orientation: *beyond, over, past,* etc
Most prepositions listed in 6.10 and 6.14 can be used in a static sense of orientation. This brings in a third factor apart from the two things being spatially related: *viz* a 'point of orientation', at which (in reality or imagination) the speaker is standing. *Beyond* (='on the far side of') is a preposition whose primary meaning is one of orientation; furthermore, *over* (BrE), *past, across,* and *through* can combine the meaning of 'beyond' with more specific information of dimension-type, etc, on the lines described in 6.13:

    He lives *across* the moors (*ie* 'from here')
    The village *past* the bus-stop/*through* the wood, etc

Up, down, along, across, and *(a)round* (see 6.14) are used orientationally with reference to an axis in

The shop *down* the road (*ie* towards the bottom end of . . .)
His office is *up/down* the stairs (*ie* at (or towards) the top/bottom of . . .)
There's a hotel *across/along* the road (*ie* on the other side/towards the other end of . . .)
He lives *(a)round* the corner

6.16
Resultative meaning

All prepositions which have motional meaning can also have a static resultative meaning indicating *the state of having reached* the destination:

$$I \text{ managed to get } \left\{ \begin{array}{l} over \text{ the fence} \\ across \text{ the river} \end{array} \right\} (ie \text{ so that I was then} \\ \text{on the other side})$$

So too with the verb *be:*

The horses are *over* the fence (*ie* are now beyond)

Resultative meaning is not always distinguishable out of context from other static meanings; its presence is often signalled, however, by certain adverbs: *already, just, at last, (not) yet,* etc.

6.17
Pervasive meaning: *all over, throughout,* etc

Over (dimension-type 1/2) and *through* (dimension-type 2/3), especially when preceded by *all,* have pervasive meaning (either static or motional):

That child was running *all over* the flower borders
Chaos reigned *all through* the house

Throughout, substitutable for *all through,* is the only preposition whose primary meaning is 'pervasive'. Occasionally the 'axis' type prepositions of 6.14 are also used in a pervasive sense:

There were crowds (all) *along* the route
They put flowers (all) *around* the statue

6.18
Seven senses of *over*

Let us now see how one preposition (*over*) may be used in most of the senses discussed:

POSITION:	A lamp hung over the door
DESTINATION:	They threw a blanket over her

PASSAGE:	They climbed over the wall
ORIENTATION:	They live over (='on the far side of') the road
RESULTATIVE:	At last we were over the crest of the hill
PERVASIVE (STATIC):	Leaves lay thick (all) over the ground
PERVASIVE (MOTION):	They splashed water (all) over me

6.19
Verbs containing prepositional meaning

When a verb contains within it the meaning of a following preposition, it is often possible to omit the preposition; the verb then becomes transitive, and the prepositional complement becomes a direct object. For example, *climb* (*up*), *jump* (*over*), *flee* (*from*), *pass* (*by*): 'He climbed (up) the hill'.

6.20
Metaphorical or abstract use of place prepositions

Many place prepositions have abstract meanings which are clearly related, through metaphorical connection, to their locative uses. Very often prepositions so used keep the groupings (in terms of similarity or contrast of meaning) that they have when used in literal reference to place. This is often true, for example, of temporal usage (6.21).

One may perceive a stage-by-stage extension of metaphorical usage in such a series as:

- (i) *in shallow water* (purely literal)
- (ii) *in deep water* (also metaphorical='in trouble')
- (iii) *in difficulties* (the preposition is used metaphorically)
- (iv) *in a spot* (='in a difficult situation'; both the preposition and the noun are metaphorical, since literally *spot* would require *at*: 6.7)

Examples in relation to the literal meanings are:

IN/OUT OF; AMID (rare)/AMIDST (formal)
position → state, condition:
   in/out of danger; amidst many troubles
enclosure → abstract inclusion:
   in stories/plays; in a group/party; in/out of the race

ABOVE/BELOW/BENEATH
   vertical direction → abstract scale:
   such behaviour is beneath (not *below*) *him; he's above me in salary*

UNDER
   vertical direction → subjection, subordination:
   under suspicion/orders/compulsion

UP/DOWN
> movement on vertical axis → movement on list or scale:
> *up/down the scale; up/down the social ladder*

FROM/TO
> starting point/destination → originator/recipient:
> *a letter/present from Browning to his wife* (6.29–30)

BEYOND/PAST/OVER
> resultative meaning; physical → abstract:
> *beyond/past endurance; we're over the worst*

BETWEEN/AMONG, AMONGST (esp BrE)
> relative position → abstract relation between participants:
> *a fight between two boys; they agree among(st) themselves*

Note
A few prepositions (chiefly *in* and *out of*) can operate in an apparently converse relationship. For example:

The horse is *in* foal (= The foal is *in* the horse['s womb])
The office is *out of* envelopes (= There are *no* envelopes *in* the office)

Cf also (*a ship*) *in ballast, out of breath.*

Time
6.21
Time *when: at, on, in*
At, on, and *in* as prepositions of 'time *when*' are to some extent parallel to the same items as positive prepositions of position (6.7), although in the time sphere there are only two 'dimension-types', *viz* 'point of time' and 'period of time'.

At is used for points of time, chiefly clock-time (*at ten o'clock, at 6.30 pm, at noon*, etc); also, idiomatically, for holiday periods (*at the weekend* (BrE), *at Christmas, at Easter*); and for phrases *at night, at the/that time,* etc.

On is used with phrases referring to days (*on Monday, on the following day, on May (the) first*); otherwise *in* or, less commonly, *during* is used to indicate periods of time: *in the evening, during Holy Week, in August, in the months that followed, in the eighteenth century,* etc.

Note
On Monday morning, on the following evening, etc illustrate an exceptional use of *on* with a complement referring to a part of a day, rather than a whole day. But with phrases like *early morning, late afternoon* it is normal to use *in: in the late afternoon.*

6.22
Duration: *for,* etc
Duration is expressed by *for;* contrast:

$$\text{We camped there} \begin{cases} \textit{for} \text{ the summer (ie all through)} \\ \textit{in} \text{ the summer (ie at some time during the} \\ \quad \text{summer)} \end{cases}$$

So too in idiomatic phrases like *for ever* and *for good* ('for ever').

Over, all through, and *throughout* have a durational meaning parallel to their pervasive meaning in reference to place (6.17): *We camped there throughout the summer. Over* normally accompanies noun phrases denoting special occasions (such as holidays and festivals), and so generally refers to a shorter period of time than *all through* or *throughout.*

From . . . to is another pair of prepositions whose locative meaning is transferred to duration. The AmE alternative expression *(from) . . . through* avoids the ambiguity as to whether the period mentioned second is included in the total span of time:

> We camped there *(from)* June *through* September (AmE)
>   (= up to and including September)
> We camped there *from* June *to* (or *till*) September
>   (= up to [?and including] September)

Note

[a] Except with verbs like *stay, during* refers to a point or period within duration rather than to duration itself: *He spoke during the meeting.*

[b] Particularly with negatives and superlatives, *for* or (esp informally) *in* expresses exclusive duration: *I haven't seen him for/in years.*

6.23
Before, after, since, **and** *until/till*

As prepositions (but *cf* 11.21), these occur almost exclusively as prepositions of time, and are followed by either (a) a temporal noun phrase (*eg: before next week*), (b) a subjectless V-*ing* clause (*eg: since leaving school*), or (c) a noun phrase with a deverbal noun (App I.13, I.16, I.24) or some other noun phrase interpreted as equivalent to a clause:

> until the fall of Rome (= 'until Rome fell')
> before the war (= 'before the war started or took place')

Until specifies a terminal point with positive and a commencement point with negative predications:

> We slept until midnight (= We stopped sleeping then)
> We didn't sleep until midnight (= We started sleeping then)

6.24
Between, by, **and** *up to*

Other prepositions of time are *between, by,* and *up to:*

I'll phone you *between* lunch and three o'clock
By the time we'd walked five miles, he was exhausted
Up to last week, I hadn't received a reply

By specifies a commencement point; contrast:

By that time he was exhausted (=He was then exhausted)
Until that time he was exhausted (=He was then no longer exhausted)

This means that *by*-phrases do not co-occur with verbs of durative meaning:

He lay there $\left\{ {*by \atop until} \right\}$ midnight

Absence of prepositions of time
6.25
Prepositions of time *when* are always absent from adjuncts having the deictic words *last, next, this,* and *that;* the quantifying words *some* and *every;* and nouns which have 'last', 'next', or 'this' as an element of their meaning: *yesterday/today/tomorrow. Cf* 8.31 *ff.* For example:

I saw him *last Thursday*
I'll mention it *next time I see him*
Plums are more plentiful *this year*
Every summer she returns to her childhood home

The preposition is usually optional with deictic phrases referring to times at more than one remove from the present, such as (*on*) *Monday week* (BrE), (*in*) *the January before last,* (*on*) *the day before yesterday.* So too with phrases which identify a time before or after a given time in the past or future: (*in*) *the previous spring,* (*at*) *the following weekend,* (*on*) *the next day.* On the whole, the sentence without the preposition tends to be more informal and more usual.

Note
Informally, we also have omission of the temporal preposition in sentences such as *I'll see you Sunday,* where the preposition *on* is omitted before a day of the week standing on its own. Another informal type of omission is in initial position preceding a plural noun phrase:

Sundays we go into the country

6.26
The preposition *for* is often omitted in phrases of duration:

We stayed there (for) three months
The snowy weather lasted (for) the whole time we were there
(For) a lot of the time we just lay on the beach

The omission almost invariably takes place with phrases which begin
with *all*, such as *all day, all (the) week:*

We stayed there all week (*not* *for all week)

In other cases, however, the omission is impossible: for example, where
the action of the verb is clearly not continuously co-extensive with the
period specified:

I lived there three years   I lived there for three years
*I taught him three years   I taught him for three years

Initial position in the clause also seems to discourage omission: *For 600
years, the cross lay unnoticed.*

Prepositional phrase chiefly as adjunct
Cause ~ purpose
6.27
CAUSE, REASON, MOTIVE: *BECAUSE OF*, etc
At one end of the spectrum of cause ~ purpose, we have prepositions
expressing either the material cause or the psychological cause (motive)
of a happening:

Because of the drought, the price of bread was high that year
On account of his wide experience, he was made chairman
I hid the money, *for fear of what my parents would say*
The survivors were weak *from exposure and lack of food*
Some people support charities *out of duty*

Phrases of cause, reason and motive answer the question 'Why . . . ?'

6.28
PURPOSE, INTENDED DESTINATION: *FOR*

He'll do anything *for money*
Everyone ran *for shelter*
He died *for his country*

The notion of 'purpose' can be seen from the possibility of paraphrase
by a clause (*in order*) *to* . . . (see 11.31): *for money*='in order to gain
money'.
  Phrases of purpose or destination answer the questions 'Why . . . ?',
'What . . . for?', 'Where . . . for?', or 'Who . . . for?'. They frequently
occur as postmodifiers as well as adverbials: *the scenery for the play*, etc.

6.29

RECIPIENT, GOAL, TARGET: *FOR, TO, AT*

He made a beautiful doll *for his daughter*

So used for 'intended recipient' (his daughter may or may not have actually received the doll), the *for* phrase can often be equated with an indirect object (7.6, 12.28): *He made his daughter a beautiful doll*. In contrast, a *to* phrase usually expresses the 'actual recipient':

He gave a beautiful doll *to his daughter*

(which entails that his daughter actually received the doll). Here again there is a transformational relationship with the indirect object construction (7.9):

$$I \begin{Bmatrix} \text{gave} \\ \text{lent} \\ \text{sold} \end{Bmatrix} \text{ the book } \textit{to my friend} \leftrightarrow I \begin{Bmatrix} \text{gave} \\ \text{lent} \\ \text{sold} \end{Bmatrix} \textit{my friend} \text{ the book}$$

At, in combinations such as *aim at* (where the prepositional phrase is complementary to the verb), expresses INTENDED GOAL or TARGET:

After aiming carefully *at the bird*, he missed it completely

A vicious mongrel was snapping *at his ankles*

As the first sentence shows, the intended goal need not be achieved. A contrast in many cases (*kick at, charge at, bite at, catch at, shoot at, chew at*) may be drawn between this use of *at*, in which some idea of 'aim' is implied, and the direct object construction, which indicates attainment of the goal or consummation of the action as planned. In other cases, *to* must be used if the attainment of the goal is to be stressed: *He ran at me/He ran to me*. Similarly, *point at/to, throw at/to*.

Note

There is a comparable difference between *at* and *to* when combined with verbs of utterance such as *roar, bellow, shout, mutter, growl: He shouted at me* suggests that I am being treated merely as a target (*eg* of abuse), while *He shouted to me* implies that the shouter is communicating with me, *ie* that I am the recipient of the message. *At* here usually suggests hostility.

6.30

SOURCE, ORIGIN: *FROM*

The converse of *to* (='goal') is *from* (='source'):

Bill lent the book *to me* ↔ I borrowed the book *from Bill*

From is also used with reference to 'place of origin':

He comes from Austria (=he is Austrian)

This type of prepositional phrase occurs not only as an adjunct, but as a postmodifier: *the man from Mars; a friend of mine from London.*

·Means ~ agentive
6.31
MANNER: *WITH, IN ... MANNER, LIKE*

We were received *with the utmost courtesy*
The task was done *in a workmanlike manner*
The army swept through the city *like a pestilence*

Note that *like* with intensive verbs, as in *Life is like a dream*, refers not to manner but to resemblance.

Note
As distinct from *like*, prepositional *as* refers to actual role:

He spoke $\begin{cases} \text{like a lawyer ('after the manner of ...')} \\ \text{as a lawyer ('in the capacity of ...')} \end{cases}$

6.32
MEANS, INSTRUMENT: *BY, WITH, WITHOUT*
By can express the meaning 'by means of':

I usually go to work *by bus/train/car*
The thief must have entered and left the house *by the back door*
By working the pumps, we kept the ship afloat for another 40 hours

With, on the other hand, expresses instrumental meaning:

He caught the ball *with his left hand*
Someone had broken the window *with a stone*

There is a correspondence between these sentences (which normally require a human subject and a direct object) and sentences containing the verb *use: He used his left hand to catch the ball; Someone had used a stone to break the window*. There is also an alternative construction in which the noun phrase denoting the instrument becomes the subject: *His left hand caught the ball; A stone had broken the window*. (On 'instrumental' subjects, see 7.10.)

For most senses of *with*, including that of instrument, *without* expresses the equivalent negative meaning: *I drew it without a ruler* (ie 'I did not draw it with a ruler').

Phrases of means and instrument answer the question 'How ...?':

A: How did he do it? B: By working hard.

Note
[a] Mode of transport is expressed by *on* as well as *by: on the bus/the train/a ship/a plane*. These are not purely locative phrases (location in such cases would be expressed by *in* rather than *on*: 6.7), but rather indicate the condition of being 'in

transit'. Thus, *I go to work on the bus* can be an alternative to *I go to work by bus*. *On* is used instead of *by* in the phrases *on foot, on horseback*.

[b] *Of* is used with *die* in expressions like *He died of hunger*.

6.33
INSTRUMENT, AGENTIVE: *WITH, BY*

While the 'instrument' is the inert and normally inanimate cause of an action (the ball that breaks a window), the 'agentive' is its animate (normally human) initiating cause (the boy who threw the ball). In a passive sentence, the agentive or instrument can be expressed by a *by*-phrase, but only the instrument can be expressed by a *with* phrase:

The window was broken $\begin{cases} \text{by a ball/by a boy} \\ \text{with a ball/*with a boy} \end{cases}$

The agentive *by*-phrase also occurs as a postmodifier to signify authorship or the like: *a novel by Tolstoy, a picture by Degas*, etc.

6.34
STIMULUS: *AT*

The relation between an emotion and its stimulus (normally an abstract stimulus) can often be expressed by *at* or by the instrumental *by*:

I was alarmed at/by his behaviour

Both of these can be treated as passive equivalents of *His behaviour alarmed me*, and the noun phrase following *at* may be treated as a 'quasi-agent'. See further 12.11. Other prepositions introducing stimuli are illustrated in the examples *resentful of, disappointed with, sorry about*.

Note

[a] A number of other prepositions may introduce 'quasi-agents' after certain participles:

　I'm worried *about this* (~ This worries me)
　He's interested *in history* (~ History interests him)
　Cf also: His plans were known *to everyone* (Everyone knew his plans)

[b] In BrE, *with* rather than *at* is used when the 'stimulus' is a person or object rather than an event: *I was furious with* (not *at*) *John; I was delighted with* (not *at*) *the present*. But in AmE, *I was furious/angry/livid at John* is quite usual. With abstract nouns, *at* is unrestrictedly acceptable: *I was furious at John's behaviour*.

6.35
Accompaniment: *with*

Especially when followed by an animate complement, *with* has the meaning 'in company with' or 'together with':

I'm so glad you're coming *with us*
Jock, *with several of his friends*, was drinking till 2 am

In the second sentence, the *with* phrase serves a function very close to coordination with *and:* 'Jock and several of his friends were . . .'.

An example of a phrase of accompaniment as postmodifier is:

Curry *with rice* is my favourite dish

In this as in most other senses (but *cf* 6.36) *without* is the negative of *with: They're going without us; You never see him without* (*ie* 'unaccompanied by') *his dog.*

6.36
Support, opposition: *for, with, against*

Are you *for* or *against the plan?* (*ie* Do you support or oppose the plan?)

It is prudent to go *with* rather than *against the tide of public opinion*

For conveys the idea of support, *with* that of solidarity or movement in sympathy; *against* conveys the contrary idea of opposition. In this use, there is no negative *without* contrasting with *with.*

6.37
Prepositional phrase chiefly as postmodifier
'**Having**': *of, with, without*
Beside the following examples:

(1)	(2)
(a) a man of courage	the courage of the man
(b) a man with large ears	the man's large ears

a comparable relation exists paraphrasable with *have:* 'The man has courage', 'The man has large ears'. The two columns differ in that (1) makes *a man* the centre of attention, while (2) makes something about him the centre of attention. They also differ in the definiteness attributed to *man* (4.20), such that column (2) presupposes previous specification. The preposition *of* in (1a) is normally used with abstract attributes, while *with* in (1b) is more general and is especially common with concrete attributes. The correspondence of the *of-* and *-s* genitive in column (2) is also to be noted (4.69 *ff*).

The negative of *with* is again *without;*

women *without children* ('childless women')
the house *without a porch* ('. . . which has no porch')

The correspondence between phrases with *with* or *without* and relative clauses with *have* applies also to clauses in which *have* is followed by a quasi-clausal object (13.19):

the girl with a boy friend in the navy
(~ . . . who has a boy friend in the navy)

6.38
Prepositional phrase chiefly as disjunct or conjunct
Concession: *in spite of, despite, for + all, with + all, notwithstanding*

>I admire him, *in spite of his faults*
>He lost the fight, *for all his boasting*

In spite of is a general-purpose preposition of concession; *despite* is rather more formal and *notwithstanding* is formal and rather legalistic in style. The combinations *for all* and *with all* (*all* being an obligatory predeterminer with this meaning) are chiefly colloquial.

6.39
Reference: *with regard to, with reference to* (formal), *as to* (BrE), *as for*

>*With reference to your letter of April 29th*, I confirm . . .
>*As for the burglar*, he escaped through the attic window

As to and *as for* (= 'returning to the question of . . .') are less formal than the other complex prepositions in this group. Other prepositions within the same general area of meaning are *regarding, in regard to, with respect to, in respect of*, and *on the matter of*. Most can be used in postmodifying phrases as well as in disjuncts: *I'd like to know your opinion as to/with regard to the burglar's behaviour.*

6.40
Exception: *except for, but*, etc

>All the students *except/but* John passed the test

Commonly the complement is itself a prepositional phrase:

>The weather is good today, except *in the south-east*

Except, excepting, and *but* function generally (in the case of *but* exclusively) in postmodifying phrases. Thus *but* cannot occur initially as a preposition: **But me, everyone was tired*. The prepositional phrase, in such constructions, is often separated from its noun head, and postponed to the end of the clause (*cf* 14.30):

>Everyone *but me* was tired ~ Everyone was tired *but me*

Except for, with the exception of, and *apart from* are used primarily in disjuncts.

Note
The resemblance and the contrast between *but* as a preposition and *but* as a conjunction (10.36) are brought out in:

>$\left\{\begin{array}{l}\text{All the students had a good time } but \text{ John} \\ \text{Most of the students had a good time } \left\{\begin{array}{l} but \ not \text{ John} \\ but \text{ John } did \ not \end{array}\right.\end{array}\right.$

6.41

Negative condition: *but for*

It is to be noted that *but for* is not used in the sense of exception, but rather that of 'negative condition': *But for Gordon, we should have lost the match* (*ie* 'If it hadn't been for Gordon ...', 'If Gordon hadn't played as he did ...', etc).

Prepositional phrase chiefly as complementation of verb or adjective
6.42

Subject matter: *about, on*

> He told me *about his adventures*
> He's lecturing *on new techniques of management*

With the meaning 'on the subject of, concerning', *about* and *on* can combine with a considerable range of verbs and adjectives, including:

> speak about/on   silent about/on

On tends to refer to deliberate, formal linguistic communication (speaking, lecturing, writing, etc), and is therefore inappropriate for verbs like *chat* or *quarrel*.

This difference of meaning occurs also with postmodifying phrases:

> a book about/on butterflies   a story about a princess

Note

[a] *Of* is a somewhat rarer and more literary alternative to *about* in *tell ... of; speak of; talk of; inform ... of;* etc. Both *about* and *of* are possible with *think*, but with a difference of meaning: *He thought about the problem*='He pondered/considered the problem'; *He thought of the problem*='He brought the problem to his mind'.

[b] A less usual alternative to *about* and *on* is *concerning*, which is formal to the point of being rather stilted: *a dispute concerning land rights.*

6.43

Ingredient, material: *with, of, out of*

After verbs of 'making', *with* indicates an ingredient, whereas *of* and *out of* signify the material or constituency of the whole thing:

> You make a cake *with eggs* (*ie* 'eggs are one of the ingredients')
> He made the frame (*out*) *of wood* (*ie* 'wood was the only material')

The same contrast of meaning is seen with *build* and *construct:*

> The terminal was built/constructed *with reinforced concrete*
> The terminal was built/constructed (*out*) *of reinforced concrete*

With also enters into expressions such as *paved with brick, filled with water, loaded with hay.*

Of (used with nouns denoting 'material') is found in a postmodifying function as well as in adverbials: *a bracelet of solid gold, a table of polished oak* (*ie* 'made/consisting of polished oak'); here it may also be used metaphorically: *a man of steel; a heart of stone.*

6.44
Respect, standard: *at, for*

A gradable adjective implies some standard or norm (5.19): *big* means something different in *This elephant is big, This cat is big,* since 'big for an elephant' presupposes a larger scale, and a larger norm, than 'big for a cat'. We can make the norm explicit by a *for* phrase:

He's not bad *for a youngster* (*ie* considering he is a youngster)
That dog is long-legged *for a terrier*

A further way in which a prepositional phrase may specify the meaning of a gradable adjective is to use *at* to introduce the respect in which the adjective is appropriate to its noun phrase:

He's bad/hopeless/terrible *at games*

These two prepositional uses are not restricted to adjectival complementation:

I'm a complete dunce *at mathematics*
For an Englishman, he speaks foreign languages remarkably well
It's a dreadfully expensive toy *for what it is*

6.45
Reaction: *to*

Instead of regarding *John's blunder* in *my surprise at John's blunder* as the stimulus of the surprise (as in 6.34), we can regard the surprise as the reaction to the blunder. If we make the main clause represent the event acting as a 'stimulus', we can express the REACTION by the preposition *to* followed by an abstract noun of emotion: *To my annoyance, they rejected the offer. To my annoyance* in this context is an attitudinal disjunct, comparable with adverbs such as *annoyingly, surprisingly* (8.50 *ff*).

Alternatively, we can use a *to*-phrase to identify the PERSON REACTING: *To me, their rejection of the offer was a surprise.* In this last sense, *to* is not limited to emotive reactions; it applies equally to intellectual or perceptual responses:

To a mind based in common sense, his ideas are utterly absurd
It looked *to me* like a vast chasm

6.46
Modification of prepositional phrases

It is worth noting that prepositional meanings (particularly of time and place) are subject to modification as regards degree and measure, and that prepositions may therefore (like many adjectives and adverbs) be preceded by intensifiers. For example:

He had wandered *right* (='completely') off the path
Now their footsteps could be heard *directly* above my head

There is doubt in such cases as to whether the intensifier should be treated as applying to the whole prepositional phrase, or to the preposition alone. Occasionally, the possibility of placing the intensifier after the phrase suggests that it is the phrase as a whole that is qualified:

Few people are against public ownership *completely*

Bibliographical note
For some theoretical discussion of prepositional roles, see Fillmore (1968). On English prepositions, see Aksenenko (1956); Close (1962); Leech (1969a), Chapter 8, on prepositions of place; Quirk (1968), on complex prepositions.

SEVEN

THE SIMPLE SENTENCE

Clause patterns
7.1
Simple and complex sentences

It was pointed out in 2.4 that elements such as V(erb) and O(bject) were constituents of sentences and also of clauses within sentences. From now on, we shall speak of *clauses* and *clause structure* whenever a statement is true both for sentences and for the clauses of which it is composed:

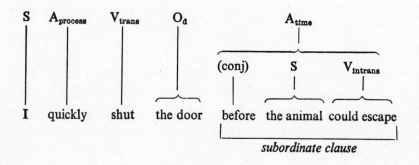

In the present chapter, however, we shall be dealing only with simple sentences: that is, sentences consisting of only one clause.

7.2
Clause types

Concentrating on those elements that are normally obligatory, we can usefully distinguish seven clause types which we may designate in italics with the abbreviations explained in 2.4–10:

(1) *SVA* S V_{intens} A_{place}
  Mary is   in the house

(2) *SVC* S V_{intens} C_s
  Mary is $\begin{cases} \text{kind} \\ \text{a nurse} \end{cases}$

(3) *SVO* S $V_{monotrans}$ O_d
  Somebody caught   the ball

(4) *SVOA* S $V_{complex\ trans}$ O_d A_{place}
  I put   the plate on the table

(5) *SVOC* S $V_{complex\ trans}$ O_d C_o
  We have proved him $\begin{cases} \text{wrong} \\ \text{a fool} \end{cases}$

(6) *SVOO* S $V_{ditrans}$ O_i O_d
  She gives   me expensive presents

(7) *SV* S $V_{intrans}$
  The child laughed

Note

[a] Most obligatory adjuncts are A_{place}, but there are many cases in which the term 'place' applies only in a broad metaphorical sense:

  He is *without a job*   We kept him *off cigarettes*

  while some are not A_{place} at all: 'They treated him *kindly*'

[b] Among the relatively minor patterns not accounted for here, we might mention S V O_i C_s: *John made Mary a good husband* (ie 'John was a good husband to Mary').

7.3
Complementation

The elements O_d, C, and A in the above patterns are *obligatory* elements of clause structure in the sense that they are required for the complementation of the verb. By this we mean that, given the use of a particular verb in a particular sense, the sentence is incomplete if one of these elements is omitted: **I put the book* (Type *SVOA*) and **He resembled* (Type *SVO*) are unacceptable. In some cases, however, a direct object or object complement in one of these patterns may be considered grammatically optional:

  He's eating – *cf* He's eating an apple (Type *SVO*)

  He made her career – *cf* He made her career a success (Type *SVOC*)

  He's teaching – *cf* He's teaching German (Type *SVO*), He's teaching the boys (German) (Type *SVOO*)

Our approach, however, will be to regard these as cases of conversion (App I.30), whereby a verb such as *eat* is transferred from the transitive to the intransitive category. Thus *He's eating* is an instance of clause-type *SV* rather than of *SVO* (with optional deletion of the object).

7.4
Optional adverbials

The patterns of 7.2 can be expanded by the addition of various optional adverbials; cf 2.10. For example (optional adverbials are bracketed):

> SV: (A)   S   V   (A)
>   (Sometimes) she sings (beautifully)
>
> SVA: (A)   S   V (A)   A
>   (In America) most students are (now) on vacation
>
> SVOO: S   (A)   V O   O
>   She (kindly) sent us some photographs

7.5
Transformational relations

One way of distinguishing the various clause types is by means of 'transformational' relations, or relations of grammatical paraphrase.

Clauses containing a noun phrase as object are distinguished by their ability to be converted into passive clauses, the object noun phrase assuming the function of subject (V_{pass} = passive verb phrase), the subject appearing (if at all) in an optional *by*-phrase, symbolized here as [A]:

> Many critics disliked the play (S V O_d) ↔ The play was disliked (by many critics) (S V_{pass} [A])

Where the passive draws more attention to the result than to the action or agency, the 'resulting' copula *get* (12.8) frequently replaces *be*, though chiefly in rather informal usage:

> The window *was* broken by my younger son
> I know how the window *got* broken

A more gradually achieved result can be sometimes expressed by *become:*

> With the passage of time, the furniture *became* covered in dust

The following examples illustrate the passive with other clause types:

> Queen Victoria considered him a genius (S V O_d C_o) ↔ He was considered a genius by Queen Victoria (S V_{pass} C_s [A])
> An intruder must have placed the ladder there (S V O_d A_{loc}) ↔ The ladder must have been placed there by an intruder (S V_{pass} A_{loc} [A])
> My father gave me this watch (S V O_i O_d)
> ↔ { I was given this watch by my father (S V_{pass} O_d [A])
>   { This watch was given me by my father (S V_{pass} O_i [A])

As Type *SVOO* clauses have two objects, they often have two passive forms, as shown above – one in which the direct object becomes subject, and another (more common) in which the indirect object becomes subject.

There is sometimes equivalence between Types *SV*, *SVC*, and *SVA* as is shown by occasional equivalences of the following kind:

S V ↔ S V C$_s$
The baby is sleeping ↔ The baby is asleep
Two loaves will suffice ↔ Two loaves will be sufficient

S V ↔ S V A
He hurried ↔ He went fast

S V C$_s$ ↔ S V A
He is jobless ↔ He is without a job

On the whole, English prefers to avoid the plain *SV* pattern where alternatives are available (14.33).

7.6
Intensive relationship
An *SVOC* clause is often equivalent to a clause with an infinitive or *that*-clause (12.20 *ff*):

I imagined *her beautiful* ↔ $\begin{cases} \text{I imagined } her \text{ to be beautiful} \\ \text{I imagined } that \text{ she was beautiful} \end{cases}$

This equivalence shows that the O and the C of an *SVOC* clause are in the same relation to one another as the S and C of an *SVC* clause. The relation is expressed, wherever it is expressed at all, by an intensive verb. The intensive relationship is important in other aspects of grammar apart from clause patterns. It underlies, for example, relations of apposition (9.45 *ff*).

Further, we may extend the concept of intensive relationship to the relation of subject to adverbial and object to adverbial in *SVA* and *SVOA* patterns respectively. (For *SVOA* patterns, see 8.29, 8.44.)

SVOO clauses can be transformed into *SVOA* clauses by the substitution of a prepositional phrase for the indirect object, with a change of order (12.28):

She sent *Jim* a card ↔ She sent a card *to Jim*
She left *Jim* a card ↔ She left a card *for Jim*

To and *for*, in their recipient senses (6.29), are the prepositions chiefly involved, but others, such as *with* and *of*, are occasionally found:

I'll play *you* a game of chess ↔ I'll play a game of chess *with/
against you*
She asked *Jim* a favour ↔ She asked a favour *of Jim*

7.7
Multiple class membership of verbs
It must be borne in mind that one verb can belong, in various senses, to a number of different classes (App I.30), and hence enter into a number of different clause types. The verb *get* is a particularly versatile one, being excluded only from Type *SV* (and not even from this universally):

> *SVC:* He's getting angry
> *SVA:* He got through the window
> *SVO:* He'll get a surprise
> *SVOC:* He got his shoes and socks wet
> *SVOA:* He got himself into trouble
> *SVOO:* He got her a splendid present

Through the multiple class membership of verbs, ambiguities can arise: *I found her an entertaining partner*, like *She called him a steward*, could be interpreted either as *SVOC* or as *SVOO*.

7.8
Clause elements syntactically defined
A SUBJECT
> (a) is normally a noun phrase (4.1) or a clause with nominal function (11.13 *ff*);
> (b) occurs before the verb phrase in declarative clauses, and immediately after the operator (2.3) in questions (but *cf* 7.53, 14.12 *ff*);
> (c) has number and person concord, where applicable (7.18, 7.26), with the verb phrase.

An OBJECT (direct or indirect)
> (a) like a subject, is a noun phrase or clause with nominal function;
> (b) normally follows the subject and the verb phrase (but *cf* 7.53, 7.63, 14.11);
> (c) by the passive transformation, assumes the status of subject (7.5), but *cf* 12.16.

An INDIRECT OBJECT, where both objects are present, precedes the DIRECT OBJECT (except in rare instances like BrE *Give it me*), and is semantically equivalent to a prepositional phrase (7.6).

A COMPLEMENT (subject or object)
> (a) is a noun phrase, an adjective phrase, or a clause with nominal function, having a co-referential relation with the subject (or object);
> (b) follows the subject, verb phrase, and (if one is present) object (but *cf* 7.53, 14.11, 14.28);
> (c) does not become subject through the passive transformation.

An ADVERBIAL (see 8.1)

(a) is an adverb phrase, adverbial clause, noun phrase, or prepositional phrase;
(b) is generally mobile, *ie* is capable of occurring in more than one position in the clause;
(c) is generally optional, *ie* may be added to or removed from a sentence
without affecting its acceptability, but *cf* the obligatory adverbial
of the *SVA* and *SVOA* patterns (7.2).

Clause elements semantically considered
7.9
Agentive, affected, recipient, attribute

The most typical semantic role of a subject is AGENTIVE; that is, the animate being instigating or causing the happening denoted by the verb:

John opened the letter

The most typical function of the direct object is that of the AFFECTED
participant; *ie* a participant (animate or inanimate) which does not cause
the happening denoted by the verb, but is directly involved in some other
way:

Many MPs criticized *the Prime Minister*

The most typical function of the indirect object is that of RECIPIENT;
ie an animate participant being passively implicated by the happening or
state:

I've found *you* a place

The role of the subject complement is that of attribute of the subject,
whether a current or existing attribute (with stative verbs) or one resulting
from the event described by the verb (with dynamic verbs).

CURRENT ATTRIBUTE: He's *my brother;* He seems *unhappy*
RESULTING ATTRIBUTE: He became *restless;* He turned *traitor*
(12.8 *f*)

The role of the object complement is that of attribute of the object,
again either a current or resulting attribute:

CURRENT ATTRIBUTE: I ate the meat *cold;* I prefer coffee *black*
RESULTING ATTRIBUTE: They elected him *President;* He painted the
wall *blue* (12.26 *f*)

Note
Although *I've found a place for the magnolia tree* and *I've found a place for Mrs Jones*
appear to be grammatically equivalent, only the second can be transformed into a
clause with indirect object:

> I've found Mrs Jones a place
> *I've found the magnolia tree a place

This is because a tree is inanimate and cannot adopt a recipient role. With the verb *give*, however, there can be exceptions (*cf* 7.16):

> I've given the bathroom a thorough cleaning

7.10
Agentive and instrumental subject

Apart from its agentive function, the subject frequently has an instrumental role; that is, it expresses the unwitting (generally inanimate) material cause of an event:

> *The avalanche* destroyed several houses

With intransitive verbs, the subject also frequently has the AFFECTED role that is elsewhere typical of the object:

> *Jack* fell down
> *The pencil* was lying on the table

We may also extend this latter function to subjects of intensive verbs:

> *The pencil* was on the table

It is now possible to see a regular relation, in terms of clause function, between adjectives or intransitive verbs and the corresponding transitive verbs expressing CAUSATIVE meaning:

$S_{affected}$ V	$S_{agent/instr}$ V $O_{affected}$
The door opened	John/The key opened the door
The flowers have died	The frost has killed the flowers
$S_{affected}$ V C	$S_{agent/instr}$ V $O_{affected}$
The road became narrower	They narrowed the road
I got angry	His manner angered me
$S_{agentive}$ V	$S_{agentive}$ V $O_{affected}$
My dog was walking	I was walking my dog

7.11
Recipient subject

The subject may also have a recipient role with verbs such as *have*, *own*, *possess*, *benefit* (*from*), as is indicated by the following relation:

> Mr Smith has bought/given/sold his son a radio → So now his
> son has/owns/possesses the radio

The perceptual verbs *see* and *hear* also require a 'recipient' subject, in contrast to *look at* and *listen to*, which are agentive. The other perceptual

verbs *taste*, *smell*, and *feel* have both an agentive meaning corresponding
to *look at* and a recipient meaning corresponding to *see:*

> Foolishly, he tasted the soup
> *Foolishly, he tasted the pepper in the soup

The adverb *foolishly* requires the agentive; hence, the second sentence,
which can only be understood in a non-agentive manner, does not make
sense.

Verbs indicating a mental state may also require a recipient subject:

> I thought you were mistaken (*cf* It seemed to me . . .)
> I liked the play (*cf* The play gave me pleasure)

Normally, recipient subjects go with stative verbs (3.35). Some of them
(notably *have* and *possess*) have no passive form:

> They have a beautiful house ↔ *A beautiful house is had by them

7.12
Locative, temporal and eventive subjects
The subject may have the function of designating place or time:

> This path is swarming with ants (= Ants are swarming *all over*
> *this path*)
> The bus holds forty people (= Forty people can sit *in the bus*)

Unlike *swarm*, the verbs in such sentences do not normally admit the
progressive (*The bus is holding . . .*) or the passive (*Forty people are
held . . .*).

Temporal subjects can usually be replaced by the empty *it* (7.13), the
temporal expression becoming adjunct:

> Tomorrow is my birthday (= It is my birthday *tomorrow*)
> The winter of 1970 was exceptionally mild (= It was exceptionally
> mild *in the winter of 1970*)

Eventive subjects (with abstract noun heads designating arrangements
and activities) differ from others in permitting intensive complementation
with a time adverbial (*cf* 12.10):

> The concert is on Thursday (*but* *The concert hall is on Thursday)

7.13
Empty *it* subject
Finally, a subject may lack semantic content altogether, and consist only
of the meaningless 'prop' word *it*, used especially with climatic predications:

> It's raining/snowing, etc   It's getting dark   It's noisy in here

Note

The 'prop' subject *it* as discussed here must be distinguished from the 'anticipatory' *it* of sentences like *It was nice seeing you* (14.24 *ff*), where the 'prop' subject is a replacement for a postponed clausal subject (= *Seeing you was nice*).

Locative and effected object
7.14

We turn now to roles of the DIRECT OBJECT. Apart from the AFFECTED OBJECT (7.9), semantic types of direct object are the LOCATIVE OBJECT and the EFFECTED OBJECT. An example of the 'locative object' is:

The horse jumped the fence ('. . . jumped *over* the fence')

There are similar uses of such verbs as *turn, leave, reach, surround, penetrate, mount, cross, climb* (see also 6.19).

An effected object is one that refers to something which exists only by virtue of the activity indicated by the verb:

Baird invented television   I'm writing a letter

With agentive subject and an affected object, one may always capture part of the meaning of a clause (*eg: X destroyed Y*) by saying 'X did something to Y'; but this does not apply to an effected object – *Baird invented television* does not imply 'Baird did something to television'.

One may include in this category also the type of object (sometimes called 'cognate') which repeats, partially or wholly, the meaning of the verb, as in *sing a song*.

Note

A more dubious category of object consists of phrases of extent or measure, as in

He ran *a mile*   It costs *ten dollars*   It weighs *almost a ton*

As these clauses do not generally permit the passive transformation, there is reason to analyse them as *SVA* rather than *SVO*. However, the final element behaves at least marginally like a direct object, as is shown by question forms with *What* alongside *How much*:

What does it weigh? How much does it weigh?

The ambiguity of sentences such as *We ate a lot*, which may be *SVO* or *SVA*, is discussed in 8.18.

7.15

A third type of effected object takes the form of a verbal noun preceded by a common verb of general meaning, such as *do, make, have, take, give*. This construction is often more idiomatic, especially in colloquial English, than an equivalent construction with an intransitive verb (see further 14.33):

He did little work that day ('He worked little that day')
He made several attempts to contact me ('He attempted several times to contact me')

The prisoner made no comment
He's having a bath/a holiday (BrE)/a smoke
He took a rest/a vacation (AmE)/a dislike to her/a dive into the
water
He gave a jump/a yell, etc

Have and *take* in these examples have agentive subjects (*have* being the typical British, and *take* the typical American form), while *give* usually has an involuntary force and therefore accompanies an 'affected' subject.

Note
Have can more easily have an affected subject than *take* (*The baby had/*took a bath*), but *cf: He took a beating*.

7.16
Affected indirect object
There is only one exception to the rule that the indirect object has the role of 'recipient': this is when *give* (or sometimes related verbs like *pay, owe*) has an 'effected' object as direct object and an 'affected' object as indirect object:

I paid her a visit ('I visited her')
I gave the door a couple of kicks ('I kicked the door a couple of
times')

These clauses, as the paraphrases make clear, are equivalent to clauses with a direct object as 'affected' object.

7.17
Summary
Although the semantic functions of the elements (particularly S and O) are quite varied, there are certain clear restrictions, such as that the object cannot be 'agentive' or 'instrument'; that a subject (except in the passive) cannot be 'effected'; that an indirect object can have only two functions – those of 'affected' and 'recipient'. The assignment of a function to the subject seems to have the following system of priorities:

If there is an 'agentive', it is S; if not,
If there is an 'instrument', it is S; if not,
If there is an 'affected', it is S; if not,
If there is a 'locative' or 'temporal' or 'eventive', it may be S; if not,
The prop word *it* is S.

Naturally, where the passive transformation applies, it transfers the role of the direct or indirect object to the subject.

Note
The above treatment of sentence elements does not include discussion of clauses as S, O, and C.

Concord
7.18
Subject-verb concord

The most important type of concord in English is concord of number between subject and verb. Thus (3) and (4) are ungrammatical:

(1) The window is open   (3) *The window are open
    (sing + sing)   (sing + plur)
(2) The windows are open   (4) *The windows is open
    (plur + plur)   (plur + sing)

A clause in the position of subject counts as singular for purposes of concord: *How they got there doesn't concern me; To treat them as hostages is criminal.* The same is true of prepositional phrases, etc, acting as subject: *After the exams is the time to relax,* etc. Nominal relative clauses on the other hand, since they are equivalent to noun phrases (11.13), may have plural as well as singular concord: *What were once human dwellings are now nothing but piles of rubble.*

Note

[a] In fact, it is possible to generalize the rule as 'A subject which is not definitely marked for plural requires a singular verb'. This would explain, in addition to clausal and adverbial subjects, the tendency in informal speech for *is/was* to follow the pseudo-subject *there* in existential sentences such as *There's hundreds of people on the waiting list* (14.19 *ff*).

[b] Apparent exceptions to the concord rule arise with singular nouns ending with the *-s* of the plural inflection (*measles, billiards, mathematics,* etc, 4.32), or conversely plural nouns lacking the inflection (*cattle, people, clergy,* etc, 4.35):

Measles *is* sometimes serious   Our people *are* complaining

[c] Plural words and phrases (including coordinate phrases, see 7.21) count as singular if they are used as names, titles, quotations, etc (see further 9.57):

Crime and Punishment is perhaps the best-constructed of Dostoyevsky's novels; but *The Brothers Karamazov* is undoubtedly his masterpiece.
'The Cedars' has a huge garden
'Senior Citizens' means, in common parlance, people over sixty

The titles of some works which are collections of stories, etc, however, can be singular or plural: *The Canterbury Tales exist/exists in many manuscripts.*

7.19
Notional concord, and proximity

Two factors interfere with concord as presented in 7.18. 'Notional concord' is agreement of verb with subject according to the *idea* of number rather than the actual presence of the grammatical marker for that idea. Thus *the government* is treated as plural in *The government have broken all their promises* (BrE), as is shown not only by the plural verb *have,* but also by the pronoun *their.*

The principle of 'proximity' denotes agreement of the verb with whatever noun or pronoun closely precedes it, sometimes in preference to agreement with the headword of the subject:

No one except his own supporters *agree* with him
One in ten *take* drugs

7.20
Collective nouns

In BrE, collective nouns, notionally plural but grammatically singular, obey notional concord in examples such as the following where AmE usually has the singular:

The public are tired of demonstrations   [1]
The audience were enjoying every minute of it   [2]

Although singular and plural verbs are more or less interchangeable in these contexts, the choice is based, if on anything, on whether the group is being considered as a single undivided body, or as a collection of individuals (*cf* 4.62). Thus plural is more likely than singular in [2], because consideration is being given to the individual reactions of members of the audience. Contrastingly, singular has to be used in sentences like *The audience was enormous.*

Coordinated subject
7.21

When a subject consists of two or more noun phrases coordinated by *and*, a distinction has to be made between appositional and non-appositional coordination. Under NON-APPOSITIONAL COORDINATION we include cases that can be treated as an implied reduction of two clauses. These have a verb in the plural:

Tom and Mary *are* now ready (↔ Tom is now ready and Mary is now ready)
What I say and what I think *are* my own affair (↔ What I say is ... and what I think is ...)

A singular verb is used with conjoinings which represent a single entity:

The hammer and sickle *was* flying from a tall flag pole

Conjoinings expressing a mutual relationship, even though they can only indirectly be treated as reductions of clauses in this way, also take a plural verb:

Your problem and mine *are* similar (↔ Your problem is similar to mine and mine is similar to yours)

With the less common APPOSITIONAL COORDINATION, however, no such reduction is possible at all, for the coordinated structures refer to the same thing. Hence a singular verb is used:

> This temple of ugliness and memorial to Victorian bad taste
>   *was* erected at the Queen's express wish

The two opening noun phrases here both refer to the same thing. The following example, however, is ambiguous and could have either a singular or plural verb according as the brother and editor are one person or two:

> His younger brother and the subsequent editor of his collected
>   papers *was/were* with him at his death-bed

Some latitude is allowed in the interpretation of abstract nouns since it is not always easy to decide if they represent one quality or two:

> Your fairness and impartiality *has/have* been much appreciated

7.22

A single noun head with coordinate modifiers may imply two separate sentences (*cf* 9.33), with the result that a plural verb may follow a singular non-count noun subject quite legitimately:

> Good and bad taste *are* inculcated by example
>   (↔ Good taste is . . . and bad taste is . . .)

A similar collapsing of coordinate subjects into a single structure is observed when the subject is a clause:

> What I say and think *are* no business of yours
>   (↔ What I say is . . . and what I think is . . .)

where the alternative with *is* would mean

> That which I say and think is no business of yours

7.23

Concord involving (*either* . . .) *or* is illustrated as follows:

> Either the Mayor or his deputy *is* bound to come   [1]
> Either the strikers or the bosses *have* misunderstood   [2]
> ?Either your brakes or your eyesight *is* at fault   [3]
> Either your eyesight or your brakes *are* at fault   [4]

No problem arises with [1] and [2], but with [3] there is divided usage, neither singular nor plural seeming right. So too: 'He asked whether one lecture or two *?was/ ?were* to be given'. With [4], the principle of proximity intervenes and the plural phrase determines the number of the verb.

Note

[a] The negative correlatives *neither . . . nor,* although disjunctive in meaning, behave in colloquial speech more like *and* than like *or* as regards concord (*cf* 9.19):

    Neither he nor his wife *have* arrived

is more natural in spoken idiom than the form preferred by some:

    Neither he nor his wife *has* arrived

[b] Grammatical concord is usually obeyed for *more than:*

    More than a thousand inhabitants *have* signed the petition
    More than one person *has* protested against the proposal

Thus although *more than one person* is notionally plural, a singular verb is preferred because (*one*) *person* operates as head of a singular noun phrase.

Indefinite expressions of amount
7.24

Another area of ambivalence is that of indefinite and negative expressions of amount. For example, in

    I've ordered the shrubs, but none (of them) have/has yet arrived

grammatical concord would suggest that *none* is singular; but notional concord (we might paraphrase as '*they* have not arrived') invites a plural verb. *Has* is therefore more conventionally 'correct', but *have* is more idiomatic in speech. These comments may be extended to *neither* and *either* as indefinite pronouns:

    I sent cards to Mavis and Margery but neither (of them) has/have
        replied; in fact, I doubt if either (of them) is/are coming.

If a prepositional phrase with a plural complement follows the indefinite construction, a plural verb is favoured not only because of notional concord but because of the proximity rule:

    none of *them* are . . .   either of *the girls* are . . .

7.25

The same proximity principle may lead to plural concord even with the indefinites *each, every, everybody, anybody,* and *nobody,* which are otherwise undoubtedly singular:

    ?Nobody, not even the teachers, were listening
    ?Every member of that vast crowd of 50,000 people were pleased to
        see him

Although these sentences might well be uttered in casual speech, or inadvertently written down, most people would probably regard them as ungrammatical, because they flatly contradict grammatical concord.

Other, more acceptable, instances of 'attraction' arise with singular nouns of kind and quantity:

A large number of people have applied for the job
Those kind/sort/type of parties are very enjoyable (informal)

The latter illustrates an idiomatic anomaly: there is lack of number concord between the noun and the determiner *those*, as well as with the verb. The awkwardness can be avoided by rephrasing as *Parties of that kind . . .*

Note
The proximity principle, if taken to mean that agreement is determined by whatever immediately precedes the verb, can explain a singular verb in cases of inversion or of an adverbial quasi-subject: *Where's the scissors?; Here's John and Mary; There's several bags missing.* As what precedes the subject here is not marked for plural (7.18 Note *a*), the singular verb follows by attraction. These are colloquial examples; in formal English *are* would be substituted.

7.26
Concord of person
As well as concord of number, there is concord of person between subject and verb:

I am your friend (1st PERSON SINGULAR CONCORD)
He is ready ⎫
He knows you ⎭ (3rd PERSON SINGULAR CONCORD)

Following the principle of proximity, the last noun phrase of a coordinate subject (where the coordinator is *or, either . . . or*, or *neither . . . nor*) determines the person of the verb:

Neither you, nor I, nor anyone else knows the answer
Either my wife or I am going

Because many people find such sentences unacceptable, they often prefer to use a modal auxiliary, which is invariable for person, *eg: Either my wife or I will be going.*

Note
In cleft sentences (14.15 *f*), a relative pronoun subject is usually followed by a verb in agreement with its antecedent: *It is I who am to blame.* But 3rd person concord prevails (in informal English) where the objective case pronoun *me* is used: *It's me who's to blame.*

Other types of concord
7.27

SUBJECT-COMPLEMENT CONCORD

Subject-complement concord of number (but not of person) exists between S and C in clauses of type *SVC*; thus:

The child was an angel ⎱
The children were angels⎰ *but not* ⎰*The child was angels
                                    ⎱*The children were an angel

This type of concord arises naturally from the denotative equivalence in the intensive relationship. There are, however, exceptions:

What we need most is books
They turned traitor (*but* They became traitors)
Good manners are a rarity these days

There is an equivalent type of concord between object and object complement in *SVOC* clauses; *eg: He thinks these girls the best actors.*

Note
We sometimes find the verb in agreement with the complement: *What we need most are books; Good manners is a rarity these days.* Such sentences are probably ascribable to the workings of notional concord, the idea of plurality being dominant in the first and that of singularity in the second.

7.28

SUBJECT-OBJECT CONCORD

Subject-object concord of number, person, and gender is necessary, as well as subject-complement concord, where the second element is a reflexive pronoun (4.84*f*):

He injured *himself* in the leg
You should give *yourself* another chance.

The same concord relation holds when the reflexive pronoun occurs in other functions (*eg* as prepositional complement), or when the reflexive genitive *his own*, etc is used:

She's making a sweater for herself
They're ruining their own chances

In BrE, collective noun subjects permit plural concord: *The navy congratulated themselves on the victory.*

7.29

PRONOUN CONCORD

Personal pronouns in the 3rd person agree with their antecedents both in number and (with the singular pronouns *he, she,* and *it*) in gender:

John hurt his foot   John and Beatrice hurt their feet
Beatrice hurt her foot   The climbers hurt their feet

By contrast, *John hurt her foot* would mean that John hurt someone else's foot (the someone else having been previously mentioned).

7.30
English has no sex-neutral 3rd person singular pronoun, and so the plural pronoun *they* is often used informally, in defiance of number concord, as a substitute for the indefinite pronouns *everyone, everybody, someone, somebody, anyone, anybody, no one, nobody*.

> *Everyone* thinks *they* have the answer   [1]
> Has *anybody* brought *their* camera?   [2]
> *No one* could have blamed *themselves* for that   [3]

The plural pronoun is a convenient means of avoiding the dilemma of whether to use the *he* or *she* form. The same dilemma can arise with co-ordinate subjects and with some indefinite noun phrase subjects, but here, resort to the evasive device of the plural pronoun is perhaps not so acceptable:

> ? *Either he or his wife* is going to have to change *their* attitude
> ? *Not every drug addict* can solve *their* problem so easily

The use of *they* in sentences like [1–3] is frowned upon in formal English, where the tendency is to use *he* as the 'unmarked' form when the sex of the antecedent is not determined. The formal equivalent of [1] is therefore:

> *Everyone* thinks *he* has the answer   [1a]

There is a still more pedantic alternative, the rather cumbersome device of conjoining both masculine and feminine pronouns:

> Every student has to make up *his or her* own mind

Note
On concord involving relative pronouns, see 13.5.

The vocative
7.31
A vocative is a nominal element added to a sentence or clause optionally, denoting the one or more people to whom it is addressed, and signalling the fact that it is addressed to them:

> JŎHN, I WÀNT you (voc S V O$_d$)
> It's a lovely DÀY, Mrs JŎHNson (S V C$_s$ voc)
> YÒU, my FRÍEND, will have to work HÀRDer (S voc V A)

These three sentences show how a vocative may take an initial, medial, or final position in the sentence; in its optionality and freedom of position, it is more like an adverbial than any other element of clause structure.

Intonationally, the vocative is set off from the rest of the clause, either by constituting a separate tone-unit or by forming the post-nuclear part of a tone unit (App II.7). The most characteristic intonations are shown above: fall-rise for an initial vocative; rise for a medial or final vocative.

7.32
In form, a vocative may be

(1) A single name with or without title: *John, Mrs Johnson, Dr Smith*
(2) The personal pronoun *you* (markedly impolite); *eg: Behave yourself, you.* Or an indefinite pronoun; *eg: Get me a pen, somebody.*
(3) Standard appellatives, usually nouns without pre- or postmodification (not even the possessive pronoun):

> FAMILY RELATIONSHIPS: *mother, father, uncle:* or more familiar forms like *mom(my)* (AmE), *mum(my)* (BrE), *dad(dy), auntie*
> ENDEARMENTS: (*my*) *darling/dear/honey* (AmE)/*love*
> TITLES OF RESPECT: *sir, madam, My Lord, Your Excellency, Your Majesty, ladies and gentlemen*
> MARKERS OF PROFESSION OR STATUS: *doctor; Mr/Madam Chairman; Mr President₁ (Mr) Prime Minister; Father* (for priest)*; Bishop*

(4) A nominal clause (very occasionally): *Whoever said that, come out here.*
(5) Items under (1), (2), or (3) above with the addition of modifiers or appositive elements of various kinds:

> (1) *My dear Mrs Johnson; young John*
> (2) *You with the red hair; you over there* (impolite); informal but not impolite: *you boys; you* (*young*) *fellows; you guys* (AmE)
> (3) *Old man/fellow* (familiar); *young man/woman*

One obvious function of a vocative in English is to seek the attention of the person addressed, and especially to single him out from others who may be within hearing. A second function, less obvious but certainly no less important, is to express the attitude of the speaker towards the addressee. Vocatives are generally used as a positive mark of attitude, to signal either respectful distance or familiarity (varying from mild friendliness to intimacy).

Negation
7.33
The negation of a simple sentence is accomplished by inserting *not, n't* between the operator and the predication:

The attempt has succeeded ～ The attempt has not succeeded
We may win the match   ～ We may not win the match
He is coming   ～ He isn't coming
We have been defeated   ～ We have not been defeated

In these instances, there is an item in the positive sentences that can serve as operator. When this is not so, the auxiliary *do* is introduced and this, like modal auxiliaries, is followed by the bare infinitive:

She sees me every week   ～ She doesn't see me every week
They understood the problem ～ They did not understand the problem

Sentences with lexical *be* behave exactly as when *be* is auxiliary: *She is a teacher* ～ *She isn't a teacher*. Lexical *have* usually has *do* as operator (though in BrE it often need not, and informally *got* is often added):

He has enough money $\begin{cases} \text{He doesn't have enough money (esp AmE)} \\ \text{He hasn't (got) enough money (esp BrE)} \end{cases}$

7.34
Abbreviated negation
In circumstances where it is possible to abbreviate the operator by the use of a contracted form enclitic to the subject (usually only a pronoun), two colloquial and synonymous forms of negation are possible (3.19–21):

He isn't coming   ～ He's not coming
We aren't ready   ～ We're not ready
They haven't caught him   ～ They've not caught him
She won't miss us   ～ She'll not miss us
He wouldn't notice anything ～ He'd not notice anything

Note
[a] As there is no contracted form of *am not*, *I'm not coming* has no alternative of the kind given in the left-hand column above. Another consequence of this gap is that there is no universally accepted colloquial question form corresponding to the stiltedly formal *Am I not correct?* The contraction *aren't* is sometimes substituted: *Aren't I correct?* In AmE, *ain't* has considerable currency in both declarative and interrogative use.
[b] Restrictions on certain negative forms, especially *mayn't*, *mustn't*, *oughtn't*, *daren't* and *needn't*, are noted in 7.42.

7.35
Non-assertive forms
There are numerous items that do not naturally occur outside negative, interrogative, and conditional clauses; for example:

We haven't seen *any* soldiers
*We have seen *any* soldiers

These items (which may be determiners, pronouns, or adverbs) are the non-assertive forms (*cf* 4.93), and the following examples will illustrate their range:

We've had *some* (lunch)	~ We haven't had *any* (lunch)
I was speaking to *someone*	~ I wasn't speaking to *anyone*
I saw him *somewhere*	~ I didn't see him *anywhere*
She was *somehow* surprised	~ She wasn't *in any way* surprised
They *sometimes* visit us	~ They *rarely/never/don't ever* visit us
He helped *to some extent*	~ He didn't help *at all*
They've arrived *already*	~ They haven't arrived *yet*
John is coming *too*	~ John isn't coming *either*
They ate *too* many (cakes)	~ They didn't eat *very* many (cakes)
He's *still* there	~ He isn't there *now/any longer*
I like her *a great deal*	~ I don't like her *much*
He's been *a long way*	~ He hasn't been *far*
She was away *a long time*	~ She wasn't away *long*
He saw *one or other* of them	~ He didn't see *either* (*one*, AmE) of them

In several of the negative sentences, the negative particle and the non-assertive form can combine to produce a negative form (*ever ~ never*) or can be replaced by a negative form (*He hadn't anything ~ He had nothing*).

Note

Non-assertive forms cannot normally be subject in a negative sentence (but *cf* 4.93):

John didn't see anyone ~ { No one was seen by John / *Anyone wasn't seen by John }

7.36
Negative intensification

There are various ways of giving emotive intensification to a negative. For example, *by any means* and (informally) *a bit* are common alternatives to *at all* as non-assertive expressions of extent. Negative determiners and pronouns are given emphasis by *at all, whatever*: *I found nothing at all the matter with him; You have no excuse whatever. Never* is repeated for emphasis, or else combined with an intensifying phrase such as *in* (*all*) *his/her* etc *life*: *I'll never, never go there again; I've never in all my life seen such a crowd.* The combinations *not one* and *not a* (*single*) are emphatic alternatives to *no* as determiner with a count noun.

7.37
Alternative negative elements

Instead of the verb, another element may be negated:

An honest man would not lie	I didn't see any birds
No honest man would lie	I saw no birds

The scope of negation (7.40) is however frequently different, so that

    Many people did not come

does not mean the same as

    Not many people came ('Few people came')

When negative adjuncts are made initial there is inversion of subject and operator:

    I will never make that mistake again
    Never again will I make that mistake (formal)

7.38
More than one non-assertive form

If a clause contains a negative element, it is usually negative from that point onward. This means that the non-assertive forms must normally be used in place of every assertive form that would have occurred in the corresponding positive clause:

    I've never travelled *anywhere* by air *yet*
    I haven't *ever* been on *any* of the big liners, *either*
    No one has *ever* said *anything* to *either* of us
    Not many of the refugees have *anywhere* to live *yet*

The non-assertive forms even occur in positive subordinate clauses following a negative in the main clause:

    Nobody has promised that *any* of you will be released *yet*
    That wouldn't deter anyone who had *any* courage

Assertive forms, however, are equally likely in such cases; and more generally, assertive forms do occur following a negative, so long as they fall outside the scope of negation (7.40).

Note

[a] Occasionally two negatives occur in the same clause: *I can't not obey* ('I have to obey'); *Not many people have nowhere to live* ('Most people have somewhere to live'); *No one has nothing to offer to society* ('Everyone has something to offer to society').

[b] In substandard English, there is an entirely different kind of 'multiple negation', where more than one negative form is used, but the meaning is that of a single negative: *No one never said nothing* (Standard English, *No one ever said anything*).

7.39
Seldom, rarely, etc

There are several words which are negative in meaning, but not in appearance. They include:

seldom and *rarely*
scarcely, hardly, barely
little and *few* (in contrast to the positive *a little* and *a few*)
only

They have the following similarities to the ordinary negative items:

(1) They are followed by non-assertive rather than assertive forms:

> I seldom get *any* sleep
> I've spoken to hardly *anyone* who disagrees with me
> Few changes in government have *ever* taken so many people
>   by surprise
> Only two of us had *any* experience at sailing

(2) When in pre-subject position, some of them can cause subject-operator inversion:

> Rarely does crime pay so well as Mr Jones seems to think
> Scarcely ever has the British nation suffered so much obloquy
> Little need I dwell upon the joy of that reunion

The inversion, as before, is literary or rhetorical in tone.

(3) They are followed by positive rather than negative tag-questions (7.48 *f*):

> She scarcely seems to care, does she?

In addition, there are verbs, adjectives, or prepositions with negative meaning that take non-assertive forms:

> He *denies* I ever told him   *Without* any delay
> I *forgot* to ask for any change   *Against* any changes
> *Unaware* of any hostility

7.40
Scope of negation
A negative form may be said to govern (or determine the occurrence of) a non-assertive form only if the latter is within the SCOPE of the negation, *ie* within the stretch of language over which the negative meaning operates (shown here with a horizontal bracket). The scope of the negation normally extends from the negative word itself to the end of the clause, or to the beginning of a final adjunct. The subject, and any adjuncts occurring before the predication, normally lie outside it. (The operator is sometimes within, and sometimes outside, the scope: 7.42.) There is thus a contrast between:

I definitely didn't speak to him ('It's definite that I did not')
|_____|

I didn't definitely speak to him ('It's not definite that I did')
|_____|

When an adverbial is final, however, it may or may not lie outside the scope (*cf* 8.8):

I wasn't Lìstening all the TÌME (*ie* I listened none of the time)
|_____|

I wasn't listening ÀLL the time (*ie* I listened some of the time)
|_____|

If an assertive form is used, it must lie outside the scope:

I didn't listen to some of the speakers (*ie* I listened to some)
|_____|

I didn't listen to any of the speakers (*ie* I listened to none)
|_____|

As we have seen (7.38), the scope can sometimes extend into a subordinate clause: *I didn't know that anyone was coming.*

7.41
Focus of negation

We need to identify not only the scope, but the FOCUS of negation. A special or contrastive nuclear stress falling on a particular part of the clause indicates that the contrast of meaning implicit in the negation is located at that spot, and also that by implication the rest of the clause can be understood in a positive sense:

HÀRry didn't attack the Labour Góvernment
    (*ie* '*Someone* attacked . . ., but it wasn't Harry')
Harry didn't *atTÀCK* the Labour Góvernment
    (*ie* 'He did *something* to the Labour Government but he didn't attack it')
Harry didn't attack the *LÀBour* Góvernment
    (*ie* 'He attacked *some* government, but it wasn't the Labour one')

Scope and focus are interrelated such that the scope must include the focus. From this it follows that one way of signalling the extent of the scope is by the position of the focus. Indeed, since the scope of the negation is often not otherwise clearly signalled, we can indicate it by where we place the information focus. One example of this is when, atypically, the scope of the negation is extended to include a subordinate clause of reason, with a contrastive fall + rise to emphasize this:

I didn't leave HÓME, because I was afraid of my FÀther

(= 'Because I was afraid of my father, I didn't leave home')
I didn't leave home because I was afraid of my FÀther

(= 'I left home, but it wasn't because I was afraid of my father')

Intonation may be crucial also in marking the extension of the scope backwards to include the subject: an occasional phenomenon found in subjects which contain one of the 'universal' items *all* or *every:*

All cats don't like wÀter (*ie* 'All cats dislike water')

ÀLL cats don't like wÀter (*ie* 'Not all cats like water')

7.42
Negation of modal auxiliaries

The negation of modal auxiliaries requires some attention, in that here the scope of the negation may or may not include the meaning of the auxiliary itself. We therefore distinguish between AUXILIARY NEGA-TION and MAIN VERB NEGATION:

AUXILIARY NEGATION:
  may not (= 'permission')
  You may not go swimming ('You are not allowed . . .')

  cannot, can't (in all senses)
  You can't be serious ('It is not possible that . . .')

  You can't go swimming ('You are not allowed . . .')

  She can't ride a bicycle ('She is not able to . . .')

  need not, needn't
  You needn't pay that fine ('You are not obliged to . . .')

  It needn't always be my fault ('It is not necessary that . . .')

MAIN VERB NEGATION:
  may not (= 'possibility')
  They may not bother to come if it's wet ('It is possible that they

  will not bother to come . . .')

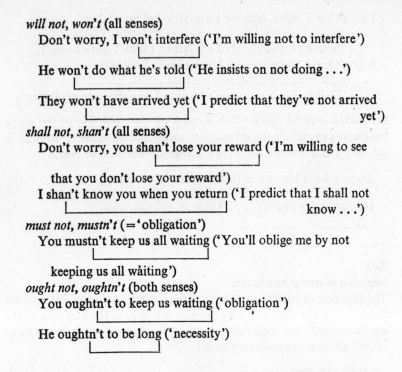

will not, won't (all senses)

Don't worry, I won't interfere ('I'm willing not to interfere')

He won't do what he's told ('He insists on not doing . . .')

They won't have arrived yet ('I predict that they've not arrived
                                                                    yet')

shall not, shan't (all senses)

Don't worry, you shan't lose your reward ('I'm willing to see

that you don't lose your reward')

I shan't know you when you return ('I predict that I shall not
                                                                know . . .')

must not, mustn't (= 'obligation')

You mustn't keep us all waiting ('You'll oblige me by not

keeping us all wàiting')

ought not, oughtn't (both senses)

You oughtn't to keep us waiting ('obligation')

He oughtn't to be long ('necessity')

Certain auxiliaries (*can* and *need*) follow the pattern of auxiliary negation, while others (*will, shall, must*) follow that of main verb negation.
May belongs to the former group in its 'permission' sense, but to the
latter group in the sense of 'possibility'. *Mustn't* is not used at all (and
must not only rarely) in the 'necessity' sense; instead, we can use *can't* in
the sense of 'impossibility'. Thus the negation of *You must be telling lies*
is *You can't be telling lies.* A common auxiliary negation of *must* is *needn't*,
which has the two meanings of non-obligation and non-necessity:

A: Must we pack now? B: No, we needn't till tomorrow.

Because of the diametric opposition of meaning between 'permission'
and 'obligation', an odd-seeming equivalence exists between *may not*
('non-permission') and *mustn't* ('obligation-not-to'):

You may not go swimming today
You mustn't go swimming today

On the whole, the past tense negative auxiliaries (*mightn't, couldn't,
wouldn't, shouldn't*) follow the same negative pattern as their present
tense equivalents, subject to the provisions described in 3.48 *ff.*

Statements, questions, commands, exclamations
7.43
Simple sentences may be divided into four major syntactic classes, whose use correlates with different communicative functions:

(1) STATEMENTS are sentences in which the subject is always present and generally precedes the verb:

John will speak to the boss today

On exceptional statements not containing a subject, see 9.6.

(2) QUESTIONS are sentences marked by one or more of these three criteria:

(a) the placing of the operator immediately in front of the subject:

Will John speak to the boss today?

(b) the initial positioning of an interrogative or *wh*-element:

Who will you speak to?

(c) rising intonation:

You will speak to the BÓSS?

(3) COMMANDS are sentences which normally have no overt grammatical subject, and whose verb is in the imperative (3.2):

Speak to the boss today

(4) EXCLAMATIONS are sentences which have an initial phrase introduced by *what* or *how*, without inversion of subject and operator:

What a noise they are making!

We use the following adjectives for these four types: (1) DECLARATIVE, (2) INTERROGATIVE, (3) IMPERATIVE, and (4) EXCLAMATORY.

Note
There is an important exception to (2a) above. It is only in relatively formal use that negative questions (7.47) have the subject immediately after the operator: *Did John not send the letter?* Normally the negative particle comes between operator and subject, but almost invariably with contraction: *Didn't John send it? (?*Did not John send it?).* Focusing adjuncts (8.8 *ff*) can also appear between operator and subject, and they make it possible for a preceding *not* to remain uncontracted: *Did not even a single student come to the lecture?* (formal).

Questions
7.44
Questions can be divided into three major classes according to the type of answer they expect:

(1) those that expect only affirmation or rejection (as in *Have you finished the book?*) are YES-NO questions;
(2) those that expect a reply supplying an item of information (as in *What is your name? How old are you?*) are WH- questions;
(3) those that expect as the reply one of two or more options presented in the question are ALTERNATIVE questions; for example

> Would you like to go for a WÁLK or stay at HÒME?

7.45
Yes-no questions

Yes-no questions are usually formed by placing the operator before the subject and giving the sentence a rising intonation:

> The boat has LÈFT ~ Has the boat LÉFT?

If there is no item in the verb phrase that can function as operator, *do* is introduced as with negation (7.33):

> He likes Mary ~ Does he like Mary?

Again as with negation, lexical *be* acts as operator; in BrE this is often true for *have* also and informally *got* is added:

> John was late ~ Was John late?

> He has a car ~ $\begin{cases} \text{Does he have a car? (esp AmE)} \\ \text{Has he (got) a car? (esp BrE)} \end{cases}$

Note
By placing the nuclear stress in a particular part of a *yes-no* question, we are able to 'focus' the interrogation on a particular item of information which, unlike the rest of the sentence, is assumed to be unknown (*cf* focus of negation, 7.41). Thus the focus falls in different places in the following otherwise identical questions:

Was he a famous actor in THÓSE days?
  ('I know he was once a famous actor – but was it then or later?')
Was he a FÁmous actor in those days?
  ('I know he was an actor in those days – but was he a famous one?')

7.46
Positive orientation

Another typical characteristic of *yes-no* questions is the use of the non-assertive forms *any*, *ever*, etc that we have already seen in operation in negative statements (7.35):

Someone called last night	Did *anyone* call last night?
I suppose *some* of the class will be *already* here	Do you suppose *any* of the class will be here *yet*?

Like the use of the *do* auxiliary, non-assertive forms point to common ground between questions and negative statements. This ground is not hard to explain: clearly a question has neutral polarity, in the sense that it leaves open whether the answer is positive or negative. Hence questions, like negatives, belong to the class of 'non-assertions' (2.20).

On the other hand, a question may be presented in a form which is biased towards a positive or negative answer. A question has positive orientation, for example, if it uses assertive forms rather than the usual non-assertive forms:

> Did *someone* call last night? ('Is it true that someone called last
>   night')
> Has the boat left *already?*
> Do you live *somewhere* near Dover?
> Would you like *some* cake?

These questions indicate that the speaker thinks that the answer is yes: he merely asks for confirmation of that assumption.

7.47
Negative orientation
Negative orientation is found in questions which contain a negative form of one kind or another:

> Can't you give us any hope of success? ('Is it really true
>   that you can't ... ?')   [1]
> Isn't your car working?   [2]
> Does no one believe me?   [3]

Negative orientation is complicated, however, by an element of surprise or disbelief which adds implications of positive meaning. Thus [2] means 'Is it really true that your car isn't working? I had assumed that it was.' Here there is a combining of a positive and a negative attitude, which one may distinguish as the OLD ASSUMPTION (positive) and NEW ASSUMP-TION (negative). Because the old assumption tends to be identified with the speaker's hopes or wishes, negative-oriented questions often express disappointment or annoyance:

> Can't you drive straight? ('I'd have thought you'd be able to, but
>   apparently you can't')
> Aren't you ashamed of yourself? ('You ought to be, but it appears
>   you're not')
> Hasn't the boat left yet? ('I'd hoped it would have left by now, but
>   it seems that it hasn't')

A second type of negative question combines *not* (the formal signal of negative orientation) with the assertive items which are the formal signals of positive orientation:

Didn't someone call last night?
Hasn't the boat left already?

Such questions are similar in effect to type [I] tag questions (7.48) and to statements showing disbelief: 'Surely someone called last night!'

Tag questions
7.48
The tag question consists of operator plus pronoun, with or without a negative particle (10.29); the choice and tense of the operator are determined by the verb phrase in the superordinate clause:

The boat hasn't left, *has it?*
Joan recognized you, *didn't she?*

As these examples illustrate, if the superordinate clause is positive, the tag is negative, and vice versa. The nuclear tone of the tag occurs on the operator and is either a rise or a fall. Four main types of tag question emerge from the observance of these rules:

	RISING TONE	FALLING TONE
	[I]	[III]
POSITIVE+NEGATIVE	He likes his JÒB, DÓEsn't he?	He likes his JÒB, DÒEsn't he?
	[II]	[IV]
NEGATIVE+POSITIVE	He doesn't like his JÒB, DÓES he?	He doesn't like his JÒB, DÒES he?

The meanings of these sentences, like their forms, involve a statement and a question; each of them, that is, asserts something then invites the listener's response to it. Sentence [I], for example, can be rendered 'I assume he likes his job; am I right?'. [II] means the opposite: 'I assume he doesn't like his job; am I right?'. Clearly, these sentences have a positive and a negative orientation respectively. A similar contrast exists between [III] and [IV]. But it is important, again, to separate two factors: an ASSUMP-TION (expressed by the statement) and an EXPECTATION (expressed by the question). On this principle, we may distinguish the four types as:

[I] Positive assumption + neutral expectation
[II] Negative assumption + neutral expectation
[III] Positive assumption + positive expectation
[IV] Negative assumption + negative expectation

The tag with the falling tone, it will be noted, invites confirmation of the statement, and has the force of an exclamation rather than a genuine question. In this, it is like (though perhaps not so emphatic as) exclamatory *yes-no* questions with a falling tone (7.56): *Isn't it gorgeous WÈAther!*

7.49

Among less common types of tag question, one may be mentioned in which both statements and question are positive:

> Your car is outsÌDE, ís it?
> You've had an ÀccIdent, HÁVE you?

This tag always has a rising nucleus, and the situation is characteristically preceded by *oh* or *so*, indicating the speaker's arrival at a conclusion by inference, or by recalling what has already been said. The tone may sometimes be one of sarcastic suspicion:

> So THÀT's your little game, ís it?

7.50

Declarative questions

The declarative question is an exceptional type of *yes-no* question identical in form to a statement, except for the final rising question intonation:

> You've got the expLÓsive?
> They've spoken to the ambÁssador?
> You realize what the RÍSKS are?
> Boris will be THÉRE, I suppose?
> He didn't finish the RÁCE?

Notice the occurrence of *I suppose*, impossible in normal questions. Declarative questions show their assertive character in the inadmissibility of non-assertive forms:

> The guests have had $\begin{Bmatrix} \text{nothing} \\ \text{something} \end{Bmatrix}$ to eat?
>
> *The guests have had anything to eat?

They are similar in force to type [I] or type [II] tag questions, except for a rather casual tone, which suggests that the speaker takes the answer *yes* or *no* as a foregone conclusion.

7.51

Yes-no questions with modal auxiliaries

The formation of *yes-no* questions with modal auxiliaries is subject to certain limitations and shifts of meaning. The modals of 'permission' (*may*, esp BrE, and *can*) and of 'obligation' (*must*, esp BrE, and *have to*) involve the speaker's authority in statements and the listener's authority in questions:

$$\left\{ \begin{array}{l} \text{A:} \left\{ \begin{array}{l} \text{May} \\ \text{Can} \end{array} \right\} \text{I leave now?} \quad (\text{'Will you permit me} \ldots \text{'}) \\[2ex] \quad \text{B: Yes, you} \left\{ \begin{array}{l} \text{may} \\ \text{can} \end{array} \right\}. \quad (\text{'I will permit you} \ldots \text{'}) \end{array} \right.$$

$$\left\{ \begin{array}{l} \text{A:} \left\{ \begin{array}{l} \text{Must I} \\ \text{Do I have to} \end{array} \right\} \text{leave now?} \quad (\text{'Are you telling me} \ldots \text{'}) \\[2ex] \quad \text{B: Yes, you} \left\{ \begin{array}{l} \text{must} \\ \text{have to} \end{array} \right\}. \quad (\text{'I am telling you} \ldots \text{'}) \end{array} \right.$$

A similar switch from listener to speaker takes place with *shall* ('volition') which (especially in BrE) implicates the speaker's will in statements, but the listener's will in questions:

You shall suffer for this! ('I intend to make you suffer . . .!')
Shall I switch off the television? ('Do you want me to . . .?')

The direct-question use of *shall*, however, is virtually restricted to first person subjects. With *we*, it has both exclusive and inclusive senses:

Shall we carry your suitcases? ('Would you like us to . . .?')
Shall we have dinner? ('Would you like us [including you] to . . .?')

May ('possibility') is not employed at all in questions; *can* (or more commonly, in AmE, *could*) takes its place:

$$\text{A:} \left\{ \begin{array}{l} \text{Can} \\ \text{Could} \end{array} \right\} \text{they have missed the bus?} \quad \text{B: Yes, they} \left\{ \begin{array}{l} \text{may have.} \\ \text{might have.} \end{array} \right.$$

Need (in BrE) is a non-assertive auxiliary in clauses where the corresponding positive form is *must*. Hence in questions:

$$\text{A: Need it happen?} \ (cf \text{AmE/BrE: Does it} \left\{ \begin{array}{l} \text{need to} \\ \text{have to} \end{array} \right\} \text{happen?})$$

$$\text{B: Yes, it} \left\{ \begin{array}{l} \text{must.} \\ \text{has to.} \end{array} \right.$$

If, on the other hand, *must* had occurred in A's question, it would have had 'positive orientation': 'Is it a fact that it must happen?' Compare *Need it ever happen?* with *Must it always happen?*, where the assertive form has to be retained.

Wh-questions
7.52
Wh-questions are formed with the aid of one of the following interrogative words (or Q-words):

who/whom/whose, what, which
when, where, how, why

As a rule,

(1) the Q-element (*ie* clause element containing the Q-words) generally
comes first in the sentence;
(2) the Q-word itself takes first position in the Q-element.

The only exception to the second principle is when the Q-word occurs in a
prepositional complement. Here English provides a choice between two
constructions, one formal and the other less so. In formal style, the
preposition precedes the complement, whereas in colloquial style, the
complement comes first and the preposition retains the position it has
in a declarative sentence:

On what did you base your prediction? (formal)
What did you base your prediction *on?*

We may perhaps express this difference more neatly by saying that colloquial English insists that the Q-word comes first, while formal English
insists that the Q-element as a whole comes first.

7.53

The following are sentences in which the Q-element operates in various
clause functions:

Who opened my LÈTter?   (Q-element: S)
Which books have you LÈNT him?   (Q-element: O_d)
Whose beautiful antÌQUES are these?   (Q-element: C_s)
How wide did they make the BÒOKcase?   (Q-element: C_0)
When will you come BÀCK?   (Q-element: A_{time})
Where shall I put the GLÀsses?   (Q-element: A_{place})
Why are they always compLÀINing?   (Q-element: A_{reason})
How did you MÈND it?   (Q-element: $A_{process}$)
How much does he CÀRE?   (Q-element: $A_{intensifying}$)
How long have you been WÀITing?   (Q-element: $A_{duration}$)
How often do you visit New YÒRK?   (Q-element: $A_{frequency}$)

As the examples indicate, falling intonation, not rising intonation, is
usual for *wh*-questions.

We see above that normal statement order of elements is upset in *wh*-
questions not only by the initial placing of the Q-element, but by the inversion of subject and operator in all cases except that in which the Q-element is subject, where the rule of initial Q-element takes precedence over
the rule of inversion.

Subject-operator inversion is the same in its application to *wh*-questions as in its application to *yes-no* questions; if there is no auxiliary in the equivalent statement, *do* is introduced as operator in the question. Lexical *be* (and sometimes, in BrE, *have*) acts as an operator: *How are you? Who have we here?*

Note

[a] Adjuncts of instrument, reason, and purpose are normally questioned by the prepositional constructions:

> *What* shall I mend it *with?*   *What* did you do that *for?*

Although the latter could be replaced by *Why did you do that?*, it has no alternative with a preposed preposition: **For what did you do that?* In this respect it is like informal questions with *be* followed by a final preposition: *What was it in?* (but not **In what was it?*).

[b] Abbreviated questions consisting of Q-word and final preposition (which in this construction bears nuclear stress), *Where to? What for/with? Who with/by?*, are as popular in colloquial speech as questions consisting of the Q-word only: *Where? Who? Why?* There is a common abbreviated negative question *Why not?* (10.36).

[c] Although there is no Q-word for the verb, the content of the predication can be questioned by *what* as the object of the generalized agentive verb *do*:

> A: What are you doing? B: I'm reading.
> A: What have you done with my book? B: I've hidden it.

[d] An indirect object cannot act as Q-element: instead of **Who(m) did you give the present?*, the equivalent prepositional complement construction is used: *Who(m) did you give the present to?* or *To whom did you give the present?*

Alternative questions
7.54

There are two types of alternative question, the first resembling a *yes-no* question, and the second a *wh*-question:

> Would you like CHÓcolate, vanÍLla, or STRÀwberry (ice-cream)?   [1]
> Which ice-cream would you LÌKE? CHÓcolate, vanÍLla, or
> STRÀwberry?   [2]

The first type differs from a *yes-no* question only in intonation; instead of the final rising tone, it contains a separate nucleus for each alternative: a rise occurs on each item in the list, except the last, on which there is a fall, indicating that the list is complete. The difference of intonation between alternative and *yes-no* questions is important, in that ignoring it can lead to misunderstanding – as the contrast between these replies indicates:

> *alternative:* A: Shall we go by BÚS or TRAÌN? B: By BÙS.
> *yes-no:* A: Shall we go by bus or TRAÍN? B: No, let's take
>   the CÀR.

The second type of alternative question is really a compound of two separate questions: a *wh*-question followed by an elliptical alternative question of the first type. Thus [2] might be taken as a reduced version of:

Which ice-cream would you LÌKE? Would you like CHÓcolate,
vanílLla, or STRÀwberry?

Any positive *yes-no* question can be converted into an alternative question by adding *or not?* or a matching negative clause:

> *yes-no:* Are you CÓMing?
>
> *alternative:* $\begin{cases} \text{Are you CÓMing or NÒT?} \\ \text{Are you CÓMing or ÀREn't you (coming)?} \end{cases}$

The alternative variant, by spelling out the negative aspect of the question, is rather petulant in tone, but is otherwise indistinguishable in meaning from the *yes-no* question.

7.55

The structure of alternative *yes-no* questions follows the pattern of clausal
coordination (9.21 *ff*); that is, two or more separate questions are col-
lapsed together, wherever convenient, by ellipsis (shown here by parentheses):

> Did Ìraly win the World Cup or (did) BrazÌL (win the World Cup)?

Often the elliptical part of an alternative question is placed within the first
question:

> Did Ìraly or BrazÌL win the World Cup?
> ÁRE you or ÀREn't you coming?

Where there is no repeated structure, no ellipsis is possible, and so the
second question appears in its full form:

> Is it RÁIning or has it STÒPPED?

Minor types of question
7.56
EXCLAMATORY QUESTION
The exclamatory question is a question in form, but is functionally like an
exclamation (7.63). The most characteristic type is a negative *yes-no* question with a falling instead of rising tone:

> Hasn't she GRÒWN!
> Wasn't it a marvellous CÒNcert!

These invite the listener's agreement to something on which the speaker
has strongly positive feelings.

A positive *yes-no* question, also with a falling tone, is another (but very
informal) way of expressing a strong positive conviction:

> ¹Am ¹I HÙNGry! ¹Did ¹he look anNÒYED! ¹Has ¹she GRÒWN!

Both operator and subject usually receive emphatic stress.

7.57

RHETORICAL QUESTION

The rhetorical question is one which functions as a forceful statement.
More precisely, a *positive* rhetorical question is like a strong *negative*
assertion, while a *negative* question is like a strong *positive* one.

POSITIVE:

> Is that a reason for desPÁIR? ('Surely that is not a reason . . .')
> Can anyone doubt the wísdom of this action? ('Surely no one
> can doubt . . .')

NEGATIVE:

> Is no one going to deFÉND me? ('Surely someone is going to
> defend me')

Unlike exclamatory questions, these rhetorical questions usually have the
normal rising intonation of a *yes-no* question.

There is also a rhetorical *wh*-question, which is equivalent to a statement in which the Q-element is replaced by a negative element:

> Who KNÔWS? ('Nobody knows')
> What DÍFference does it make? ('It makes no difference')

Again, the intonation is that of an ordinary *wh*-question, except that a
rise-fall tone is likely.

Commands
7.58
Commands without a subject

We begin with the most common category of command, that which differs from a statement in that

(1) it has no subject,
(2) it has an imperative finite verb (the base form of the verb, without
     endings for number or tense).

Otherwise the clause patterns of commands show the same range and
ordering of elements as statements; for example:

SV: Jump (V)
SVC: Be reasonable (V C)
SVOA: Put it on the table (V O_d A_{place})

The imperative verb, however, is severely restricted as to tense, aspect,
voice, and modality. There is no tense distinction or perfect aspect, and
only very rarely does the progressive form occur:

> Be preparing the dinner when he comes in

A passive is equally rare, except when the auxiliary is some verb other than *be*, as in *Get washed*. These restrictions are connected with the understandable incongruity of combining an imperative with a stative non-agentive verb: **Sound louder!* Modal auxiliaries do not occur at all in imperative sentences.

Commands are apt to sound abrupt unless toned down by markers of politeness such as *please: Please eat up your dinner; Shut the door, please*. Even this only achieves a minimum degree of ceremony; a more tactful form of request can only be arrived at if one changes the command into a question or a statement: *Will you shut the door, please? I wonder if you would kindly shut the door; I wonder whether you would mind shutting the door;* etc.

Note

Stative verbs can be interpreted as dynamic, however, in special contexts: *Know the answer by tomorrow!* (= 'Get to know . . .', 'Learn . . .').

7.59
Commands with a subject

It is implied in the meaning of a command that the omitted subject of the imperative verb is the 2nd person pronoun *you*. This is confirmed by the occurrence of *you* as subject of a following tag question (*Be quiet, will you*), and by the occurrence of *yourself* and of no other reflexive pronoun as object: *Behave yourself*, not **Behave himself*.

There is, however, a type of command in which the subject *you* is retained, differing from the subject of a finite verb in always carrying stress:

> *You* be quiet!
> *You* mind your own business, and leave this to me!

These commands are usually admonitory in tone, and frequently express strong irritation. As such, they cannot naturally be combined with markers of politeness, such as *please: *Please, you be quiet!* They may be used, however, in another way, to single out (by pointing) two or more distinct addressees: *You come here, Jack, and you go over there, Mary*. A 3rd person subject is also possible:

> *Somebody* open this door
> *Everybody* shut their eyes
> *Jack and Susan* stand over there

It is easy to confuse the subject, in these commands, with a vocative noun phrase (7.31). Whereas the subject always precedes the verb, the vocative (as we saw earlier) is an element that can occur in final and medial, as well as initial, positions in the sentence. Another difference is that the vocative, when initially placed, has a separate tone-unit (typically fall-rise); the subject merely receives ordinary word-stress:

VOCATIVE: MĂRY, play on MỲ side
Play on MỲ side, MÁRY
SUBJECT: ¹Mary play on MỲ side

The distinctness of vocative and imperative subject is confirmed by the possibility of their co-occurrence: JÓHN, ¹you listen to MÈ!

7.60
Commands with let
First person imperatives can be formed by preposing the verb *let*, followed by a subject in (where relevant) the objective case:

> *Let us* all work hard (more usually: *Let's . . .*)
> *Let me* have a look

The same applies to 3rd person subjects:

> Let each man decide for himself ·
> If anyone shrinks from this action, let him speak now

7.61
Negative commands
To negate 2nd and 3rd person imperatives, one simply adds an initial *Don't*, replacing assertive by non-assertive forms where necessary:

> Open some windows   ~ *Don't* open *any* windows
> You open the door   ~ *Don't you* open the door
> Someone open the door ~ *Don't anyone* open the door

1st person imperatives, on the other hand, have two possibilities:

$$\text{Let's open the door} \sim \begin{cases} \textit{Let's not} \text{ open the door} \\ \textit{Don't let's} \text{ open the door (informal and esp} \\ \quad \text{BrE)} \end{cases}$$

and the second of these is available for 3rd person imperatives:

> *Don't let anyone* fool himself that he can get away with it

7.62
Persuasive imperatives
A persuasive or insistent imperative is created by the addition of *do* (with a nuclear tone) before the main verb:

> Do have some more sherry   Do let's go to the theatre

Note
[a] *Do,* like *don't* and *let's,* acts as an introductory imperative marker, and is not identical with the emphatic *do* of statements (14.35). To see this, notice that neither *do* nor *don't* in commands fulfils the conditions of the *do* construction in questions and negations; they are not introduced to make good the lack of an operator and can

indeed be used with the verb *be: Do be seated; Don't be silly.* (Contrast the unacceptability of **He doesn't be silly!*) This peculiarity of imperative *do* is also found in the quasi-imperative *Why don't you* construction: *Why don't you be careful!*

[*b*] *Do, don't,* and *let's* are used in isolation as elliptical commands:

A: Shall I open the door? B: $\begin{cases} \text{Yes, do.} \\ \text{No, don't.} \end{cases}$

A: Shall we watch the game? B: Yes, let's.

7.63
Exclamations

In discussing exclamations as a formal category of sentence (but *cf* 7.56), we restrict our attention to exclamatory utterances introduced by *what* (plus noun phrase) or *how*. These express an extreme degree of some variable factor (*How beautiful!*), but the variable may be left implicit. Thus *What a book!* could refer to a very bad or to a very good book.

Exclamations resemble *wh*-questions in involving the initial placement of an exclamatory *wh*-element (the X-element). The syntactic order is therefore upset to the extent that the X-element (which may be object, complement, or adverbial, as well as subject) may be taken from its usual (statement) position and put into a position of initial prominence. On the other hand, in contrast to *wh*-questions, there is generally no subject-operator inversion:

X-element as subject: *What an enormous crowd* came! (S V)
X-element as object: *What a time* we've had today! (O$_d$ S V A)
X-element as complement: *How delightful* her manners are! (C$_s$ S V)

X-element as adverbial: $\begin{cases} \textit{How} \text{ I used to hate geography! (A S V O}_d\text{)} \\ \textit{What a long time} \text{ it lasted! (A S V)} \end{cases}$

The X-element, like the Q-element of the *wh*-question, can also act as prepositional complement, the preposition normally being postposed:

What a mess we're in!

7.64
Formulae

There are some sentences which, though appearing to belong to one of the major classes, in fact enter into few of the relations of substitutability that are common to members of those classes. For instance, the greeting formula (appropriate to a first meeting) *How do you do?* cannot be subordinated as an indirect question (**They asked him how he did*) or answered in a corresponding statement form (**I do very well*). Two slightly less restricted kinds of *wh*-question are the question without an auxiliary *why* (+*not*)+predication:

Why get so upset? *Why not* enjoy yourself?

and the *how/what about* type of question:

> *What about* the house? *How about* joining us?

These are not formulaic in the previous sense, but are irregular in that they lack some of the elements normally found in a *wh*-question.

There are also patterns which are defective in terms of regular clause or sentence structure, such as the verbless imperatives:

> *Off with* the lid! *Out with* it! *Down with* the bosses!

To this we may add a number of exclamatory types:

> *If only* I'd listened to my parents!   (with modal past: 3.47, 11.48)
> *To think* I was once a millionaire!
> *Oh for* a drink! *Oh to* be free!   (archaic except when jocular)
> *You and your* statistics! *John and his* ideas!
> *Now for* some fun!

Apart from such cases, there are sentences which contain fossilized elements no longer productively used in present-day English: for example, the subjunctive combined with inversion in

> Far be it from me to (spoil the fun)
> Suffice it to say (we lost)
> Long live (anarchy)!   (archaic except when jocular)

and without inversion in

> God save the Queen! (God) Bless you!

A slightly less archaic formula for expressing a wish is *may*+subject+ predication: *May the best man win! May you be happy!*

Note
In very familiar style we find the question formula *How come* (*you missed the bus*)? Also familiar is the greeting formula *How goes it ?*, without *do*-periphrasis.

7.65
Aphoristic sentences
Among other minor sentence types is the aphoristic sentence structure found in many proverbs:

> The more, the merrier   [1]
> Least said, soonest mended   [2]
> Handsome is as handsome does   [3]
> Easy come, easy go   [4]

These all have one structural feature in common: the balancing of two equivalent constructions against each other. While they must all be considered grammatically anomalous, example [1] has a fairly productive pattern which will be dealt with under proportional clauses (11.34).

7.66
Block language
In addition to the formulae of colloquial conversation, there is a whole realm of usage where, because of its rudimentary communicative role, language is structured in terms of single words and phrases, rather than in terms of the more highly organized units of clause and sentence.

Language so used may be termed 'block language'. It appears in such functions as labels, titles, headings, notices, and advertisements. Simple block-language messages most often consist of a noun or noun phrase or nominal clause in isolation: no verb is needed, because all else necessary to the understanding of the message is furnished by context. Examples are:

ENTRANCE	ENGLISH DEPARTMENT	DANGER: FALLING ROCKS
PURE LEMON JUICE	FRESH TODAY	HIGHLY RECOMMENDED
A GRAMMAR OF CONTEMPORARY ENGLISH		WHERE TO GO IN LONDON
HOW TO WIN FRIENDS AND INFLUENCE PEOPLE	THE FIRST LUXURY BOUND COLLECTOR'S EDITION OF AGATHA CHRISTIE'S WORK TO BE AVAILABLE IN THIS COUNTRY	

In newspaper headlines, abbreviated clause structures have been developed:

(1) FILM-STAR MARRIES EX-PRIEST (S V O_d)
(2) ELECTION A LANDSLIDE FOR SOCIALISTS (S C_s)
(3) NIXON TO MEET ASIAN PREMIERS (S V O_d)
(4) SHARE PRICES NOW HIGHER THAN EVER (S A C_s)
(5) JACKLIN BEATEN BY BONALLACK (S V A)
(6) CHANCES OF MIDDLE-EAST PEACE IMPROVING (S V)

These differ from orthodox clause structures in having different tense conventions, and in omitting closed-system words of low information value, such as the articles and the finite forms of the verb *be*.

Note
Prohibitions on notice boards often assume the special block-language form of a noun phrase introduced by *No*. For example, *No smoking; No entry; No unauthorized entry after dark.*

Bibliographical note

On clause elements, see Anderson (1971); Fillmore (1968); Halliday (1967–8); Huddleston (1971); Lyons (1968), especially Chapter 8. On negation, see Klima (1964). On questions, see Bolinger (1957); Malone (1967). On commands, see Bolinger (1967a); Thorne (1969).

EIGHT
ADJUNCTS, DISJUNCTS, CONJUNCTS

8.1
Units realizing adverbial functions
The functions of the adverbial are realized by:

(1) Adverb phrases, *ie* phrases with adverbs as head or sole realization:

> Peter was playing *as well as he could*
> We'll stay *there*

(2) Noun phrases (less common):

> Peter was playing *last week*

(3) Prepositional phrases:

> Peter was playing *with great skill*

(4) Finite verb clauses:

> Peter was playing *although he was very tired*

(5) Non-finite verb clauses, in which the verb is

(a) infinitive:

> Peter was playing *to win*

(b) *-ing* participle:

> *Wishing to encourage him*, they praised Tom

(c) *-ed* participle:

> *If urged by our friends*, we'll stay

(6) Verbless clauses:

> Peter was playing, *unaware of the danger*

8.2
Classes of adverbials: adjuncts, disjuncts, conjuncts
Adverbials may be *integrated* to some extent into the structure of the

clause or they may be *peripheral* to it. If integrated, they are termed ADJUNCTS. If peripheral, they are termed DISJUNCTS and CONJUNCTS, the distinction between the two being that conjuncts have primarily a connective function.

An adverbial is integrated to some extent in clause structure if it is affected by such clausal processes as negation and interrogation. For example, it is an adjunct if

either (1) it cannot appear initially in a negative declarative clause:

> *Quickly they didn't leave for home

or   (2) it can be the focus of a question or of clause negation:

> Does he write to his parents *because he wants to* (or does he write to them *because he needs money*)?
> We didn't go to Chicago *on Monday*, (but we did go there *on Tuesday*)

In contrast, a disjunct or a conjunct is not affected by either of these clausal processes. For example, the disjunct *to my regret* can appear initially in a negative declarative clause:

> *To my regret*, they didn't leave for home

and cannot be the focus of a question or of clause negation:

> *Does he write to his parents, *to my regret*, (or does he write to them, *to my relief*)?
> *We didn't go to Chicago, *to my regret*, (but we did go there, *to my relief*)

Items can belong to more than one class. For example, *naturally* is an adjunct in

> They aren't walking *naturally* ('in a natural manner')

and a disjunct in

> *Naturally*, they are walking ('of course')

8.3
Definitions of positional terms

We distinguish four positions of adverbials for the declarative form of the clause:

Initial position (*ie* before the subject)
Medial position:
   M1: (a) immediately before the first auxiliary or lexical *be*, or (b) between two auxiliaries or an auxiliary and lexical *be*.

M2: (a) immediately before the lexical verb, or (b) in the case of lexical *be*, before the complement.

Final position: (a) after an intransitive verb, or (b) after any object or complement.

If there are no auxiliaries present, *M1* and *M2* positions are neutralized:

They sometimes watch television

If the subject is ellipted, initial and medial positions are neutralized:

I've been waiting outside his door the whole day and *yet* haven't seen him

Final position includes any position after the stated clause elements, *eg:*

I paid *immediately* for the book
I paid for the book *immediately*

Adjuncts
8.4
Syntactic features of adjuncts
Certain syntactic features are general to adjuncts.

(1) They can come within the scope of predication pro-forms or predication ellipsis (10.29 *ff*). For example, in

John *greatly* admires Bob, and so *does* Mary

the pro-form in the second clause includes the adjunct of the first clause, so that the sentence means the same as

John *greatly* admires Bob, and Mary *greatly* admires Bob

(2) They can be the focus of limiter adverbials such as *only* (8.8 *ff*):

They only want the car *for an HÒUR* ('for an hour and not for longer')

(3) They can be the focus of additive adverbials such as *also* (8.8 *ff*):

They will also meet *ᴀFterwards* ('afterwards in addition to some other time')

(4) They can be the focus of a cleft sentence (14.15 *f*):

It was *when we were in Paris* that I first saw John

8.5
Adverb phrases as adjuncts
Adverb phrases as adjuncts can often

(1) constitute a comparative construction

John writes *more clearly than his brother does*

(2) have premodifying *however* to form the opening of a dependent adverbial clause:

> *However strongly* you feel about it, you should be careful what you say

(3) have premodifying *how*, a pro-form for intensifiers in questions or exclamations:

> *How often* does she wash her hair?
> *How cautiously* he drives!

(4) have premodifying *so* followed by subject-operator inversion and a correlative clause:

> *So monotonously* did he speak that everyone left

8.6
Subclassification of adjuncts

It is convenient to discuss adjuncts under classes that are essentially semantic. *Fig* 8:1 gives the classes and their subclasses.

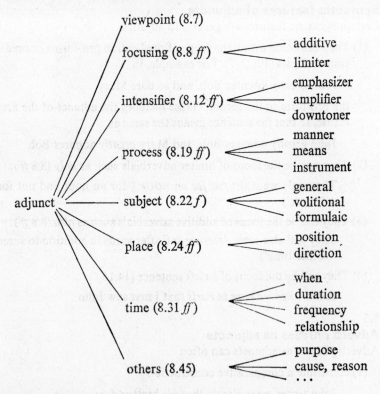

Fig 8:1 Adjuncts

8.7
Viewpoint adjuncts
Viewpoint adjuncts can be roughly paraphrased by 'if we consider what we are saying from a [adjective phrase] point of view' or 'if we consider what we are saying from the point of view of [noun phrase]'.

Adverbs functioning as viewpoint adjuncts are most commonly derived from adjectives by the addition of a *-ly* suffix:

> *Geographically, ethnically, and linguistically,* these islands are closer to the mainland than to their neighbouring islands
>
> To tap a private telephone line is not *technically* a very difficult operation

Viewpoint adjuncts derived from nouns by the addition of the suffix *-wise* (especially AmE) are considered informal:

> *Program-wise,* the new thing on TV last night was the first instalment of a new science series

All *-ly* viewpoint adjuncts have a corresponding participle clause with *speaking, eg: visually ~ visually speaking,* and a corresponding prepositional phrase with the frame *from a* [adjective phrase] *point of view, eg: morally ~ from a moral point of view.* Other examples of viewpoint adjuncts:

> Many of these people have suffered, *economically speaking,* because of their political affiliations
>
> *As far as mathematics is concerned,* he was a complete failure
>
> *Looked at politically,* it was not an easy problem

Viewpoint adjuncts, whatever their structure, are usually in initial position.

Focusing adjuncts
8.8
Focusing adjuncts indicate that what is being communicated is limited to a part that is focused – LIMITER ADJUNCTS – or that a focused part is an addition – ADDITIVE ADJUNCTS. Most focusing adjuncts are adverbs.

LIMITERS
(a) EXCLUSIVES restrict what is said to the part focused *eg: alone, just, merely, only, purely, simply*
(b) PARTICULARIZERS restrict what is said particularly or mainly to the part focused *eg: chiefly, especially, mainly, mostly; in particular*

ADDITIVES
also, either, even, neither, nor, too; as well as, in addition

Examples of their use with an indication of the part that is focused:

> You can get a B grade *JUST for that answer*
> *The workers, IN PARTICULAR*, are dissatisfied with the government
> We bought *some beer AS WELL*

Focusing adjuncts cannot be modified: **very only*, **extremely also*. Most of them cannot be coordinated: **just and exactly*, **equally and likewise*. But we have one cliché coordination:

> He is doing it *PURELY AND SIMPLY for your benefit*

Position and focus
8.9

Sentences such as

> John *only* phoned Mary today
> John *also* phoned Mary today

are ambiguous, the meaning varying with the intonation we give the sentence. In more formal English varying positions can distinguish most of the meanings, with a nucleus on the focused part in speech:

> |John ŏNly| |phoned MÀry today|=Only JOHN phoned Mary today
>   (Nobody but John phoned Mary today)
> |John only phoned MÀry today|=John phoned only MÀry today
>   (John phoned Mary today but nobody else)

> | John only phoned Mary toDÀy|=John phoned Mary $\begin{cases} \text{only toDÀY} \\ \text{toDÀY only} \end{cases}$

>   (John phoned Mary today but not at any other time)
> |John ÀLso phoned Mary today|=JÓHN, ÀLSO, phoned Mary today
>   (John as well as somebody else phoned Mary today)
> |John also phoned MÀry today|=John phoned also MÀry today
>   (John phoned Mary as well as somebody else today)

> | John also phoned Mary toDÀy|=John phoned Mary $\begin{cases} \text{also toDÀY} \\ \text{toDÀY also} \end{cases}$

>   (John phoned Mary today as well as at some other time(s))

In speech, a nucleus on the lexical verb gives an unambiguous interpretation when *only* and *also* are before the lexical verb:

> |John only PHÒNed Mary today| (John did nothing else with respect to Mary but phone her)
> |John also PHÒNed Mary today| (John phoned Mary today in addition to something else he did with respect to Mary today)

But in the written form, this position remains ambiguous, since (for example) *only* can have as its focus *phoned* (did nothing else but phone), *Mary* (phoned nobody but Mary), or *today* (on no other day). However, in practice the context usually makes it clear which interpretation is required.

8.10
Positions of focusing adjuncts
Most limiters can either precede or follow the part on which they are focused, though it is more usual for them to precede. *Just, merely, purely,* and *simply* must normally precede:

You can get a B grade JUST/MERELY/PURELY/SIMPLY *for that answer*

On the other hand, *alone* must normally follow the part on which it is focused, *eg: You can get a B grade for that answer ALONE.*

The following additives normally precede a focused part in the predicate but follow a focused subject: *again, also, equally, similarly, in addition.* On the other hand, *too* and *as well* normally follow a focused part, wherever in the clause it may be, while *even* normally precedes:

I know your family has expressed its support. *We TOO/AS WELL* will do what we can for you.
Yesterday the Robinsons were here with their new baby. They brought *their other children TOO/AS WELL.*
My father won't give me the money. He won't *EVEN lend* it to me.

Neither and *nor* are restricted to initial position and non-assertive *either* (7.35) to final position:

They won't help him, but *NEITHER/NOR* will they *harm* him
They won't help him, but they won't *harm* him *EITHER*

8.11
Focusing adjuncts in correlative constructions and cleft sentences
With certain limiters – *just, simply,* and most commonly *only* and *merely* – there can be subject-operator inversion when they follow an initial *not* in a correlative construction. Besides the normal

He *not only* protested: he (also) refused to pay his taxes

we can also have

Not only did he protest: he (also) refused to pay his taxes

The focus can be on the subject or predicate or on some part of either of them. The second correlative clause, which often has (*but*) *also*, may be implied rather than expressed. *Not only* (and less commonly *not* plus one of the other limiters) can appear initially in this construction without subject-operator inversion, with focus on the subject:

NOT ONLY he protested: ...

In a non-correlative construction, *not even* can also occur initially, but only with normal subject-verb order. The focus is on the subject:

NOT EVEN John protested

If the focus of *even* is to be on the predication (or part of it), *not even* must follow the operator:

John may *NOT EVEN have been protesting*

Focusing adjuncts can appear within the focal clause of a cleft sentence:

It was *only/also* John who protested

We should distinguish the cleft sentence from the correlative structure which it resembles but from which it differs prosodically:

It was *not* that John protested; it was *merely* that he was rude
It's *not just* that he's young; it's *surely* that he's inexperienced

The adverbials are here functioning within the superordinate clauses in which the *that*-clauses are complement. Limiters, additives and some disjuncts (*eg: possibly, probably*) occur in this correlative structure.

Intensifiers
8.12
Intensifiers can be divided into three semantic classes: emphasizers, amplifiers, downtoners. Intensifiers are not limited to indicating an increase in intensity; they indicate a point on the intensity scale which may be high or low. Emphasizers have a general heightening effect; amplifiers scale upwards from an assumed norm; downtoners have a lowering effect, usually scaling downwards from an assumed norm. The three classes are shown with their subclasses:

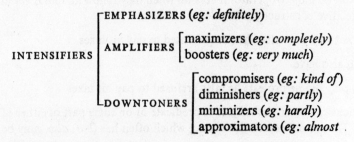

Most of the common intensifiers are adverbs, but there are also some noun phrases and a few prepositional phrases.

8.13
Emphasizers
Common emphasizers include:

[A] *actually, certainly, clearly, definitely, indeed, obviously, plainly, really, surely, for certain, for sure, of course*

[B] *frankly, honestly, literally, simply; fairly* (BrE), *just*

Examples of the use of emphasizers:

I *honestly* don't know what he wants
He *actually* sat next to her
I *just* can't understand it
They *literally* tore his arguments to pieces
I *simply* don't believe it

While emphasizers in Group A seem to be free to co-occur with any verb or predication, those in Group B tend to be restricted. For example, *honestly* tends to co-occur with verbs expressing attitude or cognition:

They *honestly* admire her courage
He *honestly* believes their accusation

Most emphasizers normally precede the item they emphasize (medial positions for verb phrases) but *for certain* and *for sure* are exceptional in being postposed.

Note
[*a*] Certain emphasizers appear in restricted environments:
(1) *always* when preceded by *can* or *could* in a positive declarative clause:
You *can always* sleep on the FLÓOR ('You can certainly . . .')
(2) *well* when preceded by *can, could, may,* or *might* in a positive declarative clause:
It *may well* be true that he beat her
('It may indeed be true . . .')
[*b*] *Indeed* can be postposed:
I appreciate your help *indeed*
This is more common after a complement of *be* which is realized by an adjective (particularly if modified by another intensifier) or a degree noun:
He was very tired *indeed* ('He was extremely tired')
It was a sacrifice *indeed* ('It was a great sacrifice')

Amplifiers
8.14
Amplifiers are divided into (a) MAXIMIZERS, which can denote the upper

extreme of the scale, and (b) BOOSTERS, which denote a high point on the scale. Boosters are very much an open class, and new expressions are frequently created to replace older ones whose impact has grown stale.

Most amplifiers can be contrasted in alternative negation with *to some extent:*

He didn't ignore me *completely*, but he did ignore me *to some extent*

Some common amplifiers are given below, with examples of their use.

MAXIMIZERS
absolutely, altogether, completely, entirely, fully, quite, thoroughly, utterly; in all respects; most

eg I can *perfectly* see why you are anxious about it
We *absolutely* refuse to listen to your grumbling
· He *quite* forgot about her birthday
I *entirely* agree with you

BOOSTERS
badly, deeply, greatly, heartily, much, so, violently, well; a great deal, a good deal, a lot, by far; exclamatory how; more

eg They like her *very much*
I *so* wanted to see her ('I wanted to see her so much')
I can *well* understand your problem

M2 (8.3) and final positions are open to most adverbs that are amplifiers; noun phrases and prepositional phrases are restricted to final position. In positive declarative clauses, final position is preferred for maximizers, but *M2* position is preferred for boosters, including maximizers when used as boosters, *ie* when they denote a high point on the scale rather than the upper extreme. Hence, the effect of the maximizer *completely* in *M2* position in *He completely denied it* is close to that of the booster *strongly* in *He strongly denied it*. On the other hand, when *completely* is final, as in *He denied it completely*, the intention seems to be closer to *He denied all of it*.

In negative, interrogative and imperative clauses, final position is normal in all cases.

Note

[a] There is a prescriptive tradition inhibiting the use of *very* or the comparative with *completely* and *perfectly* and with their respective adjective forms.

[b] The adverbs *extremely, most*, and (when no comparative clause follows) *more* are restricted to final position.

[c] Some adverbs as boosters occasionally appear in *M1* position (8.3) usually when they are themselves intensified or before an emphatic auxiliary:

I *very much* would prefer to see you tomorrow
I *so* did want to meet them
I *well* can understand your problem

But *M2* position, *eg: I would very much prefer to see you tomorrow*, is normal.

8.15
CO-OCCURRENCE RESTRICTIONS ON AMPLIFIERS
Amplifiers co-occur only with gradable verbs, whereas emphasizers can co-occur with non-gradable verbs such as *drink* or *judge:*

He *really* drinks beer
He will *definitely* judge us

When amplifiers co-occur with non-gradable verbs they function as other types of adjunct:

He drinks beer *a lot* ('often')
He will judge us *severely* ('in a severe manner')

However, a non-gradable verb can become gradable when the main concern is with the result of a process. For example, if the perfective particle *up* is added to *drink* or the perfective aspect of the verb is used, we can add an amplifier such as *completely:*

He *completely* drank up his beer
He has *completely* drunk his beer

Similarly, while *judge* is non-gradable, *misjudge* is gradable, since the latter is concerned with the result of the judging:

*He *badly judged* the situation
He *badly misjudged* the situation

Certain amplifiers tend to co-occur predominantly with certain verbs for example:

entirely + agree   completely + forget
badly + need, want   greatly + admire, enjoy

Amplifiers may occur with a semantic class of verbs, for example *greatly* with verbs having a favourable implication and *utterly* with verbs having an unfavourable implication. Some, such as *deeply*, occur with the class of 'emotive' verbs:

They wounded him *deeply* (emotional wounding)
They wounded him *badly* (physical wounding)

Note
[a] If *badly* is used with *judge*, it is interpreted as a process adjunct (perhaps expressing a blend of process with result) and must be put in final position:

He judged the situation *badly* ('in a way that was bad and with bad results')

The gradable/non-gradable distinction between *judge* and *misjudge* is found in other morphologically related verbs, *eg* :

NON-GRADABLE: calculate, estimate, rate, represent, behave, manage
GRADABLE: miscalculate, overestimate, underestimate, overrate, underrate, misrepresent, misbehave, mismanage

[b] *Much* is largely used as a non-assertive (7.35), unless premodified or in the compared forms. With some attitudinal verbs, unpremodified *much* can be used, but only in *M2* position (8.3):

We would have *much* preferred/appreciated her taking that position
They will *much* admire/regret your methods

Downtoners
8.16

Downtoners have a lowering effect on the force of the verb. They can be divided into four groups:

COMPROMISERS have only a slight lowering effect

DIMINISHERS ⎫
MINIMIZERS ⎬ scale downwards considerably

APPROXIMATORS serve to express an approximation to the force of the verb

COMPROMISERS
kind of/sort of (informal, esp AmE), *quite/rather* (esp BrE), *more or less*

eg I *kind of* like him (informal, esp AmE)
I *quite* enjoyed the party, but I've been to better ones (esp BrE)

DIMINISHERS
partly, slightly, somewhat; in part, to some extent; a little

eg The incident *somewhat* influenced his actions in later life
We know them *slightly*

MINIMIZERS
a bit; negatives (7.36): *barely, hardly, little, scarcely;* non-assertives (7.35): *in the least, in the slightest, at all*

eg I didn't enjoy it *in the least*
A: Do you like her? B: *A bit.*

APPROXIMATORS
almost, nearly, as good as, all but

eg I *almost* resigned

Noun phrases are quite common as non-assertive minimizers, *eg:* 'I didn't sleep *a wink* last night'; 'I don't owe you *a thing*'.

Most downtoners favour *M2* position (8.3) but can also occur finally, *eg:* 'He *more or less* agrees with you', 'He agrees with you *more or less*'. Some are restricted to *M2: quite, rather, as good as, all but; eg* 'I *quite* like him'. Others tend to be restricted either to *M2* or to *M1(b)*, the position between two auxiliaries: *barely, hardly, scarcely, practically, virtually;* hence we may have 'He could *hardly* be described as an expert'. A few are restricted to *M2* in a positive clause, but can precede a negative phrase in *M1: kind of, sort of, almost, nearly; eg* 'I *almost* didn't meet him'. A few others favour final position – *a bit, at all* – or are restricted to it – *enough, a little; eg* 'I didn't enjoy it *at all*', 'He hasn't worked *enough*'. A few can appear initially: *in part, in some respects, to some extent; eg* '*To some extent* he prefers working at home'.

8.17
Approximators imply a denial of the truth-value of what is denoted by the verb. Hence we can say, with the approximator *almost*,

I *almost* resigned, but in fact I didn't resign

The negative minimizers partially deny the truth-value of what is said:

I can *scarcely* ignore his views; in fact I can't ignore his views

The second clause converts the partial denial in the first clause into a full denial.

Compromisers reduce the force of the verb. If we say

I *kind of* like him (informal, esp AmE)

we do not deny liking him, but we seem to be deprecating what we are saying, 'I might go as far as to say I like him'.

Diminishers are not usually the focus of negation, but when they are, the effect is to push the scaling towards the top:

They didn't praise him SLÍGHTly ('They praised him a lot')

On the other hand, the effect of negation on those minimizers that accept negation is to deny the truth-value of what is denoted by the verb:

We don't like it *a* BÍT ('We don't like it')

Four of the minimizers – *barely, hardly, little, scarcely* – are themselves negative and cannot be negated.

Note
Certain minimizers appear in restricted environments:

(1) *possibly* and *conceivably* when they co-occur with *can* or *could* in a non-assertive clause:

They *can't possibly/conceivably* leave now ('They can't under any circumstances leave now')

(2) *never* is a negative minimizer in

> You will *never* catch the train tonight ('It is utterly impossible that you will catch the train tonight')

> In questions, *ever* can replace *never* as minimizer:

>> Will he *ever/never* go to bed tonight?

8.18
Homonyms of intensifiers: quantifiers, time *frequency* adjuncts, time *duration* adjuncts

Many items that are intensifiers are also used to denote a measure of quantity or of time duration or time frequency: all the minimizers; the compromisers *enough, sufficiently;* the boosters *much, a lot, a good deal, a great deal;* the diminishers *a little, least, somewhat, to some extent.* We can therefore contrast several uses of (say) *a lot:*

> I like them *a lot* ('to a great extent' – booster intensifier)
> I paid him *a lot* for his work ('a large amount' – quantifier)
> I see him *a lot* ('often' – time *frequency* adjunct)
> I slept *a lot* last night ('a long time' – time *duration* adjunct)

Some of the quantifiers must be analysed as direct objects, because they can be made the subject of the passive form of the sentence:

> They paid *a lot* for these pictures ↔ *A lot* was paid (by them) for these pictures

Process adjuncts
8.19

Process adjuncts define in some way the process denoted by the verb. They can be divided into at least three semantic subclasses:

MANNER   MEANS   INSTRUMENT

Common pro-forms for process adjuncts are *in that way, that way* (informal), *like that.*

Process adjuncts co-occur with dynamic verbs, but not with stative verbs (3.35):

He likes them⎫ ⎧*skilfully
He owns it   ⎭ ⎩*awkwardly

Process adjuncts favour, final position, since they usually receive the information focus. Indeed, no other position is likely if the process adjunct is obligatory for the verb:

⎧They live *frugally*   ⎧They treated his friend *badly*
⎩*They *frugally* live   ⎩*They *badly* treated his friend

Since the passive is often used when the need is felt to focus attention on the verb, process adjuncts are commonly placed in *M2* position (8.3) rather than finally when the verb is in the passive:

Tear gas was *indiscriminately* sprayed on the protesters

Process adjuncts realized by units other than adverb phrases often occur initially, that position being preferred if the focus of information is required on another part of the sentence:

By pressing this button you can stop the machine

8.20
Manner adjuncts
Examples of the use of manner adjuncts:

They sprayed tear gas *indiscriminately* on the protesters
She replied to questions *with great courtesy*
He spoke *in a way that reminded me of his father*
He always writes *in a carefree manner*
They walked (*in*) *single file*
You should write *as I tell you to*

Manner adjuncts are realized mostly by adverb phrases and prepositional phrases (6.31), but also by noun phrases and clauses (11.33).

Noun phrases with *way*, *manner*, and *style* as head tend to have the definite article:

$$\text{She cooks chicken} \begin{cases} the \text{ way I like} \\ in \begin{Bmatrix} the \\ a \end{Bmatrix} \text{way I like} \end{cases}$$

As the above example illustrates, we can regard such noun phrases as having omitted the preposition *in* (cf 6.25 f, 8.21).

An adverb manner adjunct can usually be paraphrased by *in a ... manner* or *in a ... way* with its adjective base in the vacant position. Where an adverb form exists, it is usually preferred over a corresponding prepositional phrase with *manner* or *way*. Hence, 'He always writes *carelessly*' is more usual than 'He always writes *in a careless manner/way*'.

Adverbs as heads of manner phrase adjuncts are an open class. The main method of forming manner adverbs is by adding a *-ly* suffix to an adjective. Three minor methods are by adding *-wise*, *-style*, or *-fashion* to a noun, *eg: snake-wise, cowboy-style, peasant-fashion*. With these forms the prepositional paraphrase would include postmodification: *in the manner of a snake, in the style of cowboys, in the fashion of peasants*.

Note

Some adjuncts express a blend of manner with some other meaning.

(1) Manner with result and intensification:

> The soldiers wounded him *badly* ('in such a way and to such an extent that it resulted in his being in a bad condition')

(2) Manner with time *duration:*

> He was walking *slowly* ('in such a way that each step took a long time')

Such items are more fully time adjuncts when they appear initially or medially:

> *Suddenly*, I felt free again ('it suddenly happened')
> My brother *quickly* despised his school ('My brother soon came to despise')

(3) Manner with time *when:*

> Put it together *again* ('in the way that it was before')

8.21
Means and instrument adjuncts

Examples of the use of means adjuncts:

> He decided to treat the patient *surgically*
> I go to school *by car*
> He gained entry into the building *by means of a bribe to the guard*

Examples of the use of instrument adjuncts:

> He examined the specimen *microscopically*
> You can cut the bread *with that knife*
> The injured horse was humanely killed *with a rifle bullet*

Most means and instrument adjuncts are prepositional phrases (6.31 *f*), but some are adverb phrases and others are noun phrases without an article. We can consider the noun phrases as related to prepositional phrases (8.20):

> He sent it (*by*) *air mail*   Fly$\left(\left\{ \begin{matrix} with \\ by \end{matrix} \right\}\right)$*Air France*

> He travelled to Washington (*by*) *first class*

Note

Adverbs as means and instrument adjuncts cannot be modified. Hence, *microscopically* in 'He examined the specimen *very microscopically*' can only be a manner adjunct ('in microscopic detail'), although without the premodifier *very* it can be a means or instrument adjunct ('by means of a microscope' or 'with a microscope').

Subject adjuncts
8.22

Subject adjuncts relate to the referent of the subject in an active clause (or the agent in a passive clause) as well as to the process or state denoted by the verb. All are either adverb or prepositional phrases. Three groups can be distinguished: general, volitional, and formulaic. The last group will be separately discussed in 8.23.

General subject adjuncts:

> *Resentfully*, the workers have stood by their leaders ('The workers have stood by their leaders and were resentful about it')
> *With great unease*, they elected him as their leader ('They were very uneasy when they . . .')

Volitional subject adjuncts:

> He left his proposals vague *on purpose* ('It was his purpose to . . .')
> He *deliberately* misled us ('He was being deliberate when he . . .')

> Common volitional subject adjuncts: *deliberately, (un)intentionally, purposely, reluctantly, voluntarily, wilfully, (un)willingly, on purpose, with reluctance*

The subject adjuncts show their relationship to the subject by the paraphrase they allow. For example, we must provide a different paraphrase for the subject adjunct *bitterly* from its homonyms as manner adjunct and booster intensifier:

> *Bitterly*, he buried his children ('He was bitter when he . . .')
> He spoke *bitterly* about their attitude ('He spoke in a bitter way . . .')
> He *bitterly* regretted their departure ('He very much regretted . . .')

Volitional subject adjuncts differ from other subject adjuncts in that

(1) they express the subject's intention or willingness, or the reverse

(2) they can often occur with intensive verbs:

> He is *deliberately* being a nuisance

(3) they can more easily appear before clause negation:

> *Intentionally*, he didn't write to them about it

Subject adjuncts require an animate subject:

> Joan *resentfully* packed their luggage
> *The water *resentfully* boiled

However, in the passive form it is the agent (whether present or not) that must be animate:

> Their luggage was *resentfully* packed (by Joan)

Subject adjuncts tend to occur initially or medially, but *M2* position (8.3) is probably preferred.

8.23
Formulaic adjuncts

Except for *please*, formulaic adjuncts tend to be restricted to *M2* position (8.3). They are a small group of adverbs used as markers of courtesy. All except *please* are modifiable by *very*. The most common are exemplified below:

> He *kindly* offered me a ride ('He was kind enough to . . .')
> We *cordially* invite you to our party ('We express our cordiality to you by inviting . . .')
> She announced that she will *graciously* consent to our request ('. . . she will be gracious enough to . . .')
> He *humbly* offered his apologies ('He was humble enough to offer . . .')
> Take a seat *please* ('Please me by taking . . .')

Kindly and *please* are the only formulaic adjuncts to appear freely before imperatives. *Kindly* is restricted to initial position in imperatives:

> *Kindly* leave the room

Please, however, is mobile:

> *Please* leave the room   Open the door *please*

Unlike the other formulaic adjuncts, *please* is normally limited to sentences having the function of a command, or containing a reported command, or constituting a request:

> Will you *please* leave the room?
> You will *please* leave the room
> I wonder whether you would mind leaving the room *please*
> I asked him whether he would *please* leave the room
> May I *please* have my book back?

Please and (to a lesser extent) *kindly* are very commonly used to tone down the abruptness of a command.

Place adjuncts
8.24

Place adjuncts denote static position and also direction, movement, and passage, here brought together under the general term 'direction'. Most place adjuncts are prepositional phrases (6.7 *ff*), but clauses (11.22), adverb phrases and noun phrases are frequently used:

> He lives *in a small village*
> The church was built *where there had once been an office block*
> They are not *there*
> She works *a long way from here*

               position

He ran *past the sentry*
They followed him *wherever he went*
I took the papers *from the desk*
He threw it *ten yards*
$\left.\right\}$ direction

Position adjuncts can normally be evoked as a response to a *where* question:

A: Where is he staying? B: *In a hotel.*

The appropriate question for direction adjuncts is *where* plus the relevant directional particle, except that for 'direction towards' the particle *to* is commonly omitted:

A: *Where* are you going (*to*)? B: (*To*) *the park.*
A: *Where* have you come *from?* B: (*From*) *the supermarket.*

Adverbs commonly used for both position and direction: *above, along, anywhere, around, away, back, below, by, down, east* (and other compass points), *elsewhere, everywhere, far, here, home, in, locally, near, off, opposite, out, over, past, round, somewhere, there, through, under, up, within.*

A few adverbs denote direction only: *aside, backward(s), downward(s), forward(s), inward(s), left, outward(s), right, sideways, upward(s).*

Where in its various uses is a place adjunct; *here* and *there* are pro-forms for place adjuncts.

Note
[a] For *here, above,* and *below* as signals in discourse reference, see 10.38.
[b] *Anywhere* and (normally) *far* are non-assertive (7.35).

8.25
Co-occurrence restrictions on place adjuncts
Direction adjuncts are used only with verbs of motion or with other dynamic verbs (3.35) that allow a directional meaning:

He jumped *over the fence*
She was whispering softly *into the microphone*

On the other hand, position adjuncts can be used with most verbs, including stative verbs (3.35).

Position adjuncts are used as predicative adjuncts with the intensive verb *be:*

Your sister is *in the next room*
The house you want is *on the other side of the street*

Some direction adjuncts are also used with *be,* but with a resultative meaning, indicating the state of having reached the destination (6.8).

Some place adjuncts are obligatory, providing verb complementation to verbs other than *be:*

We don't *live here*   They *put* the cat *out*
I'll *get below*   You should *set* that dish *in the middle*

Place adjuncts are used also non-literally in phrasal verbs (12.2 *f*):

The light *is on* ('is shining')
When John heard what happened, he *blew up* ('became very angry')
They *turned down* the suggestion ('rejected')

Up, in particular, is used as an intensifier or perfectively:

You must *drink up* quickly ('finish drinking')
They *closed up* the factory ('closed completely')

For the transferred or abstract use of place prepositions, see 6.20.

8.26
Position and direction adjuncts in the same clause

Position and direction adjuncts can co-occur, with the position adjunct normally following the direction adjunct in final position:

The children are running *around* (A_1) *upstairs* (A_2)

The position adjunct can be put in initially to avoid giving it end-focus (14.11):

Upstairs the children are running *around*

A prepositional phrase may be put in that position, as in

In the park some of the children are walking *to the lake*

to prevent it from being interpreted as a postmodifier of a previous noun phrase. There are other ways of avoiding such an interpretation, *eg:*

Some of the children are *in the park* and walking *to the lake*

Two position adjuncts or two direction adjuncts can be coordinated:

We can wait for you *here or in the car*
They went *up the hill and into the station*

But a position and a direction adjunct normally cannot be coordinated. Hence in

The baby was crawling *upstairs and into his parents' bedroom*

upstairs can be interpreted only as a direction adjunct since it is coordinated with a phrase that has only a directional function.

8.27
Hierarchical relationship
Two position adjuncts can co-occur:

Many people eat *in restaurants* (A_1) *in London* (A_2)

Only the adjunct denoting the larger place can be moved to initial
position:

In London many people eat *in restaurants*
*In restaurants many people eat *in London*

Initial position may be preferred in the case of a prepositional phrase
that can also be interpreted as postmodifier of a previous noun phrase, as
possibly with (*restaurants*) *in London* (*cf* 8.26).
    Two direction adjuncts can also co-occur:

He came *to London from Rome*
He went *from Rome to London*

The normal order of these direction adjuncts accords with the interpretation of the verb. *Come* concerns arrival, and therefore the destination
(*to London*) is normally mentioned before the point of departure (*from
Rome*), whereas *go* concerns departure and therefore the reverse order is
normal.
    The normal order of juxtaposed direction adjuncts otherwise follows
the same order as the events described:

They drove *down the hill* (A_1) *to the village* (A_2)

Similarly, only the adjunct relating to the earlier event can be transposed
to initial position:

And then *from Alexandria* the party proceeded *to Cairo*

8.28
Positions of place adjuncts
Both types of place adjunct favour final position:

position $\begin{cases} \text{I'll meet you } downstairs \\ \text{You'll find the sugar } where\ the\ coffee\ is \end{cases}$

direction $\begin{cases} \text{I'll go } downstairs \\ \text{We're moving some new furniture } into\ the\ kitchen \end{cases}$

Position adjuncts, particularly prepositional phrases, often appear
initially. They may be put there to avoid end-focus (14.11), or to avoid
misinterpretation (8.26), or to avoid a clustering of adjuncts at final position, though it is not usually possible to isolate any one reason.

Outside, children were jumping and skipping

Here . . . *be* and *There* . . . *be* with a personal pronoun as subject and the verb in the simple present are commonly used to draw attention to the presence of somebody or something:

> *Here* I am/*Here* it is/*There* she is/*There* you are

Speakers sometimes put position adjuncts (especially *here*, *there*, and compounds with *-where*) in *M2* and more rarely in *M1* (8.3):

> Life is *everywhere* so frustrating
> We are *here* enjoying a different kind of existence

Place adjuncts can take the position between verb and object if the object is long:

> They $\begin{Bmatrix} \text{moved } into \\ \text{found } in \end{Bmatrix}$ *the kitchen* every conceivable kind of furniture

Some direction adjuncts are put initially to convey a dramatic impact. They normally co-occur with a verb in the simple present or simple past:

> *Away* he goes   *On* they marched

If the subject is not a pronoun but a noun (and therefore has greater information value), subject-verb inversion is normal when any place adjunct is initial (14.12):

> *Away* goes the servant   *On the very top of the hill* lives a
>   hermit

Here + *be* and *there* + *be* with the verb in the simple present are common in speech:

> *Here are* the tools   *There's* your brother

Direction adjuncts are put in initial position virtually only in literary English and in children's literature. A few exceptions occur in informal speech, mainly with *go*, *come*, and *get* in either the imperative with the retained subject *you* or in the simple present:

> In (the bath) $\;\Big\}$ $\begin{Bmatrix} \text{come} \\ \text{go} \\ \text{get} \end{Bmatrix}$
> Over (the fence) $\;\Big\}$ you
> Under (the bridge) $\;\Big\}$

> On $\;\Big\}$ There they $\begin{Bmatrix} \text{go} \\ \text{come} \end{Bmatrix}$ Here $\begin{Bmatrix} \text{I} \\ \text{we} \end{Bmatrix}$ go
> Under $\;\Big\}$ you go
> Round $\;\Big\}$ Here he comes

Note
[a] There are some idiomatic expressions with *here* and *there*:

$\left.\begin{array}{l}\textit{Here} \\ \textit{There}\end{array}\right\}$ *you are* = This is for you

Here we are = We've arrived at the expected place

There you are = That supports or proves what I've said

[b] Certain direction adjuncts are commonly used as imperatives, with an implied verb of motion:

> *Out(side)!, In(side)!, (Over) Here!, (Over) There!, (Right) Back!,*
> *Down!, Off!, Up!, Under!, Left!, Right!, Away!*
> *Up the stairs!, Out of the house!, To bed!*

This applies also to some other adjuncts, *eg: Quickly!, Slowly!, Carefully!*

8.29
Position adjuncts in relation to subject and object

Position adjuncts normally indicate where the referent of the subject and (if present) of the object are located, and usually the place is the same for both referents:

I met John *on a bus* (John and I were on the bus)

But sometimes the places can be different:

I saw John *on a bus* (John was on the bus but I need not have been)

With verbs of placing, the reference is always to the place of the object and normally that will differ from the place of the subject (*cf* 8.44, and complex transitive complementation, 12.26 *f*):

I *have/keep/put/park/shelter* my car *in a garage*

With certain verbs of saying, arranging, expecting, position adjuncts are resultative and are like predicative adjuncts of the direct object (*cf* 12.14 Note):

I want *my car IN THE GARAGE* ('to be in the garage')
They plan *a meeting AT MY HOUSE* ('that there should be a meeting at my house')
They offered *a barbecue NEARBY* ('to have a barbecue nearby')
I like *my dinner IN THE KITCHEN* ('to have my dinner in the kitchen')

The position adjunct may sometimes refer to the object in a conditional relationship:

I only like *barbecues ON THE BEACH* ('if they are held on the beach')

Time adjuncts
8.30

Time adjuncts that are clauses (11.21) or prepositional phrases (6.21 *ff*) or noun phrases (6.25 *f*) are discussed elsewhere.

Time adjuncts can be divided into four main semantic classes:

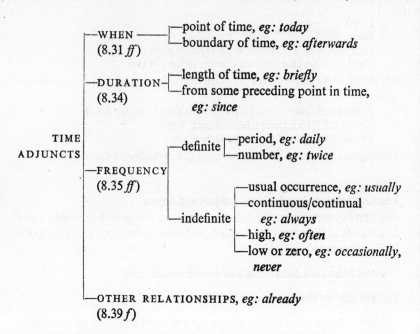

Time *when* adjuncts
8.31

Most time *when* adverbs can serve as a response to a *when* question:

A: When did he arrive?   B: $\begin{cases} \textit{Last night.} \\ \textit{While you were at the library.} \end{cases}$

When in its various uses is in part pro-form for the time adjuncts. For *then* as a pro-form for these time adjuncts, see 10.5, 10.28.

Time *when* adjuncts can be divided into

[A] those denoting a point of time
[B] those denoting a boundary of time, *ie* a point of time but also implying the point from which that time is measured

Common adverbs in these two groups include:

Group A
   again ('on another occasion'), *just* ('at this very moment'), *late* ('at a late time'), *now* ('at this time'), *nowadays* ('at the present time'), *presently* ('at the present time', esp AmE), *then* ('at that time'), *today*

Group B
   afterwards, *before*, *eventually* ('in the end'), *formerly*, *just* ('a very short time ago'), *lately* ('a short time ago'), *momentarily*

('in a moment', AmE), *previously* ('before'), *presently*
('soon'), *recently* ('a short time ago'), *since* ('after that'), *soon*,
then ('after that')

Examples of the use of time *when* adjuncts:

Group A

I was in New York *last year* and am *now* living in Baltimore
I'm *just* finishing my homework
I was awarded my Bachelor of Arts degree *in 1970*
I'll tell you all the news *when I get back home*

Group B

I haven't any time at the moment but I'll see you *soon*
Take a drink and *then* go to bed
Will you be there *after lunch?*
He owed me a lot of money and wouldn't pay me back until I got my
   lawyer to write to him. He has paid me back in full *since then*
She left him *after he struck her*

Most time *when* adjuncts in Group A normally occur finally, but *just*
is restricted to *M2* position (8.3), *eg: I've just heard that you are leaving us.*
Nowadays and *presently* commonly occur initially, *eg: Nowadays, many*
teenagers have long hair. Those in Group B commonly occur initially or
at *M2* position.

Note

[a] *Earlier* and *later* are synonymous with *before (that)* and *afterwards* respectively:

He remembered the many insults that he had *earlier* experienced
He handed in his resignation, and *later* regretted his hasty action

[b] *Presently* is synonymous with *soon* where there is a modal auxiliary or (for some
speakers) when the verb is in the past:

They $\begin{cases} \text{will } \textit{presently} \text{ call on him} \\ \textit{presently} \text{ called on him} \end{cases}$

(Some find *presently* unacceptable when it co-occurs with a verb in the past.)
   On the other hand, when the verb is in the present, it is synonymous with *at*
present (esp AmE):

They are *presently* staying with him

8.32

Most adverbs in Group B are used as correlatives to denote temporal
sequence; as such they tend to occur initially or medially:

First they petitioned the Governor, but heard nothing from him. *Then*
   they wrote to the President, and received a polite but vague reply
   from some official. They *next* organized a peaceful demonstration.
   And *finally* they picketed all Federal buildings in the city.

8.33

Time *when* adjuncts can be in a hierarchical relationship:

I'll see you *at nine* (A$_1$) *on Monday* (A$_2$)

The order of final adjuncts depends in part on information focus, but the tendency is for the superordinate adjunct (the one denoting the more extended period) to come last. However, the order may be reversed if the other adjunct is considerably longer:

I was in New York *last year* (A$_1$) *before the first snow fell* (A$_2$)

Only the superordinate adjunct can occur initially (8.27, 8.36):

On Monday I'll see you *at nine*
*At nine I'll see you *on Monday*

8.34
Time *duration* adjuncts
Time *duration* adjuncts can be divided into two groups:

[A] those denoting length of time
[B] those denoting duration from some preceding point of time

Time *duration* adjuncts in Group A can serve as a response to a (*for*) *how long* question:

A: How long are you staying (for)?   B: $\begin{cases} (For)\ About\ a\ month. \\ Till\ I\ can\ get\ my\ car\ repaired. \end{cases}$

Adverbs in Group B cannot serve as a response to such a question though prepositional phrases and clauses can do so:

A: (For) How long have you been collecting stamps?
B: *Since/*Recently/*Since last month*/*Since I was a child*

Those in Group B co-occur with perfect aspect (*cf* 11.49):

His studies $\begin{cases} haven't\ been \\ *weren't \end{cases}$ improving *lately/recently/since*

Common adverbs in the two groups include:

Group A
always, long, momentarily ('for a moment'), *permanently, temporarily*

Group B
lately/recently ('during a recent period')
since ('from some time in the past')

Examples of the use of time *duration* adjuncts:

Group A
> I have *always* lived here
> I'll be in California *for the summer*
> Was it noisy *the whole night?*
> There was no trouble *while we were there*

Group B
> He insulted me last year and I haven't spoken to him *since*
> Things haven't become any better *lately*
> I have been waiting for the books to be delivered *ever since I came to this apartment*

Time *duration* adjuncts are normally positioned finally, except for three adverbs normally positioned at *M2* (8.3): *momentarily, permanently, temporarily.*

Note

[a] When *lately* and *recently* are time *when* adjuncts (8.31), they can co-occur with simple past as well:

> He *lately/recently* moved into a new apartment

Since requires perfect aspect even when it is a time *when* adjunct:

> He $\left\{ \begin{array}{l} \text{has since moved} \\ \text{*since moved} \end{array} \right\}$ into a new apartment

[b] Uninflected *long* is normally a non-assertive form (7.35) and positioned finally, but it can be an assertive form when it co-occurs with certain verbs and is then usually positioned at *M2*. The verbs seem to be mainly verbs of belief or assumption (11.58), attitudinal verbs, and some verbs of speaking:

> I have *long* admired his style of writing
> He has *long* thought of retiring at the age of 55

[c] *Since when* and *until* (or *till*) *when* are used to form questions:

A: *Since when* have you known him? B: Since he joined our club.
A: *Until when* are you staying? B: Until next Monday.

These are the normal positions for *since* and *until/till*, postposition being unacceptable for *since* and *until*: *When have you known him since?, *When are you staying until?, and the less common position for *till*: *?When are you staying till?* In this respect, they contrast with *how long ... for; for* is normally postposed, the initial position being a formal variant.

Time *frequency* adjuncts
8.35

Most time *frequency* adjuncts can serve as a response to a *how often* question:

A: How often do you wash your car? B: $\left\{ \begin{array}{l} \textit{Every Sunday.} \\ \textit{Whenever I find a spare} \\ \quad \textit{half-hour.} \end{array} \right.$

Time *frequency* adjuncts are usually adverb phrases or noun phrases, and they can be divided semantically into two major subclasses:

[I] those naming explicitly the times by which the frequency is measured: DEFINITE FREQUENCY

[II] those not doing so: INDEFINITE FREQUENCY

Each of these subclasses can in turn be subdivided. In each case we list common adverbs.

[I] DEFINITE FREQUENCY

[A] PERIOD FREQUENCY

Committee meetings take place *weekly*

If so desired, rent can be paid *per week* instead of *per month*

common adverbs: *hourly, daily, weekly, monthly, annually*

[B] NUMBER FREQUENCY

I have been in Singapore ÒNCE (only)

He *again* demanded a refund ('for a second time')

common adverbs: *again, once* ('one time only'), *twice, etc;*
otherwise phrases, *eg: three times, on five occasions*

[II] INDEFINITE FREQUENCY

[C] USUAL OCCURRENCE

We *normally* don't go to bed before midnight

As usual, nobody asked anything at the end of the lecture

common adverbs: *commonly, generally, invariably, normally,*
usually

[D] CONTINUOUS/CONTINUAL FREQUENCY

Does she *always* dress well?

He is *continually* complaining about the noise

common adverbs: *always, constantly, continually, continuously*

[E] HIGH FREQUENCY

I have *often* told them to relax more

Have you been drunk *many times?*

common adverbs: *frequently, often, regularly, repeatedly*

[F] LOW OR ZERO FREQUENCY

I *sometimes* think she doesn't know what she's talking about

I have been in his office *on several occasions*

common adverbs: *infrequently, occasionally, rarely, seldom,*
sometimes; never, ever ('at any time')

Time *frequency* adjuncts in Groups A and B normally occur finally. Those in Groups C–F are normally positioned at *M2*, but are often found at *M1* (8.3). Phrases (apart from those consisting of an adverb or a pre-modified adverb) are normally initial for Group C (*eg: as usual, as a rule, for the most part*) and final for Groups D–E (*eg: at all times, many times, now and again*).

Note
We should add to Groups E and F items that are used as intensifiers (8.18):

    [E] *much, a lot, a good deal, a great deal* (all equivalent to *often* or *very often*)
    [F] *a little* ('very occasionally'), *little* ('hardly at any time'),
      less ('less frequently'), *least* ('least frequently'),
     a bit ('occasionally'); *barely, hardly, scarcely*
     eg I don't see him *very much* ('very often')
      I go there *very little* ('very infrequently')

As frequency adjuncts, *hardly* and *scarcely* tend to co-occur with non-assertive *ever* ('at any time'):

    I *hardly/scarcely* ever go there

8.36
Adjuncts of definite frequency in Group A denote the period of time by which the frequency is measured, while those in [B] express the measurement in number of times. Items from each group can co-occur, normally with the item from [B] coming first:

    You should take the medicine *twice* [B] *daily* [A]

Those in [A] can also co-occur with each other in a hierarchical relationship:

    She felt his pulse *hourly* [A] *each day* [A]

The order of the adjuncts in final position depends in part on information focus, but only the one denoting the longer period can occur initially (*cf* 8.27, 8.33):

    Each day she felt his pulse *hourly*

Those in [B] can likewise co-occur with each other in a hierarchical relationship with a momentary verb (3.35):

    I hit him *twice on two occasions* ('two times on each of two occasions')

As here, the superordinate adjunct tends to follow the subordinate adjunct; but it can be initial:

    On two occasions I hit him *twice*

Adjuncts in [B] can often be the response to the question *How many times?*:

    A: How many times did you hit him?   B: *Twice*.

8.37

Adjuncts of indefinite frequency in Group C denote usual occurrence. They differ from most of the other adjuncts of indefinite frequency in that they can precede the clausal negative, in which case they indicate that it is normal for something *not* to occur:

> *Generally/Normally/Usually*, he doesn't take medicine

Those in [E] and [F] that precede negation express a high or low frequency. It is not contradictory to assert that it is frequent (or infrequent) for something to occur and at the same time that it is frequent (or infrequent) for it not to occur:

$$\begin{bmatrix} Often \\ Occasionally \end{bmatrix} \text{he doesn't take medicine, but} \begin{bmatrix} often \\ occasionally \end{bmatrix} \text{he does}$$
$$\text{(take medicine)}$$

We can see from this example that *often* does not necessarily imply the majority of times, and the same is true for *frequently*. However, except for *invariably*, those in [C] do imply the majority of times; they also allow for exceptions, so that we can say:

> *Generally/Normally/Usually*, he doesn't take medicine, but *sometimes* he does (take medicine)

Frequency adjuncts in [D] normally cannot precede negation:

$$\text{*He} \begin{Bmatrix} always \\ constantly \end{Bmatrix} \text{doesn't pay his debts on time}$$

Instead we use *never, not ... ever*, or *not ... at all:*

$$\text{He} \begin{Bmatrix} never \text{ pays} \\ doesn't \text{ } ever \text{ pay} \end{Bmatrix} \text{his debts on time}$$

He did*n't* drink whisky *at all*

8.38

TIME *FREQUENCY* ADJUNCTS AND QUANTIFIERS

If the subject is generic (4.18), many adjuncts of indefinite frequency, particularly when positioned initially or medially, are equivalent to certain predeterminers (4.7 *ff*) or to certain quantifiers (4.13 *ff*) in the noun phrase of the subject. For example, in

> Sailors drink rum *often* ('on many occasions')

often refers to the frequency of the drinking of rum. However,

$$\begin{Bmatrix} \text{Often sailors} \\ \text{Sailors often} \end{Bmatrix} \text{drink rum ('it often happens that ...')}$$

is very similar to

Many sailors drink rum

Other examples:

Universities *sometimes* have linguistics departments
   = *Some* universities have linguistics departments

Students *occasionally* fail this course
   = *A few* students fail this course

Officers *never* get drunk while on duty
   = *No* officers get drunk while on duty

If the direct object is generic, the adjunct may be equivalent to a predeterminer or quantifier in the noun phrase of the direct object:

I *often* find spelling mistakes in students' essays
   = I find *many* spelling mistakes in students' essays

Other time relationships
8.39
Adjuncts included here express some relationship in time other than those specified in 8.31–38. One group consists of adjuncts concerned with the sequence within the clause of two time relationships, and they co-occur with time *when* adjuncts. Many of the same items are also used as correlatives to denote temporal sequence between clauses or between sentences (8.32):

These techniques were *originally* used in the Second World War
It wasn't until last night that I was *finally* introduced to her
She broke her leg *for the first time* when she was ten

Adverb phrases normally appear in *M2* (8.3) and other phrases in final position. Common adverbs in this group include *afterwards, eventually, finally, first, later, next, originally, subsequently, then.*

8.40
Another group consists of adjuncts that are similar to time *duration* adjuncts in that they express duration up to or before a given or implied time; they are related by assertive/non-assertive contrasts (7.35):

assertive forms: *already, still, by now*
non-assertive forms: *yet, any more, any longer*
negative forms: *no more, no longer*

They have finished their work *by now*
We haven't *yet* eaten
He would stay *no longer*

Most of these adjuncts occur either in *M2* position (8.3) or finally, but *already* is normally in *M2* position.

The three items *yet*, *already*, and *still* are in particular closely related. In contrast to non-assertive *yet*, *already* and *still* cannot lie within the scope of clause negation (7.40) except in questions. *Still*, unlike *already*, can precede negation. We therefore have the following possibilities:

DECLARATIVE POSITIVE
    I *already* like him ('I have by this time come to like him')
    *I *yet* like him
    I *still* like him ('I continue to like him')

DECLARATIVE NEGATIVE (adverb preceding negation)
    *I *already* haven't spoken to him
    *I *yet* haven't spoken to him
    I *still* haven't spoken to him ('I haven't spoken to him so far')

DECLARATIVE NEGATIVE (adverb following negation)
    *He can't *already* drive
    He can't drive *yet* ('He can't drive up to this time')
    ?He can't *still* drive ('He can't continue to drive')

INTERROGATIVE POSITIVE
    Have you *already* seen him? (That was quick)
    Have you seen him *yet*? (You've been here ages)
    Do you *still* see him? ('Do you continue to see him?')

INTERROGATIVE NEGATIVE
    Haven't you seen him *already*?⎫ ('Haven't you by this time seen
    Haven't you seen him *yet*?   ⎬   him?')
    Don't you *still* see him? ('Don't you continue to see him?')

Note

[a] The difference between *already* and *yet* in questions is that *already* expects an affirmative answer whereas *yet* leaves open whether the answer is negative or positive (7.46 *f*).

[b] *Yet* can be assertive in certain contexts where it is similar in meaning to *still*:

    I have *yet* to find out what he wants ('I have still to . . .')
    I can see him *yet* ('I can *still* see him')
    There's plenty of time *yet* ('There's plenty of time *still*')

[c] *Still* often blends concessive and temporal meanings (*cf* 8.53). For example, in

    It's very late and he's *still* working ('He's continuing *even so* to work')

8.41
Relative positions of time adjuncts
Adjuncts from the three major subclasses that can co-occur in final position – time *when*, time *duration*, and time *frequency* – tend to occur in the order

time *duration* (D) – time *frequency* (F) – time *when* (W)

The following sentences exemplify the normal order (but *cf* 8.46):

I was there *for a day or so* (D) *every year* (F) *during my childhood* (W)
I'm paying my rent *monthly* (F) *this year* (W)
Our electricity was cut off *briefly* (D) *today* (W)

8.42
Coordination

Time adjuncts in the same subclass can be coordinated:

TIME *WHEN*
    today and tomorrow   now or later

TIME *DURATION*
    permanently or temporarily   for the week or (for the) month

TIME *FREQUENCY*
    once or twice   each day and (each) night

Note
Now and then and *now and again* are common coordinated expressions used for time *frequency* ('from time to time', 'occasionally'). Similarly, *again and again* and *over and over* are used to denote frequent repetition and not just two repetitions (5.33).

8.43
Time adjuncts and time reference

Time adjuncts play a part in specifying the time reference of the verb phrase. Thus, *now* determines that the reference in

He is playing *now*

is present, and *tomorrow* that it is future in

He is playing *tomorrow*

Some time adjuncts cannot co-occur with particular forms of the verb phrase. Thus, *tomorrow* does not co-occur with the simple past:

*He played *tomorrow*

For further discussion of this topic, see 3.30.

Note
An apparent exception is with those verbs of saying, arranging, expecting, or wanting whose object has future reference. In such cases, though the expressed verb is in the past, there may be a time adjunct with future reference to the object:

She wanted the book *tomorrow* (=She wanted to have the book tomorrow)

The adjunct can co-occur with another that has past reference to the verb:

As far back as March, they predicted a crisis *next month* (*ie* their prediction of a crisis next month was made as far back as March).

8.44
Time adjuncts as predicative adjuncts with *be*
Time adjuncts can co-occur with all verbs, including *be:*

It's much warmer *now*

Many of them can also be used as predicative adjuncts with *be:*

TIME *WHEN*
The meeting will be *tomorrow*

TIME *DURATION*
The show is *from nine till twelve*

TIME *FREQUENCY*
Interviews are *every hour*

Be in such cases is equivalent to 'take place', and the subject must be eventive. For example in

The opera will be *tonight*

the opera is interpreted as 'the performance of the opera'.
The reference of the time adjunct may be to the object (*cf* 8.29). There are two types of such references:

(1) The verbs denote the placing or movement of the object, and a place adjunct is present indicating the resulting place of the action. The time adjuncts denote time *duration*.

They threw him in prison *for life* ('He will be in prison for life')

(2) The verbs are of saying, arranging, expecting, or wanting where the object has future reference. The adjuncts denote time *when*, time *duration*, and time *frequency*.

TIME *WHEN* (*cf* 8.43 Note)

TIME *DURATION*
They offered us the house *for the summer* ('that we could use the house for the summer')

TIME *FREQUENCY*
I suggest an informal discussion *occasionally* ('that there should be an informal discussion occasionally')

8.45
Other classes of adjuncts
Some classes of adjuncts are realized by prepositional phrases or clauses and either rarely or not at all by adverb phrases. For example, there are

adjuncts expressing purpose (6.28, 11.31), but there are few adverbs used in this way. (See Note below.) Other classes of adjuncts are realized by prepositional phrases only; for example, adjuncts expressing source or origin (6.30), as in

He took the book *from me*

Note

Perhaps *symbolically* ('for a symbolic purpose', 'as a symbol') and *experimentally* ('for an experimental purpose', 'as an experiment') in the following sentences are instances of adverbs used to denote purpose:

They *symbolically* buried the car as a protest against pollution
The teacher *experimentally* called the students by their first names

8.46
Relative positions of adjuncts
Where adjuncts cluster in final position, the normal order is

process – place – time

This order is exemplified in

He was working *with his shears* (process) *in the garden* (place) *the whole morning* (time).

Three other general principles apply to relative order whether within a class or between classes:

(1) The normal relative order can be changed to suit the desire for end-focus (14.2)

(2) A clause normally comes after other structures, since otherwise these would be interpreted as adjuncts of the clause:

We stood talking *for a very long time* (A$_1$) *where the fire had been* (A$_2$)

(3) Longer adjuncts tend to follow shorter adjuncts:

I was studying *earlier* (A$_1$) *in the university library* (A$_2$)

This principle often coincides with (1) and (2).

Adjuncts that can occur initially are often put in that position for reasons of information focus, but also to avoid having too many adjuncts in final position. We might, therefore, have moved the time adjunct in the first example of this section to initial position:

The whole morning he was working *with his shears in the garden*

It is not usual for more than one adjunct to be in initial position, but time and place adjuncts sometimes co-occur there:

> *In London, after the war,* damaged buildings were quickly demolished
>   and replaced by new ones

Viewpoint adjuncts also co-occur with other adjuncts in initial position:

> *Economically, in this century* our country has suffered many crises

Disjuncts
8.47
Most disjuncts are prepositional phrases (6.38 *ff*) or clauses (11.23 *ff*).
Disjuncts can be divided into two main classes: STYLE DISJUNCTS (by
far the smaller class) and ATTITUDINAL DISJUNCTS. Style disjuncts
convey the speaker's comment on the form of what he is saying, defining
in some way under what conditions he is speaking. Attitudinal disjuncts,
on the other hand, comment on the content of the communication.

Style disjuncts
8.48
Examples of the use of style disjuncts:

> *Seriously,* do you intend to resign?
> *Personally,* I don't approve of her
> *Strictly speaking,* nobody is allowed in here
> There are twelve people present, *to be precise*
> *If I may say so,* that dress doesn't suit you

The adverb phrase as style disjunct implies a verb of speaking of which
the subject is the *I* of the speaker. Thus, *very frankly* in

> *Very frankly,* I am tired

is equivalent to *I tell you very frankly.* In a question, *eg*

> *Very frankly,* is he tired?

the disjunct may be ambiguous. Here, *very frankly* corresponds to *I ask
you very frankly* or to the more probable *Tell me very frankly.*
  Common adverbs as style disjuncts include: *bluntly, briefly, candidly,
confidentially, frankly, generally, honestly, personally, seriously.*
  Style disjuncts normally appear initially.

8.49
For some adverb phrases as style disjuncts, we have a series corresponding to them in other structures. For example, in place of *frankly* in

> *Frankly,* he hasn't a chance

we could put:

> prepositional phrase – *in all frankness*
> infinitive clause – *to be frank, to speak frankly, to put it frankly*
> *-ing* participle clause – *frankly speaking, putting it frankly*
> *-ed* participle clause – *put frankly*
> finite verb clause – *if I may be frank, if I can speak frankly, if I can put it frankly*

For all of the adverbs listed in 8.48, corresponding particle constructions with *speaking* are available as style disjuncts, *eg: seriously ~ seriously speaking*. Many have infinitive clauses of the form *to be* plus the stem adjective, *eg: bluntly ~ to be blunt*. Those allowing such infinitive clauses have a corresponding finite clause with *if, eg: if I may be blunt*.

Note

[a] The style disjunct *generally* is to be distinguished from the time *frequency* adjunct *generally*, synonymous with *usually* (8.35). The style disjunct is exemplified in

> The committee interviewed the two writers. *Generally*, the writers were against censorship.

[b] The style disjunct *personally* is to be distinguished from the intensifier *personally*, which is synonymous with the appropriate reflexive form of the pronoun:

> I *personally/myself* have never been to New York

These are both to be distinguished from the adjunct *personally:*

> He signed the document *personally* ('in person')

Attitudinal disjuncts
8.50

Attitudinal disjuncts convey the speaker's comment on the content of what he is saying (*cf* 6.45, 11.45 *f*). They can generally appear only in declarative clauses:

> *Obviously*, nobody expected us to be here today
> *Understandably*, they were all annoyed when they read the letter
> He is *wisely* staying at home today
> They arrived, *to our surprise*, before we did
> *Of course*, nobody imagines that he will repay what he borrowed
> *To be sure*, we have heard many such promises before
> *Even more important*, he has control over the finances of the party
> They are not going to buy the house, *which is not surprising in view of its exorbitant price*
> *What is even more remarkable*, he manages to inspire confidence in the most suspicious people

Many of the adverb phrases are paraphrasable by constructions in which the adjective base is subject complement, expressing an attribute of the subject. The subject is the content of the original sentence or (the more usual form) anticipatory *it* with the original sentence postposed:

> *Unfortunately*, Bob rejected the offer
> $= \begin{cases} \text{That Bob rejected the offer } \textit{was unfortunate} \\ \textit{It was unfortunate} \text{ that Bob rejected the offer} \end{cases}$

Other such paraphrases are sometimes possible, *eg*
> *Rightly*, Bob rejected the offer
> $=$ *It was right* for Bob to reject the offer

And similar paraphrases, including some using the verb base, are possible for many prepositional phrases:

> *To our regret*, Bob rejected the offer
> $=$ *We regretted* that Bob rejected the offer

Common adverbs as attitudinal disjuncts are given below in semantic groups.

Group I: speaker's comment on the extent to which he believes that what he is saying is true.

(a) These express primarily a subjective view on the truth of what is said, usually the view of the speaker:

> *Certainly*, they have no right to be there ('I am certain that . . .')
> He has *probably* left by now ('I consider it probable that . . .')

Those expressing conviction: *admittedly, certainly, definitely, indeed, surely, undeniably, undoubtedly, unquestionably*
Those expressing some degree of doubt: *quite (etc) likely, maybe* (informal), *perhaps, possibly, presumably, reportedly, supposedly*

(b) These present degrees of conviction as open to objective evidence:

> *Obviously*, they have no right to be there ('It is obvious to me and to everybody else that . . .')

Those expressing conviction: *clearly, evidently, obviously, plainly*
Those expressing some degree of doubt: *apparently*

(c) These refer to the reality or lack of reality in what is said:

Those asserting the reality of what is said: *actually, really*
Those expressing a contrast with reality: *only apparently, ideally, nominally, officially, superficially, technically, theoretically*
Those expressing that what is being said is true in principle: *basically, essentially, fundamentally*

Group II: comment other than on the truth-value of what is said.

(a) These convey the attitude of the speaker without any necessary implication that the judgment applies to the subject of the sentence or indeed to the speaker. Thus,

> *Fortunately*, John returned the book yesterday

might imply that John was fortunate in doing so (perhaps he would have needed to pay a large fine otherwise) or that someone else (possibly, but not necessarily, the speaker) was fortunate as a result of John's action.

> *annoyingly, curiously, fortunately, funnily enough* (*enough* usual in BrE, obligatory in AmE), *happily* (formal), *hopefully* (esp AmE), *luckily, naturally, not unnaturally, preferably, strangely, surprisingly, understandably, unfortunately, unhappily* (formal), *unluckily*

(b) These convey the speaker's attitude, with an implication that the judgment applies to the subject of the sentence. Thus,

> *Wisely*, John returned the book yesterday

implies that the speaker considers the action as wise and he also considers John wise for doing the action.

> *rightly, wrongly, foolishly, wisely*

Adverbs with an *-ing* participle base, *eg: surprisingly*, are the most productive class of adverbs as attitudinal disjuncts.

While attitudinal disjuncts can appear in almost any position, the normal position for most is initial. However, some adverb phrases in [Ia], *eg: probably, possibly*, and all in [IIb], *eg: rightly*, normally occur at *M2* (8.3).

8.51
The semantic distinction between adverbs in Groups I (*eg: certainly, clearly*) and II (*eg: fortunately, wisely*) is reflected in the fact that it is possible to use putative *should* (3.50) in the correspondences of Group II. If *should* is inserted in correspondences of Group I, it conveys obligation and alters the meaning of the sentence radically.

Group I
> *Clearly*, he is behaving well
>> = *It is clear* that he is behaving well
>> ≠ *It is clear that* he *should* be behaving well ('ought to be behaving well')

Group II

Fortunately, he is behaving well

$$= It\ is\ fortunate\ that\ he \begin{Bmatrix} is \\ should\ be \end{Bmatrix} behaving\ well$$

Putative *should* is excluded from Group I correspondences, where the factual basis of what is said is asserted or questioned, whereas it is admitted in Group II correspondences, where an opinion is expressed.

Note

[a] *Surely* is commonly used to invite agreement from the person or persons addressed.

[b] *Naturally* and *not unnaturally* are paraphrasable by 'as might have been expected' or 'of course'. They do not correspond to *it is natural* or *it is not unnatural*.

8.52

The difference in meaning between Subgroups IIa (*eg: surprisingly*) and IIb (*eg: rightly*) is reflected in the fact that only in IIb can we make a paraphrase that relates to the subject of the clause:

Subgroup IIa

> *Surprisingly*, John returned the money
> = *It was surprising* that John should have returned the money
> ≠ **John was surprising* to return the money

Subgroup IIb

> *Rightly*, John returned the money
> = *It was right* that John should have returned the money
> = *John was right* to return the money

The predication applies to the agent in a passive sentence, whether the latter is present or recoverable or indefinite. Hence, we can have the following paraphrases:

> *Rightly*, the money was returned (by John/someone)
> = *John/someone was right* to return the money

Conjuncts
8.53

Most conjuncts are adverb phrases or prepositional phrases. For distinctions between conjuncts and conjunctions, see 9.10 *ff*.

Examples of the use of conjuncts are given below, followed by a list of common conjuncts, which are grouped according to their subclasses with references to the sections in Chapter 10 where their role is discussed:

I'd like you to do two things for me. *First*, phone the office and tell them I'll be late. *Secondly*, order a taxi to be here in about half an hour.

You can tell him from me that I'm not going to put up with his complaints any longer. *What's more*, I'm going to tell him that myself when I see him tomorrow.

I see that you've given him an excellent report. You're satisfied with his work *then*, are you?

I took him to the zoo early this morning and then we went to see a circus. *All in all*, he's had a very good time today.

It was a very difficult examination. *Nevertheless*, he passed it with distinction.

He doesn't need any money from us. *On the contrary*, we should be going to him for a loan.

ENUMERATIVE (10.10): *first, second, third . . .; first(ly), secondly, thirdly . . .; one, two, three* (especially in learned and technical use); *a, b, c* (especially in learned and technical use); *for one thing . . . (and) for another (thing); for a start* (informal); *to begin with, to start with; in the first place, in the second place; next, then; finally, last, lastly; to conclude* (formal)

REINFORCING (10.11): *also, furthermore, moreover, then* (informal, especially spoken), *in addition, above all, what is more*

EQUATIVE (10.11): *equally, likewise, similarly, in the same way*

TRANSITIONAL (10.13): *by the way, incidentally*

SUMMATIVE (10.14): *then, (all) in all, in conclusion, to sum up*

APPOSITION (10.15, *cf.* also 9.48): *namely* (often abbreviated to *viz* in formal written English), *in other words, for example* (often abbreviated to *e.g.* or *eg*), *for instance, that is* (often abbreviated to *i.e.* or *ie* in specialized written English), *that is to say*

RESULT (10.16): *consequently, hence* (formal), *so* (informal), *therefore, thus* (formal), *as a result,* [*somehow* ('for some reason or other')]

INFERENTIAL (10.17): *else, otherwise, then, in other words, in that case*

REFORMULATORY (10.18): *better, rather, in other words*

REPLACIVE (10.18): *alternatively, rather, on the other hand*

ANTITHETIC (10.20): *instead* (blend of antithetic with replacive), *then, on the contrary, in contrast, by comparison, (on the one hand . . .) on the other hand*

CONCESSIVE (10.21 *ff*): *anyhow* (informal), *anyway* (informal), *besides* (blend of reinforcing with concessive), *else, however, neverthe-*

less, still, though, yet, in any case, at any rate, in spite of that, after all, on the other hand, all the same

TEMPORAL TRANSITION (10.5): *meantime, meanwhile, in the meantime*

Note

[a] *Somehow* has been listed with result conjuncts because it is closest to them semantically. It differs from all other conjuncts in not indicating a relationship between its clause and what precedes:

Somehow I don't trust him ('for some reason or other')

Somehow is used when the reason is not made explicit in the preceding context.

[b] *On the other* is an alternative form of *on the other hand* when it is correlative to *on the one hand.*

8.54
Positions of conjuncts

The normal position for most conjuncts is initial. In that position they are usually separated from what follows by a tone unit boundary in speech or a comma in writing. In other positions, they may be in an independent tone unit or enclosed in commas to prevent confusion with homonyms or contribute towards indicating information focus.

Some conjuncts are restricted, or virtually restricted, to initial position: *again, also, altogether, besides, better, else, equally, further, hence, likewise, more, only, overall, similarly, so, still, then* (antithetic), *yet.*

Medial positions are rare for most conjuncts, and final position rarer still. Those that readily occur finally include *anyhow, anyway, otherwise,* and (commonly) *though.* The last two frequently appear medially.

Virtually all conjuncts can appear with questions, most of them initially:

Anyway, do you know the answer?
Will you *therefore* resign?

Note

So, yet, only, and *else* are distinguished by the punctuation convention that allows them to be separated from the previous clause by a comma where other conjuncts would require a more major mark of punctuation (App III.2), *eg: They thought he wasn't coming, so they left without him.* Compare: *They thought he wasn't coming; therefore they left without him,* where at least a semi-colon is required between the two clauses. (Notice that *else* is normally, though not necessarily, preceded by the coordinator *or, eg: They must be satisfied, or else they would have complained by now.*)

So, yet, and *else* usually occur without intonation or punctuation separation from what follows. However, when *so* signals a general inference from the previous linguistic context and might be paraphrased by 'it follows from what has been said', it is often marked by punctuation and intonation separation:

So, you think you know best (informal)

For *so* and *yet* in relation to coordinators, see 9.10–15.

8.55
Conjuncts as correlatives

Sometimes the logical relationship between a subordinate clause and the following superordinate clause is emphasized by adding a conjunct to the latter:

Though he is poor, *yet* he is satisfied with his situation

The sentences with the subordinator alone and the conjunct *yet* alone are similar in meaning:

Though he is poor, he is satisfied with his situation
He is poor, *yet* he is satisfied with his situation

The major difference is that the second states his poverty as a fact, whereas in the first his poverty is presupposed as given information (*cf* 14.4).

The conjuncts that reinforce particular subordinators (11.7) are shown below. It is more usual to reinforce condition and concession subordinators than cause and time subordinators.

condition: if ... then
concession: although/(even) though/ ⎫ ⎰yet/still/however/
            while/granted (that)/ ⎬ ... ⎱nevertheless/nonetheless/
            even if   ⎭   ⎰notwithstanding/anyway/
                                         ⎱anyhow
cause: because/seeing (that) ... ⎰therefore/hence/accordingly/
                                ⎱ consequently
time: while ... meanwhile/meantime

Correlations with concession and cause are chiefly found in formal use.

Note
Certain other expressions with concessive force may correlate with a concessive conjunct, for example, *true, clearly,* or *certainly, cf* 10.22.

8.56
Conjunctions for clauses with conjuncts

A clause containing a conjunct may be linked to a preceding clause by one of the coordinators (*and, or, but*). The following conjuncts seem to be limited to the specified coordinators:

and so   *or + else/again* (replacive)

but + however/then (antithetic)/*though*
and/but + besides/still/yet/nevertheless

Two of these conjuncts – *however* and *though* – cannot follow the conjunction immediately. That is to say, if *but* is the coordinator, *however* and *though* cannot be initial, although either can be if there is no preceding conjunction. We can therefore have:

You can phone the doctor if you like, *but* I very much doubt,
however, whether he will come out on a Saturday night.
You can phone the doctor if you like. *However*, I very much
doubt whether he will come out on a Saturday night.

but not

*You can phone the doctor if you like, *but*, *however*, I very much doubt
whether he will come out on a Saturday night.

Conjuncts occasionally occur in dependent finite clauses; *eg*

(a) Adverbial clauses:

I met him in the park, when, *however*, we had no time to speak

(b) Restrictive relative clauses:

He was considered a man who might *anyway* break his promise

(c) Non-restrictive relative clauses:

I'm inviting Peter, who is a student, and who *therefore*
cannot afford to spend too much money.

Bibliographical note

Some recent contributions on adverbs: Bolinger (1972); Greenbaum (1969) and (1970);
Jacobson (1964).

NINE
COORDINATION AND APPOSITION

9.1

This chapter is devoted primarily to coordination and apposition. But since these often involve ellipsis, it seems convenient to bring together here other cases of ellipsis except those discussed under sentence connection (10.29 *ff*, 10.44 *ff*), comparison (11.37 *ff*), the adjective as head of noun phrase (5.6 *ff*), and the genitive (4.75).

Ellipsis is most commonly used to avoid repetition, and in this respect it is like substitution. For example, we can avoid the repetition of *sing* in

She might sing, but I don't think she will (sing)

not only by the ellipsis of the word but also by the use of a pro-form:

She might sing, but I don't think she will *do so*

Another important reason for ellipsis is that by omitting shared items attention is focused on new material:

A: Have you spoken to him?   B: (I have) Not yet (spoken to him).

Ellipsis dependent on linguistic context
9.2
Adverbial finite clause

In adverbial finite clauses the whole of the predication or part of it can be omitted (*cf* 9.23 *ff*):

I'm happy *if you are* (happy)
Mary is dusting the furniture *because Alice won't* (dust the furniture)

But we cannot ellipt merely the object:

*I'll open an account *if you'll open* (an account)

or merely the subject complement if the verb is other than *be:*

*He became a member, *since she became* (a member).

9.3
Adverbial non-finite and verbless clauses
The subject (co-referential with that of the superordinate clause) and an appropriate form of *be* are ellipted in:

(1) participle clauses (11.3 *f*)

> *Although (he was) told to stop*, he kept on working

If the subordinator is not present, more than one subordinator can be supplied and there may be several possibilities for tense and aspect:

> *(If/When they are) Punished*, they will not cooperate
> *Although living many miles away*, he attended the course
> = *Although he is living/was living/lives/lived many miles away*, he attended the course

(2) verbless clauses (11.5)

> *While (he was) at Oxford*, he was active in the dramatic society

9.4
Postmodification
Postmodifying clauses or phrases (13.5 *ff*) can often be considered reduced relative clauses:

(1) postmodifying participle clauses:

> The police rounded up men *(who are/were) known to have been in the building at that time*
> The man *owning that car* will be fined for illegal parking ('who owns that car')

(2) postmodifying adjective phrases:

> The men *(who were) responsible for the administration of the school* refused to consider the matter

(3) postmodifying prepositional phrases:

> He spoke to *the girl (who was) from New York*

9.5
Supplementing and appended clauses
A supplementing clause can be regarded as an elliptical clause (usually parenthetic or an afterthought) for which the *whole* of the preceding or interrupted clause constitutes the ellipsis:

> I caught the train – *just*
> (= I caught the train. I only *just* caught the train.)

In an appended clause only *part* of the preceding or interrupted clause constitutes the ellipsis, and an additional clause constituent is present:

> They are meant to wound, *perhaps to kill*
> (= They are meant to wound. They are *perhaps* meant *to kill*.)

9.6
Ellipsis not dependent on linguistic context
Some types of informal ellipsis are not dependent on the linguistic context. For example, *Serves you right* can be expanded to *It serves you right*. In most cases it is the initial word or words of a sentence that are ellipted. Other examples are given, with an indication of what is ellipted:

(I) Beg your pardon	(You) Had a good time?
(I am) Sorry I couldn't be there	(Are you) Looking for anybody?
(It's) Good to see you	(Is) Anything the matter?
(I've) Got to go now	(Does) Anybody need a lift?

Determiners, operators, and pronouns are commonly omitted in block language (7.66), *eg* in headlines, titles, notices. They are also commonly omitted in personal letters, in familiar style, in notes (*eg* of lectures), diaries, and (very drastically) in telegrams.

Note
Several other types of ellipsis found only in familiar style in speech involve particular lexical items:

(1) ellipsis of an article: (*The*) *Fact is we don't know what to do;*
(2) ellipsis of a preposition: (*Of*) *Course he's there;* ellipsis that includes part of a word: *'Fraid* (= *I'm afraid*) *I won't be there*. In contrast to the last example, there are many instances where the clipped form of a word is used in all but the most formal styles (App I.44): (*tele*)*phone, photo*(*graph*).

Coordination
9.7
Syndetic and asyndetic coordination
The term *coordination* is used by some grammarians for both syndetic coordination, as in [1] – when *coordinators* (*coordinating conjunctions*) are present – and asyndetic coordination, as in [2] – when coordinators are absent but could be supplied:

> *Slowly and stealthily*, he crept towards his victim [1]
> *Slowly, stealthily*, he crept towards his victim   [2]

Coordinated units are termed *conjoins*.

9.8
Coordination and subordination

Explicit indicators of subordination are termed *subordinating conjunctions* or *subordinators*. Both coordination and subordination involve the linking of units; but, with the latter, one of the units is subordinated to the other. Thus, in *his first and best novel* each of the coordinated adjectives is a premodifier of *novel*. On the other hand, in *his first good novel* the adjective *first* does not modify *novel* directly; it modifies *good novel* and *good* in turn modifies *novel*. Thus, there is a hierarchy in relationships (*cf* 13.38) and *first good* are not coordinated.

Similar semantic relationships are found in both coordination and subordination:

> He tried hard, *but* he failed   [1]
> *Although* he tried hard, he failed   [2]

The concessive–result relationship is the same for [1] and [2], though the ordering of the relationship is different. Moreover, the same semantic relationship between the clauses may be indicated by a conjunct (8.2). Thus, the conjunct *yet* in [3] has a very similar force to *but* in [1]:

> He tried hard, *yet* he failed   [3]

Sentence [3] is an asyndetic coordination which can become syndetic with the addition of *but:*

> He tried hard, *but yet* he failed

Clausal coordination
Coordinators
9.9

In what follows we are concerned with clausal coordination. For the use of conjunctions in phrasal coordination, see 9.31 *ff*. There are three coordinators: *and, or, but*. *And* and *or* are the central coordinators from which *but* differs in some respects. On the gradient between the 'pure' coordinators and the 'pure' subordinators are *for* and *so that* (in the sense 'with the result that').

9.10
RESTRICTED TO INITIAL POSITION
The clause coordinators are restricted to initial position in the clause:

> John plays the guitar, *and* his sister plays the piano

This is generally true of conjunctions and also of some conjuncts (notably *yet* and *so*), but it is not true of most conjuncts, *eg: moreover:*

> John plays the guitar; his sister, *moreover*, plays the piano.

Note

The conjunctions *though*, *as*, and *that* are exceptional in appearing non-initially in certain circumstances (11.9):

   Though he is poor, he is happy ~ Poor *though* he is, he is happy

Although, unlike *though*, is immobile:

   *Poor *although* he is, he is happy

9.11

COORDINATED CLAUSES SEQUENTIALLY FIXED

Clauses beginning with a coordinator cannot be moved in front of the preceding clause without producing unacceptable sentences or at least changing the relationships of the clauses:

   They are living in England *or* they are spending a vacation there
   Or they are spending a vacation there, they are living in England

This is also true for conjuncts, but not for most subordinators:

   **Nevertheless* John gave it away; Mary wanted it
   Although Mary wanted it, John gave it away

For and *so that* behave like coordinators. Contrast:

   **For* he was unhappy, he asked to be transferred
   Because he was unhappy, he asked to be transferred

Note

When clauses are linked by the coordinators and by *for* and *so that*, a pronoun in the first clause cannot have cataphoric (*ie* forward) reference to a noun in the second clause. For example, *she* cannot refer to *Mary* in

   She was very tired, *but Mary* stayed the whole evening

On the other hand, the pronoun can (but need not) have cataphoric reference when the clauses are joined by a subordinator:

   Although she was very tired, *Mary* stayed the whole evening

9.12

CONJUNCTIONS PRECEDING

The coordinators and also *for* and *so that* do not allow another conjunction to precede them. On the other hand, subordinators as well as conjuncts can be preceded by conjunctions. In [1] two clauses linked by the conjunct *yet* are also linked by *and*:

   He was unhappy about it, *and yet* he did what he was told   [1]

In [2] two subordinate clauses are linked by *and*, which precedes the second subordinator *because*:

   He asked to be transferred, *because* he was unhappy *and*
      because he saw no prospect of promotion   [2]

9.13
ELLIPSIS OF SUBJECT
The coordinators allow ellipsis of the subject of the clause they introduce
if the subject is co-referential with that of the preceding linked clause:

> I may see you tomorrow *or* (I) may phone later in the day

However, this does not apply to other conjunctions, including *for* and *so
that*, or to conjuncts other than *yet*, *so*, or *then* ('after that'):

> *He did not want it, *for* was obstinate
> They didn't like it, *yet* (they) said nothing

Note
A subordinator does not allow ellipsis even when its clause is linked by a coordinator:

> *She didn't tell him the bad news *because* he was tired *and because* looked unwell

If the second subordinator in the above sentence is omitted, ellipsis is normal:

> She didn't tell him the bad news *because* he was tired and looked unwell

Conjuncts otherwise not allowing ellipsis will do so if preceded by a coordinator:

> *He went to bed early, *nevertheless* felt tired
> He went to bed early, and nevertheless (he) felt tired

9.14
LINKING OF SUBORDINATE CLAUSES
As well as linking two main clauses, *and* and *or* can link subordinate
clauses:

> I wonder *whether* you should speak to him personally about the
>   matter *or whether* it is better to write to him

Such linking is not possible for conjuncts or for the other conjunctions
except *but*. *But*, however, is restricted to linking a maximum of two
clauses, and, even so, can link only certain types of subordinate clauses:

> He said *that* John would take them by car *but that* they might be late

9.15
LINKING OF MORE THAN TWO CLAUSES
Unlike *but*, and unlike the subordinators and the conjuncts, *and* and *or*
can link more than two clauses, and all but the final instance of these two
conjunctions can be omitted. Thus

> John might take them by car, Mary might go with them by bus,
>   *or* I might order a taxi for them

is interpreted as

> John might take them by car, *or* Mary might go with them by bus,
>   *or* I might order a taxi for them

9.16

SEMANTIC IMPLICATIONS OF COORDINATION BY *AND*

And denotes a relationship between the contents of clauses. We can usually make the relationship explicit by adding an adverbial. We illustrate this with parenthesized items in most of the following examples.

(1) The event in the second clause is a consequence or result of the event in the first:

> He heard an explosion *and* he (therefore) phoned the police

(2) The event in the second clause is chronologically sequent to the event in the first:

> She washed the dishes *and* (then) she dried them

(3) The second clause introduces a contrast. *And* could be replaced by *but* when this implication is present:

> Robert is secretive *and* (in contrast) David is candid

(4) The second clause is a comment on the first:

> They disliked John – *and* that's not surprising

(5) The second clause introduces an element of surprise in view of the content of the first:

> He tried hard *and* (yet) he failed

Here too, *but* could replace *and*.

(6) The first clause is a condition of the second:

> Give me some money *and* (then) I'll help you escape

The implication is shown by the paraphrase:

> Give me some money. If you do, (then) I'll help you escape

For the conditional implication to apply, it is usual that

> (a) The second clause has a modal auxiliary
> (b) The verb of the first clause is an imperative or contains a modal auxiliary.

(7) The second clause makes a point similar to the first:

> A trade agreement should be no problem, *and* (similarly) a cultural exchange could be arranged

(8) The second clause is a 'pure' addition to the first:

> He has long hair *and* (also) he wears jeans.

9.17
SEMANTIC IMPLICATIONS OF COORDINATION BY *OR*

(1) Usually *or* is EXCLUSIVE, expressing the idea that only one of the possibilities can be realized:

> You can sleep on the couch, *or* you can go to a hotel, *or* you can go back to London tonight

When the content of the sentence allows the realization of more than one alternative, we can exclude the combination by adding *either*:

> You can *either* boil an egg, *or* you can make some cheese sandwiches

Even so, a third clause can be added which explicitly allows both alternatives:

> You can *either* boil an egg, *or* you can make some cheese sandwiches, *or* you can do both

Some speakers avoid a sentence such as the last, because of prescriptive teaching that insists that *either* should accompany only two alternatives.

(2) Sometimes *or* is understood as INCLUSIVE, allowing the realization of a combination of the alternatives, and we can explicitly include the third possibility by a third clause:

> You can boil an egg, *or* you can make some cheese sandwiches, *or* you can do both

(3) The alternative expressed by *or* may be a restatement or a correction of what is said in the first conjoin:

> He began his educational career, *or*, in other words, he started to attend the local kindergarten
> They are enjoying themselves, *or* at least they appear to be enjoying themselves

(4) *Or* may imply a negative condition. Thus,

> Give me some money *or* I'll shoot

can be paraphrased by

> Give me some money. *If you don't*, I'll shoot.

This use of *or* is the negative of one use of *and* (9.16), but (unlike *and*) it does not require an imperative or modal auxiliary in the first clause:

> They liked the apartment *or* they wouldn't have stayed so long

9.18

SEMANTIC IMPLICATIONS OF COORDINATION BY *BUT*
But denotes a contrast.

(1) The contrast may be because what is said in the second conjoin
is unexpected in view of what is said in the first conjoin:

John is poor, *but* he is happy
He didn't want their help, *but* he had to accept it

(2) The contrast may be a restatement in affirmative terms of what has
been said or implied negatively in the first conjoin (9.20):

John didn't waste his time in the week before the exam, *but*
studied hard every evening

With this relationship, it is normal to ellipt the repeated subject in the
second clause.

With the first type of contrast, we can insert in the *but* clause concessive
conjuncts such as *yet ;* with the second type, we can insert the antithetic
conjunct *on the contrary* (*cf* 10.20).

9.19

Either . . . or, both . . . and, neither . . . nor
There are three common correlative pairs: *either . . . or*, where *either*
anticipates the alternative introduced by *or* (9.17); *both . . . and*, where
both anticipates the addition introduced by *and;* and *neither . . . nor*,
where *neither* negates the first clause and anticipates the additional negation introduced by *nor*. Thus, two clauses with *neither* in the first and *nor*
in the second are the equivalent of two negative clauses conjoined by *and:*

David *neither* loves Joan *nor* wants to marry her
= David does *not* love Joan and does *not* want to marry her

The position of the anticipatory element – *either, both, neither* –
generally indicates the scope of the alternative, addition, or additional
negation respectively, while the second element – *or, and, nor* – generally
introduces a truncated clause that has corresponding scope:

$$\text{He} \begin{bmatrix} either \\ both \\ neither \end{bmatrix} \text{has long hair} \begin{bmatrix} or \\ and \\ nor \end{bmatrix} \text{wears jeans}$$

$$\text{I can} \begin{bmatrix} either \\ both \\ neither \end{bmatrix} \text{knit} \begin{bmatrix} or \\ and \\ nor \end{bmatrix} \text{sew}$$

He smoked $\begin{bmatrix} either \\ both \\ neither \end{bmatrix}$ cigars $\begin{bmatrix} or \\ and \\ nor \end{bmatrix}$ cigarettes

You can write $\begin{bmatrix} either \\ both \\ neither \end{bmatrix}$ elegantly $\begin{bmatrix} or \\ and \\ nor \end{bmatrix}$ clearly

But, unlike *both*, anticipatory *either* and *neither* can be placed before the lexical verb even when the scope does not include the whole of the predication:

He $\begin{bmatrix} either \\ neither \end{bmatrix}$ smoked cigars $\begin{bmatrix} or \\ nor \end{bmatrix}$ cigarettes

You can $\begin{bmatrix} either \\ neither \end{bmatrix}$ write elegantly $\begin{bmatrix} or \\ nor \end{bmatrix}$ clearly

When *either* and *neither* are in the position before the lexical verb, the correlative clause introduced by *or* and *nor* can be a full clause, but in that case *nor* is followed by subject-operator inversion:

You can $\begin{bmatrix} either \\ neither \end{bmatrix}$ write elegantly, $\begin{bmatrix} or\ you\ can \\ nor\ can\ you \end{bmatrix}$ write clearly

Either differs from the other two anticipatory elements in that it can be positioned initially when the scope extends over the whole clause or over part of it. In such cases, the clause introduced by *or* is a full clause:

> *Either* John sleeps on the couch, *or* you must book a hotel room for him
> *Either* you can write elegantly, *or* you can write clearly
> *Either* Bob damaged the furniture *or* Peter did

Where, as in the last example, the predicates are identical, a near-equivalent but less common construction has phrasal coordination in the subject:

> *Either* Bob *or* Peter damaged the furniture

With *both* and *neither*, on the other hand, it is usual to have phrasal coordination in the subject (*cf* 9.42):

$\begin{bmatrix} Both \\ Neither \end{bmatrix}$ Bob $\begin{bmatrix} and \\ nor \end{bmatrix}$ Peter damaged the furniture

9.20
Other correlatives

Nor and (less commonly) *neither* correlate with an actual or implied negative in the previous clause. In this use, they are roughly interchangeable, and can be linked to preceding sentences by the conjunctions *and* or *but*, a possibility which excludes them from the class of coordinators (9.12). Both conjuncts require subject-operator inversion:

> He did *not* want to ask them for help; (but) *nor* could he do without
>   their help
> We owe *no* money, (and) *neither* do they

A clause introduced by either of these conjuncts can be separated from the previous clause by a heavier mark of punctuation than the comma.

Common anticipatory correlatives with *but* are *not* (and enclitic *-n't*) and *not only:*

> He did*n't* come to help, *but* to hinder us
> They *not only* broke into his office and stole his books, *but* they
>   (*also*) tore up his manuscripts

A more dramatic effect is achieved by positioning *not only* initially, with consequent subject-operator inversion:

> *Not only* did they break into his office and steal his books, *but* they
>   *also* tore up his manuscripts

Note

In a formal and mannered style, *nor* is occasionally found after an affirmative clause:

> It was hoped that all would be agreeable to that proposal. *Nor* was this hope
>   disappointed.

Ellipsis in coordinated clauses
9.21
ELLIPSIS OF SUBJECT (AND AUXILIARIES)
Identical subjects of coordinated clauses are ellipted:

> Peter ate a cheese sandwich and (Peter) drank a glass of beer

If the subjects and the auxiliaries are identical, ellipsis of both is normal:

> Mary has washed the dishes, (Mary has) dried them, and (Mary has)
>   put them in the cupboard

As is usual for ellipsis in coordination, the realized items are in the first clause and the ellipsis is in subsequent clauses.

Note

In subordinate clauses, ellipsis of subject alone or of subject with auxiliaries is generally not allowed (but *cf* 9.3 *f*):

> Jack was looking well although *he had* slept little
> *Jack was looking well although (had) slept little

9.22
ELLIPSIS OF AUXILIARY ONLY
If the subjects of coordinated clauses are different, there may be ellipsis of
an identical auxiliary:

> John *should* clean the shed and Peter (should) mow the lawn

If there is more than one auxiliary, it is normal for all to be ellipted:

> John *must have been* playing football and Mary (must have been) doing
> her homework

ELLIPSIS OF PREDICATE OR PREDICATION
9.23
Ellipsis of first part of predicate or predication
The first part of the predicate or of the predication may be ellipted,
and the subject may be ellipted as well. For pro-forms, see 10.29 *ff*.

(1) Verb phrase only or (less commonly) lexical verb only:

> Yesterday John *was given* a railway set, and Sue (was given)
>   a doll
> I *work* in a factory, and my brother (works) on a farm
> *She* will *work* today, and (she) may (work) tomorrow

If the clause contains an object with an object complement, the
subject must be ellipted as well:

> His suggestions made John happy, but (his suggestions made)
>   Mary angry
> **His suggestions made* John happy, but *his suggestions* Mary
>   angry

(2) Verb phrase plus subject complement:

> John *was the winner* in 1971, and Bob (was the winner) in 1972
> *It's cold* in December in England, but (it's cold) in July in New
>   Zealand

(3) Verb phrase/lexical verb plus direct object:

> Peter *is playing football* for his school and Paul (is playing
>   football) for his club
> Joan will *cook the meals* today and Barbara may (cook the
>   meals) tomorrow
> John will *meet my family* tonight and (John) will (meet my
>   family) again tomorrow

In certain contexts there can be ambiguity as to whether the subject and verb are ellipted or the verb and object are ellipted. For
example, the sentence

> Bob will interview some candidates this morning and Peter
>   this afternoon

can be interpreted as having either of these two kinds of ellipsis:

> *Bob will interview* some candidates this morning and (Bob will
>   interview) Peter this afternoon
> Bob *will interview some candidates* this morning and Peter
>   (will interview some candidates) this afternoon

9.24
Auxiliaries in predication ellipsis

The ellipted form of the auxiliary or lexical verb sometimes varies from
that of the realized form when one is 3rd person singular present and the
other is not:

> I *work* in a factory and my brother (work*s*) on a farm

In general, most co-occurrences of auxiliaries are allowed, for example:

> His friends already *belong* to the club and he will (*belong* to the
>   club) soon [present and modal]
> John may be *questioning* our motives, but Peter hasn't (*questioned*
>   our motives) [progressive and perfect]
> I *saw* your parents last week, but (I) haven't (*seen* your parents)
>   since [past and perfect]

One major exception is that an ellipted passive does not co-occur with
any of the other forms:

> Paul *denied* the charge, but the charge wasn't *denied* by his friends
> *Paul *denied* the charge, but the charge wasn't by his friends

9.25
Ellipsis of whole of predication

If the predication is ellipted completely, it is usual to have the predication
realized in the first clause and ellipted in subsequent clauses:

> George will *take the course* and Bob might (take the course) too
> *They* can *pay the full fee*, and (they) certainly should (pay the full fee),
>   but (they) probably won't (pay the full fee)

However, it is also possible to have the predication ellipted in the first
clause, in which case it is realized in some subsequent clause:

> George will (take the course), and Bob might, *take the course*

When the predication is ellipted in the first clause and the subject is ellipted in a subsequent clause, we have COMPLEX ELLIPSIS (*ie* ellipsis with both previous and subsequent realizations):

> *John* could have been (watching television), but (John) wasn't, *watching television*
> *They* no doubt can (pay the full fee), and (they) certainly should (pay the full fee), but (they) probably won't, *pay the full fee*
> *They* can (pay the full fee) and (they) should *pay the full fee*, but (they) won't (pay the full fee)

Note
The co-occurrence of auxiliaries with predication ellipsis is the same as when only the first part of the predication is ellipted (9.24), provided that the realized predication is in the first clause. However, if the realized predication is in the last clause, then only auxiliaries that take the same head of the verb phrase will normally co-occur. Occasionally one or more of the auxiliaries is also ellipted:

> *They* could (have saved more), and (they) should, *have saved more*

9.26
Ellipsis of direct object or subject complement
If the direct object alone is ellipted, the realized items must be in the last clause:

> John likes (Mary), and Peter hates, *Mary*
> *George* opened (the door) and (George) closed *the door*

Similarly, if the subject complement alone is ellipted, and the verb in the last clause is other than *be*, the realized items must be in the last clause:

> George was (angry), and Bob certainly seemed, *angry*
> *George* has been (the chairman), and (George) obviously could again become, *the chairman*

But it would be more common to have the pro-form *so* (10.36) in the second clause than to have any ellipsis:

> George was angry, and Bob certainly seemed *so*

When the verb in the last clause is *be*, the realized items can be either in the first clause or in the last clause:

> Bob seemed *angry*, and George certainly was (angry)
> John has recently become (a very hardworking student), and his brother always was, *a very hardworking student*

9.27
Ellipsis of adverbial
It is often more satisfactory to say that the scope of the adverbial is extended to subsequent clauses than to say that it is ellipted. This is

particularly so when the adverbial is positioned initially. For example, *unfortunately* in

Unfortunately, John is not at home and Sally is too busy to see you

appears to apply to a combination of the circumstances described in the two clauses rather than separately to each circumstance.

Conjuncts (8.53 *ff*), disjuncts (8.47 *ff*), and adjuncts of viewpoint (8.7), time (8.30 *ff*), and place (8.24 *ff*) commonly have extended scope:

If John is a member, *then* we should call on him and (we should) ask him to take us along [conjunct]
To my surprise, they didn't appoint him, and they didn't even interview him [disjunct]
Theoretically, I have no objections to his proposal and neither have any of my colleagues [viewpoint adjunct]
This afternoon Mary intends to take the children to the beach, but I am going to wash my car [time adjunct]
In our school, students and teachers get on well together, but this harmony is comparatively recent [place adjunct]

Initial position of these adverbials is usually interpreted as implying an extension of scope to subsequent coordinated (or for that matter, subordinated) clauses.

If the adverbials are in the middle of the clause or at the end of any but the last clause, they are generally interpreted as applying only to the clause in which they actually appear:

Joan is *perhaps* shopping and the children are at school
Joan is shopping, *perhaps*, and the children are at school
Joan is shopping, and the children are *perhaps* at school

However, if there is an ellipsis that links the two clauses more closely, the scope of the adverbial is extended to the second clause:

Mary is *perhaps* inside the supermarket and John outside

Process adjuncts (8.19 *ff*) are occasionally ellipted, with the realized items present in the last clause:

Bill drinks (sparingly), and Peter smokes, *sparingly*

If there is no comma or intonation break, the adjunct applies only to the second clause:

Mary spoke and John answered *rudely*

9.28
Ellipsis of head of noun phrase and of prepositional complement
The head of a noun phrase can be ellipted:

We wanted fried *fish*, but they gave us boiled (fish)
She wore the red *dress*, but the blue (dress) suits her better

This type of ellipsis is not limited to coordination:

He prefers Dutch *cheese* to Danish (cheese)

The complement of a prepositional phrase can be ellipted, with the realized complement in the second clause:

Bob is bored with (music), but Peter enjoys, *music*

9.29
Intonation and punctuation marking of ellipsis
The point where ellipsis has taken place is often marked in speech by an intonation break, that is to say, it co-occurs with the end of an intonation unit (App II.7).

When the ellipsis is in the second and subsequent clauses there is no intonation or punctuation marking for the ellipsis of the subject, or of the subject and immediately following elements:

Peter cooks his own meals and (Peter) washes his own clothes

It appears that a 'gap' is not felt when the ellipsis immediately follows the coordinator. In contrast, intonation marking is usually present in other cases of ellipsis, though punctuation marking is frequently absent:

John likes Mary, and Peter (likes) Susan
The men were drinking and the women (were) listening to music

When the ellipsis is in the first clause, there is usually intonation or punctuation marking both at the point of ellipsis and at the corresponding point in the fully realized clause:

Gerald likes (Sylvia), but Peter hates, Sylvia
He looked (tired), and (he) indeed was, tired
They can (be disciplined), (they) should (be disciplined), and (they) will be, disciplined

However, intonation and punctuation marking may be absent if the ellipsis results in the linking of two lexical verbs:

John found (a valuable stamp) and sold a valuable stamp

If the first verb can be interpreted as either transitive with ellipsis of the object or as intransitive, the presence of intonation or punctuation marking after the first verb suggests that it is intransitive and that there is therefore no ellipsis. Thus

Joan writes, and sings ballads

suggests that Joan writes various things and not necessarily ballads.

9.30
Semantic effect of ellipsis in coordinated clauses
Often the effect of ellipsis is no more than to suggest a closer connection
between the content of the clauses, but sometimes the effect is to indicate
that there is a combined process rather than two separate processes
(*cf* 9.41 *f*). Thus

Did Peter tell lies and hurt his friends?

implies that Peter's telling lies had the result that he hurt his friends.
The sentence is one question, and may be answered by *yes* or *no*. There is
no such implication in

Did Peter tell lies, and did he hurt his friends?

where Peter's telling lies and his hurting his friends are regarded as two
separate processes and there are two separate questions. Sometimes,
intonation may also be a factor. For example,

Shall we take the car or go by BÚS?

will probably be regarded as one question and could be answered by *No,
let's go by taxi*. On the other hand,

Shall we take the CÁR or go by BÙS?
Shall we take the CÁR or shall we go by BÙS?

would both be regarded as alternative questions (7.54 *f*), requiring as an
answer a choice between taking the car or going by bus.

The combinatory effect is common when the coordinated clauses are
direct or indirect questions or subordinate to another clause, or when
negation is involved.

Phrasal coordination
9.31
And and *or* are the main coordinators for phrasal coordination. *But*
is used only to link adjective phrases and adverb phrases:

A very long *but* unusually interesting journey
He wrote to them politely *but* firmly

Although we have suggested that there is ellipsis of the rest of the clause
when the verb phrases or parts of them are directly linked, we do not
posit ellipsis of the rest of the clause when other phrases are directly
conjoined by *and* and *or*. For example,

Peter and John played football

is not regarded as elliptical for

Peter played football and John played football

though, of course, the two sentences can be synonymous. Instead we regard *Peter and John* as a coordinated plural phrase functioning as subject of the sentence, analogous to *the boys* or the pro-form *they*. This type of coordination is phrasal coordination.

Note

Most subordinators cannot be used to link phrases, but two – *if* and *though* – are used quite freely to link adjective phrases and adverb phrases, as is the conjunct *yet*:

> A very pleasant *if* talkative child
> A shabby *though* comfortable armchair
> A simple *yet* devout prayer
> He looked at me kindly *if* somewhat sceptically
> He spoke firmly *though* pleasantly
> He drove quickly *yet* safely

Noun phrases
9.32
Noun phrases are commonly conjoined (13.37):

> *Peter and John* were there
> I write articles on current affairs for *newspapers and magazines*

If *I* (or its case variant) realizes one of the conjoins, conventions of politeness require that *I* should always appear last, and it is also common for *you* to be put first:

> *you or I; you or they; my friend and me; you, John, and me*

9.33
Within the noun phrase there may be ellipsis of the head. For example, in

> *Old and young men* were invited

the subject is elliptical for *old men and young men*.
   In contrast, there is no ellipsis, for the normal interpretation, in

> *Honest and clever students* always succeed

where the same students are both honest and clever. *Honest and clever* are therefore conjoined adjectives. Similarly, there is no ellipsis of the noun head with appositional coordination (7.21), as in

> I like teaching *a studious or hard-working undergraduate*

If merely two adjectives are conjoined, the coordinator *and* can be omitted with non-elliptical premodifying adjectives only. Contrast

> *Old, young men were invited
> Honest, clever students always succeed

The head of the noun phrase is very occasionally ellipted in the second conjoin when an adjective is present (*cf* 9.28):

> The strong nations and the weak (nations)

9.34

Ellipsis of a noun phrase head can occur with modifiers other than adjectives. For example, with postmodifying prepositional phrases:

> He has *workers from Ireland and* (*workers*) *from France* in his factory

and with numerals:

> I think there were *two* (*Prime Ministers*) *or three Prime Ministers*
>   who were assassinated, but I forget which

But phrasal coordination with numerals may express approximation, in which case there is no ellipsis: *one or two reasons, a bottle or two, ten or eleven students, three or four hundred people.*

There is a similar set of coordinate expressions of approximation with a pro-form in the second conjoin:

> They waited ten *or so* years
> He had a dollar *or so* to spend $\Big\}$ [units of measurement]

> He's drunk brandy *or something*
> He's drunk *or something* $\Big\}$ [nouns/adjectives/verbs]
> He coughed *or something*

> He went to New Orleans *or* $\left\{\begin{array}{l}\textit{somewhere}\\ \textit{some place}\ (\text{esp AmE})\end{array}\right\}$ [place adjunct]

> He left at ten *or some such time* [time adjunct]

For non-coordinate means of expressing approximation, see 5.26 *f*, 8.16 *f*.

9.35

As pro-forms, demonstratives can be linked to each other or to other determiners in the noun phrase, but the singular forms of the demonstratives are normally not linked to their corresponding plurals:

> this (book) and that book   these (chairs) and those chairs
> that (reason) or some other reason   these (students) or other students

A noun phrase can be linked to a pro-form in the second conjoin:

> his friends and mine   that method and the other
> her idea and John's   your proposals and others

Note

Possessive pronouns are not normally linked, except *his* followed by *her:*

> his or her friends   *but*   *our and their work

9.36

An article realized in the first conjoin of a noun phrase is often ellipted in the second conjoin:

a boy or (a) girl   the boys and (the) girls

When premodifiers are present, there can also be ellipsis of the head of the noun phrase in the first conjoin:

the old (men) and (the) young men

Other determiners can also be ellipted in the second conjoin:

my brother or (my) sister   other boys and (other) girls

9.37

It is normal for a premodifier realized in the first conjoin of a noun phrase to be ellipted in subsequent conjoins:

young boys and (young) girls

If we ellipt the premodifier, we must ellipt an accompanying determiner:

the young men and (the young) women

Hence,

the young men and the women

does not have ellipsis of the premodifier *young* in the second conjoin.

Similarly, a postmodifier is commonly ellipted, but it must be realized in the last conjoin and ellipted in previous conjoins:

boys (studying at this school) and girls studying at this school
cows (kept on our farm), bulls (kept on our farm), and pigs kept
 on our farm

If a determiner is present in the first conjoin, it can be either ellipted or retained in subsequent conjoins without affecting the ellipsis of the postmodifier:

the boys (studying at this school) and (the) girls studying at this school

Ellipsis can occur even if the determiners in the conjoins differ:

many boys (studying at this school) and some girls studying at this
 school

We can prevent the postmodifier from applying to the first conjoin by reversing the order of the conjoins:

some girls studying at this school and many boys

It is also possible to combine ellipsis of premodifier and postmodifier. For example, in place of

> the older boys studying at this school and the older girls studying at this school

we can have

> the older boys and the older girls studying at this school

with ellipsis of the postmodifier in the first conjoin; or

> the older boys and older girls studying at this school

with the additional ellipsis of the determiner in the second conjoin; or

> the older boys and girls studying at this school

with ellipsis of the premodifier as well. As we have seen before, separate determiners in the two conjoins do not allow the interpretation that there is ellipsis of any premodifier, and therefore

> the older boys and the girls studying at this school

does not have ellipsis of the premodifier *older* in the second conjoin.

9.38

And and *or* can link more than two noun phrases (*cf* 9.15), and all but the final instance of the conjunctions can be omitted:

> We thanked John, Peter, and Robert ('. . . John and Peter and Robert')
> They will employ John, Peter, or Robert ('. . . John or Peter or Robert')

The same applies to the coordination of other units:

> He was tall, dark and handsome
> You can spend your vacation at a hotel, in a cottage by the sea, or at a summer camp

9.39

Units other than noun phrases

  (1) Prepositional phrases:

> The attacks *in June and in July* failed
> He climbed *up the wall and over the wall*

If the two or more prepositions are identical, then those subsequent to the first can be ellipted:

> John complained *to Mary and Peter*

There are further possibilities of ellipsis:

He climbed *up and over the wall*
He climbed *up the wall and over*

(2) Other adverbials and dependent clauses:

You can wash it *manually or by using a machine*
They can call *this week or whenever they wish*

If two or more conjunctions are identical, those subsequent to the first can be ellipted:

If I can find the letter and (if) you are interested in it, I'll let you have it

On the other hand, if two clauses are identical except for their conjunctions, one of the clauses can be ellipted, normally the first, so that two conjunctions are linked:

I am prepared to meet them *when (they like) and where they like*

Sometimes the second clause is ellipted:

They will be arriving *before the show begins or after (the show begins)*

With relative clauses introduced by a preposition and *whom*, ellipsis of the rest of the first clause is not uncommon:

I want to know *by whom (it was ordered) and for whom it was ordered*

(3) Adjectives:

Adjectives can be conjoined when they are predicative:

She is *young and beautiful*

or attributive (*cf* 9.33):

His *clear and forceful* delivery impressed the audience

There can be ellipsis of a premodifier or of complementation:

very cheap and (very) gaudy
I am loath (to do it) and afraid to do it

Note

[a] In philosophical and mathematical discourse, *if and only if* (abbreviated *iff*) is a common combination with ellipsis of the first clause.

[b] *If and when* is a stereotyped expression conveying a strong possibility that the condition in the clause will be realized:

If and when he buys the car, I'll try to persuade him to buy the insurance from me

Other institutionalized conjoinings of conjunctions are *as and when, unless and until.*

9.40
Order in Phrasal Coordination
The relatively fixed order for subclasses of adjectives in premodification does not apply to coordinated strings, whether or not a coordinator is present. But the order of conjoined words can be influenced by a tendency for the shorter word to come first, *eg: big and ugly, cup and saucer*. There are also stereotyped coordinations where the conjoins are in virtually irreversible order, *eg: odds and ends; bread and butter; law and order; by hook or by crook; through thick and thin; knife, fork, and spoon*.

Combinatory and segregatory coordination
9.41
When conjoined phrases function in the clause, they may involve combinatory or segregatory coordination (*cf* 7.21 *f*, 9.30). The distinction applies to various types of conjoined phrases, but is perhaps clearest with noun phrases. When the coordination is segregatory, we can paraphrase the original sentence with two or more coordinated clauses. For example,

> *John and Mary* have a cold

is equivalent to

> John has a cold and Mary has a cold

But no analogous paraphrase is available for the combinatory coordination in

> *John and Mary* make a pleasant couple

Other examples of combinatory coordination:

> He gave all his books to *Tom and Alice*
> *Mary and Susan* are sisters

Among adjectives involving combinatory coordination, colour adjectives in particular allow a 'particoloured' interpretation:

> Our flag is *red, white, and blue* ('partly red, partly white, and partly blue')

In

> He painted the cars *black and white*

there is a combined process if each car is painted black and white, and separate processes if some cars are painted black and others white.

Note
[a] The distinction applies also to plural or collective noun phrases. Hence we find combined process in *They look alike* and separate process in *The children have a cold,*

while there is ambiguity in *They are married* (to each other or each to another person).

[*b*] For singular concord with some subjects involving combinatory coordination, see 7.22.

9.42

Certain markers explicitly indicate that the coordination is segregatory: *both, each, neither . . . nor, respective* (formal), *respectively* (formal).

While *John and Mary have won a prize* is ambiguous, we are left in no doubt that two prizes were won in

> *John and Mary each* have won a prize
> *John and Mary* have *each* won a prize
> *John and Mary* have won a prize *each*
> *Both John and Mary* have won a prize
> *John and Mary both* have won a prize
> *John and Mary* have *both* won a prize

Similarly, while *John and Mary didn't win a prize* is ambiguous, the sentence *Neither John nor Mary won a prize* makes it clear that two prizes are involved.

Respective is used as a premodifier in a plural noun phrase to indicate separate processes. For example, *John and Bob visited their respective uncles* can only mean that John visited his uncle or uncles and that Bob visited his uncle or uncles. Separate processes are similarly indicated if the subject is a plural noun phrase: *The boys visited their respective uncles.* The related noun phrases can even be in different clauses or in different sentences:

> *Bob and I* have had some serious trouble at school lately. *Our respective parents* are going to see the principal about the complaints.

Respectively is used to indicate which constituents go with which in the separate processes, the order of one linked set corresponding to the order of the other linked set. For example:

> John, Peter, and Robert play football, basketball, and baseball *respectively*
>   = John plays football, Peter plays basketball, and Robert plays baseball
> John and Peter are going to Paris and to Amsterdam *respectively*
>   = John is going to Paris and Peter is going to Amsterdam

9.43
Coordination of identical items
Identical items may be conjoined an indefinite number of times. With

comparatives of adjectives and adverbs susceptible of intensification or gradability, the effect is to express a continuing increase in degree (5.33):

He felt *more and more angry* = He felt increasingly angry
He drove *slower and slower* = He drove increasingly slowly

With verbs and the absolute forms of adverbs, the effect of coordination of identical items is to express a continuing or repetitive process:

They *knocked and knocked* (= They knocked repeatedly)
He talked *on and on and on* (= He talked on continuously)

If a noun is repeated once, the effect may be to suggest that different types can be distinguished:

There are *teachers and teachers* (= There are good and bad teachers)

9.44
Structures relating to coordination

There are several QUASI-COORDINATORS, most of which are related to comparative forms (11.37 *ff*):

as well as, as much as, rather than, more than

They sometimes resemble coordinators:

He publishes *as well as* prints his own books
He was pitied *rather than* disliked

But they can also have a prepositional or subordinating role, as in

As well as printing the books, he publishes them
Rather than cause trouble, I'm going to forget the whole affair

In subject position they do not normally bring about plural concord unless the first noun phrase is plural:

John, *as much as* his brothers, was responsible for the loss

In this respect, they resemble prepositions such as *with* or *in addition to*:

John, *with* his brothers, was responsible for the loss

Non-restrictive relative clauses have been considered as semantically equivalent to coordinate clauses. Such an assignment seems reasonable when the relative clause has the superordinate clause as its antecedent (13.12). Thus,

John didn't go to the show, *which is a pity*

is semantically equivalent to

John didn't go to the show, *and that is a pity*

Apposition
9.45

Apposition resembles coordination in linking units having grammatical affinity. But, in addition, for units to be *appositives*, they must normally be identical in reference or else the reference of one must be included in the reference of the other. For example, in

> *A neighbour, Fred Brick,* is on the telephone

a neighbour is identified as Fred Brick. The relationship underlying apposition is therefore an intensive relationship (7.6):

> *Fred Brick* is *a neighbour*

In many cases the co-reference and grammatical similarity will permit the omission of either appositive unit with a resultant acceptable and synonymous sentence:

> *A neighbour* is on the telephone
> *Fred Brick* is on the telephone

This is true even where, as commonly, the appositives are discontinuous:

> *An unusual present* awaited him, *a book on ethics*
> ~ *An unusual present* awaited him
> ~ *A book on ethics* awaited him

In some of the attribution examples (9.54), where an additional clause element is present in one of the units, it is not possible to meet the condition:

> *Norman Jones, at that time a student,* wrote several novels

Nor is it possible in other instances where the apposition is only partial:

> *The reason he gave, that he didn't notice the other car,* was unconvincing

where *The reason he gave was unconvincing* is not synonymous with *That he didn't notice the other car was unconvincing.* The two appositives need not have the same grammatical form to meet this condition. Thus, in the following sentence one of the appositives is a noun phrase, the other a non-finite clause:

> *Playing football on Sunday, his favourite exercise,* kept him fit

9.46
Non-restrictive and restrictive apposition

Apposition may be NON-RESTRICTIVE or RESTRICTIVE (*cf* 13.3). The appositives in non-restrictive apposition are in different information units, and the two appositives have different information value, one of them being subordinate in the distribution of information. Non-restrictive apposition is indicated in speech by separate tone units for the appositives and in writing by commas or more weighty punctuation, with one of the appositives marked as parenthetic. For example, the apposition is non-restrictive in

Mr Campbell, the lawyer, was here last night

while it is restrictive in

Mr Campbell the lawyer was here last night (*ie* Mr Campbell the lawyer as opposed to any other Mr Campbell we know)

9.47
More than two units

Occasionally there may be more than two units in apposition, as in

They returned to *their birthplace, their place of residence, the country of which they were citizens*

There may also be a hierarchy of appositional relationships, indicated in the following sentence by the various types of bracketing:

We now find { a new type of student: [the revolutionary – ⟨(the radical bent on changing the system) and (the anarchist bent on destroying it)⟩]}

9.48
Indicators of apposition

A number of expressions explicitly indicate apposition. They can be inserted between appositives, for example *namely* in

The passenger plane of the 1980s, namely *the supersonic jet,* will transform relations between peoples of the world

The indicators express certain semantic relationships between the appositives and therefore cannot be used for all cases of apposition. Common indicators are listed below, those marking the same or similar relationship being grouped together.

that is to say, that is, ie (formal and written); *namely, viz* (formal and written); *to wit* (formal, especially legal); *in other words; or, or rather, or better; and; as follows; for example, for instance, eg* (formal and written), *say, including, included, such as; especially, particularly, in particular, notably, chiefly, mainly, mostly; of*

Some of these indicators either precede or (less commonly) follow the second appositive:

The President of the United States, *in other words* Richard Nixon,
    was on television last night
The President of the United States, Richard Nixon *in other words*,
    was on television last night

But others can only precede the second appositive: *namely, and, or*
(*rather/better*), *as follows, including, such as, of,* and the abbreviated
forms, *ie, viz,* and *eg:*

Many professions, *such as* the legal profession, have established
    their own codes of professional conduct

Included can only follow the second appositive:

Many people, my sister *included,* won't forgive him for that

Non-restrictive apposition
9.49
Apposition is typically exemplified by noun phrases in non-restrictive
apposition. The semantic relationships between the appositives are dis-
played below, with one or two representative indicators of relation.

$$
\begin{cases}
\text{EQUIVALENCE} \\
(\textit{ie, in other words})
\end{cases}
\begin{cases}
\text{appellation } (\textit{namely; who/which}+\text{BE}) \\
\text{designation } (\textit{who/which}+\text{BE}) \\
\text{identification } (\textit{namely}) \\
\text{reformulation } (\textit{or})
\end{cases}
$$

ATTRIBUTION
(*who/which*+BE)

INCLUSION $\begin{cases} \text{exemplification } (\textit{for example}) \\ \text{particularization } (\textit{especially}) \end{cases}$

9.50
Appellation
With appellation, there is unique reference between the two appositives.
Both appositive noun phrases are commonly definite and the second is
typically a proper noun, but need not be:

The company commander, (that is to say) *Captain Madison,*
    assembled his men and announced their mission

The second appositive can be replaced by a corresponding relative clause:

The company commander, who was Captain Madison, assembled
    his men and announced their mission

It is more specific than the first, and hence the use of *namely,* an indicator
that introduces a more specific appositive:

The passenger plane of the 1980s, (namely) *the supersonic jet*, will
transform relations between peoples of the world

The second appositive is often a finite clause:

He told them *the good news:* (namely) *taxes are to be reduced*

9.51
Designation
With designation, there is also unique reference, but the second appositive is less specific than the first. Both appositives are commonly definite
noun phrases:

Captain Madison, (that is to say) *the company commander*, assembled
his men and announced their mission

Replacement of the second appositive by a corresponding relative clause
is again possible.

9.52
Identification
With identification, there is no unique equivalence. The second appositive
is more specific, identifying what is given in the first, which is typically
an indefinite noun phrase:

A company commander, (namely) *Captain Madison*, assembled his
men and announced their mission

Unlike the two previous types of equivalence apposition, replacement of
the second appositive by a corresponding relative clause is not possible.
A similar relationship obtains if the first appositive is, or contains, a pronoun referring to the second appositive:

We – (that is to say) *John and I* – intend to resign

Note
[a] There are obvious affinities between the second example of identification apposition and substitution constructions (restricted to informal spoken English) containing a pronoun and an appended noun phrase to which the pronoun refers
(14.38):

He's a complete idiot, *that brother of yours*
It went on far too long, *your game*

On a somewhat similar construction in familiar or dialectal use – *He's a complete
idiot, John is* – see 14.38.

There are also similarities between non-restrictive apposition and extraposed
constructions with anticipatory *it* (14.25 *f*):

It was good *to see you again*

[b] We sometimes have the converse of the substitution referred to in Note *a:* anticipatory substitution. In this type of construction (also restricted to informal spoken

English), a noun phrase is positioned initially, marked off by intonation or punctuation from what follows, and a pronoun substitutes for it in the relevant position within the sentence:

Your friend John, I saw *him* here last night
That play, *it* was terrible

[c] There are appositives other than noun phrases that in general resemble identification apposition, *eg*

They *summoned help – called the police*
They bought it *cheaply, for three dollars*

9.53
Reformulation

Reformulation is a rewording in the second appositive of the content of the first.

If the reformulation is based on linguistic knowledge, the second appositive is a synonymous expression:

a terminological inexactitude, in other words a lie
sound units of the language, technically phonemes

An example with appositive adjectives:

He drew a *triacontahedral*, or *thirty-sided*, figure

A synonymous word or phrase may replace the first formulation in order to avoid misinterpretation or provide a more familiar or a more technical term.

In addition to the markers it shares with other types of reformulation, this type admits a large range of expressions that specifically mark linguistic reformulation, *eg:*

(*more*) *simply, to put it simply, in more technical terms,*
   technically (*speaking*)

Apposition involving linguistic reformulation includes translations from foreign languages:

savoir (*know* in English)

If the reformulation is based on knowledge about the external world, the second appositive is a co-referential expression:

Fred – or Ginger as he is usually called
The United States of America, or America for short

The reformulation may be a correction of what was said. The correction may be due to an attempt at greater accuracy and precision in formulation:

His party controls *London, Greater London* that is to say

Examples with appositives other than noun phrases:

> She is *happier, very much happier,* than he is
> *Thirdly* and *lastly,* they would not accept his promise

9.54
Attribution

Attribution involves predication rather than equivalence. We can replace the second appositive by a corresponding relative clause. The second appositive is commonly an indefinite noun phrase:

> *The house, an imposing building,* dominated the street

But it can be definite:

> *Many soldiers, the cream of the battalion,* died in the attack

Certain kinds of construction are found only in attributive apposition:

(1) An article is absent from the second appositive:

> *Robinson, leader of the Democratic group on the committee,*
> refused to answer questions

This type is common in newspapers and magazines.

(2) An adverbial that is a clause constituent is added to the second appositive:

> *Your brother, obviously an expert on English grammar,* is
> highly praised in the book I am reading

(3) The second appositive has an internal structure of subject and either complement or adjunct. The participle *being* can be inserted between the two constituents of the appositive:

> *Jones and Peters, both (being) of unknown address,* were
> charged with the murder of Williamson
> At the entrance there are *two pillars, one (being) on each side*

Note

An attribution appositive is to be distinguished from a verbless adverbial clause (11.5) of which the following are examples:

> *An even-tempered man, Paul* nevertheless became extremely angry when
> he heard the news ('Though he was an even-tempered man')
> *The heir to a fortune, his friend* did not need to pass examinations ('Since he was
> the heir to a fortune')

These constructions differ from identification appositives (9.52) in that when they occur initially the subject of the sentence is not marked off from the predicate by intonation or punctuation separation.

9.55
Inclusion
Inclusion applies to cases of apposition where the reference of the first appositive is not identical with that of the second, but instead includes it. There are two types of inclusion: exemplification and particularization.

In exemplification, the second appositive exemplifies the more general term in the first appositive:

> *His excuses,* say *the breakdown of his car,* never seemed plausible

The explicit indicators of exemplification apposition are those in the group headed by *for example* in 9.48. Sometimes there may be ambiguity between exemplification and identification (9.52) if no indicator is present:

> *Famous men* (*De Gaulle, Churchill, Roosevelt*) have visited this
>   university

The two types of relationship are distinguished by the explicit indicators. Unlike exemplification, particularization requires an explicit indicator:

> The children liked *the animals,* PARTICULARLY *the monkeys*

The explicit indicators of particularization apposition are those in the group headed by *especially* in 9.48.

We should perhaps include here instances where a numeral or quantifier in the second appositive indicates the particularization (*cf* 9.54):

> *The two men,* ONE *a Dane,* were awarded medals
> *The soldiers,* SOME *drunk,* started fighting each other

Restrictive apposition
9.56
Strict restrictive apposition of noun phrases can take three forms of which the first is the most common:

(1) The first appositive is the more general expression and is preceded by a definite determiner (and possibly premodifier):

> that famous critic Paul Jones   the number three
> the novel *Great Expectations*   my good friend Bob

(2) The second appositive is preceded by a determiner, always *the,* and is more general than the first, as in *Paul Jones the critic.*

(3) Type 3 is like (1) but with omission of the determiner (esp AmE):

> Critic Paul Jones   Democratic leader Robinson

For titles with personal names, such as *Professor Brown,* see 4.25 for geographical names, see 4.27.

9.57

An important use of the first form of restrictive apposition is found with citations and names of books, films, etc:

the term 'heavy water'   the novel *Crime and Punishment*
the word 'if'

The first appositive is often absent:

'If' is a conjunction
'John and Mary' is a coordinated noun phrase
I'm reading *Crime and Punishment*

In such cases, we may assume an ellipsis of some general phrase such as 'the expression' or 'the citation form', or of an appropriate term in the case of titles, such as 'the book'. The singular number concord with 'John and Mary' can only be explained if we assume the ellipsis of a singular first appositive. (For further examples see 7.21.)

9.58

Restrictive apposition is common with such general noun phrases as *the fact, the idea, the view:*

The fact that he wouldn't betray his friends is very much to his credit
I don't agree with *the view that there is no advantage in being patient*
The question whether to confess or not troubled him
Your duty to report the accident takes precedence over everything else

With participle clauses, and sometimes with *wh*-clauses, *of* is used as an indicator:

The thought of playing against them arouses all my aggressive instincts
He didn't accept *the idea of working while he was studying*
His account of what he had done that year did not satisfy his colleague

Bibliographical note
Some recent contributions to coordination in general: Gleitman (1965); Hudson (1970); Karlsen (1959); Lakoff, R. (1971); Stockwell *et al* (1973), Ch 6. On the distinctions between coordinators, subordinators, and conjuncts, see Greenbaum (1969).

TEN

SENTENCE CONNECTION

Factors in sentence connection
10.1

There are many factors that interact in pointing to links between sentences. We illustrate this by examining a single paragraph. For ease of reference, the sentences are numbered.

[i] We sometimes thoughtlessly criticize a government announcement which refers to 'male persons over the age of eighteen years'. [ii] What ridiculous jargon, we think; why couldn't this pompous official have used the word 'man'! [iii] But the official may be forced into a jargon by the lack of precision of ordinary words. [iv] 'Man' may seem to be exactly the same as 'male person over the age of eighteen years', but would the latter be our automatic interpretation if the word 'man' had been used? [v] We often use it of even younger males of sixteen or seventeen, and it can be applied to a school-boy of ten ('the team is a man short'). [vi] It may simply mean 'brave person', as when we tell a little boy of four to 'stop crying and be a man'. [vii] Or it may mean 'human being', without regard to sex, as in a phrase like 'not fit for man or beast'. [viii] It may even mean a wooden disc – as in the game of draughts.

We shall refer to three factors that enter into sentence connection in the above paragraph: implication in the semantic content, lexical equivalence, and syntactic devices.

In speech, there are also prosodic features of connection (14.2 *ff*, App II.9, 11), which are ignored in the present treatment.

10.2

A reader searches for semantic relationships implied between sentences that are next to each other. For example, he finds that sentences [vi], [vii], and [viii] present a series of alternatives linked to the joint content of [v], but only in [vii] do we find the coordinator *or* marking the alternatives.

10.3

We can expect successive sentences to show some relationship through their vocabulary, some equivalence in the lexical items. The simplest form for such lexical equivalence is through the repetition of words or phrases. For example *man*, which first appears in [ii], recurs twice in [iv], and once in [v], [vi], and [vii].

Lexical equivalents are often synonyms or near-synonyms. Of course, the whole point of the paragraph is the degree of closeness in meaning between 'male persons over the age of eighteen years' – [i] and [iv] – and 'man'.

However, the lexical equivalents need not be synonyms. A more general term may be used as the equivalent of a more specific term (*human being* [vii] ~ *man* or *woman*). Or the relationship may be established in the context (*a government announcement* in [i] ~ *this pompous official* in [ii]). Or (to go outside the present illustration) it may depend on factual knowledge or pre-suppositions that the speaker assumes that his audience shares with him (*Paris* ~ *the capital of France; the youth* ~ *the nation's most precious asset*).

Furthermore, lexical connection between sentences may involve antonyms. For example, the connection between the following two sentences is largely dependent on the antithesis between *men* and *women:*

> Discrimination is undoubtedly practised against *women* in the field of scientific research. We don't find *men* complaining that they are not being interviewed for positions that they are clearly qualified to fill.

Finally, lexical items belonging to a particular set of items tend to co-occur. For example, *birth* and *baby:*

> We heard that the *birth* was easy. The *baby* is smaller than expected, but is in good health.

10.4

Our illustrative paragraph also contains syntactic devices for sentence connection. As we have said, *man* appears in five of the sentences. But 'man' as a word is also referred to by the pronoun *it* – twice in [v] and once in each of [vi], [vii], and [viii]. Thus *man* and its equivalents, lexical or syntactic, form a motif running through the paragraph.

In what follows we shall be primarily concerned with syntactic devices that help to connect sentences.

Time relaters
10.5
Time-relationships between sentences can be signalled by temporal adjec-

tives or adverbials or by tense, aspect and modality in verbs. Once a time-reference has been established, certain adjectives and adverbials may order subsequent information in relation to it. There are three major divisions of time-relationship:

(1) previous to given time-reference:

ADJECTIVES: *earlier, former, preceding, previous*

> *eg* He handed in a good essay. His *previous* essays were all poor. ('previous to that good essay')

ADVERBIALS: *already, as yet, before, earlier, first, formerly, previously, so far, yet;* phrases with pro-forms: *before that, before then, until now*

> *eg* I shall explain to you what happened. But *first* I must give you a cup of tea. ('before explaining what happened')

(2) simultaneous with given time-reference:

ADJECTIVES: *contemporary, simultaneous*

> *eg* The death of the president was reported this afternoon on Cairo radio. A *simultaneous* announcement was broadcast from Baghdad. ('simultaneous with the report of the death of the president on Cairo radio')

ADVERBIALS: *at present, at this point, meantime, meanwhile, in the meantime, now, presently* (esp AmE), *simultaneously, then,* relative *when*

> *eg* Several of the conspirators have been arrested but their leader is as yet unknown. *Meanwhile* the police are continuing their investigations into the political sympathies of the group. ('at the same time as the arrests are being made')

(3) subsequent to given time-reference:

ADJECTIVES: *following, later, next*

> *eg* I saw him on Friday and he seemed to be in perfect health. The *following* day he died. ('following the Friday just mentioned')

ADVERBIALS: *afterwards, again* ('after that'), *immediately, later next, since, then, after that*

> *eg* The manager went to a board meeting this morning. He was *then* due to catch a train to London. ('after the board meeting')

Words with temporal significance do not always have a connective function. Thus, somebody may say

John's *previous* wife died last year

without any prior mention of John's subsequent or present wife.

10.6

The ordinals constitute a temporal series of adjectives: *first, second, third* ..., with *next* as a substitute for any of the middle terms when moving up the series, and *final* or *last* as a substitute for the term for the end of the series. There is a corresponding series of adjuncts with *first* (also *at first* and, less commonly, *firstly*) as the beginning of the set; *next, then, later, afterwards,* as interchangeable middle terms; and *finally, lastly,* or *eventually* as markers of the end of the set.

10.7

Tense, aspect, and modality are discussed in 3.26 *ff.* Here we merely illustrate two features of the more obvious time-relationships signalled by these features of the verb phrase:

He *telephoned* the police. There *had been* an explosion.   [1]
Alice *turned on* the radio. John *was taking* a shower.   [2]

The past perfect of the verb in one sentence and the simple past in the other fix the temporal sequence of the information conveyed in the two sentences of [1]. The past perfect form allows the two sentences to appear in reverse sequence without any obscurity. In [2] the verb forms indicate that the action described in the first sentence took place during that described in the second sentence.

10.8
Place relaters

Words denoting place-relationship can play a part in sentence connection:

He examined the car. The *front* was slightly damaged. ('front *of the car*')

A few place adverbs, *here, there,* and relative *where,* are pro-forms, *eg:*

All my friends have been to Paris at least once. I am going *there* next summer for the first time. ('to Paris')

Logical connecters
10.9
And

The possible relationships between sentences linked by *and* are in general the same as those between clauses linked by *and* (9.16). *And* can link its sentence with a unit comprising several sentences, as in the following example, where *that* does not refer merely to the preceding sentence:

> It was a convention where the expected things were said, the predictable things were done. It was a convention where the middle class and the middle aged sat. It was a convention where there were few blacks and fewer beards. *And* that remains the Republican problem.

10.10
Enumeration

Enumerative conjuncts (8.53) indicate a listing of what is being said. Other listing conjuncts are also used in the set, as *furthermore* in

> He attacked the senator viciously, but he was never called before the committee. *First*, he was not an important enough figure. *Furthermore*, his criticism of the senator was public knowledge. *Finally*, there was no case for suggesting he was secretly infiltrating the government.

The addition of *far more importantly* in the following indicates that the statements are listed in ascending order of importance:

> Tom Brown is well known in this city. He has been a member of the city council for many years. *Secondly, and far more importantly*, he is a football player of national reputation.

There are several climactic additive conjuncts that mark the end of an ascending order: *above all, on top of it all, last but not least*.

We can indicate a descending order at the beginning of the series by such expressions as *first and foremost*, and *first and most important(ly)*. *Most important(ly)* and *most important(ly) of all* can occur either at the beginning or at the end of a series; they mark by their position whether the series is in ascending or descending order of importance.

It is obvious that *first(ly)*, *second(ly)*, *third(ly)*, etc, mark particular positions in a series. *To begin with, to start with*, and (informally) *for a start* can occur initially in a series, *next* and *then* only medially, and *last(ly), finally*, and (rather formally) *to conclude* only in final position. Reasons for what has been said can be linked by the correlatives *for one thing* . . . *(and) for another (thing)*, though the first of the pair can be used alone if the intention is to offer only one reason.

The enumeration may be expressed in ways that are more integrated within the structure of the sentence, as in the following formulaic expressions that are typical of formal spoken English:

> I want to begin by saying . . . I will conclude by saying . . .

The introductory expression may be related more closely to the preceding lexical content, as in *One reason is . . . the other reason is . . .* We might even have a main clause that serves as a link in the enumeration, *eg: There is still another thing* or *I want to make one final point.*

Noun phrases alone can be used for enumeration as well as the fuller forms, *eg: another thing, one final point.*

Addition
10.11
The addition relationship is often conveyed by the two subclasses of additive conjuncts, reinforcing and equative conjuncts (8.53):

> This food is very good and it's probably something that people wouldn't get at home. *Also*, it's not difficult to cook and it's quick to prepare.
> There has been no progress in the negotiations between the union and the employers. The union is determined to get more than the employers have proposed. *Equally*, the employers have absolutely no intention of increasing their final offer.

10.12
Additive adjuncts (8.8 *ff*) specify that part of the sentence is an addition to what has been previously mentioned or implied:

> The children read the play. They acted it *too*.
> He didn't explain what the letter signified. *Neither/Nor* did she.

Either, neither, and *nor* (9.20) differ from the others in requiring the two sentences they link to be negative but no other negative appears in the sentence containing *neither* or *nor*. *Too*, on the other hand, generally requires both to be positive. Thus, in the following sentences, *either, neither,* and *nor* are admissible (as are other additive adjuncts, such as *also*), but not *too:*

> A: The children didn't read the play.   B: *They didn't act it *too*.
> A: The children didn't read the play.   B: They *also* didn't act it.
> A: The children didn't read the play.   B: They didn't act it *either*.
> A: The children didn't read the play.   B: *Neither/Nor* did they act it.

10.13
Transition
Now introduces a new stage in the sequence of thought:

> We have settled that at last. *Now*, what was the other thing we wanted to discuss?

As for (in BrE also *as to*) introduces a related topic:

> Mary has several close friends. *As for* John, he is always surrounded
> by friends.

Certain other expressions mark a transition, but they can also begin discussion: *with reference to, with respect to, with regard to* (all formal).

Incidentally and *by the way* add explicitly that what is being said is a digression:

> The airlines charge half-price for students. *Incidentally*, I have already
> bought my ticket to New York.

Certain other expressions are commonly used for marking a transition to a new stage: *Let us now turn to . . .* (formal), *Regarding . . .* (formal), *To turn to . . .*; or to introduce a digression: *Talking/Speaking of . . .*, *That reminds me, . . .*

10.14
Summation

The final part of a unit may be a generalization or summing-up of what preceded. Summative conjuncts (8.53) and style disjuncts such as *in brief* (8.48 *f*) can be used to indicate this:

> The techniques discussed are valuable. Sensible stress is laid upon
> preparatory and follow-up work. Each chapter is supported by a
> well-selected bibliography. *In all*, this is an interesting and clearly
> written textbook that should prove extremely useful to geography
> teachers.

Integrated expressions include *I will sum up by saying, I shall conclude by saying.*

10.15
Apposition

Indicators of an apposition (9.48) can be used to refer back to previous sentences:

> It is important that young children should see things and not merely
> read about them. *For example*, it is a valuable educational
> experience to take them on a trip to a farm.

Integrated indications of certain types of apposition include *Another way of putting it is . . ., An example would be . . .*

10.16
Result

Several result conjuncts (8.53) indicate that a sentence expresses the consequence or result of what was said before.

They don't often use it over the weekend. *So* you can borrow it if
you want to.
They refused to pay the higher rent when an increase was
announced. *As a result*, they were evicted from their house.

Integrated indications include *The result (of that) is . . ., The consequence
(of that) was . . .*

10.17
Inference

An inference from what is implicit in the preceding sentence or sentences
can be indicated by an inferential conjunct (8.53):

A: I'm afraid there isn't much I can help you with.
  B: *In other words*, you don't want to be bothered.
A: He says he wants to marry Susan.
  B: *In that case*, he shouldn't be quarrelling with her all the time.

Other markers of inference include *If so, If not, That implies . . ., You can
conclude from that . . .*

10.18
Or: Reformulation and replacement

Or introduces a reformulation (a type of apposition, 9.53) or replacement. It can be followed by conjuncts that have the same function, or they
alone can be used.
  Examples of reformulatory conjuncts (8.53):

They are enjoying themselves. (*Or*) *Rather*, they appear to
be enjoying themselves.
You say you took the book without his permission. (*Or*) *In other
words*, you stole it.

Integrated markers of reformulation include *A better way of putting it
is . . ., It would be better to say . . .*
  Examples of replacive conjuncts (8.53):

I might do it. *Or again*, I might not.
In order to buy the car, I may draw on my savings, though I am
reluctant to do so. (*Or*) *On the other hand*, I might approach
my parents for a loan.

Integrated markers of replacement include *The alternative is . . ., It might
be better if . . .*

10.19
But

The relationships between sentences linked by *but* are the same as those

between clauses linked by *but* (9.18), though the contrast may be with a
preceding unit consisting of more than one sentence:

> More than one marriage had its beginnings in the Princess Theatre;
> more than one courtship was extended and perpetuated there.
> And it would be fair to say that a number of lives were shaped,
> to a degree, by the figures and fashions and personalities that
> flashed upon the screen. *But* years have a way of doing strange
> things to people, times and events and now the old Princess is
> little more than a misty memory.

10.20
Contrast

A contrast can be indicated by antithetic conjuncts (8.53). *On the contrary* emphasizes that the opposite is true:

> I didn't ask her to leave. *On the contrary,* I tried to persuade her to
> stay.

The other conjuncts introduce a comparison or contrast, without en-
tailing a denial of the validity of what preceded:

> He's rather foolish, I'm afraid. *By comparison,* she's a genius.
> A cut of one quarter in the total wages bill would bring only a five
> per cent saving in the ship's final cost. *By contrast,* the price
> difference between British and Japanese tankers is now as much
> as 25 per cent.

On the other hand often indicates contrast, especially when it is the second
of a correlative pair with *on the one hand:*

> *On the one hand,* you don't want to be too aggressive. *On the other
> hand,* you shouldn't be too timid.

Instead involves a contrast, though it also indicates a replacement. The
conjunct is illustrated in

> He doesn't study at all. *Instead,* he sits and day-dreams.

and the adjunct in

> He wanted a fishing-rod for his birthday. His father bought him a
> book *instead*. ('instead of a fishing-rod')

Concession
10.21

Concessive conjuncts (8.53) signal the unexpected, surprising nature of
what is being said in view of what was said before:

He has been in office for only a few months. He has, *however*,
  achieved more than any of his predecessors.
The term papers were very brief. *Still*, they were better than I
  expected.
I didn't invite your friend Bill to the party. *Besides*, he wouldn't
  have come.

Most of the concessive conjuncts can be paraphrased by a concessive
subordinate clause introduced by *though* or *although*; for example, with
the first pair of sentences above: *Though he has been in office for only a few
months, he has achieved more than any of his predecessors*. *Besides*, *anyhow*
(informal), and *anyway* (informal) indicate that an addition is being made
to a process of reasoning, but they are at the same time concessive. With
besides the additive implication is particularly prominent: it could be
paraphrased: 'if you don't find that point convincing, here's another
point.' *At any rate* may be roughly paraphrased as 'whatever happens' or
'regardless', and *after all* as 'this at least must be conceded'. When *else*
(following the conjunction *or*) is a concessive conjunct, it is equivalent
to 'even if not'.

Even is a concessive adjunct, but it is also additive:

Even John was there (John was there (surprisingly) in addition to
  others)
John will *even* sing a song if you ask him (John will sing a song in
  addition to other things he will do)

10.22

Certain disjuncts that assert the truth of their sentence are often used
to express some notion of concession, roughly equivalent to 'this at least
is true'. They include the attitudinal disjuncts *actually*, *admittedly*,
certainly, *really*, *in (actual) fact*, *of course* (8.50), and the style disjunct
strictly speaking. Sometimes the reservation is about a preceding sentence:

I wasn't called up by the army. *Actually*, I volunteered.

But the reservation may relate to what follows, and in such a case *but* or a
concessive conjunct is often found in the next sentence:

Of course, the book has some entertaining passages about the private
  lives of film stars. *But* on the whole it is extremely boring.

Integrated markers of this relationship include *I admit . . .*, *It is true
that . . .*

10.23

Several attitudinal disjuncts suggest that the context of the sentence to
which they are related may not be true in reality *eg: nominally, officially*,

technically, theoretically (8.50). A following sentence, which may then indicate what is said to be the real truth, may be marked for this purpose by *actually, really, in (actual) fact,* or *in reality.* For example:

OfFIcially, he is in charge. ÁCtually, his secretary does all the work.

Integrated markers of this relationship include *The official position was . . ., The theory was . . .*

10.24
For

The conjunction *for* (formal and usually literary) indicates that what is said is the reason for mentioning what has been said previously:

The vast majority of the competitors will be well content just to walk around at their own pace, stopping for rest or refreshment as required. *For* it is a long day's walk, and there is much to be said for enjoying the scenery at the same time.

Substitution
10.25

Like ellipsis (9.1), substitution is a device for abbreviating and for avoiding repetition. Most of the substitutes or PRO-FORMS within sentences are also used across sentences. They are normally unstressed. Hence, though a nucleus is commonly on the last word of a clause, it would not be usual to have a nucleus on a pro-form (App II.7). Contrast:

John upset a large beautiful vase. It fell and hurt BÒB.
A large beautiful vase fell on Bob's head. It was very heavy and HÙRT him.

Pro-forms for noun phrases and their constituents
10.26

The most obvious pro-forms for noun phrases are the 3rd person pronouns:

John and Mary stole a toy from my son. *Their* mother told *them* to return the toy, but *they* said it was *theirs.*
Dr Solway took *the student's* blood pressure that day. *He* also examined *his* lungs and heart.

It will be noticed that *he* substitutes for *Dr Solway* and *his* for *the student's.* We interpret the appropriate substitutions from the content of the sentences. For example, we can change the second sentence to transfer the substitutions:

Dr Solway took *the student's* blood pressure that day. *He* had
   felt sick during the night and came for *his* help as soon as the
   clinic opened.

In the second sentence, *he* now substitutes for *the student*, and *his* for *Dr
Solway's*. Where the reference of the pronoun is felt to be ambiguous, the
full form or a lexical equivalent can, of course, be used.

   The plurals of the 1st and 2nd person pronouns sometimes have as their
antecedent a noun phrase and can then be considered pro-forms:

John and I have finished our work. Can *we* start *our* lunch now?

A somewhat different situation exists when the 'antecedent' noun phrase
does not include the pronoun appearing in the next sentence:

You and John seem to be finished. Shall *we* have lunch now?

We here substitutes for an implied *you and John and I:* see further 4.82.
The singulars of the 1st and 2nd person pronouns are never pro-forms for
noun phrases: they merely replace themselves.

10.27
One can be a pro-form for a noun phrase head or for an indefinite noun
phrase (4.96). Certain other items can be pro-forms for noun phrases, in
particular *all, any, both, each, either, neither, some, none.* They can be
regarded as elliptical, since they can be expanded by *of* with some appropriate prepositional complement:

The boys applied for a scholarship. *Each (of them)* was able to
   present excellent references.
You told me there were *three pictures by Van Gogh* in the exhibition. But I didn't see *any (of his pictures)*.
My friends intend to make a career in business. *None (of my friends)*
   want to go to university.

There is an equivalent expansion which converts the pro-forms into determiners or predeterminers. This affects *all, both, each, either, neither,*
as in *all the boys, each boy.*

   The same is a pro-form for a noun phrase. The phrase it replaces must
be identical with the antecedent, but (except in dialect or archaic use) the
two phrases are usually not co-referential:

A: Can I have *a cup of black coffee with sugar,* please?
   B: Give me *the same,* please.

10.28
Pro-forms for adverbials
Some time relaters (10.5) can be pro-forms for time adjuncts, principally

then (='at that time'), but also *that* when it functions as subject and when the verb is intensive:

> We saw John *at eight on Monday evening*. We told him *then* that we
>   would be coming to the party.
> A: I'm meeting George for a drink *this evening*.
> B: *That* would be the best time to raise the subject.

Some place relaters (10.8) can be pro-forms for place adjuncts, principally *here* (='at/to this place'), and *there* (='at/to that place'), but also *that* (='that place') and *it* (='that place') when they function as subject and when the verb is intensive:

> Look *in the top drawer*. You'll probably find it *there*.
> They sat *right in front of the stage*. *That/It/There* was where the noise
>   was greatest.

The most common pro-forms for process adjuncts (8.19 *ff*) are *in that way*, *that way* (informal) and *like that:*

> She plays the piano *with great concentration and with great energy*.
>   I'm afraid she doesn't study *like that*. ('with great concentration . . .')
> *Always be frank and open to your colleagues*. *That way* you'll win
>   their trust and confidence. ('by always being frank . . .')

Pro-forms for predicate and predication
10.29
AUXILIARIES AS PRO-FORMS
Do is a pro-form for the predicate and carries tense and person distinctions:

> A: John drives a car.   B: I think BÒB *does* TÒO (=drives a car).

When functioning as operator for negation, interrogation, or emphasis (3.25), *do* can be considered as allowing ellipsis of the predication:

> A: John drives a car.   B: Bob doesn't (drive a car).

But it is convenient to treat cases of ellipsis together with the pro-form *do*.
   Other operators and auxiliaries allow ellipsis of the predication, but can also be treated together with the pro-forms:

> A: John can drive a car.   B: I think BÒB *can* (drive a car) TÒO.
> A: Was the entire building destroyed?   B: Yes, it *was* (destroyed).
> A: Have they seen the play?   B: No, they *haven't* (seen the play).
> A: I'm hungry.   B: *Are* you (hungry)?

There can be combinations of operator and auxiliaries with such ellipsis:

> A: Has the show started?   B: It *may have* (started).

A: Should she have been taking that medicine?   B: Yes, she *should* (*have* (*been* (taking the medicine))).

A: I've paid for the tickets.   B: You *shouldn't have* (paid for the tickets).

and of an operator with lexical *be* or (especially for BrE) lexical *have:*

A: Mary's in Chicago.   B: She *can't be* (in Chicago).

A: I wonder if you have a pen with you.   B: I *may* (*have* (a pen with me)).

Note

[a] The rules of co-occurrence of auxiliaries are the same for both coordinated clauses and coordinated sentences (9.24).

[b] There is also ellipsis with imperative *do* and *don't:*

    A: Can I have a piece of cake?   B: Please *do* (have a piece of cake).

10.30
Complex pro-forms

The substitute may be a COMPLEX PRO-FORM: a combination of one or more auxiliaries with the pro-forms *so*, *that*, or *it*.

The patterns of combination are exemplified below for declarative sentences. For patterns (i) and (ii), lexical *be*, passive *be*, or (especially for BrE, see Note *a* below) lexical *have* may combine with the pro-form *so*.

(i) *so do* type: *so* + auxiliary [+ subject]

    A: John drives a car.   B: *So does* BÒB.

    A: Mary will enter the competition.   B: *So will* JÒAN.

    A: Susan is obstinate.   B: *So is* SÀrah.

    A: My car was washed this morning.   B: *So was* MÌNE.

(ii) *so ... do* type: *so* [+ subject] + auxiliary

    A: Look! That man seems lost.   B: *So he* DÒES.

    A: I've found the reference.   B: *So you* HÀVE.

(iii) *do so* type: [subject +] (auxiliary +) *do* + *so*

    A: Have you sent your donation?   B: I *did so* yesterday.

    Peter can join our group.   I'm not sure whether DÀvid *can do so*.

(iv) *do that* type: [subject +] (auxiliary +) *do* + *that*

    A: Do you know who broke the television set?   B: I heard JÒHN *did that*.

    A: Sam called the meeting.   B: No, I think PÈter *may have done that*.

(v) *do it* type: [subject +] (auxiliary +) *do* + *it*

    A: Your brother said he was going to send a letter of protest to the President.   B: He *did it* last week.

    A: Gerald has told your father what you said.   B: He *shouldn't have done it*.

In BrE many allow also the possibility of adding *do* alone to (a) a modal, or (b) perfect *have:*

(a) A: Will you be attending the meeting this evening?
    B: I MÁY *do.*
(b) I didn't touch the television set. But PÈRcy *might have done.*

Note

[*a*] Lexical *have* admits the two pro-form phrases *so have* and *so . . . have* in addition to *have* alone:

A: John has a cold. B: $\begin{cases} \text{Yes, and Ì } have \text{ TòO.} \\ \text{Yes, and } so \text{ } have \text{ Ì.} \\ \text{Yes, } so \text{ he HÀS.} \end{cases}$

This use of *have* is much more common in BrE than in AmE, where it is formal as well as restricted in use (*cf* 3.19). The pro-forms *do, so do,* and *so . . . do* are also used in BrE, but are more common in AmE:

A: John has a cold. B: $\begin{cases} \text{Yes, and Ì } do \text{ TòO.} \\ \text{Yes, and } so \text{ } do \text{ Ì.} \\ \text{Yes, } so \text{ he DÒES.} \end{cases}$

[*b*] *So* is used as a synonym for *true,* but in that use it is not a pro-form:

A: Joan has very many friends. B: That isn't *so.*

10.31

PRO-FORMS IN RELATION TO VERB CLASSES

All lexical verbs allow substitution by *do* or other auxiliaries and by the complex pro-form types *so do* and *so . . . do.* But several of the verb classes established in 3.35 do not allow the full range of substitutions. For example, verbs of bodily sensation such as *feel* admit only the auxiliaries and the types *so do,* and *so . . . do:*

A: John *feels* much better.

B: $\begin{cases} \text{I KNÒW } he \text{ } does \text{ (} = \text{I know he feels much better).} \\ \text{Yes, and } so \text{ } do \text{ Ì.} \\ \text{Yes, } so \text{ he DÒES.} \end{cases}$

But we cannot substitute for them the other three types – *do so, do that,* and *do it:*

A: John *feels* much better.

B: *$\begin{cases} \text{I KNÒW he } does \text{ } so. \\ \text{Yes, he DÒES } that. \\ \text{Yes, he DÒES } it. \end{cases}$

Only activity and momentary verbs (3.35) – with other parts of the predication, if any – can be replaced by the full range of pro-forms:

A: John *abandoned* his car during the snowstorm. [activity verb]

B:
$\begin{cases} \text{I wonder \textsc{why} he } \textit{did} \left(\begin{Bmatrix} so \\ that \\ it \end{Bmatrix} \right). \\ \text{Yes, and } so\ did\ \hat{\text{I}}. \\ \text{Yes, } so \text{ he } \textsc{d\`id}. \text{ There it is.} \end{cases}$

A: Bob *kicked* the door several times. [momentary verb]

B:
$\begin{cases} \text{He \`Always } \textit{does} \left( \begin{Bmatrix} so \\ that \\ it \end{Bmatrix} \right) \text{ when he wants to attract} \\ \qquad\qquad\qquad\qquad\qquad\quad \text{attention.} \\ \text{Yes, and } so\ did\ \text{P\`eter.} \\ \text{Yes, } so \text{ he } \textsc{d\'id}. \text{ I can see the marks.} \end{cases}$

10.32
PRO-FORMS IN RELATION TO ADVERBIALS

The pro-forms need not cover a time or place adjunct in the antecedent predicate:

A: John paid for the tickets tonight.

B: Yes, he *did so* L\`AST week T\`OO. ('paid for the tickets')

The pro-forms exclude a conjunct or disjunct (8.2) that may be present in the antecedent predicate. In this respect we can contrast the adjunct *usually* with the disjunct *wisely:*

A: Bob *usually* walks to work.

B: *Does* he? (... *usually walk to work*)

A: Bob *wisely* walks to work.

B: *Does* he? (... *walk to work*)

10.33
CO-REFERENTIALITY OF SUBJECTS

The *so do* type is used only if the subject of the clause is *not* co-referential with that of the antecedent clause:

A: *John* buys his drinks at the local supermarket.

B: *So do* W\`E.

On the other hand, the *so ... do* type is used regardless of whether the subjects of the clauses are co-referential or not, though it is more common for them to be co-referential:

A: *John* buys his drinks at the local supermarket.

B:
$\begin{cases} \text{So he } \textsc{d\`oes}: \text{ I'd forgotten.} \\ So\ lots\ of\ \`other\ people\ do, \text{ I imagine.} \end{cases}$

The other substitution types are used whether or not the subject is co-referential with that of the antecedent clause.

Note
In some contexts, *so* may be ambiguous between the pro-form *so* and the result conjunct *so* (=therefore). For the latter, see 10.16.

10.34
OPERATOR IN PRO-FORMS
The *do so*, *do that*, and *do it* pro-forms require an additional *do* as operator:

A: Do they buy their drinks at the local supermarket?
    B: Yes, but WÈ *don't do so*.
A: John swims a lot.   B: *Does* BÒB *do that?*
A: Bill didn't damage his father's car.   B: Oh, but he *DÌD do it*.

Contrast other constructions where the pro-form contains or is an operator:

A: Some people can drive.   B: Yes, but PÈter *can't*.
A: Arnold has joined the club.   B: But *has* his WÍFE *done so?*

10.35
EXCLUSION OF PRO-FORM TYPES FROM CERTAIN CLAUSES
There are severe restrictions on the occurrence of auxiliaries as pro-forms in non-finite clauses:

A: Peter hunts rabbits.   B: $\begin{cases} \text{*Yes, I have noticed him } doing. \\ \text{*Yes, I have watched him } do. \\ \text{*I know. He wanted me } to\ do \text{ too.} \end{cases}$

Instead, we must use one of the complex pro-forms allowed by the particular verbs:

A: Peter hunts rabbits.   B: $\begin{cases} \text{Yes, I have noticed him } doing\ so. \\ \text{Yes, I have watched him } do\ that. \\ \text{I know. He wanted me } to\ do\ it, \text{ too.} \end{cases}$

An alternative to the pro-forms with the *to*-infinitive clause is ellipsis of the infinitive clause, *to* alone being retained:

A: Peter hunts rabbits.   B: I know. He wanted me *to*, also.

Neither the *so . . . do* nor the *so do* type can function in an imperative clause:

A: It's time to wash the dishes.   B: $\begin{cases} \text{*}So \text{ (you) } do. \\ \text{*}So\ do \text{ (you).} \\ \text{(You) } Do\ so. \end{cases}$

Pro-forms other than those from the *so do* and *so . . . do* types are commonly used in questions and in negative sentences. Where the negative sentence adds to what has been negated previously, *either* is commonly appended, or *neither/nor* placed initially (with obligatory subject-operator inversion) to achieve negation (8.10, 9.20):

A: Bob can't drive a car.   B: No, $\begin{cases} \text{jÒhn } \textit{can't do that } \text{èither.} \\ \left.\begin{array}{l} \text{Neither} \\ \text{Nor} \end{array}\right\} \textit{ can } \text{jÒhn } \textit{do that.} \end{cases}$

10.36
THE PRO-FORMS *NOT* AND *SO*

Not can be a negative pro-form for the predicate:

  A: Bill would have taken the book.
    B: Yes, but *not* tòm. (=Tom would not have taken the book)
  A: Bob will take it for you.
    B: No, *not* hìm. (=He will not take it for me)

In very formal speech the subjective case of the pronoun would be used instead of the objective case if the pronoun is the subject in the clause that is being replaced:

  A: John is a coward.   B: Yes, but not I. (=I am not a coward)

Not can also be a pro-form for the subject and part of the predicate:

  A: John wanted to pay for the tickets.
    B: True, but *not* for the dinner. (=but John did not want to pay for the dinner)

Not in *why not* and *if not* is a negative pro-form for the whole clause, while *so* is the pro-form for the equivalent of the whole clause in the case of *if so*, and (less commonly) *why so:*

  A: I don't want to go in.
    B: Why *not?* (=Why don't you want to go in?)

So is used as a pro-form for a direct object clause:

  Oxford is likely to win the next boat race. All my friends say *so*.
  (=that Oxford is likely to win the next boat race)

Not can often serve as the negative of *so* in this use:

  Many people believe that there will be another world war before the end of the century. My father thinks *so*, but I believe *not*.
  (My father thinks *that there will be another . . .*, but I believe *that there will not be another . . .*)

In this use, *not* is restricted mainly to verbs of belief or assumption (*cf* 11.58), while *so* extends also to some verbs of speaking. Verbs that commonly allow both *so* and *not* as pro-forms for the direct object clause include: *assume, believe, expect, fancy, guess, hope, imagine, presume, suppose, think, understand.*

So is also commonly used as a pro-form for a subject complement with the intensive verbs *become, appear, seem;* the last two also allow *not* as a pro-form:

A: I didn't think she was exceptionally shy.
  B: She wasn't at one time, but she has become *so* recently. (= become *exceptionally shy* recently)
A: Are they ready? B: It appears *not*. (= It appears *that they are not ready*)

Where transferred negation is possible (*cf* 11.58), it is preferred in informal use: *I don't think so.* The pro-form *not* is occasionally used with the verbs *say* and *tell*, but the use of the pro-form *so* with these verbs is much more frequent. Not all verbs of speaking allow even *so*. For example, we cannot say **He asked so.*

So in this use can take initial position with several verbs, particularly *say* (and also *believe* and *understand*, especially with *I* or *we* as subject):

So all my friends say *So* I understand

Note
Tell requires the presence of an indirect object before the pro-form (*cf* 12.31):

I told you so   *I told so

Discourse reference
10.37
There are a number of signals marking the identity between what is being said and what has been said before. They have been brought together here because they have in common a 'deictic' reference, that is to say, they point back (ANAPHORIC) or forward (CATAPHORIC) in discourse.

10.38
Sentence/clause reference
Common signals for sentence or clause reference:

anaphoric and cataphoric: *here, it, this*
anaphoric only: *that, the foregoing* (formal)
cataphoric only: *as follows, the following, thus*

ANAPHORIC EXAMPLES
Many years ago their wives quarrelled over some trivial matter, now long forgotten. But one word led to another and the

quarrel developed into a permanent rupture between them.
That's why the two men never visit each other's houses.
Many students never improve. They get no advice and therefore
they keep repeating the same mistakes. *It*'s a terrible
shame.
Students want to be shown connections between facts instead
of spending their time memorizing dates and formulas.
Reflecting *this*, the university is moving away from large
survey courses and breaking down academic fences in order
to show subjects relating to one another.

CATAPHORIC EXAMPLES
This should interest you, if you're still keen on boxing. The world
heavyweight championship is going to be held in Chicago
next June, so you should be able to watch it live.
Here is the news. A diplomat was kidnapped last night in
London ... (radio announcement)
It never should have happened. She went out and left the baby
unattended.
My arguments are *as follows* ...

Above and *below* are used in formal written discourse to indicate where
units of varying length and illustrations are to be found: *the arguments
given below* (perhaps referring to several sentences), *the diagrams below
illustrate* ... There is no determinable limit to the distance between them
and the place they refer to. *The above* is used with anaphoric reference
(but *the below has no corresponding use):

The above illustrates what we mean by ...

Note
The non-restrictive relative clause with sentential antecedent (13.12) is sometimes
made into a separate orthographic sentence:

*She has borrowed a history book. Which suggests that her teacher is having some
influence on her.*

Noun-phrase reference
10.39
Certain determiners can be used to signal that a noun phrase is referen-
tially equivalent to a previous noun phrase: *the, this, these, that, those*.
The noun phrases may have identical heads, but may be co-referential
without the heads being identical:

He bought *a battered, old black van* in 1970. What a lot of money
he earned with *that vehicle*.
Students are free to select *optional courses from any field that touches
on American studies. These options* are very popular.

The co-reference of two noun phrases may be emphasized by use of *identical, same, selfsame* (formal), *very:*

> He spoke to a meeting of *striking workers* that evening. *Those same workers* had previously refused to listen to his speeches.

These determiners and adjectives can be used to indicate identity of type rather than co-reference:

> He bought *a Jaguar XJ6*. I ordered *that same car* the previous year.

Such (5.27) is used specifically to indicate identity of type:

> They regularly get *The Daily Courier*. I wouldn't read *such a paper*.

Like plus *that* or *those* is also used anaphorically for identity of type, and postmodifies the noun-phrase head:

> They regularly take *The Daily Courier*. I wouldn't read *a paper like that*.

Like this and (informally) *this way* are used cataphorically:

> He told it $\begin{Bmatrix} like\ this \\ this\ way \end{Bmatrix}$: George was running down the road and . . .

10.40
The demonstratives can be used as pro-forms for noun phrases:

> I hear that you dislike his latest novel. I read *his first novel. That* was very boring, too.

Normally, demonstratives replace noun phrases with a human referent only in intensive clauses with a nominal complement:

> Will you try and help me find *Peter Williams? That*'s the man I was telling you about.

10.41
Former and *latter* (both mainly formal written English) are used anaphorically to single out one of two previous noun phrases:

> Bob and John were at the meeting. *The former* brought his wife with him. ('Bob')

If *the latter* were used instead, the reference would be to *John*. These two terms can also be used as reference signals when they premodify:

> Bill Singer and Tom Patterson were charged with being drunk and disorderly. *The latter student* had two previous convictions on such charges.

Similarly, when there are more than two previous noun phrases that might be referred to, the ordinals *first, second,* etc, and *last* can be used anaphorically to single out one of several phrases.

The ordinals and *former* and *latter* can also refer back to clausal units as well as noun phrases:

> He explained that he had lost a lot of money and that he had also quarrelled with his wife. *The former* seemed to have upset him more than *the latter.*

10.42

So and (rather informally) *that* can have anaphoric reference when they are intensifiers premodifying an adjective:

> There were two thousand people in the theatre. I didn't expect it to be *so/(all) that* full.

Such is used more commonly than *so* or *that* when the adjective is in a noun phrase (*cf* 5.27):

> ... I didn't expect *such* a large audience.

10.43
Comparison

The most obvious comparison signal is found in adjectives and adverbs, whether in the inflected forms or in the periphrastic forms with *more, most, as, less, least.* If the basis of comparison (5.32) is not made explicit in the clause, it can often be inferred from the previous context:

> Mary used to listen to records most of the time. Sally was a *more hardworking* student. (*than Mary was*)
> There were ten boys in the class. Bob was by far *the best.* (*of the ten boys in the class*)

Likewise, we must often look at the previous context for the basis of similarity or difference:

> John was the victim of a confidence trick. Bill was tricked *in the same way.* (*as John was tricked*)
> Tom had to be sent home. However, the *other* boys had behaved well. (*the boys other than Tom*)

Ellipsis in dialogue
10.44

Ellipsis in dialogue may take place under three conditions, which can occur in various combinations:

(1) REPETITION: the second speaker repeats what is said by the first.
(2) EXPANSION: the second speaker adds to what is said by the first.
(3) REPLACEMENT: the second speaker replaces what is said by the first with new material.

There is usually a choice in repetition between ellipsis, substitution, and the full form. We show the choice, giving optional items in parentheses and alternatives in braces. The categorization is not intended to be exhaustive, but to give typical examples of ellipsis.

Note
Ellipsis in coordinated clauses is dealt with in detail in 9.21 *ff*, and much of what is discussed there applies to ellipsis across sentences. Ellipsis of predicate and predication has been discussed in the relevant sections in this chapter (10.29 *ff*). Moreover, other instances of what could be considered ellipsis have been referred to in the course of this chapter, *eg* 10.8, 10.27, 10.43. Some of the examples that we give for dialogue could, of course, equally occur in sentences spoken or written by the same person.

10.45
Question and response
The usual function of a question in discourse is to request the listener to respond verbally with information that the questioner seeks. The link between question and response is often reinforced by ellipsis in the response, thereby avoiding repetition of material from the question and focusing attention on what is new.

(1) REPETITION
> A: Have you spoken to the doctor?
>
> B: (Yes,) *I have* $\left(\left\{\begin{array}{l} \text{spoken to} \left\{\begin{array}{l} \text{the doctor} \\ \text{him} \end{array}\right\} \\ \text{done so} \end{array}\right\}\right)$.

(2) EXPANSION
> A: Will they lose the game?
> B: *Probably* (they will (lose (the game)))

(3) REPLACEMENT
This most commonly occurs with *wh*-questions (7.52 *f*), where the Q-element is normally replaced in the response:

> A: Who told your father?   B: *Mary* $\left(\left\{\begin{array}{l} \text{told} \left\{\begin{array}{l} \text{my father} \\ \text{him} \end{array}\right\} \\ \text{did (so)} \end{array}\right\}\right)$.

COMBINATIONS include expansion and replacement:

A: When did he lose the key?

$$\text{B: } \textit{Probably } \left(\text{he} \left\{ \begin{array}{l} \text{lost} \left\{ \begin{array}{l} \text{the key} \\ \text{it} \end{array} \right\} \\ \text{did so} \end{array} \right\} \right) \textit{ last night.}$$

Where the response is merely repetition, *yes* alone is used as a substitute for repetition. *No* alone is a substitute for negation of repetition.

Neither ellipsis nor substitution need be factors in the connection between a question and the response to it. For example:

A: Can I help you, madam?
   B: Well, I'm looking for a pair of white gloves.

10.46
Statement and question
Questions are usually prompted by what was said before, though they may be stimulated by the situational context.

(1) REPETITION
   A: I'm studying grammar.   B: *ÁRE you* (studying grammar)?

(2) EXPANSION
   A: Peter will be there.

$$\text{B: } \textit{Are you SÚRE} \left(\left\{ \begin{array}{l} \text{(that)} \left\{ \begin{array}{l} \text{Peter} \\ \text{he} \end{array} \right\} \text{will (be there)} \\ \text{of that} \end{array} \right\} \right) ?$$

(3) REPLACEMENT
   A: It cost me twenty-five dollars.
   B: *HÓW much* (did it cost (you))?

COMBINATIONS include repetition and replacement:

   A: John told me what you did.

$$\text{B: } \textit{WHÓ told you} \left(\left\{ \begin{array}{l} \text{what I did} \\ \text{that} \end{array} \right\} \right) ?$$

10.47
Statement and statement
(1) REPETITION
   A: He's studying Latin.
   • B: (He's studying) *LÁTin!* He doesn't know his *ÒWN* language.

(2) EXPANSION
   A: He won't play.

$$\text{B: } \textit{I'd like to know why} \left(\left\{ \begin{array}{l} \text{he won't (play)} \\ \text{not} \end{array} \right\} \right).$$

(3) REPLACEMENT

A: They want the key now.

B: *No,* $\left(\text{they want} \left\{\begin{matrix}\text{the key}\\ \text{it}\end{matrix}\right\}\right)$ *tonight.*

COMBINATIONS include repetition, expansion, and replacement:

A: They paid fifty dollars for it.

B: *Oh no, they paid more* $\left(\left(\text{than} \left\{\begin{matrix}\text{fifty dollars}\\ \text{that}\end{matrix}\right\}\right) \text{(for it)}\right).$

10.48
Structural parallelism

If two or more sentences have identical or very similar structure, this parallelism connects the sentences, the connection being further reinforced by lexical equivalences and implications of semantic relationship (usually of contrast):

John put his career before his family. Bill put his family before his career.

Devices of structural parallelism are particularly common in mannered style. The parallel between sentences is more transparent (and hence the connection is more strongly indicated) if the word order is not the normal one, even if otherwise there is little structural similarity:

My paintings the visitors admired. *My sculptures* they disliked.

An apparent similarity in structure is sufficient to suggest an affinity between sentences:

My paintings the visitors admired. *My sculptures* irritated them.

The impression of a link between the two initial noun phrases (the first a direct object and the second a subject) is reinforced by the use of *my* in both phrases and the lexical set to which both *painting* and *sculpture* belong. The two sentences are further linked by semantic parallelism and by the pro-form *them* in the second sentence.

The last example above illustrates a combination of several devices: syntactic parallelism, semantic parallelism, lexical relationships, and substitution by a pro-form. The example serves to remind us of a point which we made at the beginning of the chapter, but which may have been obscured by our attention to devices in isolation: several devices – some of them perhaps syntactic – may be interacting to form links between sentences.

Bibliographical note

Some recent contributions on sentence connection in general: Crymes (1968), Karlsen (1959). On conjuncts and disjuncts, see Greenbaum (1969).

ELEVEN
THE COMPLEX SENTENCE

11.1
Coordination and subordination

Subordination is a non-symmetrical relation, holding between two clauses in such a way that one is a constituent or part of the other. Compare the coordination in

```
1                  1              2                   2
[I like John]     and           [John likes me]
1                  1              2                   2
['independent']                  ['independent']
```

with the subordination in

```
1                 2                          21
[I like John      [because John likes me]]
1                                            1
['superordinate' or 'independent' or 'main']
                  2                          2
                  ['subordinate' or 'dependent']
```

The above examples also illustrate the terms commonly associated with the clausal units distinguished.

The device of subordination enables us to organize multiple clause structures. Each subordinate clause may itself be superordinate to one or more other clauses, so that a hierarchy of clauses, one within another, may be built up, sometimes resulting in sentences of great complexity. A relatively simple example:

```
     X-        Y-              Z-          -Z-Y-X
    ( I think [ that you can do it { if you try } ] )
```

Here the clause beginning at Z- is subordinate to the clause beginning at Y-, which in turn is subordinate to the clause beginning at X-. Both Y and

Z are dependent clauses, while X is the independent clause, and is identical with the sentence as a whole: *I* as S, *think* as V, *that you can do it* as O, and *if you try* as A.

Dependent clauses may be classified either by STRUCTURAL TYPE, *ie* in terms of the elements they themselves contain, or by FUNCTION, *ie* the part they play in the superordinate clause.

11.2
Finite, non-finite, and verbless clauses
Analysing by structural type, we arrive at three main classes:

FINITE CLAUSE: a clause whose V element is a finite verb phrase (3.23)

> *eg: John has visited New York*
> *Because John is working*, he ...

NON-FINITE CLAUSE: a clause whose V element is a non-finite verb phrase (3.23)

> *eg: Having seen the pictures*, he ...
> *For John to carry the parcels* was a ...

VERBLESS CLAUSE: a clause containing no V element (but otherwise generally analysable in terms of one or more clause elements)

> *eg: Although always helpful*, he ...
> John, *then in New York*, was ...

All clauses – finite, non-finite, or verbless – may of course themselves have subordinate clauses which are finite, non-finite, or verbless. *Eg* the following verbless clause has a finite clause within it:

Although always helpful *when his father was away*, he ...

11.3
Finite and non-finite clauses
The finite clause always contains a subject as well as a predicate, except in the case of commands (7.58 *ff*) and ellipsis (9.21, 10.44 *ff*). As nearly all independent clauses (in discursive English, though not in 'block language': 7.66) are finite clauses, it is these that are most clearly related to the clauses dealt with in Chapter 7. In contrast, non-finite clauses can be constructed without a subject, and usually are. The four classes of non-finite verb phrase (3.23) serve to distinguish four classes of non-finite clause:

[I] INFINITIVE WITH *to*
> without subject: The best thing would be *to tell everybody*
> with subject: The best thing would be *for you to tell everybody*

The use of *for* to introduce the subject should be noted. The infinitive clause with *to* and with a subject is found characteristically in anticipatory *it* constructions (14.25): *It would be better (for you) to tell everybody.*

[II] INFINITIVE WITHOUT *to*
without subject: All I did was *hit him on the head*
with subject: Rather than *John do it*, I'd prefer to give the job to Mary

[III] *-ing* PARTICIPLE
without subject: *Leaving the room*, he tripped over the mat
with subject: *Her aunt having left the room*, I declared my passionate love for Celia

[IV] *-ed* PARTICIPLE
without subject: *Covered with confusion*, I left the room
with subject: We left the room and went home, *the job finished*

When the subject of adverbial participial clauses is expressed, it is often introduced by *with*:

With the tree $\begin{Bmatrix} growing \\ grown \end{Bmatrix}$ *tall*, we get more shade

The normal range of clause types (7.2) is available, with active and passive forms broadly as in the corresponding finite clauses, but there is a restriction on the *-ed* participial clause, which is both syntactically and semantically passive, and therefore admits only the four passive clause types SV_{pass}, $SV_{pass}C$, $SV_{pass}A$, and $SV_{pass}O$:

Defeated, he slunk from the room
Type $(S)V_{pass}$ $(=$ active Type $SVO)$

11.4
Structural 'deficiencies' of non-finite clauses

The absence of the finite verb from non-finite clauses means that they have no distinctions of person, number, or modal auxiliary. Together with the frequent absence of a subject, this suggests their value as a means of syntactic compression. Certain kinds of non-finite clause are particularly favoured in the careful style of written prose, where the writer has the leisure to make a virtue out of compactness. But the advantage of compactness must be balanced against the stumbling block of ambiguity; for the absence of a subject leaves doubt as to which nearby nominal element is *notionally* the subject:

We met you [*when you?/we? were*] leaving the room

When no referential link with a nominal can be discovered in the linguistic context, an indefinite subject 'somebody/something' may be inferred, or else the 'I' of the speaker:

> *To be an administrator* is to have the worst job in the world
>   ('For a person to be . . .')
> The prospects are not very good, *to be honest*
>   ('. . . if I am to be honest')

Note

[a] In negative non-finite clauses, the negative particle is placed immediately before the verb:

> It's his fault for *not* doing anything about it
> The wisest policy is (for us) *not* to interfere

It should be observed that the *not* precedes the *to* of the infinitive.

[b] The inseparability of *to* from the infinitive is also asserted in the widely held opinion that it is bad style to 'split the infinitive'. Thus rather than:

> ?He was wrong to *suddenly* leave the country

many people (especially in BrE) prefer:

> He was wrong to leave the country *suddenly*

It must be acknowledged, however, that in some cases the 'split infinitive' is the only tolerable ordering, since avoiding the 'split infinitive' results in clumsiness or ambiguity. For example:

> I have tried to *consciously* stop worrying about it

11.5
Verbless clauses

With the verbless clause, we can usually infer ellipsis of the verb *be;* the subject, when omitted, can be treated as recoverable from the context:

> Dozens of people were stranded, *many of them children* (many of them
>   *being* children)
> *Whether right or wrong*, he always comes off worst in an argument
>   (Whether *he is* right or wrong . . .)

Verbless clauses can also, on occasion, be treated as reductions of non-finite clauses:

> *Too nervous to reply*, he stared at the floor
>   (*Being* too nervous to reply . . .)

Here the verbless clause itself contains a non-finite clause, *to reply*.

As with participle clauses (11.3), the subject is often introduced by *with:*

> *With the tree now tall*, we get more shade

Since the verbless clause is basically an elliptical intensive verb clause (Type *SVC* or *SVA:* 7.2), the variations of its structure are somewhat limited. The following, however, are among possible combinations:

She marched briskly up the slope, *the blanket across her shoulder*

$$S \; [V_{intens}] \; A$$

When ripe, these apples will be delicious   *when* + [S V_{intens}] C_s

His gaze travelled round, *irresolute*   [S V_{intens}] C_s

Optional adverbials may also be added, either initially or finally:

She looked with disgust at the dog, *quiet now in Dinah's grasp*

$$[S \; V_{intens}] \; C_s \; A_{time} \; A_{place}$$

11.6
Formal indicators of subordination

In general, subordination is marked by some indication contained in the subordinate rather than superordinate clause. Such a signal may be of a number of different kinds: it can be a subordinating conjunction; a *wh*-element; the item *that;* inversion; or (negatively) the absence of a finite verb form. Especially in *wh*-items (*where*, *when*, etc), we can see a fusion of conjunction and pro-adjunct.

11.7
Subordinators

Subordinators (or more fully 'subordinating conjunctions') are perhaps the most important formal indicators of subordination. Like prepositions, which they resemble in having a relating or connecting function, subordinators forming the core of the class consist of a single word; and again as with prepositions, there are numerous compound items which act, to various degrees, like a single conjunction. In addition, there is a small class of correlative subordinators, *ie* combinations of two markers, one (a conjunction) occurring in the subordinate clause, and the other (normally an adverb) occurring in the superordinate clause.

SIMPLE SUBORDINATORS
after, (al)though, as, because, before, if, once, since, that, until, when, where, while, etc

COMPOUND SUBORDINATORS
ending with *that:*
in that, so that, such that, except that, etc; *in order that* (or *to* + infinitive clause)
ending with optional *that:*
now (that), provided (that), supposing (that), considering (that), seeing (that), etc

ending with *as:*

> *as far as, as long as, as soon as, so long as*, etc;
> *so as* (+ *to* + infinitive clause)

ending with *than:*

> *sooner than* (+ infinitive clause), *rather than* (+ non-finite or
> verbless clause)

other:

> *as if, as though, in case*

CORRELATIVE SUBORDINATORS

> *if . . . then; (al)though . . . yet/nevertheless; as . . . so*
> *more/-er/less . . . than; as . . . as; so . . . as; so . . . (that);*
>   *such . . . as; such . . . (that); no sooner . . . than*
> *whether . . . or*
> *the . . . the*

Note

[a] Some subordinators (*as, since, until, till, after, before, but*) also function as prepositions: *since the war*, etc.

[b] *For, with,* and *without*, elsewhere prepositions, might be added to the list of subordinators when they introduce the subject of a non-finite or verbless clause:

> *for* him to interfere (11.3); *with* so many people there (11.3, 11.5)

[c] Some of the above-listed subordinators introduce non-finite and verbless clauses
(*eg: if a nuisance*), others do not (**since a nuisance*). Details are given under relevant
sections (11.21, 11.22, 11.24, 11.26, 11.29).

11.8
Borderline subordinators

Three borderline categories may be mentioned: (a) habitual combinations of a subordinator with a preceding or following intensifying adverb
(*just as, if only*); (b) participle forms (*supposing . . .*), bearing a resemblance to participle clause disjuncts like *judging from . . ., speaking frankly*, etc; (c) expressions of time which, although adverbial in form, act like
a single temporal conjunction (*eg: directly/immediately/the moment (that)
I had spoken*).

11.9
Other indicators of subordination

Now we give a brief preliminary survey of other indicators of subordination, apart from subordinating conjunctions.

(a) *Wh*-ELEMENTS are initial markers of subordination in, for example,
    dependent interrogative clauses. The *wh*-words (such as *who*) func-
    tion as or within one of the clause elements subject, object, comple-
    ment, or adverbial.

(b) Subject-operator inversion (14.13) is a marker of subordination in some conditional clauses, where the operator is *had*, *were*, or *should*. Other unusual syntactic orderings also play a role in distinguishing a subordinate clause: for example, *Sad though I was* (11.26 Note).

There are only two types of subordinate clause that contain no marker within themselves of subordinate status: these are

[I] Nominal clauses which may or may not have *that* (11.13):

I suppose *you're right* (*cf* I suppose *that* you're right)

[II] Comment clauses (11.45) of a kind relatable to the *main* clause in the previous example:

You're right, *I suppose*

11.10
Functional classification of dependent clauses

Dependent clauses may function as subject, object, complement, or adverbial in the superordinate clause:

subject: *That we need more equipment* is obvious
direct object: I know *that she is pretty*
subject complement: The point is *that we're leaving*
indirect object: I gave *whoever it was* a cup of tea
object complement: I imagined him *overcome with grief*
adjunct: *When we meet,* I shall explain everything
disjunct: *To be honest,* I've never liked him
conjunct: *What is more,* he has lost the friends he had

In addition, they may function *within* these elements, as postmodifier, prepositional complement, etc; *eg*

postmodifier in noun phrase (13.5 *ff*): A friend *who remains loyal*
prepositional complement (6.2): It depends on *what we decide*
adjectival complement (12.11 *ff*): Ready *to act promptly*

Note
Dependent clauses rarely act as conjuncts, as object complements, or as indirect objects. As object complement, they must be non-finite clauses in complex-transitive complementation (12.20 *ff*). As indirect object, they must be nominal relative clauses (11.11).

11.11

Just as noun phrases may occur as subject, object, complement, appositive, and prepositional complement, so every NOMINAL CLAUSE may occur in some or all of these roles. But the occurrence of nominal clauses is limited by the fact that they are normally abstract; *ie* they refer to events, facts, states, ideas, etc. The one exception to this generalization is the nominal relative clause (11.16), which may refer to objects, people, substances, etc, and may in fact be analysed, on one level, as a noun phrase consisting of head and postmodifying relative clause, the head and relative pronoun coalescing to form a single *wh*-element (4.88).

11.12

ADVERBIAL CLAUSES (11.20–36) operate as adjuncts or disjuncts. In this respect, they are like adverbs, and are often commutable with prepositional phrases. Compare:

> *Because the soloist was ill,* they cancelled the concert
> *Because of the soloist's illness,* they cancelled the concert

COMPARATIVE CLAUSES (11.37–44), like sentential relatives, are difficult to fit into any of the major functional categories. They often have the appearance of adverbial or adjectival modifiers:

> I love you *more* deeply *than I can say*
> He's not *as* clever *a man as I thought*

They also have some features in common with adverbial clauses, however. Semantically, we may consider them, together with their correlative element (*more, as, -er*, etc) in the main clause, as equivalent to a degree adverb.

COMMENT CLAUSES (11.45*f*) perform the function of disjunct or (occasionally) conjunct, and often express the speaker's attitude to the main clause, or his manner of asserting it:

> Food is cheap in England, *I believe*

Each of these functional types will now be examined in greater detail, leaving others to later chapters: relative clauses (13.5 *ff*), clauses in structures of complementation (12.12 *ff*).

Nominal clauses
11.13
That-clauses
The *that*-clause can occur as:

> subject: *That she is still alive* is a consolation
>
> direct object: $\left\{\begin{array}{l}\text{I told him} \\ \text{I knew}\end{array}\right\}$ *that he was wrong*
>
> subject complement: The assumption is *that things will improve*

appositive: Your assumption, *that things will improve,* is unfounded
   (13.13, 9.45)
adjectival complement: I'm sure *that things will improve*

It cannot, however, occur as prepositional complement (6.2) or as object
complement.

When the *that*-clause is object or complement (or delayed subject:
14.25), the conjunction *that* is frequently omitted in informal use, leaving
a 'zero' *that*-clause:

$$\left.\begin{array}{l} \text{I knew} \\ \text{I told him} \\ \text{I'm sure} \end{array}\right\} \textit{he was wrong}$$

When the clause is subject and not extraposed, *that* cannot be omitted
and is usually expanded to *the fact that,* except in very formal English:

   (The fact) that she is still alive consoles me

Note

[a] The zero *that*-clause is particularly common when the clause is brief and uncompli-
cated. In contrast, the need for clarity discourages or even forbids the omission of
that in complex sentences loaded with adverbials and modifications. Any parenthetical material between the verb of the superordinate clause and the subject of the
that-clause is especially likely to inhibit deletion:

   We had hoped, in a moment of optimism, *that* the Government would look
      favourably on our case

The position of *that* after the second comma, rather than before the first comma, in
this sentence, is decisive in assigning the parenthetical adverbial to the main clause
and not the *that*-clause. The omission of *that* would leave the structure of the sentence unclear.

[b] Direct passive transforms of clauses with a *that*-clause object are rare, the version
with extraposition (14.25) being preferred: *It is thought that he will come.* The same
point applies to other nominal clauses.

[c] While *that*-clauses, like most other nominal clauses, cannot be object complements,
an alternative (and rather formal) *to*-infinitive construction is available with some
verbs. Contrast [1] and [2]:

   I thought his argument absurd ↔ I thought his argument *to be* absurd   [1]

   *I thought his argument   I thought his argument
      that we should pay   ↔   *to be* that we should pay   [2]

11.14
Wh-interrogative clauses
The dependent *wh*-interrogative clause occurs in the whole range of
functions available to the *that*-clause, and in addition can act as prepositional complement:

   subject: *How the book will sell* depends on its author
   direct object: I can't imagine *what made him do it*

subject complement: The problem is not *who will go*, but *who will stay*
appositive: My original question, *why he did it at all*, has not been
  answered
adjectival complement: I wasn't certain *whose house I was in*
prepositional complement: No one was consulted on *who should
  have the prize*

As regards meaning, these clauses resemble *wh*-questions (7.52 *f*) in that
they leave a gap of unknown information, represented by the *wh*-element.
Compare the negative and interrogative with the positive declarative in
the following:

I'm not sure *who* is coming
Do you know *who* is coming?
$\left.\begin{array}{l}\text{I'm sure}\\\text{I know}\end{array}\right\}$ that *John* is coming

There is also a grammatical similarity to *wh*-questions in that the *wh*-ele-
ment is placed first; indeed, apart from the absence of subject-operator
inversion in the dependent clause, the structures of the two types of
clause are in all respects parallel. We have, in the *wh*-interrogative clause,
the same choice between initial and final preposition where the prepositional complement is the *wh*-element:

He couldn't remember $\left\{\begin{array}{l}\textit{on which shelf} \text{ he kept it (formal)}\\\textit{which shelf} \text{ he kept it } \textit{on}\end{array}\right.$

An infinitive *wh*-clause can be formed with all *wh*-words except *why:*

He was explaining *how to start the motor* ('. . . how one should . . .')
I never know *where to put my coat* ('. . . where I ought to . . .').

Note
[*a*] In literary style, there is an occasional subject-operator inversion when the *wh*-
element is the A of an *SVA* type clause, or the C of an *SVC* type clause:

I told them *how strong was my desire* to visit the famous temple

There is also an informal but chiefly dialectal inversion (*eg* in Irish English), as in:

He asked me *where was I staying*

[*b*] The preposition preceding a *wh*-clause is optional in certain circumstances:

I was not certain (*of*) *what to do*

11.15
Yes-no interrogative clauses
The dependent *yes-no* interrogative clause (*cf* 7.45 *ff*) is formed with *if* or
whether:

Do you know *if/whether the banks are open?*

The dependent *alternative* question (cf 7.54 f) has *if/whether ... or:*

I don't know *whether it will rain or be sunny*
I don't care *if your car breaks down or not*

Only *whether* can be directly followed by *or not:*

I don't care $\begin{Bmatrix} \textit{whether or not} \\ \textit{*if or not} \end{Bmatrix}$ your car breaks down

A clause beginning with *whether* cannot be made negative, except as the second part of an alternative question:

I don't care $\begin{cases} \textit{if it doesn't rain} \\ \textit{*whether it doesn't rain} \\ \textit{whether it rains or (whether it does) not} \end{cases}$

On the other hand, *if* cannot introduce a subject clause:

$\begin{Bmatrix} \textit{Whether} \\ \textit{*If} \end{Bmatrix}$ it rains or not doesn't concern me

Note
With certain introductory verbs or adjectives a negative *whether*-clause is acceptable:

I wonder $\quad$ $\Big\}$ whether he doesn't expect too much from her
I'm not sure

In fact, however, such sentences have a positive rather than negative meaning: 'I think he expects too much from her'.

11.16
Nominal relative clauses
The nominal relative clause, also introduced by a *wh*-element, can be:

 subject: *What he is looking for* is a wife
 direct object: I want to see *whoever deals with complaints*
 indirect object: He gave *whoever came to the door* a winning smile
 subject complement: Home is *where your friends and family are*
 object complement: You can call me *what*(*ever*) (*names*) *you like*
 appositive: Let us know your college address (that is, *where you live
  in term time*)
 prepositional complement: Vote for *which*(*ever*) *candidate you like*

The nominal relative clause is much closer to noun phrase status than other nominal clauses are. It can normally be paraphrased by a noun phrase containing a postmodifying relative clause:

I'll give you *however much tobacco you need* ('... any amount ...
 that you need')
Quality is *what counts most* ('... the thing that counts most')

There is a difference between UNIVERSAL and DEFINITE meaning as expressed by the *wh*-form of a relative clause. We see this in the paraphrases of the examples above: the first is paraphrased in 'universal' terms (*any amount*), the second in 'definite' terms (*the thing*). Contrast with the latter:

Quality is *whatever counts most* ('. . . anything that . . .')

The form *who* is rarely used in present-day English in this nominal relative function (**Who told you that was lying*), being replaced in many contexts, for both universal and definite meanings, by *whoever*:

Whoever told you that was lying $\left\{\begin{array}{l}\text{'The person who \ldots'}\\ \text{'Anyone who \ldots'}\end{array}\right\}$

Where the *wh*-word chosen is available for both nominal relative and interrogative clauses, an ambiguity arises:

They asked me *what I didn't know* ('They asked me that which I didn't know' *or* 'They asked me "What don't you know?"')

11.17
To-infinitive nominal clauses
The *to*-infinitive nominal clause can occur as:

subject: *For a bridge to collapse like that* is unbelievable
direct object: He likes *everyone to be happy*
subject complement: My wish is *to be a pilot*
appositive: His ambition, *to be a straight actor*, was never fulfilled
adjectival complement: I'm glad *to help you* (see 12.13)

The subject of a *to*-infinitive clause is normally preceded by *for* (which is perhaps acting here more as a conjunction than as a preposition). The subject, when a pronoun, is in the objective case:

The idea is $\left\{\begin{array}{l}\text{that }we\text{ should meet on Thursday}\\ \text{for }us\text{ to meet on Thursday}\end{array}\right.$

When the clause is a direct object, however, the *for* is omitted:

He wants me to leave (*rather than:* *He wants for me to leave)

On *wh*-infinitive clauses, see 11.14.

Note
[a] The infinitive clause resembles the *that* clause (in contrast to the *-ing* clause) in never being a prepositional complement.
[b] The correspondence between 'The idea is *to meet*' and 'The idea is *that we should meet*' shows the putative nature of the infinitive clause (*cf* 11.51).

11.18
Nominal *-ing* clauses
The nominal *-ing* clause, a PARTICIPLE CLAUSE, occurs in the following positions:

subject: *Telling lies* is wrong
direct object: No one enjoys *deceiving his own family*
subject complement: His favourite pastime is *playing practical jokes*
appositive: His hobby, *collecting stamps*, absorbed him
prepositional complement: I'm tired of *being treated like a child*
adjectival complement: The children were busy *building sandcastles*

It is the commonest type of participle clause, that which has no subject, that is illustrated above. When a subject is required, there is sometimes a choice as follows (but *cf* 12.24):

GENITIVE case in formal style:

I'm surprised at *his/John's* making that mistake

OBJECTIVE or COMMON case (for personal pronouns or nouns, respectively) in informal style:

I'm surprised at *him/John* making that mistake

It is commonly claimed that the genitive is the only 'correct' form, but in fact it frequently has a stilted effect, and is particularly unsuitable when the subject is an inanimate or abstract noun phrase which would not normally take the genitive case, or a 'group' genitive phrase (13.74):

? The crisis has arisen as a result of *recent uncontrolled inflation's* having outweighed the benefits of devaluation

On the other hand, a pronoun in the objective case is disliked in subject position:

Him being a Jesuit was a great surprise (very informal)

Many prefer to avoid both possibilities where alternatives are available:

It was a great surprise that he was a Jesuit

Note
As compared with the *-ing* clause, the genitive is obligatory where the *-ing* item constitutes the head of a noun phrase:

His/him criticizing John was very unfair
His/*him criticizing of John was very unfair
See 13.20, 23 Note.

11.19
Bare infinitive and verbless clauses

The *to* of the infinitive is optionally omitted in a clause which supplies a predication corresponding to a use of the pro-verb *do:*

All I did was (*to*) *turn off the gas*

When the infinitive clause is initial, *to* has to be omitted: *Turn off the tap was all I did.*

Note
In the following sentence, the lack of concord between *carpets* and *is* shows that the subject is not a noun phrase:

Wall-to-wall carpets in every room is very expensive

Rather, it should be seen as a nominal verbless clause, paraphrasable as 'Having wall-to-wall carpets in every room'. On the other hand, the similarity often causes these verbless clauses to be given the concord demanded with noun phrases:

Are *fast cars in cities* really very wise?

Adverbial clauses
11.20

Adverbial clauses, like adverbials in general (8.3), are capable of occurring in a final, initial, or medial position within the main clause (generally in that order of frequency, medial position being rather rare). Attention will be drawn, in the paragraphs that follow, to modifications of this general statement. On problems of tense, aspect, and mood, see 11.47 *ff.*

11.21
Clauses of time

Finite adverbial clauses of time are introduced by such subordinators as *after, before, since, until, when:*

When I last saw you, you lived in Washington
Buy your tickets *as soon as you reach the station*
Our hostess, *once everyone had arrived,* was full of good humour

The *-ing* clause may be introduced by *after, before, since, until, when*(*ever*), and *while; -ed* clauses by *once, until, when*(*ever*), and *while;* and verbless clauses by *as soon as, once, when*(*ever*), and *while:*

He wrote his greatest novel *while working on a freighter*
Once published, the book caused a remarkable stir
When in difficulty, consult the manual

In addition, *-ing* clauses without a subject are also used to express time relationship:

Nearing the entrance, I shook hands with my acquaintances
('when/as I neared . . .')

The stranger, *having discarded his jacket,* moved threateningly
towards me ('after he had discarded . . .')

Temporal clauses are common in initial position.

Note

[a] With *until* and its variant *till,* the superordinate clause is negative if the time reference is to a commencement point (*cf* 6.23 *f*):

*He started to read *until he was ten years old*
He didn't start to read *until he was ten years old*
He walked in the park *till it was dark*

In the negative sentence, *not* (. . .) *until* means the same as *not* (. . .) *before.*

[b] There is no semantic subordination with a type of *when*-clause which occurs finally
in sentences in formal narrative style and in which *when* means rather *and then:*

The last man was emerging from the escape tunnel *when a distant shout
signalled its discovery by the guards*

[c] Infinitive clauses of 'outcome' may be placed among temporal clauses:

I awoke one morning *to find the house in an uproar*

Such sentences could be paraphrased by switching the relationship of subordination, and using a *when*-clause:

When I awoke one morning, I found the house in an uproar

Their restriction to final position suggests an analogy between these infinitive
clauses and result clauses (11.32), which they resemble in meaning.

11.22
Clauses of place

Adverbial clauses of place are introduced by *where* or *wherever:*

They went *wherever they could find work*
Where the fire had been, we saw nothing but blackened ruins

Non-finite and verbless clauses occur with both the subordinators:

Where(ver) known, such facts have been reported
Where(ver) possible, all moving parts should be tested

Note

In this last example, as in the *When in difficulty* example of 11.21, we see a general contingency relation similar to conditions: *wherever possible, whenever possible, if possible.*
This generality of meaning is characteristic of verbless and non-finite clauses (*cf* 11.36)
but is common also in finite clauses (*Whenever anyone finds this possible*), and in part
reflects fundamental similarities between several adverbial relationships.

11.23
Clauses of condition and concession

Whereas conditional clauses state the dependence of one circumstance or
set of circumstances on another:

If you treat her kindly, (then) she'll do anything for you

concessive clauses imply a contrast between two circumstances; *ie* the main clause is surprising in the light of the dependent one:

> *Although he hadn't eaten for days*, he (nevertheless) looked very fit

The parenthesized items illustrate the possibility of correlation (11.7) in both types of clause.

From this, we see that *although* as a subordinator is the approximate equivalent of *but* as a coordinator (9.18):

> He hadn't eaten for days, *but* he looked strong and healthy

The overlap between conditional and concessive clauses comes with such subordinators as *even if*, which expresses both the contingent dependence of one circumstance upon another and the surprising nature of this dependence (11.26):

> *Even if he went down on bended knees*, I wouldn't forgive him

Both conditional and concessive clauses tend to assume initial position in the superordinate clause.

11.24
Clauses of condition

Finite adverbial clauses of condition are introduced chiefly by the subordinators *if* (positive condition) and *unless* (negative condition):

> He must be lying *if he told you that*
> *Unless the strike has been called off*, there will be no trains tomorrow

The latter means roughly '*If* the strike has *not* been called off . . .'. But there is a slight difference between an *unless*-clause and a negative *if*-clause in that *unless* has the more exclusive meaning of 'only if . . . not' or 'except on condition that . . .'. It is thus the opposite of the compound conjunction *provided* (*that*) or *providing* (*that*), which means 'if and only if . . .':

> *Provided that no objection is raised*, we shall hold the meeting here

Other compound conditional conjunctions approximately synonymous with *provided* (*that*) are *as long as, so long as*, and *on condition that*.

If and *unless* often introduce non-finite and verbless clauses: *if ready; unless expressly forbidden*, etc. Also to be noted are the residual positive and negative conditional pro-clauses *if so* and *if not* (10.36).

11.25
Real and unreal conditions

A 'real' condition leaves unresolved the question of the fulfilment or non-fulfilment of the condition, and hence also the truth of the proposition expressed by the main clause. In an 'unreal' condition, on the other hand, it is clearly expected that the condition will *not* be fulfilled. Thus:

> Real: If he comes, I'll see him.   If she was awake, she certainly
> heard the noise.
> Unreal: If he came, I'd see him.   If she'd been awake, she would
> have heard the noise.

On the association of past with 'unreal', see 3.47, 11.48. On conditional clauses as disjuncts, see 8.49.

If-clauses are like questions in implying uncertainty. They tend therefore to contain non-assertive forms such as *any, ever* (see 7.35):

> If you *ever* have *any* trouble, let me know

Clauses beginning with *unless*, on the other hand, lay stress on the excluded positive option, and so normally contain assertive forms:

> I won't phone you, unless *something* unforeseen happens
> (=I'll phone you when something unforeseen happens – but we
> can exclude this as unlikely)

For the same reason, *unless*-clauses are not usually unreal conditions. Hence the negative unreal conditional clause *If I had not arrived* has no equivalent *unless*-clause, **Unless I had arrived*.

Note

[a] The combination *if only* is an intensified equivalent of *if*, typically used in preposed unreal conditions (with no non-assertive requirement) to express a wish:

> *If only somebody had told us*, we could have warned you

[b] The subjunctive or *should* (3.50) is sometimes used in formal real conditions:

> If he $\begin{Bmatrix} be \text{ found} \\ should be \text{ found} \end{Bmatrix}$ guilty, his wife will suffer terribly

[c] The infinitival clause can be used conditionally:

> You have to be strong *to lift a table like that* ('if you're going to lift')
> He'd be stupid *not to accept that offer* ('if he didn't accept')

Such clauses contain an element of purposive meaning (11.51).

[d] Conditional clauses (especially unreal) may have subject-operator inversion without a conjunction:

> *Had I known*, I would not have gone

11.26
Clauses of concession

Clauses of concession are introduced chiefly by *though* (also a conjunct: 8.53) or its more formal variant *although*. Other conjunctions include *while, whereas* (chiefly formal), *even if*, and occasionally *if*.

No goals were scored, *though it was an exciting game*
Although I enjoyed myself, I was glad to come home
Whereas John seems rather stupid, his brother is clever
Even if you dislike music, you would enjoy this concert
If he's poor, at least he's honest

Non-finite and verbless clauses of concession are often introduced by conjunctions, but not by *whereas*. For example, *though a young man; although often despairing of rescue; even if still operating; even though given every attention.*

Note

Concession is sometimes rather formally expressed with the subordinators *as*, *though*, and *that* occurring after the subject complement; less frequently other predications may be preposed:

  Naked as I was, I braved the storm
  Sneer unkindly though you may, John is very popular

11.27
Alternative conditional-concessive clauses

The correlative sequence *whether* (. . .) *or* . . . is a means of coordinating two subordinate clauses, combining conditional meaning with disjunctive meaning:

> *Whether they beat us or we beat them*, we'll celebrate tonight
> *Whether (living) in London or not*, John enjoyed himself
> *Whether or not he finds a job in New York*, he's moving there

The concessive element of meaning comes in secondarily, through the implication that if the same thing takes place in two contrasting conditions, there must be something surprising about at least one of them.

11.28
Universal conditional-concessive clauses

The universal conditional-concessive clause, introduced by one of the *wh*-compounds (*whatever*, *whoever*, etc), indicates a free choice from among any number of conditions:

> She looks pretty *whatever she wears*

That is, *even though* she were to wear overalls or a space suit. There is a subtle semantic difference between such conditional clauses and apparently identical time and place clauses:

> *Wherever you live*, you can keep a horse

The locative meaning would be 'You can keep a horse at any place where you may live'; the conditional-concessive meaning is 'It doesn't matter where you live, you can keep a horse – not necessarily in that same place'.

The longer constructions *it doesn't matter wh-* and the more informal *no matter wh-* may be added to the list of universal conditional-concessive clause introducers:

$$\left\{ \begin{array}{l} \textit{No matter} \\ \textit{It doesn't matter} \end{array} \right\} \textit{how hard I try,} \text{ I can never catch up with him}$$

Note

With an abstract noun phrase subject of an *SVC* clause, the verb *be* can be omitted from a universal conditional-concessive clause:

> *Whatever your problems (are),* they can't be worse than mine
> *However great the pitfalls (are),* we must do our best to succeed

11.29
Clauses of reason or cause

Clauses of reason or cause are most commonly introduced by the conjunctions *because, as,* or *since:*

> I lent him the money *because he needed it*
> *As/since Jane was the eldest,* she looked after the others

These different positional tendencies (characteristic of the respective conjunctions) reflect a different syntactic status: *because*-clauses are adjuncts, whereas *as*- and *since*-clauses are disjuncts. Informally, however, a final *because*-clause sometimes functions as a disjunct of reason:

> They've lit a fire, *because I can see the smoke rising*

Non-finite and verbless clauses can be used for cause (11.36), but without conjunction:

> *Being a man of ingenuity,* he soon repaired the machine

11.30
Clauses of circumstance

Clauses of circumstance express a fulfilled condition or (to put it differently) a relation between a premise (in the subordinate clause) and the conclusion drawn from it (in the main clause). *Because, since,* and *as* can convey this meaning, but in addition there is a special circumstantial compound conjunction, *seeing (that):*

> *Seeing that the weather has improved,* we shall enjoy our game

Non-finite clauses and verbless clauses are often used (11.36), but without subordinator:

> *The weather having improved,* we enjoyed the rest of the game

11.31
Clauses of purpose
Clauses of purpose are adjuncts, usually infinitival, introduced by *(in order)* *(for* N) *to, so as to:*

   I left early *to catch the train*
   They left the door open *in order for me to hear the baby*

Finite clauses of purpose may be introduced by *so that, so* (informal), or *in order that* (formal):

   John visited London $\begin{Bmatrix} \text{in order that} \\ \text{so (that)} \end{Bmatrix}$ he could see his MP

In the purpose clause, which has 'putative' meaning (11.51), the modal auxiliaries *should* and *may* (past tense *might*) are used.

Note
Negative purpose is expressed by *for fear (that)*, (in BrE) *in case*, or the now rather archaic and very formal conjunction *lest:*
   They left early for fear they would meet him (= in order that . . . not . . .)

11.32
Clauses of result
Result clauses (disjuncts, placed finally in superordinate clauses) are factual rather than 'putative'; hence they may contain an ordinary verb form without a modal auxiliary. They are introduced by *so that*, informally *so:*

   We planted many shrubs, *so (that) the garden soon looked beautiful*

11.33
Clauses of manner and comparison
Clauses of manner are introduced by *(exactly) as, (just) as:*

   Please do it *(exactly) as I instructed* ('in the way that . . .')

If an *as*-clause is placed initially, the correlative form *so*, in formal literary English, may introduce the main clause:

   (Just) as a moth is attracted by a light, (so) he was fascinated by her

Such examples provide a transition to the adverbial clauses of comparison, introduced by *as if, as though:*

   He looks *as if he is going to be ill*

If there is doubt or 'unreality', the modal past is used:

   He treated me *(just) as if he had never met me*

Note
Clauses of comparison sometimes show subject-operator inversion:
   The present owner collects paintings, *as did several of his ancestors*

11.34
Clauses of proportion and preference

Proportional clauses express a 'proportionality' or equivalence of tendency or degree between two circumstances, and are either introduced by *as* (with or without a formal correlative *so*) or by fronted correlative *the . . . the* plus comparatives:

> *As he grew disheartened,* (so) his work deteriorated
> *The more* he thought about it, *the less* he liked it
> *The harder* he worked, *the happier* he felt

Clauses of preference are introduced by *rather than, sooner than,* with a bare infinitive structure; but *rather than* is less restricted:

> $\left.\begin{array}{l}\textit{Rather than}\\ \textit{Sooner than}\end{array}\right\}$ go there by air, I'd take the slowest train

> $\textit{Rather than}\left\{\begin{array}{l}\textit{sitting quietly at home,}\text{ he preferred to visit his friends}\\ \textit{a new car,}\text{ he bought a colour television}\end{array}\right.$

Non-finite and verbless clauses
11.35
IMPLIED SUBJECT

If the subject is not actually expressed in a non-finite or verbless clause, it is assumed to be identical with the subject of the superordinate clause:

> *When ripe, the oranges* are picked and sorted
> *He* took up anthropology, *stimulated by our enthusiasm*
> *She* hesitated, *being very suspicious,* to open the door
> *He* opened his case *to look for a book*

Commonly, however, this 'attachment rule' is violated:

> ? Since leaving her, *life* has seemed empty

In this case, we would assume that the superordinate clause means 'Life has seemed empty *to me*' and that the subject of the *-ing* clause is also first person. Such 'unattached' ('pendant' or 'dangling') clauses are frowned on, however, and are totally unacceptable if the superordinate clause provides no means at all for identifying the subordinate subject. In the following sentence, for example, it cannot be *a dog:*

> *Reading the evening paper, a dog* started barking

Note

[a] The attachment rule does not need to be observed with disjuncts:

> *Speaking candidly* (S = 'I'), *John* is dishonest

[b] Tense, aspect and mood are also inferred in non-finite and verbless clauses from the sentential context. *Cf* 13.5, 13.14 *ff.*

11.36
SEMANTIC DIVERSITY

We have seen that many of the relationships (time, reason, etc) discussed earlier can be expressed by means of non-finite and verbless clauses. Where these are introduced by conjunctions, the relationship may be quite explicit: *if necessary, since being here*, etc. Where they are not so introduced, there may be considerable indeterminacy as to the relationship to be inferred:

John, $\begin{Bmatrix} \textit{soon to become a father} \\ \textit{feeling considerable anxiety} \\ \textit{told of his good fortune} \\ \textit{sad at the news} \end{Bmatrix}$, went to Mexico

In this position, the clauses could have the function merely of non-restrictive postmodifier of *John* (*cf* 13.17). But their potential relationship to the whole superordinate clause rather than only to the subject is indicated by their mobility. For example:

Soon to become a father, John went to Mexico
John went to Mexico, *feeling considerable anxiety*

Clearly, their formal inexplicitness allows considerable flexibility in what we may wish them to convey. Thus according to the context, we might want to imply a temporal relation (*eg:* '*When he was* told of his good fortune'), a causal relation (*eg:* '*Because he was* soon to become a father'), a concessive relation (*eg:* '*Although he was* soon to become a father', '*Although he was* sad at the news'). In short a CONTINGENCY is implied, but for the hearer or reader the actual nature of the contingency has to be inferred from the context.

Comparative sentences
11.37

In a comparative construction, a proposition expressed in the superordinate clause is compared with a proposition expressed in the subordinate clause by means of a 'COMP(arative) ELEMENT'. This comp-element specifies the standard of comparison (*eg: health*) and identifies the comparison as equational or differentiating. The comp-element is linked with the subordinate clause by a correlative sequence: equational *as . . . as*, or differentiating *less . . . than, more . . . than* (where the first item may be replaced where relevant by the inflectional comparative). See 5.32. *Eg:*

Jane is $\begin{Bmatrix} \textit{as healthy as} \\ \begin{Bmatrix} \textit{less healthy} \\ \textit{more healthy} \\ \textit{healthier} \end{Bmatrix} \textit{than} \end{Bmatrix}$ her sister (is)

The standard of comparison involves only a scale, without commitment to absolute values; thus, in the above examples, neither Jane nor her sister need be 'healthy'.

11.38

Like the Q-element of a question, a comp-element can be any of the main elements of clause structure (apart from the verb):

comp-element $=$ S: *More people* use this brand than (use) any
                                  other window-cleaning fluid
comp-element $=$ C_s: I'm *happier* about it than my husband (is)
comp-element $=$ O_d: He knows *more* than most people (know)
comp-element $=$ O_i (rare): That man has given *more children*
                                  happiness than anyone else (has)
comp-element $=$ A: You've been working *much harder* than I
                                  (have)

Note

[a] Constructions with *more . . . than* and *less . . . than* do not necessarily introduce comparative clauses. There is a type of non-clausal comparison in which *than* is followed by an explicit standard or yardstick of comparison, normally a noun phrase of measure, or a noun phrase implying degree:

    The books weigh *more than four pounds*
    It goes faster *than 100 miles per hour*
    The strike was nothing *less than a national catastrophe*

Here *than* is best considered a preposition, and the phrase which follows it a prepositional complement.

[b] There is a second type of *more . . . than* construction not introducing a comparative clause. This is the quasi-coordinative type of construction illustrated by

    I was more angry than frightened   (*cf* I was angry rather than frightened)

A distinguishing characteristic of this construction is the non-occurrence of the suffixal form of comparison:

    *I was angrier than frightened

11.39

Ellipsis in comparative sentences
Ellipsis of a part of the subordinate clause is likely to occur whenever that part is a repetition of something in the main clause. Since it is normal for the two clauses to be closely parallel both in structure and content, ellipsis is the rule rather than the exception in comparative constructions. It is worth while pointing out, however, that there is no necessary parallelism between the main and comparative clauses, and that the comparative clause, so long as it overlaps with the content of the main clause in respect of the comp-element, can be of independent structure. Thus we may take two *wh*-questions of disparate clause types:

{ How quickly does he speak?
{ How quickly can his secretary take dictation?

and use them to construct the comparative sentence:

He speaks more quickly than his secretary can take dictation

Optional ellipses and substitutions (by pronoun and by pro-predication) are illustrated in the following:

(a) James enjoys the theatre more than Susan enjoys the theatre
(b) James enjoys the theatre more than Susan enjoys it
(c) James enjoys the theatre more than Susan does
(d) James enjoys the theatre more than Susan

It should be noted that ellipsis of the object cannot take place unless the verb too is ellipted (9.2); thus we could not expand (d) as:

*James enjoys the theatre more than Susan enjoys

But, if the object is the comp-element itself, the verb may remain:

James knows more about the theatre than Susan (knows)

Obligatory ellipsis, on the other hand, applies to the standard of comparison which cannot be specified again in the subordinate clause (*Jane is healthier than her sister is healthy*), though different aspects of a single standard may be specified in each clause. This occurs with 'size' and 'ability' in the following examples:

The bookcase is wider than it is tall
Jane is as successful at sport as her sister is successful academically

11.40
Ambiguity through ellipsis
When normal ellipses have taken place, ambiguity can arise as to whether a remaining noun phrase is subject or object (9.23):

He loves the dog more than his wife

could mean either [1] '... than his wife loves the dog' or [2] '... than he loves his wife'. If *his wife* were replaced by a pronoun, formal or fastidious English could disambiguate this example:

He loves the dog more than she   [1]
He loves the dog more than her   [2]

Informally, however, the ambiguity would remain, since *than* plus the objective case tends to be used for both [1] and [2]. See 4.83 and *cf* 10.36, 11.38 Note *a* on the quasi-prepositional value of *than*. Since objections can be raised against both (stiffness or over-familiarity), we sometimes steer a middle course using additional pro-forms (*than she does, than he does her*).

11.41
Ellipsis and partial contrast
If the two clauses in a comparison differed solely in the comp-element (**I hear it more clearly than I hear it*), only nonsense would result, of course. But the elements in the two clauses may be lexically identical and differ only in tense or mood. In such cases it is normal to have ellipsis of all identical items except any that are necessary to express the contrast:

> I hear it more clearly than I did (*ie* hear it)
> I get up as early as I should (*ie* get up)

If the contrast lies in tense only, it may be expressed in the subordinate clause solely by an adverbial:

> She'll enjoy it more than (she enjoyed it) last year

This provides the basis for the total ellipsis of the subordinate clause in examples like

> You are slimmer (*ie* than you were)

Note

[a] In negative superordinate clauses, *as* can be replaced by *so* especially when there is total or considerable deletion in the subordinate clause:

> He's not as naughty as he was
> He's not so naughty (now)

[b] There is a second type of circumstance in which the comparative clause is omitted: this is where there is anaphoric reference to an implied or actual preceding clause or sentence (*cf* 10.43), as in:

> I caught the last bus from town; but Harry came home even *later*
> (*ie* 'later than that', 'later than I came home')

11.42
Noun phrase and comp-element
If we were to say:

> There are more intelligent monkeys than Herbert

we would normally mean that Herbert is an intelligent monkey; that is, by placing the comparative adjective in front of the noun phrase, we put the whole noun phrase in an intensive relation with the noun phrase in the comparative clause. On the other hand, if *more* and the adjective are placed after the noun, we readily admit the plausible interpretation that Herbert is a man:

> There are monkeys more intelligent than Herbert

Note

More may be the comparative quantifier:

John has more new clothes than I have

that is, a greater quantity of *new clothes*, not *newer clothes*. The modifying sequences *less/more of a* . . ., *as much of a* . . . occur with gradable noun heads (4.3 Note):

He's more of a fool than I thought (he was)

Cf the *How*-question, *How much of a fool is he?*

11.43
Enough and *too*

There are comparative constructions with *enough* and *too*, which convey the contrasting notions of 'sufficiency' and 'excess', and which are related through negation. Paraphrase pairs may be constructed, using antonymous adjectives or adverbs, as follows:

{The grass is too short (to cut)
The grass isn't long enough (to cut)

{He's not too poor (to own a car)
He's rich enough (to own a car)

The infinitive clause which follows the comp-element may be omitted if the context allows.

The negative force of *too* is shown in the use of non-assertive forms like *any* or *anything* compare:

She's *old enough* to do *some* work
She's *too old* to do *any* work

Like other infinitive clauses, the subordinate clause in these constructions may have an expressed subject:

The blade moves too quickly for most people to see (it)

As in this example, the expressed subject permits also the optional expression of an object pronoun (here representing *the blade*). When the subject is not expressed, it may be identified with the superordinate subject or with an indefinite subject:

I've lived long enough to understand these things
The writing is too faint to read

With neither subject nor object expressed, ambiguity is possible (*cf* 12.13):

The lamb is too hot $\begin{bmatrix}\text{(for us)}\\\text{(for it)}\end{bmatrix}$ to eat $\begin{bmatrix}\text{(it)}\\\text{(anything)}\end{bmatrix}$

Note

With gradable nouns, we have *enough/too much of a* . . . (*cf* 11.42 Note); *cf* also 'He was *fool enough* to go without a coat'.

11.44

So . . . (that) **and** *such . . . (that)*

The correlatives *so . . . (that)* and *such . . . (that)* are linked to *too* and *enough*, by paraphrase relations. For example:

{ It flies fast enough to beat the speed record
{ It flies so fast that it can beat the speed record

{ It's too good a chance to miss
{ It's such a good chance that we mustn't miss it

It will be observed that in these paraphrases, the verb in the *that*-clause contains a modal auxiliary; when the modal auxiliary is absent, the *so/such . . . (that)* construction has the more definitive meaning of result or outcome:

He was so wild *that we let him escape*
I so enjoyed it (*or* I enjoyed it so much) *that I'm determined to go again*

The alternation between *so* and *such* depends on grammatical function. The *that* which introduces the comparative clause is sometimes omitted in informal English:

He polished the floor so hard *you could see your face in it*

The somewhat formal construction *so/such . . . as to* plus infinitive clause is sometimes used in place of *so* or *such* followed by a *that*-clause:

His satires were *so* brilliant *as to make even his victims laugh*
The brilliance of his satires was *such as to make even his victims laugh*

Note

An emphatic fronting of the comp-element, accompanied by inversion of subject and operator, is sometimes found in formal (especially literary) English:

To such lengths *did she go* in rehearsal that two actors walked out
So strange *was his appearance* that no one recognized him

Comment clauses
11.45

Comment clauses are somewhat loosely related to a superordinate clause, and may be classed as disjuncts or conjuncts. In general, they may occur initially, finally, or medially, and have a separate tone unit (App II.7):

The SMÍTHS, | *as you probably KNÓW,* | are going to AMÈRICA |

As the following list of types shows, comment clauses vary in form:

(1) Like a main clause:

At that time, *I believe*, labour was cheap

(2) Like an adverbial clause (introduced by *as*):

> I'm a pacifist, *as you know*

(3) Like a nominal relative clause as conjunct (8.53):

> *What's more*, we lost all our belongings

(4) *To*-infinitive clause as style disjunct (8.48 *f*):

> I'm not sure what to do, *to be honest*

(5) *-ing* clause as style disjunct (8.48 *f*):

> I doubt, *speaking as a layman*, whether television is the right medium

(6) *-ed* clause as style disjunct (8.48 *f*):

> *Stated bluntly*, he has no chance of winning

11.46

In the first type of clause, which is perhaps the most important, the verb or adjective requires an indirect statement as complementation (11.13, 11.55, 12.17). We may therefore set up a one-to-one relationship between sentences containing such clauses, and indirect statements:

$$\left\{ \begin{array}{l} \text{At that time, I believe, labour was cheap} \\ \text{I believe that, at that time, labour was cheap} \end{array} \right.$$

To convert an indirect statement into a sentence with comment clause, one has to reverse the relation of subordination between the two clauses, making the *that*-clause into the main clause and the main clause into the comment clause. Because of this reversal of syntactic roles, the two examples above are not exact paraphrases; but the relationship between them illuminates the function of the comment clause.

Since the *that* of a *that*-clause is normally deletable (11.13), cases arise in which only the intonation (reflected by comma separation in writing) distinguishes which is the superordinate and which the subordinate clause:

> You KNOW, | I | think you're WRONG |⎫   (*You know* is a comment
> You know, I | think you're WRONG | ⎭   clause)

> You | know (that) I think you're WRONG | (*You know* has an object
>   clause)

Quite a number of Type 1 comment clauses introduced by 1st or 2nd person subjects are the stereotyped *I see, you know*, etc, inserted to give informality or warmth. Outside this group, however, clauses can be fairly freely constructed, and variations of tense and aspect, additions of adjuncts, etc, are permitted:

The Indian railways (*my uncle was telling me some time ago*) have
always made a profit

The subordinator *as* may be added to Type 1 clauses converting them to
Type 2, with virtually no change of meaning:

The Indian railways (*as my uncle was telling me some time ago*)
have always made a profit

Note

[a] There are also comment clauses which may be related to a main clause introducing
an indirect question:

What's he doing, *I wonder?*   (*cf* I wonder what he's doing)

Sometimes a comment clause is itself in the form of a direct question:

What's he doing, *do you think?*

[b] Clauses which introduce direct speech (11.52) may be considered comment clauses
of Type 1:

'It's time we went,' *I said*

The verb phrase in dependent clauses
11.47
The present tense with subordinators

To express future meaning, the present tense is used in preference to the
auxiliary *will/shall* in certain types of adverbial clauses:

$$not \begin{cases} \text{*When} \\ \text{*Before} \\ \text{*If} \end{cases} \text{he } \textit{will arrive,} \text{ the band will play the National Anthem}$$

$$but \begin{cases} \text{When} \\ \text{Before} \\ \text{If} \end{cases} \text{he } \textit{arrives,} \text{ the band will play the National Anthem}$$

The subordinators chiefly involved belong to the temporal and conditional (in part also, concessive) categories:

TEMPORAL: *after, as, before, once, till, until, when(ever), as soon as*
OTHER: *if, unless, provided* (*that*), *given* (*that*), *assuming* (*that*),
           presuming (*that*), *even if, in case, as* (manner), *whatever,*
           etc

Thus:

Even if tomorrow's match *is* cancelled, Newcastle will still be
top of the league
He will come in case we *need* him
Next time I'll do as he *says*

Nominal *that-* and *wh*-clauses tend to contain present tense verbs when
the main clause (as well as the subordinate clause) refers to the future; but

when the main clause refers to the present, the future *will* is likely to be used in the subordinate clause. Contrast:

> I shall ask him what he *wants* tomorrow
> The question is what he *will want* tomorrow

However, there are exceptional verbs like *hope, suppose* (in the imperative), and *assume*, after which the simple present can often be used as readily as *will:*

> I hope that the parcel *comes* in time
> Let's assume our opponents *win* the election

Note

There are two exceptions to the rule that *will/won't* cannot appear in *if*-clauses (and in some of the other types of clause mentioned above):

(i) Where *will/won't* has a volitional or habitual meaning, rather than a pure future meaning:

> If you *won't* (=' refuse to ') help us, all our plans will be ruined

(ii) Where even though the *if*-clause refers to the future, the condition expressed by the whole sentence obtains in the present:

> If he *won't* arrive before nine, there's no point in ordering dinner for him
> If it *will* make any difference, I'll gladly lend you some money

In both these sentences, the future contingency expressed in the *if*-clause determines a present decision.

11.48
The modal past

The past tense is used, as already explained (11.25), in unreal conditional sentences:

> If we *had* enough money, I wouldn't have to work so hard

The corresponding superordinate verb phrase is *would/should*+infinitive, except when the past of another modal auxiliary is used:

> If we had enough money, we *could* buy a tape-recorder

Other constructions in which the modal past is used are illustrated below (on the subjunctive *were*, see 3.46):

> It's time you *were* in bed
> He behaves as though he *was/were* a millionaire
> It's not as though we *were* poor
> Just suppose/imagine someone *was/were* following us
> I'd rather we *had* dinner now
> If only I *had* listened to my parents!

From each of these sentences a negative inference can be drawn: 'but you're not in bed', 'but he isn't a millionaire', etc. Unreal meaning in past time is indicated by *had* plus the *-ed* participle:

> We could have got married today, if you'*d* really *wanted* to
> If he *had listened* to me, he wouldn't have made the mistake

With past reference, the unreal meaning is more absolute than in the present, and amounts to an implied rejection of the condition: 'but in fact you didn't want to'; 'but in fact he didn't listen'. With present and future reference, the meaning may be merely one of improbability and negative expectation:

> If you *listened* to me, you wouldn't make mistakes
>   ('... but I don't suppose you will listen to me')

11.49
Perfect aspect with *since*, etc

When *since* is used in a temporal sense, the perfect is used in the superordinate clause, also sometimes in the subordinate clause, in referring to a stretch of time up to (and potentially including) the present:

> Since we have owned a car, we *have gone* camping every year
>   (*or possibly:* ... we *go* camping, *where* own *implies duration*)
> She *has been drinking* Martinis ever since the party started
>   (*not:* She *is drinking* ..., *where* start *excludes duration*)

The same applies to *since* as preposition and as prepositional adverb:

> Scholars *have been writing* English grammars since the sixteenth
>   century

After and *when*, in referring to a sequence of past events, can be followed either by a past perfect or by a simple past tense verb:

$$\left.\begin{array}{c}\text{After}\\\text{When}\end{array}\right\} \text{he} \left\{\begin{array}{c}\text{had returned}\\\text{returned}\end{array}\right\} \text{from work, his wife served dinner}$$

All four of these are acceptable, and mean roughly the same. The only difference is that *when* with the simple past tense (probably the most popular choice) suggests that the one event followed *immediately* on the other. There may however be a contrast:

$$\text{He went away when I} \left\{\begin{array}{c}\text{visited}\\\text{had visited}\end{array}\right\} \text{her}$$

The variant with the past tense would normally mean 'as soon as I visited her' or 'at the time that I was visiting her', that with the past perfect 'after I had visited her'.

Note

If the verb phrase of the main clause is progressive in aspect, or contains a stative verb, *when* indicates the simultaneity, rather than successivity of the events:

> When he returned from work, his wife was (working) in the kitchen.

11.50
Present subjunctive in conditional clauses, etc

The present subjunctive (3.46) is used very occasionally and in rather formal use, as we have seen, in real conditional clauses and concessive clauses:

> *Whatever be the reasons for it*, we cannot tolerate this disloyalty
> (*cf* Whatever *may be* the reasons . . .)

Clauses of concession and purpose may also very occasionally contain a verb in the subjunctive mood to express 'putative' meaning (see 11.51):

> Though he $\left\{\begin{matrix} is \\ be \end{matrix}\right\}$ the President himself, he shall hear us

The subjunctive is also possible in *that*-clauses expressing wish, hope, or intention (though *should* would be more usual):

> Congress has voted/decided/decreed/insisted that the present law
> *be* maintained

The present subjunctive is more common in AmE than in BrE, where it is rare outside legal style.

The past subjunctive *were* is used in formal clauses of hypothetical meaning, such as those introduced by *if, as if, as though, though*, and the imperative verbs *suppose* and *imagine:*

> Suppose he *were* here . . .
> If the truth *were* known . . .

11.51
Putative *should*

The modal auxiliary *should* is used quite extensively in *that*-clauses to express not a subordinate statement of fact, but a 'putative' idea. It can usually be replaced by the indicative without much difference of meaning. Compare:

> I am surprised that he *should feel* lonely (=he feels)
> I am told that he *feels* lonely (≠he should feel)

The first sentence alludes to a report over which doubt may be allowed to linger, while the second accepts the report as a fact.

Other superordinate constructions which introduce a *that*-clause with *should* can be illustrated as follows:

It's a pity
I'm surprised
It's disgraceful } that he should resign
It's unthinkable
It worries me

Most of these are constructions in which the *that*-clause is an extraposed subject (14.24*f*, 12.12, 12.17). Notice that in the first two cases, despite the *should*, the event is assumed to have taken place already. This is because the 'factual' bias of the main clause construction overrides the doubt otherwise implicit in the *should* construction. Nonetheless, there is still a difference of feeling between *I'm surprised that he should resign* and *I'm surprised that he has resigned:* in the first, it is the 'very idea' of resignation that surprises; in the second, it is the resignation itself, as an assumed fact.

Note
Putative *should* also occurs in some idiomatic questions and exclamations:

How *should* I know?
Why *should* he be resigning?
That he *should* dare to attack me!
Who *should* come in but the mayor himself!

11.52
Direct and indirect speech
The difference between direct speech and indirect (or reported) speech is shown in:

He said: 'I am very angry'   (DIRECT SPEECH)
He said that he was very angry   (INDIRECT SPEECH)

Indirect speech subordinates the words of the speaker in a *that*-clause within the reporting sentence. In the case of direct speech, his words are 'incorporated' (in writing by quotation marks) within the reporting sentence and retain the status of an independent clause. Nevertheless, the 'incorporated' speech has in part the function of an element in the clause structure of the reporting sentence:

He said *this* (O_d), namely '*I am very angry*'

Structurally, the reporting clause, in direct speech, may be classed as a comment clause (11.46). It may occur before, within, or after the speech itself. Except when it occurs in initial position, there is likely to be an inversion of the subject and a reporting verb in the simple present or past tense:

'I am your friend,' $\begin{cases} \textit{said John} \\ \textit{John said} \\ \textit{he said} \end{cases}$

Inversion is unusual and archaic, however, when the subject of the reporting clause is a pronoun: ... *said he*. The medial placing of the reporting clause is very frequent:

'As a result,' said John, 'I am very angry'

Note
'Direct and indirect speech' will be used here as traditionally, but 'speech' must be allowed to include unspoken mental activity when the reporting verb may be *think, believe, feel*, etc; but *cf* 11.58. It should also be noted that indirect report frequently involves paraphrase or summary of the speech or thought it represents.

11.53
Back-shift and other changes
Several changes are made in converting direct to indirect speech (subject to the exceptions in 11.54), and their effect is one of distancing. 1st and 2nd person pronouns are changed to 3rd person:

'*I*'ll behave *myself*,' he promised
  →He promised that *he*'d behave *himself*
' *You* are beautiful,' he whispered
  → He whispered that *she* was beautiful

Frequently, there is a change from *this/these* to *that/those*, from *here* to *there*, and from *now* to *then*:

'I live *here*,' he explained → He explained that he lived *there*
'I shall do it *now*,' he said → He said that he would do it *then*

The most important alteration takes place, however, in the verb phrase: this is the change of tense that is referred to as BACK-SHIFT. When the reporting verb is in the past tense, verbs in the reported speech are changed as follows:

DIRECT	INDIRECT
(1) present	→ past
(2) past	
(3) present perfect	→ past perfect
(4) past perfect	

Thus, if we move into the past for the reporting clause, there is a corresponding shift into the past (or if necessary, further into the past) in the reported clause. Examples of each part of the rule are:

(1) 'I *am* tired,' she complained
     → She complained that she *was* tired

(2) 'The exhibition *finished* last week,' explained Ann
→ Ann explained that the exhibition *had finished* the preceding week ·

(3) 'I've *won* the match already!' exclaimed our friend
→ Our friend exclaimed that *he had won* the match already

(4) 'The whole house *had been ruined*,' said the landlord
→ The landlord said that the whole house *had been ruined*

If, on the other hand, the reporting verb is in the present, there is no tense change:

She keeps saying, 'I *am* a failure'
→ She keeps saying that she *is* a failure

11.54
Exceptions to the distancing rules
The change to the more 'distant' meaning (*eg* to 3rd person pronouns) does not always take place, in that the use of forms appropriate to the reporting situation must take precedence over those appropriate to the reported speech situation. For example:

' *You* are wrong, John,' said Mary
→ [John reporting] 'Mary said that *I* was wrong'

Analogously, the rule of back-shift can be ignored in cases where the validity of the statement reported holds for the present time as much as for the time of utterance. Thus, while back-shift is obligatory in the first of the following examples, it is optional in the second:

'I *am* a citizen, not of Athens, but of the world,' said Socrates
→ Socrates said that he *was* a citizen, not of Athens, but of the world

'Nothing *can* harm a good man,' said Socrates

→ Socrates said that nothing $\begin{Bmatrix} could \\ can \end{Bmatrix}$ harm a good man

11.55
Indirect statements, questions, exclamations, and commands
Our examples have so far been of indirect statements. Questions, exclamations, and commands are converted into indirect speech as follows:

INDIRECT QUESTION: dependent *wh*-clause or *if*-clause
INDIRECT EXCLAMATION: dependent *wh*-clause
INDIRECT COMMAND: *to*-infinitive clause (without subject)

For example:

> 'Are you ready yet?' asked Joan   (*yes-no* QUESTION)
>   → Joan asked (me) *whether I was ready yet*
> 'When will the plane leave?' I wondered   (*wh*-QUESTION)
>   → I wondered *when the plane would leave*
> 'What a hero you are!' Margaret told him   (EXCLAMATION)
>   → Margaret told him *what a hero he was*
> 'Keep still!' she said to the child   (COMMAND)
>   → She told the child *to keep still*

What has been said about back-shift applies to questions and exclamations as well as to statements. Indirect commands, in contrast, cannot incorporate back-shift, as they contain no finite verb. The reporting verb, in the case of indirect commands, has to be followed by an indirect object or prepositional object: for the indirect speech version of '*Sit down*,' *I snapped*, one would write not **I snapped to sit down*, but *I snapped at him to sit down*. With a verb like *sneer* one could render an indirect command with *tell* and an appropriate adverbial:

> 'Go back to the nursery,' he sneered
>
> → He told them $\begin{Bmatrix} \text{sneeringly} \\ \text{with a sneer} \end{Bmatrix}$ to go back to the nursery

Note
Alternative questions are made indirect with *whether . . . or* on a model similar to *yes-no* questions:

> Are you satisfied or not?   → I asked him *whether or not he was satisfied*

11.56
The modal auxiliaries and indirect speech
Although *He would go* is not the past of *He will go* (3.51), it is the back-shifted form in indirect speech. So too with the other modal auxiliaries:

> '*May I go?*' she asked → She asked if *she might go*

If a modal auxiliary in direct speech has no past tense equivalent (this includes auxiliaries which are already past, such as *could*, *might*, as well as *must, ought to, need*, and *had better*), then the same form remains in indirect speech:

> 'I would like some tea,' he said → He said (that) he *would like* some tea

The element of speaker involvement which is often present in the meaning of some modal auxiliaries (*eg: may*='permission', 3.49) is naturally assigned in indirect speech to the subject of the indirect statement. Thus,

John said that I might go would mean that John was giving me permission to go (corresponding to the direct 'You may go'), whereas *I might go* outside indirect speech would mean that I was considering the possibility of going.

Note

If the reporting verb phrase is modal and perfective (I + II, 3.24), it counts as past for purposes of the back-shift rule. Compare:

He *asks* what John *is* doing   He *has asked* what John *is* doing

but

He *may have asked* what John *was* doing

11.57
Free indirect speech

Free indirect speech is a half-way stage between direct and indirect speech, and is used extensively in narrative writing. It is basically a form of indirect speech, but (1) the reporting clause is omitted (except when retained as a parenthetical comment clause), and (2) the potentialities of direct-speech sentence structure (direct question forms, vocatives, tag questions, etc) are retained. It is therefore only the back-shift of the verb, together with equivalent shifts in pronouns, determiners, and adverbs, that signals the fact that the words are being reported, rather than being in direct speech:

> So that was their plan, was it? He well knew their tricks, and would show them a thing or two before he was finished. Thank goodness he had been alerted, and that there were still a few honest people in the world!

Very often, in fiction, free indirect speech represents a person's stream of thought rather than actual speech. It is quite possible, therefore, that *he thought* would be the appropriate reporting clause to supply for the above passage, rather than *he said*.

11.58
Transferred negation

There are several ways in which 'indirect speech' involving mental activity verbs (*he thought*, etc) differs from that where the reporting verb is one of language activity (*he said*, etc). A very important difference involves negation; thus, while both clauses can be made independently negative with *say*, etc:

He did not say that Mary was pretty
He said that Mary was not pretty

(so that these two sentences are sharply different in meaning), it is usual

with *think, believe, suppose, imagine, expect*, etc for a superordinate negative to apply also in the subordinate clause. For this reason, the following
pairs of sentences would normally be regarded as virtually synonymous:

$\begin{cases} \text{He didn't think that Mary was pretty} \\ \text{He thought that Mary wasn't pretty} \end{cases}$

$\begin{cases} \text{I don't suppose he has paid yet} \\ \text{I suppose he hasn't paid yet} \end{cases}$

The transfer of the negation can be seen clearly in the second pair above,
with the non-assertive *yet* (7.35) appearing in the subordinate clause even
when the verb in this clause is not negated. Another indication is the form
of the tag question (7.48 *f*) in:

I don't suppose (that) he CÀRES, *DÒES* he?

(*cf* He doesn't CÀRE, *DÒES* he?)

The tag question in this sort of sentence is attached to the *that*-clause
rather than to the independent clause, as is clear from the tag subject, *he*.
Since a tag question with a falling tone contrasts in positive/negative
terms with its main clause, however, we would expect *DÒESn't he?* in this
context. That in fact a positive tag question occurs is thus evidence of the
negativeness of the *that*-clause.

Note

[a] Not all verbs in the semantic field of belief, uncertainty, etc, take transferred negation:

I don't assume that he came $\neq$ I assume that he didn't come

So too *surmise, presume*. Conversely, a few verbs outside the field of mental activity
(for example, *seem, happen*) permit the transfer.

[b] A condensed sentence like *I don't think so* contains transferred negation, and is thus
synonymous with *I think not; cf* 10.36.

Bibliographical note

On nominal clauses, see Lees (1960a); Vendler (1968), especially Part I. On comparative clauses, see Huddleston (1971). On non-finite clauses, see Hudson (1971).

TWELVE

THE VERB AND ITS COMPLEMENTATION

12.1

This chapter will deal with units which complement the verb and which are, in general, obligatory in clause structure (but *cf* 7.3 *f*, and also the possibilities for ellipsis discussed in 9.21 *ff*). We have earlier (2.7 *f*) distinguished between different categories of verbs with respect to their potentialities for complementation. We shall here discuss these categories in greater detail, concentrating in turn on intransitive verbs, intensive verbs, and transitive verbs. But before we do so, we shall consider cases where the main verb and one or more particles seem to combine as a multi-word verb.

12.2

Intransitive phrasal verbs

One common type of multi-word verb is the intransitive phrasal verb consisting of a verb plus a particle, as exemplified in

The children were *sitting down*	He is *playing around*
Drink up quickly	*Get up* at once
The plane has now *taken off*	Did he *catch on?*
The prisoner finally *broke down*	He *turned up* unexpectedly
When will they *give in?*	The tank *blew up*

Most of the particles are place adjuncts or can function as such (8.25). Normally, the particle cannot be separated from its verb (** Drink quickly up*), though particles used as intensifiers or perfectives (8.25) or referring to direction can be modified by intensifiers (*Go right on*).

A subtype of intransitive phrasal verb has a prepositional adverb (6.5) as its particle, the particle behaving as a preposition with some generalized ellipsis of its complement:

He *walked past* (the object/place)
They *ran across* (the intervening space)

In some instances, the particles form the first element in a complex preposition:

Come along (with us/me)
They *moved out* (of the house)

Phrasal verbs vary in the extent to which the combination preserves the individual meanings of verb and particle. In instances like *give in* ('surrender'), *catch on* ('understand'), and *turn up* ('appear'), it is clear that the meaning of the combination cannot be predicted from the meanings of the verb and particle in isolation.

12.3
Transitive phrasal verbs
Many phrasal verbs can take a direct object:

We will *set up* a new unit
Find out whether they are coming
Drink up your milk quickly
They *turned on* the light
They *gave in* their resignation
He can't *live down* his past

They are *bringing over* the whole family
She is *bringing up* her brother's • children
They *called off* the strike
I can't *make out* what he means
He *looked up* his former friends

As we see from the examples here and in 12.2, some combinations (*drink up, give in*) can be either transitive or intransitive, with or without a difference of meaning (*cf* App I.30).

With most transitive phrasal verbs, the particle can either precede or follow the direct object:

They *turned on* the light ~ They *turned* the light *on*

although it cannot precede personal pronouns: *They turned it on* and not **They turned on it* (except, rarely, with contrastive stress: App II.5). The particle tends to precede the object if the object is long or if the intention is that the object should receive end-focus (14.2).

Many transitive phrasal verbs have prepositional adverbs:

They *dragged* the case *along* (the road)
They *moved* the furniture *out* (of the house)

In these examples the particles have literal meanings. We can contrast

She *took in* the box ('brought inside')
She *took in* her parents ('deceived')

As with the intransitives, transitive phrasal verbs vary in the extent to which they form idiomatic combinations. For example, the verb and

particle in *put out the cat* preserve their individual meanings in that combination and in a wide range of other combinations (*eg: put + down/out-
side/away/aside; take/turn/bring/push/send/drag + out*). There are fewer
alternative combinations that the verb and particle in *turn out the light*
can enter (*turn + on/off/down/up; switch + on*). Finally, in *put off* ('postpone') the verb and particle are fused into a new idiomatic combination,
which does not allow for contrasts in the individual elements.

Note
With *put N out* we can compare *put N straight* and other complex transitive constructions (12.26).

Prepositional verbs
12.4
The preposition in a prepositional verb must precede its complement.
Hence, we can contrast the prepositional verb *call on* ('visit') with the
phrasal verb *call up* ('summon'):

They *called on* the man	They *called up* the man
They *called on* him	*They *called up* him
*They *called* the man *on*	They *called* the man *up*
*They *called* him *on*	They *called* him *up*

On the other hand, the prepositional verb allows an inserted adverb
after the verb and a relative pronoun after the preposition:

They *called* early *on* the man	*They *called* early *up* the man
The man *on* whom they *called*	*The man *up* whom they *called*

In general, prepositional verbs, such as *call on* or *look at*, plus their prepositional complements differ from single-word verbs plus prepositional
phrases, as in *They called at the hotel* and *They called after lunch*, in that
they allow pronominal questions with *who(m)* for personal noun phrases
and *what* for non-personal noun phrases but do not allow adverbial
questions for the whole prepositional phrase:

They called on the man ~ Who(m) did they call on?
   ~ *Where did they call?
They looked at the picture ~ What did they look at?
   ~ *Where did they look?
They called at the hotel (*or* after lunch) ~ *What did they call at
   (*or* after)? ~ Where (*or* when) did they call?

Many prepositional verbs allow the noun phrases to become the subject of a passive transformation of the sentence:

They called on the man ~ The man was called on
They looked at the picture ~ The picture was looked at

Other prepositional verbs do not occur in the passive freely, but will do so under certain conditions, such as the presence of a particular modal:

Visitors didn't walk over the lawn
~ ?The lawn wasn't walked over (by visitors)
Visitors can't walk over the lawn
~ The lawn can't be walked over (by visitors)

Other examples of prepositional verbs: *ask for, believe in, care for, deal with, live on, long for, object to, part with, refer to, write about.*

Like phrasal verbs, prepositional verbs vary in their idiomaticity. Highly idiomatic combinations include *go into* (*a problem*), 'investigate', *come by* (*the book*), 'obtain'.

12.5

A sentence like *He looked at the girl* can be given two analyses. In one, there is an intransitive verb (*looked*) followed by a prepositional phrase (*at the girl*) functioning as adverbial. In the other analysis, implied in the previous section, the prepositional verb *looked at* is a transitive verb and *the girl* is direct object.

ANALYSIS 1:   V   A
                He looked at the girl
ANALYSIS 2:   V   O

Analysis 1 (verb + adverbial) accounts for the similarity of such a sentence to others having a single-word verb and adverbial with respect to relative clauses and the positioning of adverbs:

The girl $\begin{cases} \text{at whom he looked/(who(m)) he looked at} \\ \text{to whom he came/(who(m)) he came to} \end{cases}$

He $\begin{cases} \text{looked nervously at the girl} \\ \text{stood nervously near the girl} \\ \text{*watched nervously the girl} \end{cases}$

Analysis 2 (prepositional verb + direct object) accounts for the similarity of the sentence to others having a transitive single-word verb with respect to passivization:

The girl was $\begin{cases} \text{looked at} \\ \text{watched} \\ \text{*stood near} \end{cases}$

The two analyses are equally valid ways of looking at the same sentence, and account for different aspects of it. In this chapter, in which we are concerned with complementation of the verb, we adopt the second analysis and consider prepositional verbs to be transitive verbs.

12.6
Phrasal-prepositional verbs
Some multi-word verbs consist of a verb followed by two particles:

He *puts up with* a lot of teasing ('tolerates')

As with prepositional verbs, we can analyse these as transitive verbs with the following noun phrase as direct object. They allow pronominal questions and under certain conditions can occur in the passive:

He can't put up with bad temper ~ What can't he put up with?
                                  ~ Bad temper can't be put up with
                                          for long

As with single-word transitives and prepositional verbs, we cannot insert an adverb immediately before the object:

*He *puts up with* willingly that secretary of his

though it is possible to do so between the particles:

He *puts up* willingly *with* that secretary of his
We *look forward* eagerly *to* your next party

In relative clauses and questions, the particles are positioned after the verb:

The party we were *looking forward to* so eagerly
Who(m) does he *put up with* willingly?

or (less commonly) the final particle can be brought into initial position:

The party *to* which we were *looking forward* so eagerly
With whom does he *put up* willingly?

  Like phrasal and prepositional verbs, these multi-word verbs vary in their idiomaticity. Some, like *stay away from* ('avoid'), are easily understood from their individual elements, though often with figurative meaning, *eg: stand up for* ('support'). Others are fused combinations, and it is difficult or impossible to assign meaning to any of the parts, *eg: put up with* ('tolerate'). There are still others where there is a fusion of the verb with the first particle or where one or more of the elements may seem to retain some individual meaning. For example, *put up with* can also mean 'stay with', and in that sense *put up* constitutes a unit by itself (*cf: stay with, put up at*, and the transitive phrasal verb *put up* in *I can put you up*). Similarly, *check up on (his record)*, 'investigate', is analysable as consisting of the prepositional verb *check on* plus the intensifying *up*. We also have the single-word verb *check*, and therefore three transitive verbs of similar meaning, together with the intransitive *check* and *check up*.

Other examples of phrasal-prepositional verbs: *break in on* (*the conversation*), 'interrupt'; *cut down on* (*expenses*), 'curtail'; *get away with* (*such behaviour*), 'avoid being reprimanded or punished for'; *look down on* (*somebody*), 'despise'; *look in on* (*somebody*), 'visit'; *look up to* (*somebody*), 'respect'; *walk out on* (*the project*), 'abandon'.

12.7
Intransitive verbs

There are some verbs that are always intransitive, *ie* can never take an object:

Your friends have *arrived*

Other verbs can be either intransitive:

He *smokes* every day   The tomatoes *are growing* well

or transitive, with or without a change in participant role:

He *smokes cigars* every day   He is *growing tomatoes*

In this book we regard verbs that can be either intransitive or transitive as belonging to two categories. We consider the relation between, for example, the intransitive verbs *smoke* and *grow* and the transitive verbs *smoke* and *grow* to be that of conversion (7.3, 7.10, App I.30).

Note

[a] The verb *live* takes an adjunct as an obligatory element. *Live* in the sense 'reside' requires a position adjunct (*He lives in China*) and in the sense 'maintain life' or 'subsist' a process adjunct (*He lives very comfortably*, *They live on rice*). For *live* in the sense 'be alive' a time adjunct is virtually obligatory (*They lived in the nineteenth century*). The verb *get* also has an obligatory adjunct use; in this case the obligatory adjunct is a direction adjunct (*I'll get into the car*).

[b] Some of the intransitive phrasal verbs could not be used intransitively if the particle were omitted. Besides *get* as in *get up* ('arise'), the verbs include *find* (*find out*, 'discover'), *keep* (*keep away*, 'stay away'), *set* (*set off*, 'depart').

[c] Intransitive verbs with a 'passive' sense (converted from transitive verbs: App I.30) virtually require an adjunct: *The book is selling badly*, *The door unlocks easily*.

[d] Verbs of measure require an adjunct, usually a noun phrase: *weigh* (*five pounds*), *cost* (*a dollar*), *contain* (*much*). Cf 7.14 Note.

Intensive complementation
12.8
Copulas

There is intensive complementation of the verb when a subject complement is present (7.6). The verb in such a sentence is a 'copula' or 'linking verb'. The most common copula is *be*. Other copulas fall into two main classes, according to whether the role of the subject complement is that of current attribute or attribute resulting from the event described in the verb (7.9). The most common of these are listed below. Most of them are used only with a subject complement that is an adjective phrase or a noun phrase with gradable noun head. Those that are commonly used with a noun phrase as well are followed by '(N)'.

'Current' copulas: *appear, feel* (N), *look* (N), *remain* (N), *seem* (N), *smell, sound, taste*

'Resulting' copulas: *become* (N), *get* (chiefly informal), *go, grow, turn* (N); *make* (N only)

12.9
Noun and adjective phrases as subject complement

The copulas which allow the widest range as subject complement are *be* for current attribute and *become* for resulting attribute:

$$\text{John} \begin{Bmatrix} \text{was} \\ \text{became} \end{Bmatrix} \begin{Bmatrix} \text{a doctor} \\ \text{healthier} \end{Bmatrix}$$

Like the other copulas, *be* is commonly used to introduce a characterization or attribute of the subject, as in the example just given, but with complement noun phrases it also commonly introduces an identification of the subject:

John was the doctor (that I mentioned)

The verb *feel* has two copula uses. In the meaning 'have a sensation' the subject must be personal and the complement an adjective or gradable noun:

He felt foolish/ill/a fool

In the meaning 'give a sensation', the subject is concrete but without other restriction, the complement being adjectival only:

The table felt rough

Note

[a] *Look* requires a visual feature:

The pit looked a danger to health

The smell $\begin{Bmatrix} \text{*looked} \\ \text{seemed} \end{Bmatrix}$ a danger to health

Turn is used to indicate a change of occupation or allegiance: *He turned plumber/ Democrat/traitor/nasty*. *Go*, when its complement is a noun phrase, seems to be restricted to change in political allegiance: *He has gone Democrat/socialist*. Adjectival complementation is restricted to a few items, *eg: go mad/bald*. Both *turn* and *go* are normally disparaging, and with both the indefinite article is omitted before a noun phrase.

[b] Where the subject is a clause, the subject complement must be an adjective phrase or a generic noun modified by an adjective:

$$\left.\begin{array}{l}\text{That he didn't come}\\ \text{To see him there}\end{array}\right\} \text{ was } \left\{\begin{array}{l}\text{strange}\\ \text{a strange thing}\end{array}\right.$$

Usually, of course, this structure has extraposition (14.24 *f*): *It was a strange thing . . . Cf* 12.13.

12.10
Predicative adjuncts

The only copula that allows an adverbial as complementation is *be* (5.42). The adverbials, termed predicative adjuncts in this function, are mainly place adjuncts (8.25):

The children are at the zoo/. . . are outside

but time adjuncts are also common with an eventive subject (8.44):

The party will be at nine o'clock/. . . will be tonight

Other types of predicative adjuncts:

The two eggs are for you ['recipient' adjunct: 6.29]
The drinks are for the journey ['purpose' adjunct: 6.28]
The increase in food prices this year was because of the drought
    ['cause' adjunct: 6.27]
Transport to the mainland is by ferry ['means' adjunct: 6.31 *f*]

Complementation of adjective phrase as subject complement
12.11
Adjective complementation by prepositional phrase

Some adjectives (at least when used in a particular sense) require complementation by a prepositional phrase, the preposition being specific to a particular adjective:

Joan is *fond of* them
They are *conscious of* their responsibility
We are *bent on* a vacation in Mexico

Other adjectives that must be complemented by a prepositional phrase include the following, which are listed together with the required preposition: *intent on, reliant on, averse to, liable to, subject to, inclined to, (un)familiar with.*

Many adjectives can take such complementation but are not obliged to. Usually, the prepositions are specific to a given adjective or to a given kind of complementation:

$$\text{They were afraid} \left\{\begin{array}{l}\text{of him ('They feared him')}\\ \text{for him ('They were anxious about him')}\\ \text{of leaving the house}\end{array}\right.$$

He was $\left\{ \begin{array}{l} \text{angry} \\ \text{pleased} \end{array} \right\}$ $\left\{ \begin{array}{l} \text{at Mary('s) getting married} \\ \text{with Mary for getting married} \\ \text{about the wedding} \end{array} \right.$

As these examples show, the complement of the preposition can be an -*ing* participle clause (6.2), whose subject, if introduced, may or may not be a genitive (11.18). As well as the stylistic choice there can be differences in semantic implication, *cf* 13.23 Note. Thus,

I am angry at Mary getting married

could imply anger at Mary because she has got married (*cf: I am angry at Mary for getting married*) rather than merely anger at the marriage (*cf: I am angry at the fact that Mary got married*), which would be the obvious interpretation of . . . *angry at Mary's* . . .

When -*ed* participial adjectives are used, the constructions have active analogues:

John is interested in English grammar ∼ English grammar
   interests John
We were worried about the situation ∼ The situation worried us
He was surprised at her behaviour ∼ Her behaviour surprised him

The verbs in the active have a causative feature, *eg: The situation worried us* ∼ *The situation caused us to worry.*

12.12
Adjective complementation by finite clause
Finite clauses as complementation may have

(a) indicative verb: I am sure that he is here now
(b) putative *should:* I was angry that he should ignore me
(c) subjunctive verb (3.46): I was adamant that he be appointed
    (formal in BrE, but *cf* 12.17 Note)

An indicative verb is used if the adjective is 'factual', *ie* concerned with the truth-value of the complementation. An indicative verb or putative *should* (11.51) is used if the adjective is 'emotive', *ie* concerned with attitude. A subjunctive verb or *should* (sometimes putative, but often obligational) is used if the adjective is 'volitional', *ie* expressing indirectly some command. (For adverb analogues to the first two types of adjective, see 8.50 *ff.*) The subjunctive is more usual in AmE in such cases, while BrE prefers *should.*

The finite clause is commonly a *that*-clause, but factual adjectives admit *wh*-clauses as well: *I'm not sure why he came, I'm not clear where she went.* Clauses introduced by *whether* or (less commonly) *if* are used with factual adjectives if the adjective is negative or has a negative sense:

$\left\{\begin{array}{l}\text{I'm not sure} \\ \text{I'm doubtful}\end{array}\right\}$ $\left\{\begin{array}{l}\text{whether} \\ \text{if}\end{array}\right\}$ he is here yet

Personal subject + copula + adjective phrase + finite clause:

factual adjective: I am aware that he was late

emotive adjective: He is angry that $\left\{\begin{array}{l}\text{they should be late} \\ \text{they are late}\end{array}\right.$

I am amazed that $\left\{\begin{array}{l}\text{he should have got the post} \\ \text{he got the post}\end{array}\right.$

volitional adjective: He was $\left\{\begin{array}{l}\text{keen} \\ \text{insistent}\end{array}\right\}$ that $\left\{\begin{array}{l}\text{they be present} \\ \text{(formal in BrE)} \\ \text{they should be present}\end{array}\right.$

With emotive adjectives, the complementation expresses cause. This can be shown by a variant construction in which the complementation is the subject of the sentence. It is particularly evident when the emotive adjective is participial, in which case there is a corresponding active (*cf.* 12.13):

He is angry that they should be late ~ That they should be late has made him angry

I am amazed that he got the post ~ That he got the post amazes me

Participial adjectives in this construction are commonly emotive adjectives.

12.13
Adjective complementation by *to*-infinitive clauses

We distinguish five main types of construction in which the adjective phrase is followed by a *to*-infinitive clause. They are exemplified in the following five sentences, which are superficially similar, though, as we shall see, only 2, 3, and 4 are wholly concerned with adjective complementation:

(1) Bob is splendid to wait
(2) Bob is slow to react
(3) Bob is furious to hear it
(4) Bob is hesitant to agree with you
(5) Bob is hard to convince

In Types 1–4, the subject of the sentence (*Bob*) is also the subject of the infinitive clause. We can therefore always have a direct object in the infinitive clause in these four types if the verb is transitive. For example, for Type 1 if we replace intransitive *wait* by transitive *make*, we can have *Bob is splendid to make that for you.*

Type 1 (*Bob is splendid to wait*) has an analogue with a construction involving extraposition (14.24 *f*): *It is splendid of Bob to wait*. As alternatives to the adjective phrase, we can use a noun phrase that has as its head a degree noun (4.3 Note) or a generic noun modified by an adjective: *David must be (quite) a magician to make so much money, Bob is a splendid man to wait*.

In Type 2 (*Bob is slow to react*), the sentence has an analogue in which the adjective is transformed into an adverbial:

Bob is slow to react ~ Bob reacts slowly

In Type 3 (*Bob is furious to hear it*), the head of the adjective phrase is an emotive adjective (commonly a participial adjective) and the infinitive clause expresses causation:

Bob is furious to hear it ~ To hear it has made Bob furious
~ It has made Bob furious to hear it
I was excited to be there ~ To be there excited me
~ It excited me to be there

In Type 4 (*Bob is hesitant to agree with you*), the head of the adjective phrase is a volitional adjective. Common adjectives in this type are *eager*, *keen*, *willing*, *reluctant*. Along with Type 3, this type often admits *feel* as the copula.

In Type 5 (*Bob is hard to convince*), the subject of the sentence is the object of the infinitive clause, which must therefore have a transitive verb (**Bob is hard to arrive*). We distinguish two subtypes:

(a) There is an analogue with a construction in which the adjective is complement to the infinitive clause:

Bob is hard to convince ~ To convince Bob is hard
~ It is hard to convince Bob

The adjectives used in this subtype are chiefly *hard, difficult, impossible, easy, convenient*. Unless there is ellipsis, we cannot omit the infinitive clause, and hence there is no semantic relation between the sentences *Bricks are hard to make* and *Bricks are hard*.

(b) There are no analogues of the kind that we have exemplified: *The food is ready to eat* (**To eat the food is ready*), and we can generally omit the infinitive clause: *The food is ready*.

As with Type 1, we can use a noun phrase as an alternative to the adjective phrase: *Bob is a hard man to convince; Bob is a pleasure to teach*. In both (5a) and (5b), the subject of the sentence can be the complement of a preposition in the infinitive clause: *He is easy to talk to, The paper is flimsy to write on*.

See also 12.19 Note *b*.

Transitive complementation
12.14

Monotransitive verbs require a direct object, which may be a noun phrase, a finite clause, or a non-finite clause (infinitive or participle clause). Prepositional verbs and phrasal-prepositional verbs do not admit as direct object *that*-clauses (whether *that* is retained or omitted) or infinitive clauses (6.2). We illustrate the possibilities and restrictions with the prepositional verb *approve of*:

$$
\text{Tom approved of}
\begin{cases}
\text{the meeting} \\
\text{what had been decided} \\
\text{meeting her} \\
\text{*(that) they should meet} \\
\text{*to meet her}
\end{cases}
$$

However, the restriction involving *that*-clauses applies only if the *that*-clause is direct object, and hence the preposition can be retained in the passive (*That they should meet was approved of*), even in extraposition, where the preposition immediately follows the passive verb phrase (*It was agreed to eventually that they should meet again soon*).

Note
Certain transitive verbs expressing causation of movement have an adverbial following the direct object, normally an adjunct of place:

  The hostess showed me to the door
  He saw Mary home
  John put the car into the garage
  Mary placed/set a vase on the table
  We kept them out of trouble

With the above verbs (in the senses exemplified) where the adverbial is obligatory, there is a similarity with complex transitive complementation: *cf* 12.26 *f*, 8.29, 8.44.

Noun phrases as direct object
12.15

Direct objects are typically noun phrases. It is usually possible for the direct object of an active sentence to become the subject of a passive sentence, with the subject of the active sentence as the prepositional complement in an optional *by*-phrase (7.5):

  The boy caught the ball ~ The ball was caught (by the boy)

It is, however, usual to omit the *by*-phrase, often because it is irrelevant or unknown, as in

  Order has been restored without bloodshed and without concessions
  The Prime Minister was attacked last night during the debate

or because it is redundant in the context, as in

  Jack fought Michael last night and Jack was beaten

The passive transformation is blocked when there is co-reference between subject and object, *ie* when there are reflexive, reciprocal, or possessive pronouns in the noun phrase as object:

John could see $\left\{\begin{array}{l}\text{Paul}\\\text{himself}\end{array}\right\}$ in the mirror

$\sim\left\{\begin{array}{l}\text{Paul}\\\text{*Himself}\end{array}\right\}$ could be seen in the mirror

We could hardly see each other in the fog

$\sim$*Each other could hardly be seen in the fog

The other waitress wiped $\left\{\begin{array}{l}\text{the tables}\\\text{her hands}\end{array}\right.$

$\sim\left\{\begin{array}{l}\text{The tables}\\\text{*Her hands}\end{array}\right\}$ were wiped by the other waitress

Note

[a] A shift of meaning may accompany shift of voice in verb phrases containing auxiliaries that have more than one meaning, *eg: shall, will,* and *can* (*cf* 3.48 *ff*):

John cannot do it $\sim$ It cannot be done (by John)

In the active sentence *can* would normally be interpreted as expressing ability, whereas in the passive sentence it is interpreted as expressing possibility.

[b] With dynamic verbs (3.35) we can distinguish between 'actional' passives, illustrated above in this section, and 'statal' passives. The latter express a state:

The house is already sold

Corresponding actives require an aspectual shift to the perfect (3.27 *ff*):

Someone has already sold the house   (*Someone already sells the house)

A sentence such as *They were married* is ambiguous between an actional interpretation (*They were married in church yesterday*) and a statal interpretation (*They were married when I last heard about them*).

12.16

A small group of transitive verbs, the most common of which is *have,* normally do not allow a passive transformation of the sentence:

They *have* a nice house   Will this *suit* you?
He *lacks* confidence   John *resembles* his father
The coat does not *fit* you

These verbs are sometimes considered to form a separate category of non-transitive verbs taking noun phrases as their complementation (*cf* also verbs of measure, 12.7 Note *d*). They include 'reciprocal' verbs such as *resemble, look like, equal* (*Two times three equals six*), *agree with, mean* ('*Oculist*' *means* '*eye-doctor*'); verbs of 'containing' or their opposite, such as *contain* (*The library contains a million books*), *hold* (*The audi-*

torium holds over a thousand people), comprise, lack; and verbs of 'suiting', such as *suit, fit, become (This dress becomes her). Contain* and *hold* occur in a similar sense in the passive but without a *by*-phrase: *A million books are contained in that library.*

12.17
Finite clauses as direct object

Like finite clauses as complementation of adjective phrases (12.12), finite clauses as direct object may have an indicative verb, putative *should*, or a subjunctive verb, depending on the class of the superordinate verb:

(a) factual superordinate verb, with indicative subordinate verb:

> They agree that she is pretty
> I know how he did it
> He forgot why they complained

(b) emotive verb, with indicative verb or putative *should:*

> I regret that $\begin{cases} \text{she should worry about it} \\ \text{she worries about it} \end{cases}$

(c) volitional verb, with subjunctive verb (3.46) or *should* (not clearly differentiated between its putative and obligational uses):

> I proposed that he $\begin{cases} \text{admit all applicants} \\ \text{should admit all applicants} \end{cases}$

Factual verbs that are used to convey an indirect question are followed by clauses with *whether* or (less commonly) *if:*

> He asked
> He doubted $\left.\right\} \begin{Bmatrix} \text{whether} \\ \text{if} \end{Bmatrix}$ they had arrived
> He didn't know

A verb may belong to more than one class. For example, *He suggested that she went* is ambiguous: if *suggested* is a factual verb, *she went* is a factual report, whereas if it is a volitional verb, *she went* is a suggested action. Similarly, within the class of factual verbs, *say* may be used with both a *that*-clause and (more commonly in the negative or in a question) a *whether/if* clause: *I didn't say that/whether they had arrived.*

Examples of the three classes of verbs are listed.

(a) factual verbs: *admit, agree, answer, believe, declare, deny, expect, hope, insist, know, report, say, see, suggest, suppose, think, understand*

factual verbs commonly followed by *whether/if: ask, discuss, doubt, find out, forget, (not) know, (not) notice, (not) say, wonder*

(b) emotive verbs: *deplore, prefer, regret*
(c) volitional verbs: *command, demand, insist, order, propose, recommend, suggest*

Finite clauses as direct object can become the subject of a corresponding passive sentence:

Everybody admitted that she sang well
  ~ That she sang well was admitted (by everybody)

However, it is far more usual for the passive to have extraposition with anticipatory *it* (14.24 *f*):

  ~ It was admitted (by everybody) that she sang well

Non-finite clauses as direct object
12.18
Among non-finite clauses as direct object, we distinguish between those with a subject and those without a subject, and within each type between infinitive and participle clauses:

	without subject	*to*-infinitive		*He likes to talk*
		-ing participle		*He likes talking*
non-finite clause object	with subject	infinitive	*to*-infinitive	*He wants her to come*
			bare infinitive	*He saw her come*
		participle	*-ing* participle	*He saw her coming*
			-ed participle	*He found the seats taken*

12.19
Non-finite clauses without subject
In non-finite clauses without an overt subject the verb is either an infinitive preceded by *to* or an *-ing* participle (but *cf* Note *c*). The implied subject is normally the subject of the superordinate clause. There are verbs which take

(1) only an infinitive clause:

John longed $\left\{\begin{array}{l}\text{to do}\\ \text{*doing}\end{array}\right\}$ homework

(2) only a participle clause:

John denied $\left\{\begin{array}{l}\text{having stolen}\\ \text{*to have stolen}\end{array}\right\}$ the money

(3) either an infinitive or a participle clause:

$$\text{John began} \begin{Bmatrix} \text{to write} \\ \text{writing} \end{Bmatrix} \text{a letter}$$

Where both constructions are admitted, there is usually felt to be an aspectual difference that influences the choice. The participle construction generally implies 'fulfilment' and the infinitive construction 'potentiality':

$$\text{He started} \begin{cases} \text{speaking and kept on for more than an hour} \\ \text{to speak but stopped because she objected} \end{cases}$$

Another factor influencing the choice is that the participle tends to express the progressive aspect (3.33 *ff*):

$$\text{I heard the door} \begin{cases} \text{slamming all night long} \\ \text{slam just after midnight} \end{cases}$$

The progressive aspect may also influence a preference for the participle after verbs of beginning, continuing, and ending, when multiple activities are involved:

$$\text{He began} \begin{cases} \text{opening all the cupboards} \\ \text{to open the cupboards} \end{cases}$$

While some verbs in this semantic group allow both constructions (*begin, continue, cease, start*), others allow only the participle construction (*finish, go on, keep (on), stop*).

For the three verbs *forget*, *remember* and *regret*, there is a temporal (and perhaps also modal) difference between the two constructions. The infinitive construction indicates that the action or event takes place after the mental process denoted by the verb has begun, while the reverse is true for the participle construction:

$$\begin{cases} \text{I remembered to fill out the form} \quad (\text{'I remembered that I was to} \\ \quad \text{fill out the form and then did so'}) \\ \text{I remembered filling out the form} \quad (\text{'I remembered that I had} \\ \quad \text{filled out the form'}) \end{cases}$$

$$\begin{cases} \text{I forgot to go to the bank} \quad (\text{'I forgot that I was to go to the bank} \\ \quad \text{and therefore did not do so'}) \\ \text{I forgot (about) going to the bank} \quad (\text{rare without } \textit{about;} \text{ 'I forgot} \\ \quad \text{that I went to the bank'}) \end{cases}$$

$$\begin{cases} \text{I regret to tell you that John stole it} \quad (\text{'I regret that I am about} \\ \quad \text{to tell you that John stole it'}) \\ \text{I regret telling you that John stole it} \quad (\text{'I regret that I told you that} \\ \quad \text{John stole it'}) \end{cases}$$

For one small group of verbs (*deserve, need, require,* and, less commonly, *want*), the choice involves a difference in voice, the participle construction corresponding to a passive infinitive construction:

$$\text{Your shoes need} \begin{cases} \text{cleaning} \\ \text{to be cleaned} \end{cases}$$

We list some common verbs according to the non-finite clauses that they allow, omitting the three small groups that we have discussed above:

verbs with infinitive only: *agree, arrange, ask* (see Note *d*),
   choose, decide, demand, deserve, expect, hope, learn, long,
   manage, mean, offer, pretend, promise, refuse, threaten, want,
   wish
verbs with participle only: *deny, dislike, enjoy, fancy, finish,*
   (*cannot*) *help, keep* (*on*), *don't mind, miss, put off, risk, cannot*
   stand, stop, suggest
verbs with infinitive or participle (mainly emotive verbs or verbs
   expressing striving or lack of striving): *cannot bear, delay, hate,*
   intend, like, love, neglect, omit, plan, prefer, try

There is in general no passive for sentences whose object is a non-finite clause without a subject. The exceptions are with a few verbs (notably *agree, arrange, decide*) and then only if there is extraposition:

They decided to meet in London ~ It was decided to meet in London

Note

[a] With verbs like *need*, the subject of the superordinate clause is not the implied subject of the participle clause, but rather its implied direct object: *Your shoes need cleaning* implies that you or someone needs to clean the shoes.

[b] We might consider here also several verbs with infinitive clauses which are not direct objects. With *appear, happen,* and *seem,* the infinitive clause is more plausibly seen as part of the subject: *He appears to like the show ~ That he likes the show appears* (*true*). The quasi-adverbial function of the main verb can be shown by the paraphrase *He apparently likes the show.* There are analogies with such adjectives as *sure, certain, bound* in relation to infinitive clauses: *He is certain to like the show ~ That he will like the show is certain ~ He will certainly like the show.*

[c] The verb *help* can be followed by a construction with the bare infinitive: *I helped her* (*to*) *do it.* Otherwise, the bare infinitive is found only in a few set phrases, eg: *make do, make believe,* (*live and*) *let live, let go.*

[d] Some factual verbs will permit as direct object a non-finite indirect question, but not of the *yes-no* type: *He asked/inquired how to get there.* Cf: *He arranged/forgot when to do it.*

Complex transitive complementation
12.20
Non-finite and verbless clauses with subject

When a clause as object in a monotransitive sentence (a) is non-finite or verbless, and (b) has its subject expressed, this subject behaves as though it alone were the direct object of the superordinate verb; it can therefore be the subject in a passive transformation. Compare (1a) and (2a) with (1b) and (2b):

(1a) Everyone expected *that Mary would marry John*
　　　That Mary would marry John was expected by everyone
　　　　　(*Mary* was expected by everyone *would marry John*)

(1b) Everyone expected *Mary to marry John*
　　　Mary was expected by everyone *to marry John*
　　　　　(*Mary to marry John* was expected by everyone)

(2a) John thought *that Mary was exceptionally clever*

(2b) John thought *Mary exceptionally clever*
　　　Mary was thought *exceptionally clever*

It is this divisibility of an essentially clausal object that is the outstanding characteristic of complex transitive complementation.

To-infinitive clauses with subject
12.21

Two classes of verb have to be distinguished as taking complex transitive complementation: factual and non-factual. With factual verbs the subordinate clause normally has a stative verb and (especially when the subordinate verb is other than *be*) a finite construction is preferred in ordinary usage to the non-finite, except that the latter provides a convenient passive form. The attribute of *be* in this construction is required to be 'current' (7.9):

　John believed that the stranger was a policeman
　John believed the stranger *to be a policeman*
　The stranger was believed *to be a policeman*

　The professor assumed that the student knew some French
　The professor assumed the student *to know some French* (formal)
　The student was assumed *to know some French*

Other common factual verbs: *feel, find, imagine, know, suppose, think*.

The non-factual verbs with this non-finite construction express a causative, volitional or attitudinal relationship with the subordinate clause. There is no restriction on the class of verbs in the non-finite clause and no stylistic restriction on its use:

　John intended that Mary should sing an aria
　John intended Mary *to sing an aria*
　Mary was intended *to sing an aria*

With some of the superordinate verbs no finite-clause construction of this type is possible: notably, *get, want, like:*

> John wanted Mary *to play the piano*
>> (*but* that Mary (should) play the piano *occurs in AmE*)

Other common non-factual verbs: *cause, expect, hate, mean.*

When the subject of the subordinate clause is identical with that of the superordinate one, the non-finite construction is possible with factual and causative verbs only if the reflexive is expressed (as it commonly is with *get*):

> I believed that I had won
> I believed myself to have won (rare)
> *I believed to have won

With volitional and attitudinal verbs, however, co-referential subjects are readily allowed but the subordinate subject cannot be expressed in the non-finite clause (*cf* 12.19):

> I intended that I should go
> I intended to go

Note
A few verbs, *get, hate, like, want,* do not have a corresponding passive, while a few others, in particular *say,* occur only in the passive form of the construction:

> He was said to come from Ireland ~ *They said him to come from Ireland

12.22
Prepositional verbs with *for* use *for* to introduce a *to*-infinitive clause:

> He arranged for Mary to come at once

The infinitive construction is therefore a direct object of the prepositional verb, which may be emotive or volitional. Some common verbs with this construction: *ask, call, long, plan, wait.*

Note
Prepositional verbs that are ditransitive allow another object (perhaps also introduced by a preposition) to precede the infinitive clause:

> He $\left\{ \begin{array}{l} \text{telephoned} \\ \text{arranged with} \end{array} \right\}$ John for Mary to come at once

Cf: He telephoned John/He arranged with John for another meeting.

12.23
Bare infinitive clauses with subject
Three causative verbs take a bare infinitive in their infinitive clause: *have* ('cause'), *let, make:*

> They had/let/made Bob teach Mary

Some verbs of perception take the bare infinitive in the active: *feel, hear, notice, observe, see, smell, watch*. The verbs of perception also occur with the *-ing* participle clause (12.24):

I watched Bob teach(ing) Mary

In the passive, the bare infinitive is replaced by the *to*-infinitive: *Bob was made to clean his room, They were heard to shout something*. This does not apply to *have* and *let*, which have no passive, except for perhaps as in *He was let go*. Only *let* has a passive of the infinitive clause: *They let Mary be taught (by Bob)*. With the verbs of perception, there is a passive with *being* (12.24): *I watched Mary being taught (by Bob)*. For the passive corresponding to the infinitive clause after *have* and *see* as in *I had Bob teach Mary ~ I had Mary taught (by Bob)*, see 12.25.

12.24
-ing participle clauses with subject
Verbs taking an *-ing* participle clause fall into two classes: those which permit the subordinate subject to be genitive (predominantly emotive verbs with personal nouns or pronouns) and those which disallow the genitive.

Genitive optional (*cf* 11.18):

I dislike him/his driving my car

With this type, the subject of the subordinate clause cannot be the subject of the superordinate clause in the passive: **He is disliked (by me) driving my car*. When the superordinate and subordinate subjects are co-referential, the subordinate subject is not expressed: *I dislike driving my car*.

Genitive disallowed:

I found $\left\{ \begin{array}{l} \text{him} \\ \text{*his} \end{array} \right\}$ driving my car

With this type, the subject of the subordinate clause can be the subject of the superordinate clause in the passive: *He was found driving my car*. When the superordinate and subordinate subjects are co-referential, the subordinate subject is expressed by the reflexive: *I found myself driving my car*.

Where there is a choice between *-ing* participle or infinitive (whether bare or *to*-infinitive), there is usually felt to be an aspectual difference that influences the choice (12.19):

I hate the door $\left\{ \begin{array}{l} \text{slamming all night long} \\ \text{to slam just after midnight} \end{array} \right.$

Verbs taking a non-finite clause with subject may have

(1) only an -*ing* participle clause:

   I started Bob cleaning the car

(2) either an -*ing* participle or a bare infinitive clause:

   I watched Bob $\begin{cases} \text{doing his homework} \\ \text{do his homework} \end{cases}$

(3) either an -*ing* participle or a *to*-infinitive clause:

   I hate Bob $\begin{cases} \text{working in the garden} \\ \text{to work in the garden} \end{cases}$

We list common verbs according to whether they permit or disallow the genitive, and within each class, we note the verbs which, in addition to the -*ing* construction, permit the infinitive construction, with or without *to:*

> genitive optional: (1) -*ing* participle only: (*cannot*) *afford, enjoy, forget,* (*not*) *mind, regret, remember, resent, risk,* (*cannot*) *stand;*
> (2) -*ing* participle or *to*-infinitive: *dislike, hate, like, love, prefer*
> genitive disallowed: (1) -*ing* participle only: *catch, find, keep, leave, start, stop;* (2) -*ing* participle or bare infinitive: *have* ('cause');
> verbs of perception – *feel, hear, notice, observe, see, smell, watch;*
> -*ing* participle or *to*-infinitive: *get,* informal (*I got Bob cleaning/to clean his room*)

12.25
-*ed* participle clauses with subject
We can distinguish between three types of construction involving -*ed* participle with subject:

> causative/volitional verb: *He got the watch repaired*
> factual verb expressing an event: *He saw the watch stolen*
> factual verb expressing a current state: *He found the watch stolen*

Some of the causative/volitional verbs have analogous finite clauses with a subjunctive verb or *should* (12.17): *He ordered that the watch* (*should*) *be repaired.* Similarly, the factual verbs have analogous finite clauses with an indicative verb: *He saw the watch stolen* ~ *He saw that the watch was being stolen, He found the watch stolen* ~ *He found that the watch was stolen. Have* can be either causative or factual: thus *He had a watch stolen* is ambiguous between 'He caused the watch to be stolen' and 'He suffered the loss of a watch' (14.23 Note *a*).

Common verbs of the three types are:

causative/volitional: *get, order, have* ('cause'), *want*
factual, expressing event: *see, have* ('suffer')
factual, expressing state: *find, keep, leave*

The factual verbs allow passivization:

The tourists found the chairs occupied
~The chairs were found occupied (by the tourists)

Verbless clauses with subject
12.26

In both the *-ing* and *-ed* clauses just considered, it is reasonable to see the non-finite clauses in many cases as resulting from ellipsis of infinitival *be:*

I hate *him* (*to be*) *driving my car*
They found *the chairs* (*to be*) *occupied*

With complementation by verbless clauses, we can also see underlying *be* clauses:

I consider $\begin{cases} \text{that John is a good driver} \\ \text{John to be a good driver} \\ \textit{John a good driver} \end{cases}$

The two elements of such verbless clauses are thus in an intensive *subject-complement* relation, but since the whole construction is itself the object in the superordinate clause, we do not depart from the tradition of describing them as *object* and *object complement* respectively. As with other transitive sentences, the 'object' can be the subject in a passive transformation (*John is considered a good driver*), and as with other intensive clauses, the complement element can usually be realized by either a noun phrase or an adjective phrase:

He made the girl $\begin{cases} \text{his secretary} \\ \text{much happier} \end{cases}$

When the object complement is an adjective it may be a 'current' or a 'resulting' attribute (7.9). Verbs taking a current attribute include: *call, consider, declare, find, have, keep, leave, like, prefer, think, want*:

I called him stupid
I always have my coffee hot

Verbs taking a resulting attribute: *get, make, paint*, as well as *call, declare*, etc, in their formal 'performative' use:

I made her very angry
I declare the meeting open

Some combinations of verb and adjective resemble transitive phrasal verbs (12.3) in that the adjective can precede or follow the noun phrase and (like the particle) cannot precede a personal pronoun:

She *put* the tablecloth *straight*	She *put* the tablecloth *out*
She *put* it *straight*	She *put* it *out*
She *put straight* the tablecloth	She *put out* the tablecloth
*She *put straight* it	*She *put out* it

Likewise, the adjective cannot be separated from the verb by an adverb as adjunct:

She quickly *put* the tablecloth *straight*	She quickly *put* the tablecloth *out*
*She *put* quickly the tablecloth *straight*	*She *put* quickly the tablecloth *out*
*She *put* the tablecloth quickly *straight*	*She *put* the tablecloth quickly *out*

Make is commonly the verb in such combinations: *make clear* (*the reason*), *make possible* (*the meeting*), *make plain* (*the difference*). Among adjectives, *open, loose, free,* and *clear* are particularly common: *push open, keep loose, shake free, leave clear*. In many cases, there is a close meaning relationship between verb and adjective: *cut short, wash clean, drain dry, pack tight*.

The adjective retains its potentialities for modification:

He *pushed* the door *wide open*
She didn't *wash* the shirts *as clean as Mary did*

12.27

Many of the verbs mentioned in 12.26 as taking adjective phrases as object complement will also admit noun phrases (exceptions include *get, have* and *put*). When the object complement is a noun phrase it can, as with the adjective phrase, be 'current' or 'resulting'. In general, however, the noun phrase as current attribute is uncommon and somewhat formal (unless it is indefinite with a gradable noun head and hence with an adjectival quality):

They thought John the leader (rather uncommon)
They thought John a fool

As resulting attribute, on the other hand, the noun phrase is freely used:

They $\begin{Bmatrix} \text{elected} \\ \text{made} \\ \text{appointed} \\ \text{named} \end{Bmatrix}$ John $\begin{cases} \text{(the) chairman} \\ \text{(the) ambassador to Peru} \end{cases}$

They made John a useful mechanic

The verbs *appoint, crown, elect,* and *consider* are commonly used with an alternative *as* construction:

> They elected him (as) their leader

The following verbs are among those that can have complex complementation only with *as* or (less commonly) *for: accept as, class as, describe as, intend as, interpret as, know as, mistake for, recognize as, regard as, take as/for, treat as, use as;* for example: *They recognized John as intelligent/their spokesman.*

Most verbs taking a noun phrase as object complement will also admit an adjective phrase; outstanding exceptions include verbs of appointing such as *appoint, choose, elect, name.*

Note

The object complement may precede the 'direct object' when the latter is lengthy or requires special emphasis:

> They will elect chairman anyone willing to serve
> He thought desirable most of the women in the room

Limitedly, an analogous inversion can occur with the *-ing* and *-ed* clauses of 12.24 *f.* *Cf* also 12.3.

Ditransitive complementation
12.28
Noun phrase as both indirect object and direct object

Ditransitive complementation involves two objects that are not in intensive relationship (7.6): an indirect object (normally animate), which is positioned first, and a direct object (normally concrete):

> He   gave   the girl   a doll
> S   V O_i O_d

Indirect objects can be omitted without affecting the meaning or function of the rest of the sentence:

He gave the girl a doll $\begin{cases} \sim \text{He gave a doll} \\ \sim \text{He gave the girl} \end{cases}$

He bought the girl a white hat $\begin{cases} \sim \text{He bought a white hat} \\ \sim \text{He bought the girl} \end{cases}$

They can usually be replaced by a corresponding prepositional phrase, which normally follows the direct object:

> He gave a doll to the girl
> He bought a white hat for the girl

We list some common verbs which allow the indirect object to be replaced by a prepositional phrase, the preposition concerned being indicated:

ask (a question) of (John), bring to, do (a favour) for, do (a disservice) to, find for, give to, leave for/to, lend to, make for, offer to, owe to, pay for, pour for, promise to, read to, save for, show to, teach to, tell to, throw to

A few verbs disallow the variant with a prepositional phrase: *allow, refuse, wish*. With *allow* and *wish*, it would be exceptional to have either of the noun phrases omitted.

One group of verbs (chiefly *ask, owe, pay, teach, tell, show*) taking ditransitive complementation allow either object to be omitted:

$$\text{I paid John the money} \sim \begin{cases} \text{I paid John} \\ \text{I paid the money} \\ \text{I paid the money to John} \end{cases}$$

Note

[a] The verb *give* allows considerable flexibility: the direct object can be abstract and the indirect object inanimate, though in such cases the latter has no variant with a prepositional phrase:

He gave the car a wash ('He washed the car')
 ~*He gave a wash to the car

Sentences with some ditransitive verbs have two passives:

$$\text{He gave the girl a doll} \begin{cases} \sim \text{The girl was given a doll} \\ \sim \text{A doll was given the girl} \end{cases}$$

Of these two passives, the first is the more common. The second is usually replaced by the corresponding prepositional phrase:

A doll was given to the girl

[b] The verb *make* admits several different constructions:

monotrans: She made a cake
ditrans: She made him a cake (~a cake for him)
complex trans: She made him a good husband (~him into a good husband)
intensive: She made a good wife
intensive with 'indirect object': She made him a good wife (~turned out to be
 a good wife to/for him)

12.29
Ditransitive prepositional verbs

Ditransitive verbs whose direct object must be introduced by a preposition (*ie* ditransitive prepositional verbs) normally allow only one passive, with the indirect object as subject:

We reminded him of the agreement
 ~ He was reminded of the agreement

They differ from most ditransitive verbs (*cf* 12.31) in frequently allowing the indirect object to be expressed alone: *We reminded him (of the agreement)*.

Common verbs of this type enter into constructions of the form *accuse X of Y*, where with most of the verbs X is usually a person and Y is usually a thing:

charge with, compare to, congratulate on, convince of, deprive of, inform of, introduce to, punish for, refer to, remind of, rob of, sentence to, treat to

But there are notable exceptions, such as *explain X to Y*, where X would normally be a thing and Y a person.

With several verbs (*eg: blame, provide, supply*), either of the noun phrases in the complementation can follow the verb immediately, the other requiring a preposition:

She blamed John *for* the damage ~ She blamed the damage *on* John
They provided the homeless *with* blankets ~ They provided blankets
   for the homeless
They supplied the terrorists *with* guns ~ They supplied guns *for/to*
   the terrorists

12.30
Idiomatic expressions consisting of verb+noun phrase+preposition

Some verbs form an idiomatic unit when combined with certain noun phrases followed by certain prepositions and in this respect resemble many prepositional verbs (12.4). There are two passive forms of the sentence, since either of two noun phrases can become the subject of a passive sentence:

They had *made good use of* the house
   ~ *Good use* had been *made of* the house
   ~ The house had been *made good use of* (informal)

Other examples of the latter kind of passive (chiefly informal) are:

Mary realized she was being *made fun of*
Her beauty was *made much of*
Pretty girls will always be *taken notice of*
The children were *taken good care of*

The following list includes some common idioms consisting of V + NP + prep:

catch sight of	make allowance for	put a stop to
give place to	make fun of	set fire to
give way to	make a fuss over/about	take account of
keep pace with	make room for	take advantage of
lose sight of	make use of	take care of

lose touch with   pay attention to   take note of
lose track of   put an end to   take notice of

12.31
Noun phrases as indirect object+finite clauses as direct object

With some verbs the indirect object is obligatory:

John convinced me that he was right
~ *John convinced that he was right

With other verbs, it can be omitted:

John showed me that he was honest
~ John showed that he was honest

Common verbs in this type of construction are listed according to whether the indirect object is obligatory or optional.

indirect object obligatory: *advise, assure, convince, inform, persuade, remind, tell*

indirect object optional: *ask* (+indirect question), *promise, show, teach, warn*

The indirect object often occurs without the direct (*cf.* 12.29).

The sentence can be passivized, with the indirect object as subject of the passive sentence: *I was convinced that he was right.* The verbs *show* and *tell* allow also the direct object to become subject of the passive sentence, though normally there is extraposition: *That he was an honest man was shown (to me) ~ It was shown (to me) that he was an honest man.*

Some verbs require a prepositional phrase introduced by *to* instead of the indirect object. They all allow the omission of the prepositional phrase:

John mentioned (to me) that they were sick

They allow a passive form with the direct object becoming subject of the sentence, though normally there is extraposition: *That they were sick was mentioned (to me) (by John) ~ It was mentioned (to me) (by John) that they were sick.* Common verbs used in this construction include *admit, announce, confess, declare, explain, mention, point out, remark, report, say, state, suggest.*

12.32
Noun phrases as indirect object+non-finite clauses as direct object

Many of the superordinate verbs in 12.31 will allow the clausal direct object to be a *to*-infinitive clause:

374 The verb and its complementation **12.32**

$$\text{They persuaded John} \begin{cases} \text{that he should see me} \\ \textit{to see me} \end{cases}$$

This is possible only when the indirect object is identical with the subject of the direct object clause: thus, *They persuaded John that Mary should see me* has no corresponding form with a non-finite clause as direct object. The subject of the non-finite clause can become the subject of a passive superordinate clause:

John was persuaded *to see me*

Not all verbs taking a finite clause allow the non-finite clause as direct object but among the common verbs that permit both constructions we should mention *ask* (with *wh*-indirect questions), *persuade, remind, teach, tell* and *warn*. There are several verbs which permit the non-finite clause but which do not (or do not freely) admit the finite clause; for example, *ask* (= 'request'), *encourage, force, help*, and *order:*

Mary helped John to carry the bag
(*Mary helped John that he might carry the bag)

There is a superficial similarity between certain complex transitive and ditransitive examples:

complex trans: He wanted Mary to teach Bob   [1]
ditrans: He persuaded Mary to teach Bob   [2]

The difference can be seen when the subordinate clause is made passive:

He wanted Bob to be taught by Mary   [3, = 1]
He persuaded Bob to be taught by Mary   [4, ≠ 2]

This difference depends on the fact that, with complex transitive verbs, the infinitive clause (*Mary to teach Bob*) is direct object and *Mary* is not itself a constituent of the superordinate clause. With the ditransitive verb *persuade*, however, *Mary* as indirect object is indeed a separate constituent (the subject of the infinitive clause in this instance being only implied). In [4], this indirect object function is taken over by *Bob*, and hence the radically changed meaning.

Note
When a *wh*-clause is object to a verb of stating, the subject is identical with the indirect object; with verbs of asking, however, it is identical with the superordinate subject:

He told them where to go (= where *they* should go)
He asked them where to go (= where *he* should go)

Bibliographical note
On types and problems of complementation, see Aijmer (1972); Allen (1966); Bald (1972); Halliday (1967–68); Huddleston (1971), Ch 3, 4; Macháček (1965); Poldauf (1972); Rosenbaum (1967); van Ek (1966); Stockwell *et al* (1973), Ch 8.

THIRTEEN
THE COMPLEX NOUN PHRASE

13.1

Just as the sentence may be indefinitely complex (11.1), so may the noun phrase. This must be so, since sentences themselves can be reshaped so as to come within noun-phrase structure. For example, the following sentences – simple and complex – can become one simple sentence with a very complex noun phrase as subject:

The girl is Mary Smith	[1a]
The girl is pretty	[1b]
The girl was standing in the corner	[1c]
You waved to the girl when you entered	[1d]
The girl became angry because you waved to her	[1e]

*The pretty girl standing in the corner who became angry because
  you waved to her when you entered* is Mary Smith   [2]

Moreover, starting from [2], we could unhesitatingly reconstruct any of the sentences listed in [1] – and in fact we could not understand the noun-phrase subject of [2] unless we recognized its component parts as they are set out in [1]. Yet [2] has introduced many changes. We have suppressed all or part of the verbs in [1b] and [1c] (different in tense and aspect); we have put the complement *pretty* of [1b] before the noun *girl*; we have replaced *the girl* of [1e] by *who*. The purpose of the present chapter is to state the conditions governing such changes.

13.2

In describing complex noun phrases, we distinguish three components:

(a) *The head,* around which the other components cluster and which dictates concord and other kinds of congruence with the rest of the sentence outside the noun phrase. Thus, we can have [1], [2], and [3], but not [4]:

The pretty girl *standing in the corner* ... is ...	[1]
The pretty girls *standing in the corner* ... are ...	[2]

He frightened *the pretty* girl *standing in the corner*   [3]
*He frightened *the pretty* lampshade *standing in the corner*   [4]

That is, there are no constraints affecting *frighten* and *the pretty
... standing in the corner* but only *frighten* and the head *lampshade*.

(b) *The premodification*, which comprises all the items placed before
the head – notably adjectives and nouns. Thus:

> *The pretty* girl
> *Some pretty college* girls

(c) *The postmodification*, comprising all the items placed after the head
– notably prepositional phrases, non-finite clauses, and relative
clauses:

> The girl *in the corner*
> The girl *standing in the corner*
> The girl *who stood in the corner*

13.3
Restrictive and non-restrictive
Modification can be restrictive or non-restrictive. That is, the head can be
viewed as a member of a class which can be linguistically identified only
through the modification that has been supplied (*restrictive*). Or the head
can be viewed as unique or as a member of a class that has been independently identified (for example, in a preceding sentence); any modification
given to such a head is additional information which is not essential for
identifying the head, and we call it *non-restrictive*.

In example [2] of 13.1, the girl is only identifiable as Mary Smith provided we understand that it is the particular girl who is *pretty*, who was
standing in the corner, and who *became angry*. Such modification is
restrictive. By contrast, if a man (in a monogamous society) says

Come and meet my beautiful wife

the modification *beautiful* is understood as non-restrictive. Again,

Mary Smith, who is in the corner, wants to meet you

has a non-restrictive relative clause since Mary Smith's identity is independent of whether or not she is in the corner, though the information on
her present location may be useful enough. In these examples, the modification is *inherently* non-restrictive, since the heads in question – being
treated as unique – will not normally admit restriction. But any head can
be non-restrictively modified:

The pretty girl, who is a typist, is Mary Smith

Here the only information offered to identify the girl as Mary Smith is the allusion to her prettiness; the mention of her work as a typist is not offered as an aid to identification but for additional interest.

Modification at its 'most restrictive' tends to come after the head: that is, our decision to use an item as a premodifier (such as *silly* in *The silly boy got lost*) often reflects our wish that it be taken for granted and not be interpreted as a specific identifier. Secondly, restrictive modification tends to be given more prosodic emphasis than the head; non-restrictive modification, on the other hand, tends to be unstressed in pre-head position, while in post-head position, its 'parenthetic' relation is endorsed by being given a separate tone unit (App II.7), or – in writing – by being enclosed by commas.

13.4
Temporary and permanent

There is a second dichotomy that has some affinities with the distinction between restrictive and non-restrictive but rather more with the contrast of non-progressive and progressive in predication (3.27), generic or specific reference in determiners (4.16), or permanent and temporary in agentials (App I.13 Note *b*). Modification in noun-phrase structure may also be seen as permanent or temporary (5.18), such that items placed in premodification position are given the linguistic status of permanent or at any rate characteristic features. Although this does not mean that post-modification position is committed to either temporariness or permanence, those adjectives which cannot premodify have a notably temporary reference. Thus *The man is ready* would be understood as having reference only to a specific time and this corresponds to the non-occurrence of **The ready man*. On this basis, we see that timidity and fear are contrasted in part according as the first is seen as permanent, the second as temporary:

A man who is timid ~ A timid man
A man who is afraid ~ *An afraid man

Just as some modifiers are too much identified with temporary status to appear in pre-head position, so there can be modification constrained to pre-head position because it indicates permanent status. Compare *original* in *the original version* and *his work is quite original;* in the latter, it would permit adverbial indication of time span (*now, always, . . .*), as well as use in premodification.

Postmodification
13.5
Explicitness

As we saw in 13.1, premodification is in general to be interpreted (and

...ost frequently can only be interpreted) in terms of postmodification and its greater explicitness. It will therefore be best to begin our detailed study of noun-phrase structure with the forms of postmodification.

Explicitness in postmodification varies considerably, however. It is greater in the finite relative clause

> The girl who was standing in the corner

than in the non-finite clause

> The girl standing in the corner

from which the explicit tense (*is ?/was ?*) has disappeared, though this in turn is more explicit than the prepositional phrase

> The girl in the corner

from which the verb indicating a specific posture has also disappeared. We are able (and usually must be able) to infer such facts as tense from the sentential context much as we infer the subject of non-finite adverbial clauses (11.35):

> The girl standing in the corner $\left\{ \begin{array}{l} now \\ last\ night \end{array} \right\}$ is my sister

> *Have you spoken* to the girl in the corner?

Part of the relative clause's explicitness lies in the specifying power of the relative pronoun. It is capable (a) of showing agreement with the head and (b) of indicating its status as an element in the relative clause structure.

Agreement is on the basis of a two-term 'gender' system, personal and non-personal (4.58 *ff*, 4.81):

Joan, who ...	London, which ...
The boy/people who ...	The fox/animals which ...
The human being who ...	The human body which ...
The fairy who ...	The unicorn which ...

It will be seen from these examples that 'personality' is ascribed basically to human beings but extends to creatures in the supernatural world (angels, elves, etc) which are thought of as having human characteristics such as speech. It does not extend to the body or character, in part or whole, of a human being, living or dead, when this is considered as separate from the entire person. Pet animals can be regarded as 'personal' (at least by their owners):

> Rover, *who* was barking, frightened the children

On the other hand human babies can be regarded (though rarely perhaps by their parents) as not having developed personality:

This is the baby *which* needs inoculation

Though ships may take the personal pronoun *she* (4.64), the relative pronoun is regularly non-personal:

Is *she* the ship *which* is due to leave for New York tomorrow?

It is noteworthy that collective nouns (4.62) are treated as personal when they have plural concord, non-personal when they have singular:

The $\begin{Bmatrix} \text{committee} \\ \text{group} \end{Bmatrix} \begin{Bmatrix} \textit{who were} \\ \textit{which was} \end{Bmatrix}$ responsible for this decision ...

13.6
Case in the relative pronoun
Case is used to indicate the status of the relative pronoun in its clause. There are two situations to consider. First, if the pronoun is in a genitive relation to a noun head, the pronoun can have the form *whose:*

The woman *whose* daughter you met is Mrs Brown
   (The woman is Mrs Brown; you met *her* daughter)
The house *whose* roof was damaged has now been repaired
   (The house has now been repaired; *its* roof was damaged)

In examples like the latter where the antecedent head is non-personal, there is some tendency to avoid the use of *whose* (by using, for example, *the roof of which*), presumably because many regard it as the genitive only of the personal *who.*

Secondly, with a personal antecedent, the relative pronoun can show the distinction between *who* and *whom*, depending on its role as subject of the relative clause or as object or as prepositional complement:

The girl who spoke to him	[1]
The girl to whom he spoke	[2]
The girl who(m) he spoke to	[3]
The girl who(m) he met	[4]

It will be noticed that when the governing preposition precedes its complement (*cf* 6.3) as in the rather formal [2], the choice of *whom* is obligatory. When it does not, as in the more informal [3], or when the relative pronoun is the object, as in [4], there is some choice between *who* or *whom*, the latter being preferred in written English and by some speakers, the former being widely current informally.

13.7
Relative pronoun and adverbial
The relative pronoun can be replaced by special adjunct forms for place, time, and cause:

That is the place *where* he was born   [1]
That is the period *when* he lived here   [2]
That is the reason *why* he spoke   [3]

There are considerable and complicated restrictions on these adjunct forms, however. Many speakers find their use along with the corresponding antecedent somewhat tautologous – especially [3] – and would prefer the *wh-* clause without antecedent:

That is *where* he was born
That is *when* he lived here
That is *why* he spoke

If *how* is used, such clauses cannot in any case have an antecedent noun:

That is *how* he spoke

Moreover, there are restrictions on the antecedent nouns that can occur in [1–3]. With [3], *reason* is virtually alone, and with [1] and [2], it is also the most general and abstract nouns of place and time that seem to be preferred. Thus while

The office *where* he works . . .   The day *when* he was born . . .

are acceptable to most users of English, others would prefer a prepositional phrase in each case:

The office $\begin{cases} \text{at which . . . (formal)} \\ \text{which . . . at} \end{cases}$ The day $\begin{cases} \text{on which . . . (formal)} \\ \text{which . . . on} \end{cases}$

or one of the less explicit forms that we shall now be considering (*The office he works at, The day he was born*).

Restrictive relative clauses
Choice of relative pronoun
13.8

Though most of the examples in 13.5 *ff* have been of restrictive clauses, it is in the non-restrictive relative clauses that the most explicit forms of relative pronoun are typically used. In restrictive clauses, frequent use is made of a general pronoun *that* which is independent of the personal or non-personal character of the antecedent and also of the function of the pronoun in the relative clause:

The boy *that* is playing the piano . . . (or *who*)   [1]
The table *that* stands in the corner . . . (or *which*)   [2]
The boy *that* we met . . . (or *who(m)*)   [3]
The table *that* we admire . . . (or *which*)   [4]
The boy *that* the dog ran towards . . . (or *towards whom*)   [5]
The table *that* the boy crawled under . . . (or *under which*)   [6]

Provided the relative pronoun is not the subject of the relative clause, as in [1] and [2], a further option exists in relative clause structure of having no relative pronoun at all: the clause with 'zero' ($\varnothing$) relative pronoun. The examples [3–6] could take this form:

The boy we met ... (who(m), that)
The table we admire ... (which, that)
The boy the dog ran towards ... (towards whom, who(m)/that ... towards)
The table the boy crawled under ... (under which, which/that ... under)

Some choice exists in placing a preposition which has a *wh-* pronoun as its complement (13.6); there is no such choice with *that* and zero, where the preposition must be postposed.

The choices are summarized in the diagram:

$$
\text{The}
\begin{cases} \text{man} \\ \text{table} \end{cases}
\begin{cases} \text{who} \\ \text{that} \\ \text{which} \end{cases}
\text{remained}
$$

$$
\text{The}
\begin{cases} \text{man} \\ \text{table} \end{cases}
\begin{cases} \text{who(m)} \\ \text{that} \\ \varnothing \\ \text{which} \end{cases}
\begin{cases} \text{I saw} \\ \text{I glanced at} \end{cases}
$$

$$
\text{The}
\begin{cases} \text{man at whom} \\ \text{table at which} \end{cases}
\text{I glanced}
$$

Note

Choices are not only connected with relative formality. Some prepositions cannot be postposed (**the meeting that I slept during*). *Who* is often preferred to *that* when it is subject and when the antecedent is personal (*people who visit me*); but *that* is preferred to *who(m)* when it is object, in part perhaps to avoid the *who/whom* choice (*people that I visit*). When the verb in the relative clause is *be*, the complement pronoun must be *that* or zero (*John is not the man he was*). This example illustrates one of the most favoured uses of zero: *ie* when the pronoun is object or complement, the subject is pronominal, and the relative clause is short. When the antecedent is long and complex, *wh-* pronouns are preferred:

I have interests outside my daily professional work which give me great pleasure

Just as *that* and zero are available when the relative pronoun is dominated by a preposition, so they can be used when the relative pronoun is part of a place, time, or cause adjunct. With place adjuncts, the preposition must usually be expressed:

This is the garden (that) he sunbathes in
This is the university (that) he works at

But with the time adjuncts, omission of the preposition is usual whether the pronoun is *that* or zero (*cf* 6.25 *f*):

This is the time (that) he normally arrives (at)
Monday was the day (that) he left (on)

In many cases, indeed, omission of the preposition is obligatory, especially when the antecedent is itself the head of a time adjunct phrase:

He worked the whole time (that) he lived there

But when (less frequently and more formally) the pronoun is *which*, the preposition must be expressed in these instances and it would be usual to make it precede the pronoun (*cf* 13.7):

This is the time *at which* he normally arrives
Monday was the day *on which* he left

With cause and manner adjuncts, the usual pronoun is *that* or zero, and there is no preposition:

This is the reason (that) he came
This is the way (that) he did it

But with manner adjuncts, it would not be abnormal to find *which* with a preposition in a more formal style:

This is the way *in which* he did it

13.10
Quantified heads

Beside the noun phrase *the girls that he knew*, we may have one in which the head is made quantitatively indefinite with the predeterminer *such*, the relative pronoun *that* being replaced by *as:*

Such girls *as* he knew were at the party

Compare: *As many girls as he knew* ... A further connection with comparative sentences (*cf* 11.37 *ff*) can be seen in:

$\left.\begin{array}{l}More \\ Fewer\end{array}\right\}$ girls *than* he knew were at the party

13.11
Non-restrictive relative clauses

The loose non-restrictive relationship is often semantically indistinguishable from coordination (with or without conjunction) or adverbial subordination, as we indicate by paraphrases of the examples below. The repertoire of pronouns is limited to the *wh-* items:

Then he met Mary, $\begin{cases} \textit{who} \text{ invited him to a party} \\ \textit{and she} \text{ invited him to a party} \end{cases}$

Here is John Smith $\begin{cases} \textit{, who(m)} \text{ I mentioned the other day} \\ \textit{; I mentioned } \textit{him} \text{ the other day} \end{cases}$

He got lost on Snowdon, $\begin{cases} \textit{which} \text{ was enveloped in fog} \\ \textit{when it} \text{ was enveloped in fog} \end{cases}$

He got lost on Snowdon, $\begin{cases} \textit{which} \text{ he was exploring} \\ \textit{while} \text{ he was exploring } \textit{it} \end{cases}$

Note

As a determiner, *which* appears in non-restrictive clauses that are introduced especially by temporal adjuncts, but this is largely in formal style:

He emigrated in 1840, *at which time* there was much hardship and unrest

13.12
Sentential relative clauses

One type of non-restrictive clause has as its antecedent not a noun phrase but a whole clause or sentence or even sequence of sentences. As with the clauses in 13.11, the relationship frequently resembles coordination, but these clauses are also very much like disjuncts. For example:

He admires Mrs Brown, which $\begin{cases} \text{surprises me} \\ \text{I find strange} \end{cases}$

Cf 'and this surprises me'; 'to my surprise'.

Quite often, *which* is used in these clauses as a determiner of factive nouns which represent the antecedent clause or sentence:

The train may have been held up, *in which case* we are wasting our time

13.13
Appositive clauses

The appositive clause (9.58) resembles the relative clause in being capable of introduction by *that*, and in distinguishing between restrictive and non-restrictive. It differs in that the particle *that* is not an element in the clause structure (subject, object, etc) as it must be in a relative clause. It differs also in that the head of the noun phrase must be a factive abstract noun as *fact* itself, *proposition*, *reply*, *remark*, *answer*, and the like. For example:

> The belief *that no one is infallible* is well-founded
> I agree with the old saying *that absence makes the heart grow fonder*

As with apposition generally (*cf* 9.45), we can link the apposed units with *be* (where the copula typically has nuclear prominence):

> The belief *is* that no one is infallible (. . . Ís . . .)
> The old saying *is* that absence makes the heart grow fonder

Or we may replace deverbal nouns like *belief* by the corresponding verb plus object clause: *He believes that no one is infallible*. It will be noticed that these restrictive examples have the definite article before the head noun: this is normal but by no means invariable (except with a few nouns referring to certainty, especially *fact*):

> A message *that he would be late* arrived by special delivery

Plural heads are also rare with appositive postmodification and are re-garded as unacceptable, for example, with *belief, fact, possibility*.

Note
Non-restrictive appositive clauses can less easily resemble relative clauses since irre-spective of non-restrictiveness they still involve the particle *that*, in sharp contrast with non-restrictive relative clauses:

> This fact, that *that* is obligatory, should be easy to remember

Postmodification by non-finite clauses
13.14
-*ing* participle clauses
Postmodification of the noun phrase is possible with all three of the non-finite clause types (11.3), and the correspondence between restrictive rela-tive and non-finite clauses will be illustrated.

$$\text{The man who} \begin{cases} \text{will } \begin{cases} \text{write} \\ \text{be writing} \end{cases} \\ \text{writes} \\ \text{is writing} \\ \text{wrote} \\ \text{was writing} \end{cases} \text{the obituary is my friend}$$

The man *writing the obituary* is my friend

The latter will be interpreted, according to the context (*cf* 13.15), as equi-valent to one of the former more explicit versions. So too:

> A tile *falling from a roof* shattered into fragments at his feet
> ('which *fell* from a roof')

At the station you will see a man *carrying a large umbrella*
  ('who *will be carrying* a large umbrella')
The man *writing on the board* when you came in
  ('who *was writing* . . .')

But not all -*ing* forms in non-finite postmodifiers correspond to progressive forms in relative clauses. Stative verbs, which cannot have the progressive in the finite verb phrase, can appear in participial form:

He is talking to a girl *resembling Joan* ('who *resembles* Joan' not
  '*who is resembling Joan')
It was a mixture *consisting of oil and vinegar* ('that *consisted* . . .')

In all instances, the antecedent head corresponds to the deleted subject of the non-finite verb clause; there is no non-finite postmodifier, therefore, corresponding directly to the relative clause in

The obituary *that the man is writing* will be published tomorrow

without recourse to the passive, *being written by the man* (13.15).

13.15
-*ed* participle clauses
Consider now the different versions of the following:

The only car that $\begin{cases} \text{will be repaired} \\ \text{is (being) repaired} \\ \text{was (being) repaired} \end{cases}$ by that mechanic is mine

The only car (*being*) *repaired by that mechanic* is mine

Again, the latter will be interpreted, according to the context, as equivalent to one of the former. Thus:

The only car $\begin{bmatrix} \text{repaired} \\ \text{being repaired} \\ \text{repaired} \\ \text{repaired} \end{bmatrix}$ by that mechanic $\begin{bmatrix} \text{next week} \ldots \\ \text{now} \ldots \\ \text{on Tuesdays} \ldots \\ \text{before he left} \ldots \end{bmatrix}$

Another example:

Any coins *found on this site* must be handed to the police
  ('that are found . . .' or, more precisely, 'that may be found . . .')

The antecedent head is identical with the deleted subject of the -*ed* postmodifying clause as it is with the -*ing* construction, but in this case the participle concerned is as firmly linked with the passive voice as that in the -*ing* construction is linked with the active. Hence, with intransitive verbs, there is no -*ed* postmodifier corresponding exactly to a relative clause:

train *which has arrived at platform one* is from York

ɪ̠ɪᴇ train *arrived at platform one* is from York

13.16
Infinitive clauses

The non-finite clause in

The next train *to arrive* was from York

could, in a suitable context, have precisely the same meaning as the relative clause *which arrived*. But the subject of an infinitive clause need not be the antecedent. It may be separately introduced by the *for*-device (11.3) or it may be entirely covert:

The man *for John to consult* is Wilson
The man *to consult* is Wilson

where the latter non-finite clause could be understood, according to context, as '(The man) that *you/he*, etc should consult' or 'that *everyone* should consult'. Still more elliptically, the infinitive clause may omit also an entire adjunct phrase, as in

The time *to arrive* is 8 pm
A good place *to stay* is the White Hart

where a fairly common alternative is to introduce the relative pronoun and retain the infinitive clause:

... time *at which to arrive* ... ⎫
... place *at which to stay* ... ⎬ *(the subject obligatorily absent)*

Compare *the way in which to do it* beside *the way to do it*.

Finally it should be noted that voice and mood are variable, the latter covertly:

The time *to arrive* (= at which you should arrive)
The case *to be investigated* (= that will *or* is to be investigated)
The money *to buy* food (= with which you may buy)
The procedure *to be followed* (= which must *or* should *or* will be followed)

13.17
Non-restrictive postmodification

Non-restrictive postmodification can also be achieved with non-finite clauses:

The apple tree, *swaying gently in the breeze*, had a good crop of fruit ('which was swaying ...')
The substance, *discovered almost by accident*, has revolutionized medicine ('which was discovered ...')

> This scholar, *to be seen daily in the British Museum,* has devoted
> his life to the history of science ('who can be seen . . .')

These clauses can be moved to initial position without change of meaning,
but in that case they can no longer be expanded into finite relative clauses.
Indeed, they have an implicit semantic range beyond that of a relative
clause (*cf* 11.36). Thus the non-finite clause in this example:

> The man, wearing such dark glasses, obviously could not see clearly

could be a reduction of a relative clause 'who was wearing . . .' or of a
causal clause 'because he was wearing . . .' or of a temporal clause such
as 'whenever he wore . . .'.

Note
Cf the semantic versatility noted in finite non-restrictive relative clauses, 13.11.

13.18
Appositive postmodification
Appositive postmodification is fairly common by means of infinitive
clauses. A restrictive example:

> The appeal *to join the movement* was well received

which would correspond to the finite *that people should join the movement.*
A corresponding non-restrictive example:

> This last appeal, *to come and visit him,* was never delivered

There are cases of non-finite postmodification where no corresponding
finite apposition exists:

> Any attempt *to leave early* is against regulations
> (*. . . that one should leave early . . .)
> He lost the ability *to use his hands*

In all these examples, the construction obliges us to infer the (often indefinite) subject of the infinitive clause from the context. But a subject
may be explicitly introduced by a prepositional device:

> The appeal *for John* to join . . .
> Any attempt *by John* to leave . . .

Notes
On *-ing* clauses in appositive structures, see 13.20.

Postmodification by prepositional phrases
13.19
Relation to more explicit modifiers
In 13.5 we saw that the sentence 'The girl was standing in the corner'
could yield the noun phrase, *The girl in the corner.* A prepositional phrase

is by far the commonest type of postmodification in English: it is three or four times more frequent than either finite or non-finite clausal postmodification. The full range of prepositions is involved:

> The road *to Lincoln*   Two years *before the war* —
> A tree *by a stream*   A man *from the electricity board*
> The house *beyond the church*   This book *on grammar*

including the complex prepositions (6.4):

> Action *in case of fire*   Passengers *on board the ship*

and including those having participial form:

> A delay *pending further inquiry*

Among the prepositions less commonly used in postmodification we should mention *like* in the sense 'resembling': 'The man *like John* is over there'. But it is common and fully acceptable in the sense 'such as':

> A man *like John* would never do that

It is natural to relate such prepositional postmodifications to *be* sentences ('the man in the corner' ~ 'the man *is* in the corner'), though in some instances more seems to be ellipted than the verb *be*. For example, we presumably need to regard

> The university *as a political forum*

as related to a somewhat fuller predication:

> The university is $\left\{ \begin{matrix} \text{acting} \\ \text{regarded} \end{matrix} \right\}$ as a political forum

Again, although there is no problem with

> The present *for John* cost a great deal
>   (The present is for John)

we cannot interpret so straightforwardly

> The man *for the job* is John (= the *right* man for the job . . .)

Again, it is not through *be* sentences that we must understand

> The man *with a red beard*   The girl *with a funny hat*

but rather through *have* sentences ('The man *has* a red beard'): *cf* 6.37.

13.20
The *of*-genitive
It is with *have* sentences that we find the most obvious resemblance when

we turn to the commonest prepositional postmodification of all, the *of*-phrase:

A man of courage ~ The man has courage

But, as we saw in 4.69 *ff*, many relationships find expression through the *of*-genitive, and one that deserves brief consideration here is the appositive relation which in fact resembles a *be* sentence:

The pleasure of your company ~ Your company is a pleasure

Where the postmodification has an -*ing* clause, the subject may have to be inferred from the context or it may be identified with a premodifier of the head:

The hope of winning a prize (=X hoped that X would win a prize)
John's hope of winning a prize (=*John* hoped that *he* would . . .)

But a separate subject may be introduced:

John's hope of *Mary*('s) winning a prize (=John hoped that *Mary* would . . .)

On *Mary* versus *Mary's* here, see 11.18. Where the postmodification has a deverbal noun, a specified 'subject' must, of course, be genitive:

John's hope of *Mary's* arrival (=John hoped that *Mary* would arrive)

13.21
Restrictive and non-restrictive
Prepositional phrases may thus be non-appositive or appositive, and in either function, they can be restrictive or non-restrictive:

This book on grammar   (non-appositive, restrictive)
This book, on grammar,   (non-appositive, non-restrictive)
The issue of student grants   (appositive, restrictive)
The issue, of student grants,   (appositive, non-restrictive)

But we must mention some limitations. The second example in each case is rare and rather awkward: non-restrictive appositives would more usually be without a preposition, as in

The issue, student grants

and would thus have the primary form described in 9.49 *ff*. On the other hand, if the ambiguous noun phrase

The issue of student grants

had its non-appositive meaning (objective *of:* 'someone issued student grants'), non-restrictive function would be rare and unnatural, plainly suggesting an awkward afterthought.

13.22
Position and varied relationship

As with non-finite postmodifiers when non-restrictive, so with prepositional phrases, the non-restrictive function merges with adverbial expressions; compare

The children $\begin{Bmatrix} \text{behind the fence} \\ \text{on the bus} \end{Bmatrix}$ jeered at the soldiers

which means 'Those children who were . . .'

The children, $\begin{Bmatrix} \text{behind the fence} \\ \text{on the bus} \end{Bmatrix}$, jeered at the soldiers

which may mean 'The children, who (by the way) were . . .' or, on the other hand, 'The children, now that they were (safely . . .)': *cf* 9.54 Note. It is rather this latter implication that becomes uppermost if the prepositional phrase is moved into initial position:

$\begin{rcases} \text{Behind the fence,} \\ \text{On the bus,} \end{rcases}$ the children jeered at the soldiers

Again, the prepositional phrase in the following is poised between interpretation as non-restrictive postmodifier and as adverbial:

Money, in aid of the refugees, was collected from students and staff

In the former interpretation, the money collected was in aid of the refugees, whereas in the latter, *the act* of collecting money was in aid of the refugees, since in this case the adverbial modifies the whole predication just as it would in initial position:

In aid of the refugees, money was collected . . .

13.23
Deverbal noun heads

We should not, however, exaggerate the difference between the prepositional phrase as adverbial and the prepositional phrase as postmodifier. The second of these should rather be regarded as a special instance of the first, depending for its interpretation on our ability to relate it to a sentence in which it is adjunct. In the following, for instance,

(a) A quarrel broke out *in the morning over pay*

both the prepositional phrases are introduced as adjuncts. If we wish to refer again to the quarrel, these adjuncts may now become postmodifiers:

(b) The quarrel *in the morning* ruined their friendship

(c) The quarrel *over pay* was the reason for his resignation

The relation of postmodifier to adjunct may be even clearer if instead of (a) we take a sentence in which *quarrel* occurs as a verb:

(d) They quarrelled in the morning over pay

to which we also relate (b) and (c) but in this case through conversion of the verb (App I.24). Such conversion should be distinguished from the process (11.18) whereby (d) could become a non-finite clause as subject of sentences like (b) or (c):

Their quarrelling over pay was the reason for his resignation

The subject of this sentence is a clause rather than a noun phrase, as we can see from the fact that in such cases adjective modification is often inadmissible. By contrast, a deverbal head (App I.13, I.16) will not permit premodifying adverbs:

The violent quarrel over pay   *The violently quarrel over pay
*Their safe arriving in Cairo   Their safe arrival in Cairo

Note

As well as distinguishing between the deverbal noun (*eg: quarrel, arrival, suggestion, painting* as count noun) and the corresponding verbal nouns in *-ing*, we need to recognize a complex gradience through what is traditionally called 'gerund' to the purely participial form in a finite verb phrase:

Some paintings of Brown's (*ie* some paintings that Brown owns)	[1]
Brown's paintings of his daughter (*ie* paintings owned by Brown, depicting his daughter but painted by someone else)	[2]
Brown's paintings of his daughter (*ie* they depict his daughter and were painted by him)	[3]
The painting of Brown is as skilful as that of Gainsborough (*ie* Brown's (a) technique of painting *or* (b) action of painting)	[4]
Brown's deft painting of his daughter is a delight to watch (*ie* it is a delight to watch while Brown deftly paints his daughter)	[5]
Brown's deftly painting his daughter is a delight to watch (= [4b] and [5] in meaning)	[6]
I dislike Brown's painting his daughter (*ie* I dislike *either* (a) the fact *or* (b) the way Brown does it)	[7]
I dislike Brown painting his daughter (= [7a])	[8]
I watched Brown painting his daughter (*ie: either* I watched Brown as he painted *or* I watched the process of Brown('s) painting his daughter)	[9]
Brown deftly painting his daughter is a delight to watch (= [4b] and [5])	[10]
Painting his daughter, Brown noticed that his hand was shaking (*ie* while he was painting)	[11]
Brown painting his daughter that day, I decided to go for a walk (*ie* since Brown was painting)	[12]
The man painting the girl is Brown (*ie* who is painting)	[13]
The silently painting man is Brown (*ie* who is silently painting)	[14]
He is painting his daughter	[15]

13.24
Minor types of postmodification

We come now to some relatively minor types of postmodification. These are (a) adverbial modification (*cf* 5.28); (b) the postposed adjective (*cf* 5.4*f*); and (c) the postposed 'mode' qualifier. For example,

(a) *The road back* was dense with traffic
(b) *Something strange* happened last night
(c) *Lobster Newburg* is difficult to prepare

In (a) we recognize some such sentence as '*The road* which leads *back* (to London)', from which all but the subject and an important adjunct have been dropped. Similarly '*The way* (which leads) *in* (to the auditorium)', '*The people* (who are sitting) *behind*'.

In (b), we have in fact two subtypes. The first has been illustrated. The indefinite pronouns such as *anybody*, *someone* can be followed but not preceded by adjective modification. The pronouns concerned are the *any-*, *some-*, *no-* series (4.91 *ff*) plus one or two others (*cf: what else, who next*, etc). But we are not free to postpose with indefinites all modifying items that can be preposed with ordinary noun heads:

A party official is waiting   *but not*   *Somebody party is waiting

Even adjectives need generally to be 'permanent' and hence eligible equally for attributive and predicative use (13.4; *cf* 5.13 *ff*); thus

Somebody timid   *rather than*   *Somebody afraid

The other subtype in (b) consists chiefly of the sprinkling of noun plus adjective phrases (modelled on French) like *blood royal, heir apparent*. These are of little importance in themselves, being infrequently used (though our ability to form names like *Hotel Majestic* suggests that they are more than mere fossils) and it is likely that the native speaker feels them to be very similar to compound nouns. Nevertheless, beside this subtype, there is a similar but much more general phenomenon. When a head is non-restrictively modified by a coordinated string of adjectives, it is common to postpose them:

A man, timid and hesitant, approached the official

though the potential mobility of the string allows it to be detached from the noun phrase altogether (*cf* 13.17). Even a restrictively modifying adjective can be postposed if it is itself modified (by an adjunct, not by the intensifier *very: cf* 5.5):

A man always timid is unfit for this task (*cf: *A man very timid*)

This is particularly common where the modification is of a 'temporary' nature (13.4). Thus beside *The finest available car*, we have *The finest car (currently) available*.

With (c), we again encounter a French model: *Lobster Newburg*. Though virtually confined to cuisine, it is moderately productive within these limits, perhaps especially in AmE. In BrE one finds *veal paprika* and many others, but there is some resistance to this type of postposition with other than French lexical items, as in *pâté maison, sole bonne femme*.

Though technically a prepositional phrase phenomenon, expressions involving *à la* clearly belong here. It appears in culinary formations like *chicken à la king*, and also (informally or facetiously) to designate style:

> *Another play à la Osborne* has appeared, though I forget
> who wrote it

13.25
Multiple modification

(a) A head may have more than one postmodification. Thus

> The girl in the corner   *and*   The girl talking to John

can be brought together as

> The girl in the corner (and) talking to John

Without conjunction, there would usually be a hierarchy:

> {[The girl (in the corner)] talking to John}

(b) A modification may be applicable to more than one head. Thus

> The girl in the corner   *and*   The boy in the corner

can be brought together by multiple-head rules which permit the determiner to apply to both heads (*cf* 9.37):

> The girl and boy in the corner

By bringing (a) and (b) together, we can produce complexes such as:

> The girl and boy in the corner (and) talking to John

(c) The head of a modifying phrase may itself be modified; thus

> The girl in the corner   *and*   The corner nearest the door

may be brought together as

> The girl in the corner nearest the door

By bringing (a), (b), and (c) together, we form

> The girl and boy in the corner nearest the door talking to John

though many fastidious users of English would prefer to end with a relative clause here ('. . . who are talking to John'), no doubt in response to an instinct that prompts the introduction of explicitness at a point which is relatively distant from the head.

13.26
Ambiguity and constraints on multiple modification
Frequently, careful ordering of constituents in a noun phrase is essential to communicate all (and only) one's intention. To take an obvious example, the following pair differ in meaning and are not mere stylistic variants:

The man in black talking to the girl
The man talking to the girl in black

One of the chief reasons for preferring the *of*-phrase to the *-s* genitive is to avoid discontinuity (with unwanted humour); thus

The ears of the man in the deckchair

and not

*The man's ears in the deckchair

(But *cf*, with group genitive, *The man in the deckchair's ears:* 4.74.)
  A special type of multiple modification that requires careful ordering occurs when the modifying clause becomes itself embedded in a clause. Consider the following series:

John will write a poem for you
Tom hopes (that) John will write a poem for you
I will read the poem (*which*) Tom hopes (that) *John will write for you*

In this last sentence, the relative pronoun (*which*) is object in the italicized relative clause. When, however, a relative pronoun is subject, the conjunction *that* must be omitted

A poem will be written for you
Tom hopes (that) a poem will be written for you

I will read the poem (*which*) Tom $\left\{ \begin{array}{l} \textit{hopes will} \\ \textit{*hopes that will} \end{array} \right\}$ *be written for you*

Note
Even with simpler examples and the most careful ordering, we may find clarity and acceptable grammar difficult to attain in multiple modification. Beginning with

He liked the smiles of delight on all the faces

a noun phrase based on this sentence and having *smiles* as its head may be ambiguous in one ordering:

The smiles of delight on all the faces that he liked

(was it the smiles or the faces that he liked?), and grammatically awkward in another.

Premodification
13.27
Types of premodifying item

Holding constant a lexical frame (*his ... cottage*) and non-restrictive function, we have the following range of premodifying items:

(a) ADJECTIVE
> I visited *his delightful cottage*
> (His cottage is delightful)

(b) PARTICIPLE
> I visited *his crumbling cottage*
> (His cottage is crumbling)
> I visited *his completed cottage*
> (His cottage has been completed)

(c) -*S* GENITIVE
> I visited *his fisherman's cottage*
> (The cottage belonged to a fisherman)

It should be noticed that if we had used a more normal genitive example (*his uncle's cottage*) we would have changed the relationship of *his*.

(d) NOUN
> I visited *his country cottage*
> (His cottage is in the country)

(e) ADVERBIAL
> I visited *his far-away cottage*
> (His cottage is far away)

(f) SENTENCE
> (?) I visited *his pop-down-for-the-weekend cottage*
> (*cf* His cottage is ideal to pop down to for the weekend)

This type is largely playful and familiar. Somewhat more generally used are noun phrases which can be interpreted either as having a sentence as premodifier or as being object (usually of *know*) in an embedded noun clause:

> He asked *I don't know* HÒW *many people*

13.28
Premodification by adjectives

A premodifying adjective, especially when it is the first item after the determiner, can itself be premodified in the same way as it can in predicative position (5.23):

> His *really quite unbelievably* delightful cottage

Some intensifiers tend however to be avoided with premodifying adjectives. Thus the predicative phrase in *His cottage which is so beautiful* would seem a little affected in premodification: *His so beautiful cottage*. With indefinite determiners, *so* would be replaced by *such* (*cf* 5.27):

A cottage which is so beautiful ~ Such a beautiful cottage

Or else *so* plus adjective would be placed before the determiner: *So beautiful a cottage*.

There is resistance also to transferring clause negation to a structure of premodification, and this is possible only in limited circumstances (usually *not* plus intensifier or negative affix):

The dinner was not $\begin{Bmatrix} \text{very pleasant} \\ \text{unpleasant} \end{Bmatrix}$ ~ The not $\begin{Bmatrix} \text{very pleasant} \\ \text{unpleasant} \end{Bmatrix}$ dinner

Note
On adjectives that cannot be used in premodification, see 5.18. By contrast, there are premodifying adjectives that cannot be related to clauses with a corresponding predicative usage: *cf* 5.13 *ff*.

Premodification by participles
-*ing* participles
13.29
Everything here depends on the potentiality of the participle to indicate a permanent or characteristic feature. To a lesser extent, gradability (especially as indicated through intensification by *very*) is involved.

She has a very interesting mind

shows *interesting* as fully adjectival (5.46 *f*) despite the direct relation to the verb *interest:*

Her mind *interests* me *very much*

But an item can be a premodifier and yet disallow *very:*

A roaring bull (*very roaring)

And the converse can be true:

The man was very $\begin{Bmatrix} \text{reassuring} \\ \text{shocked} \\ \text{surprised} \end{Bmatrix}$?He was a $\begin{Bmatrix} \text{reassuring} \\ \text{shocked} \\ \text{surprised} \end{Bmatrix}$ man

This last example will illustrate the crucial significance of the 'permanence' characteristic; such participles can freely premodify nouns such as *look, smile:*

He greeted me with a very $\begin{Bmatrix} \text{reassuring} \\ \text{shocked} \\ \text{surprised} \end{Bmatrix}$ expression

The man himself cannot have shock or surprise attributed permanently to him, but a particular look can of course be permanently associated with such a value. So too we may speak of *a smiling face* rather than of *a smiling person*. It is thus necessary to realize that we are not here concerned with particular participles so much as with their contextual meaning. *A wandering minstrel* is one habitually given to wandering, but if we saw a man wandering down the street, we could not say

*Who is the wandering man?

Again, someone who told good stories could be *a (very) entertaining person* but one could not say this of someone who happened, at the moment of speaking, to be entertaining his friends with a good story.

13.30
As we have noted before (13.4), the indefinite article favours the habitual or permanent, the definite article the specific or temporary. Thus

?The approaching train is from Liverpool

is strange (especially in BrE) but not

He was frightened by an approaching train

where we are concerned perhaps with what is characteristic in 'approaching trains'. Similarly, *?The barking dog is my neighbour's*, compared with the quite normal, *I was wakened by a barking dog*. On the other hand, after an indefinite head has been postmodified by an *-ing* clause, the *-ing* participle can premodify the same head plus definite article:

A proposal offending many members . . . → The offending proposal . . .

In addition, the definite article may be used generically (4.16) and hence evoke the same generality and permanence as the indefinite:

The beginning student should be given every encouragement

-ed participles
13.31
Much of what has been said of *-ing* participles applies to *-ed* participles also, but there are additional complications. In the first place, the *-ed* participle can be active or passive, but as with postmodification (13.15) the active is rarely used in premodification. Contrast

The immigrant who has arrived   *with*   *The arrived immigrant

The vanished treasure ('The treasure which has vanished') and *A retired*

teacher are exceptional, but exceptions are somewhat more general when an active participle is adverbially modified:

> The newly-arrived immigrant
> Our recently-departed friend

Within the passive we must distinguish the statal from the actional or true passive (12.15 Note *b*); a statal example:

> Some complicated machinery ~ The machinery is complicated
> (*The machinery was complicated by the designer)

Here belong also *born* and some uses of *hidden, married, troubled, darkened*, etc, but in premodification they must either have 'permanent' reference or be adverbially modified: *a married man, a newly-born child, a carefully-hidden spy*. The last example illustrates a noteworthy general contrast between *-ing* and *-ed* participles. Beside the similarity in post-modification

> A spy, carefully hidden in the bushes,⎫
> A spy, carefully hiding in the bushes, ⎬ kept watch on the house

the latter unlike the former resists premodification

> *A carefully-hiding spy

13.32

Most *-ed* participles are of the agential type and naturally only a few will easily admit the permanent reference that will permit premodifying use. We may contrast

> The wanted man was last seen in Cambridge
>   (The man goes on being wanted by the police)
> *The found purse was returned to its owner
>   (The purse was found at a particular moment)

But *a lost purse* is grammatical, because although a purse is no longer regarded as 'found' after it has been retrieved, a purse will be regarded as 'lost' throughout the period of its disappearance. So too: *the defeated army, a broken vase, a damaged car, its relieved owner*. But not: **a sold car, *the mentioned article, *a built house, *a described man*.

But there are exceptions which suggest that the semantic and aspectual factors are more complicated than here described. For example, although a sum of money can go on being needed, one does not normally say *the needed money. Modified by adverbs, of course, the starred examples become acceptable: *a recently(-)sold car*, etc.

Finally, modifiers in *-ed* may be directly denominal and not participles at all (see App I.21): *the vaulted roof, a fluted pillar, a wooded hillside*. But constraints occur (perhaps dictated merely by semantic redundancy), such that there is no *a powered engine, *a haired girl, *a legged man, though we have *a diesel-powered engine, a red-haired girl, a long-legged man*.

13.33
Premodification by genitives

A noun phrase like *a fisherman's cottage* is ambiguous: the cottage belongs to a fisherman or belonged to a fisherman (or resembles the cottage of a fisherman). As distinct from *a delightful cottage* or *a completed cottage*, the determiner need not refer forward to the head: more usually, it refers only to the genitive. If the latter, then any intermediate modifiers between the determiner and the genitive must also refer only to the genitive. Thus

> These nasty women's clothing

where *these* must predetermine the plural *women's* and the phrase must mean 'the clothing of these nasty women' and not 'the nasty clothing of these women' which would require the order *These women's nasty clothing*. If the former ('the clothing of . . .') then an intermediate modifier will be interpreted as referring to the head. Thus

> This nasty women's clothing

would mean 'this nasty clothing belonging to (or designed for) women'. Ambiguous instances are however common: *an old man's bicycle* (contrast: *a man's old bicycle*) could mean 'the bicycle belonging to an old man' or 'an old bicycle designed for a man' (or even 'a bicycle designed for an old man').

Note
On genitive modification in general, see 4.67 *ff*.

Premodification by nouns
13.34

Noun premodifiers are often so closely associated with the head as to be regarded as compounded with it (App I.34 *ff*). In many cases, they appear to be in a reduced-explicitness relation with prepositional postmodifiers:

> The question of partition ~ The par'tition question
> The door of the cupboard ~ The cupboard 'door
> A village in Sussex ~ A Sussex 'village

But not all noun premodifiers have prepositional phrase analogues:

> Bernard Miles was both actor and producer ~ The actor–pro'ducer

13.35

Attention must be drawn to two important features in noun premodifications.

(1) Plural nouns usually become singular (*cf* 4.33 Note *b*), even those that otherwise have no singular form:

> The leg of the trousers ~ The ˈtrouser leg

But while singularization is normal it is by no means universal (*cf: arms race*), especially with noun premodification that is not hardening into a fixed phrase or compound: *The committee on promotions ~ The proˈmotions committee.*

(2) According to the relationship between the two nouns, the accent will fall on the premodifier or the head; for example, *An iron ˈrod* but *A ˈwar story.* The conditions under which the latter stress pattern is adopted are by no means wholly clear but they are also connected with the conventionalizing of a sequence in the direction of compounding.

A notable constraint against making postmodifying phrases into premodifying nouns is the relative impermanence of the modification in question. Thus while *The table in the corner* will readily yield *The corner table*, we cannot do the same with

> *The girl in the corner* (spoke to me) ~ *The corner girl . . .

We must insist again that this is not a property of the lexical item (in this instance, *corner*) but of the semantic relation. Premodification confers relative permanence which befits the assignment to a corner of a table or even a waitress, but not a girl as such.

Multiple premodification
13.36

With single head

The three types of multiple modification specified in 13.27 apply to premodification also. More than one premodifier may be related to a single head, with no grammatical limit on the number:

> His brilliant book ~ His last book ~ His (. . .) book ~ His last
> brilliant (. . .) book

This is however misleading in giving the impression that the multiple modifiers constitute an unordered and coordinate string. It usually follows a recursive process:

> His book → His brilliant book → His [last (brilliant book)]

We would here mean that of several brilliant books we are speaking only of his last one; by contrast

His book → His last book → His [brilliant (last book)]

indicates that his last book was brilliant without commitment to whether any of his others were. In some instances, however, we do indeed have multiple modifications in which no priority among modifiers need be assumed; to these we may give separate prosodic emphasis or introduce commas in writing:

His LÁST BRÍLLiant BÒOK

or formally coordinate them. Thus there would be little difference between

His forceful, lucid remarks   *and*   His lucid (and) forceful remarks

When such coordinated modifiers relate to properties that are normally thought to conflict, the coordinator will probably not be *and:*

His handsome but dirty face   His dirty but handsome face

13.37
With multiple head
Modification may apply to more than one head (*cf* 9.37):

The new table
The new chairs } ~ The new table and chairs

The multiple head thus produced can now be subject to recursive or coordinate modification:

The new table and chairs → { The beautiful new table and chairs
The new (but) ugly table and chairs

If we coordinated *learned papers* and *books* as in (*He wrote*) *learned papers and books*, we would suggest that *learned* applies to both *papers* and *books*. To clarify, we can either re-order (*books and learned papers*) or introduce separate determiners (*some learned papers and some books*).

13.38
With modified modifier
We have already seen two types of modification with modified modifier:

His *really quite unbelievably delightful* cottage (13.28)
These nasty women's clothing (13.33)

In a third type, the noun premodifier can be itself premodified by either adjective or a noun and, if the latter, this can in turn be similarly pre-modified:

The office furniture → { The *small office* furniture
                        { The *tax office* furniture———┐
    ┌———The *property tax* office furniture ←————————┘
    └——→The *house property* tax office furniture

It should be noted, however, that if we were to introduce an adjective in this last noun phrase, already clumsy and improbable, (i) it would have to come immediately after the determiner, and (ii) it would normally be interpreted as relating directly to the head *furniture* rather than to *house*, the only other possibility:

The {pleasant [⟨(house property) tax⟩ office] furniture}

This is not to say however that obscurity cannot exist or that noun pre-modifiers can modify only the next following noun. Consider *A new giant size cardboard detergent carton*, where *size* does not premodify *cardboard* and *cardboard* does not premodify *detergent* but where the linear structure is rather:

A ⟨new {(giant size) [cardboard (detergent carton)]}⟩

13.39
Other complexities in premodification

A friendship between a boy and girl becomes *A boy and girl friendship*. A committee dealing with appointments and promotions can readily be described as *The appointments and promotions committee*, while one whose business is the allocation of finance can be *The allocation of finance committee*.

A noun phrase in which there is noun premodification can be given the denominal affix which puts it into the 'consisting of' class of adjectives (5.20) while retaining the noun premodifier; hence, from *party politics* we have *a party political broadcast*.

Similarly, a noun phrase having a denominal adjective may itself take a denominal affix to become a premodifier in a noun phrase. For example, beside *cerebral palsy* (= 'palsy' of the cerebrum), we have *cerebral palsied children* which has the structure (*cf* 13.32, App I.21):

{[(cerebral palsy)ed] children}   *and not*   *[cerebral (palsied children)]

Note
There are analogies in the group genitive: 4.74. Coordination gives rise to numerous difficulties in premodification. Beside the relatively explicit *children with impaired speech*, we have the premodified form *speech-impaired children*. But since speech and hearing are so often jointly impaired, we are involved in the need to have a corresponding premodification, *speech(-) and hearing(-)impaired children*, clear enough in spoken English but possibly requiring clumsy hyphenation to make it clear in writing.

Relative sequence of premodifiers
13.40
DENOMINAL AND NOMINAL

The item that must come next before the head is the type of denominal adjective often meaning 'consisting of', 'involving', or 'relating to', and this can be preceded by a wide range of premodifying items:

the $\begin{Bmatrix} \text{extravagant} \\ \text{pleasant} \\ \text{only} \\ \text{London} \end{Bmatrix}$ *social* life　　a $\begin{Bmatrix} \text{serious} \\ \text{city} \\ \text{mere} \\ \text{United States} \end{Bmatrix}$ $\begin{matrix} political \\ \text{problem} \end{matrix}$

Next closest to the head is the noun premodifier, already exemplified with *London* and *city* in the foregoing examples. When two nouns premodify, one which corresponds to the head as object to verb will follow one relating to material or agency:

a $\begin{Bmatrix} detergent \\ cardboard \end{Bmatrix} \begin{Bmatrix} \text{container} \\ \text{carton} \end{Bmatrix}$　　a *cardboard detergent* $\begin{Bmatrix} \text{container} \\ \text{carton} \end{Bmatrix}$

my $\begin{Bmatrix} \text{ciga}^{\text{l}}\text{rette} \\ {}^{\text{l}}\text{gas} \end{Bmatrix}$ lighter　　my ₁*gas ciga*ˡ*rette* lighter

　　　　　　　　　　　not　　*my cigarette gas lighter

13.41
CLASSES OF ADJECTIVES

Next before a noun modifier, the most important class of items is the adjective of provenance or style:

a *Russian* trade delegation　　　*Gothic* church architecture

and preceding this type is the participle:

a *carved* Gothic doorway　　　some *interlocking* Chinese designs

Preceding the participle, we have adjectives of colour:

a *black* dividing line　　　　a *green* carved idol

These are preceded by adjectives of age, together with the premodifiers and postmodifiers that these and other freely gradable adjectives may have:

an *old* blue dress　　　　　　a *really very elderly* trained nurse
a *very young* physics student　　a *large enough* lecture room

Next comes the large class that we may call 'general', except that between 'general' and colour (and usually all other modifiers to the right) comes the diminutive unstressed use of *little*. Thus, not **an old little blue ornament*, but:

$$a \begin{Bmatrix} \text{gracious} \\ \text{typical} \\ \text{beautiful} \\ \text{peculiar} \\ \text{handsome} \\ \text{hideous} \\ \text{splendid} \end{Bmatrix} \text{little} \begin{Bmatrix} \text{old blue ornament} \\ \\ \text{old carved Gothic doorway} \end{Bmatrix}$$

See *Fig* 13:1 which illustrates the relative positions of items in premodification.

Note

There are many qualifications to the foregoing. The 'general' adjectives, for example, are not placed randomly but comprise several subclasses. We would prefer *a small round table* to *?a round small table*; *several thick even slices* to *several even thick slices*; *a fierce shaggy dog* to *a shaggy fierce dog*; *a tall angry man* to *an angry tall man*; *a brief hostile glance* to *a hostile brief glance*. Evaluative or subjective adjectives frequently precede those that are relatively objective or measurable; size often precedes shape; within size, height often precedes girth. 'General' adjectives are themselves preceded by semantically weak items like *nice*, by non-predicable items like *mere*, by quantifiers, numerals, determiners and associated closed-system items (4.5 *ff*).

Deter-miners	general	age	colour	participle	proven-ance	noun	de-nominal	head
the	hectic						social	life
the	extrava-gant					London	social	life
a				crumbling		church		tower
a			grey	crumbling	Gothic	church		tower
some	intricate	old		inter-locking	Chinese			designs
a	small		green	carved		jade		idol
his	heavy	new					moral	responsi bilities

Fig. 13:1 Examples of premodification sequence

Discontinuous modification
13.42

It is not uncommon for the noun phrase to be interrupted by other items of clause structure. Note for instance the time adjunct between the head and postmodifier in the following:

You'll meet *a man* tomorrow *carrying a heavy parcel*

There are more striking examples:

I had *a nice glass of beer* but in *an ugly glass*

This is not as contradictory as it may seem, since it is only in the second noun phrase that *glass* is premodified by an adjective; in the first, it is better to regard *glass of beer* as a complex unit modified as a whole but with *glass* being less a concrete noun than a unit of measure. So too with *a weak cup of tea*, and phrases of the form *kind/sort of N* which take premodifiers plainly related to *N* rather than *sort*, both in semantics and in concord:

A big awkward sort of *carton*
?These big awkward kind of *cartons*

13.43

Discontinuous modification more aptly applies to examples like the following (*cf* 5.5):

Comparable facilities to ours
Different production figures from those given earlier

The prepositional phrases here do not directly relate to the head (as they do in *roads to London, people from the village*) but to the premodifying adjective: 'facilities comparable to ours', 'figures different from those'. Compare also *The tall man that I saw* with *The first man that I saw* (='The man that I saw first'); 'An *attractive* scheme *financially*' (='A scheme which is *financially attractive*'); *cf* 5.23 Note *a*.

Most discontinuities, however, are brought about by interpolating a parenthesis or the finite verb of the sentence (where the noun phrase is subject) between the head and the postmodifier; and the usual motive is to correct a structural imbalance (*cf* 14.30) as in '*The story* is told *that he was once a boxer*', or to achieve a more immediate clarity as in:

The woman is by the DÒOR, who sold me the TÍCKETS and told me
    the play doesn't begin till THRÉE

Bibliographical note
For treatment of the noun phrase as a whole, see Bourquin (1964) and Fries (1970). On adjectives and other premodifiers, see Bolinger (1967*b*); on modification in relation to function, see Aarts (1971). On relative clauses, see Jacobsson (1970); Quirk (1968); Huddleston (1971); Stockwell *et al* (1973), Ch 7.

FOURTEEN
FOCUS, THEME, AND EMPHASIS

14.1

In previous chapters, particularly Chapter 7, we have seen how English sentences are built up from various phrase types which serve a range of constructional functions within the grammar (subject, verb, adverbial, etc). We have also seen (7.9 *ff*) how the elements which have these functions have also a different kind of function (a participant role) describable in terms such as 'agentive', 'recipient', 'attribute'. In this final chapter, we come to a third way in which one may view these parts of the sentence: as items which can be manipulated within the structure of sentences for different kinds of prominence. There are three kinds to be considered: focus, theme, and emotive emphasis. Studying these aspects of linguistic structure makes one aware of language as a sequentially organized communication system, in which judicious ordering and placing of emphasis may be important for the proper understanding of the message and its implications. For illustrative purposes, we generally use independent clauses which constitute simple sentences.

Information focus
14.2
End-focus and contrastive focus

We start by considering how the English language organizes a spoken message into units of information, as signalled by intonation (*cf* App II.7 *ff*). Each tone unit represents a unit of information, and the place where the nucleus falls is the focus of information. As the clause is the unit of grammar that most closely corresponds to the tone unit, the best way to consider the positioning of the information focus is to relate it to clause structure, taking examples in which clause and tone unit correspond in extent.

The neutral position of focus is what we may call END-FOCUS, that is (generally speaking) chief prominence on the last open-class item or proper noun in the clause (App II.4):

Dylan Thomas was born in SWÀNsea

Special or contrastive focus, however, may be placed at earlier points, and so may fall on any of the non-final elements of the clause. For example:

Focus at S:

> [Who was born in Swansea?] Dylan THÒMAS was (born in Swansea)

Focus at V:

> [Dylan Thomas was married in Swansea, wasn't he?] NÒ, he was BÒRN in Swansea

Focus at O_d:

> [I hear you're painting the bathroom blue.] NÒ, I'm painting the LÌving-room blue

Focus at A:

> [Have you ever driven a Cadillac?] YÈS, I've ÒFten driven one

Contrastive focus can also be signalled by placing the nucleus on a final item which normally would not have end-focus; for instance, on closed-system items like pronouns and prepositions:

> Who are you working FÒR? (not *with*)
> He was speaking to MÈ (not to *you*)

Note
The principle that focus normally comes at the end of a tone unit explains why a parenthesis (which is normally bordered by tone-unit boundaries) can be used rhetorically to throw emphasis on a word immediately preceding it:

> And THÌS, | in SHÓRT, | is why I REFÙSED |

14.3
Contrastive focus on words and syllables
The above examples show that whichever element is contrastive receives nuclear prominence on its last fully stressed syllable. Intonation can also focus more narrowly on a particular word of a phrase, rather than phrase of a clause:

> DÝLan Thomas was born in 1914 (not *ÉDward Thomas*)
> I put them ÒN the bed (not *ÚNder it*)

or even on PART of a word, with a contrastive shift from normal word-stress:

> I'm afraid that BÙreaucracy can be worse than AÙtocracy

Normally word-stress, and hence nuclear prominence, would fall on the second syllable: *bu'reaucracy* and *au'tocracy*.

Note
Noun compounds and phrases with 'compound' stress (App II.3) are exceptional in
that end-focus does not fall on the last open-class word: *He's an insÙRance agent*. But
nuclear prominence can be transferred to the final noun for contrastive purposes: *He's
an insurance ÀGent* (*not an insurance BRÓKer*).

14.4
Given and new information
Focus is related to the difference between GIVEN and NEW information;
that is to say, between information already supplied by context and information which has not been prepared for in this way. The focus, signalled by the nucleus, indicates where the new information lies, and the
unit carrying such information has the nucleus in final position. Hence if
the nucleus falls on the last stressed syllable of the clause (according to
the end-focus principle), the new information could, for example, be the
entire clause, or the predication of the clause, or the last element of the
clause. In the following sentence, we mark three possible extents of new
information in the same sentence; each of the three questions indicates
how much is already assumed by speaker and audience before the reply
is made:

Whole clause is new (neutral information focus):

NEW
[What's on today?] We're going to the RÀCes

Predication is new:

NEW
[What are we doing today?] We're going to the RÀCes

Final adverbial is new:

NEW
[Where are we going today?] We're going to the RÀCes

By contrast, where the new item comes earlier in the clause, the prosodic
form is distinctive:

NEW
[Who's going to the races?] WÈ are going to the races

14.5
Variation in the scope of new information
Different interpretations are also possible when the nucleus occupies the
terminal part of a complex non-final element. Compare:

NEW

> William wòRDsworth is my favourite English pòet
> (not John Keats)

NEW

> William wòRDsworth is my favourite English pòet
> (not William Shakespeare)

If the nucleus comes on the final word, either the whole phrase or only the final part of it may be 'new'. 'New', therefore, may be varied in scope from a whole clause to a single word, or even to a single syllable.

Note

[a] The second half of the complex fall-plus-rise pattern (App II.10) represents subsidiary information: *eg: Pass me my còAT, jóhn* (where John is assumed to be present, although he has not been actually mentioned).

[b] Pre-final focus is habitual in some colloquial sentences, where the assumed 'givenness' of the final item derives from cultural norms (4.20); *eg*

> The kèTtle's boiling
> The mìLkman called
> Is your fÁTHER at home? (*Contrast* Is your father oÚT?)

[c] There may be more than one contrasted element in the same clause. In the following there are three:

> dŸLan Thomas was born in nineteen-fourtĔen in swÀNsea, but
>
> hŬGH Thomas was born in eighteen-eighty-THRĔe in ÀNGlesey

14.6
Focus on the operator

One type of focus so far ignored is focus on the operator (*cf* 14.35), which often has the function of signalling contrast between positive and negative meaning. Where the verb phrase is without an item that can function as operator, *do* is introduced:

> [A: I thought John worked hard.]   B: But he DÌD work hard.
> [A: Why haven't you had a bath?]   B: I HÀVE had a bath.
> [A: Look for your shoes.]   B: I ÀM looking for them.
> [A: Surely he can't drive a bus?]   B: NÒ, but he CÀN drive a cÁR.

When the operator is positive, the meaning is 'Yes in contrast to No'; when the operator is negative, the meaning is the opposite contrast:

> So you HÀVEn't lost, after ÀLL! ('I thought you had')

The operator emphasizes positiveness or negativeness when it bears the focus (as it normally does) in elliptical replies (10.29):

> [A: Have you seen my books?]   B: No, I HÀVEn't.
> [A: Does this bell work?]   B: Yes, it DÒES.

With a rise or fall-rise intonation, focus on past and future auxiliaries often puts contrastive emphasis on the tense rather than on the positive/negative polarity:

> He owns – or DĬD own – a Rolls RÒYCE
> We've sold OÙT, but we WĬLL be getting some

Similarly, the nucleus on auxiliaries such as *may* and *ought to* often signals a contrast between the supposed real state of affairs, and a state of affairs thought desirable or likely:

> The opinion polls MĂY be right ('but I suspect they're not')
> My purse OŬGHT to be HÈRE ('but it probably isn't')

14.7
Ellipsis and substitution

We have referred to the use of the operator in elliptical replies (14.6). In general, an important reason for ellipsis is to focus attention on new information by avoiding repetition of given information (9.1 *ff*, 9.21 *ff*, 10.44 *ff*):

> I haven't spoken to your brother yet, but I will later today
>   (=will speak to your brother later today)
> A: When are you seeing her?   B: Tomorrow.
>   (=I'm seeing her tomorrow)

A similar effect is achieved by substituting pro-forms for given information (10.25 *ff*):

> Give Joan the red cup and take the blue one for yourself
>   (the blue one=the blue cup)
> Susan won a prize last year and will do so again this year
>   (will do so=will win a prize)

Ellipsis and substitution are useful in unambiguously marking the focus of information in written English, where intonation is absent (*cf* 14.15).

Voice and reversibility
14.8
Voice, end-focus, and end-weight

Three factors contribute to the presentation of the content of a clause in one particular order rather than another. One is the tendency to place new information towards the end of the clause – the principle of end-focus (14.2). Another is the tendency to reserve the final position for the more complex parts of a clause or sentence – the principle of end-weight.

Since it is natural to express given information briefly (*eg* by pronoun substitution), these two principles work together, rather than against one another.

A third factor is the limitation of possible clause structures to those outlined in 7.2, with their associated sets of participant roles (7.9 *ff*). These restrictions determine, for example, that an 'agentive' role cannot be expressed by an object or complement, but only by the subject, or by the agent of a passive clause. From this, one sees the importance of the passive voice as a means of reversing the normal order of 'agentive' and 'affected' elements, and thus of adjusting clause structure to end-focus and end-weight:

A: *Who* makes these chairs? B: They're made by *Ercol*.

A finite clause as subject is readily avoided by switching from the active to the passive voice, in accordance with the principle of end-weight:

{ *That he was prepared to go to such lengths* astounded me
{ I was astounded *that he was prepared to go to such lengths*

14.9
Converses

Quite apart from the grammatical contrast between active and passive, the language possesses other grammatical or lexical means for reversing the order of roles:

{ An uncle, three cousins, and two brothers *benefited from* the will
{ The will *benefited* an uncle, three cousins, and two brothers
{ An unidentified blue liquid *was in* the bottle
{ The bottle *contained* an unidentified blue liquid
{ A red sports car was *behind* the bus
{ The bus was *in front of* a red sports car

The items or sequences in italics are converses; *ie* they express the same meaning, but with a reversal of the order of participants. The second sentence in each case is generally preferable, since the element with the definite determiner, containing given information (4.20), would normally not take terminal focus.

Theme and inversion
14.10
Theme

The initial unit of a clause (with the exception of initial adverbials referred to in 14.11 Note) may be called its THEME. Apart from the last stressed element of clause structure (that which most naturally bears information focus), the theme is the most important part of a clause from the point of view of its presentation of a message in sequence.

The expected or 'unmarked' theme of a main clause is

(1) Subject in a statement: *He* bought a new house
(2) Operator in a *yes-no* question: *Did* he buy a new house?
(3) *Wh*-element in a *wh*-question: *Which house* did he buy?
(4) Main verb in a command: *Buy* a new house

The theme may be characterized as the communicative point of departure for the rest of the clause.

The two communicatively prominent parts of the clause, the theme and the focus, are typically distinct: one is the point of initiation, and the other the point of completion. The theme of a clause is 'given information' more often than any other part of it. Yet the two can coincide; for instance, when the focus falls on the subject:

[Who gave you that magazine?] BÌLL gave it to me

14.11
Thematic fronting or 'marked theme'

One may take as theme of a clause some element not usually assuming that function. Elements placed initially for thematic prominence vary in style and effect.

In informal speech, it is quite common for an element to be fronted with nuclear stress, and thus to be 'marked' (or given special emphasis) both thematically and informationally:

C_s as theme:

JOÈ his NÁME is

C_o as theme:

RelaxÀtion you call it!

O_d as theme:

Really good CÒCKtails they made at that hotÉL

It is as if the thematic element is the first thing that strikes the speaker, and the rest is added as an afterthought. The possible insertion of a comma suggests that the non-thematic part is almost a tag (14.38) in status: *Joe, his name is*.

A second type of marked theme is found in rhetorical style, and helps to point a parallelism between two units in the clause and two related units in some neighbouring clause of contrasting meaning:

Prepositional complement as theme:

His FÀCE I'm not FÓND of (but his character I despise)

O_d as theme:

. . . but his CHĂRacter I desPÌSE

C_s as theme:

RÍCH I MÀY be (but that doesn't mean I'm happy)

Predication as theme:

(I've promised to do it,) so ¹do it I SHÀLL

A as theme:

In LÒNdon I was BÓRN, and in LÒNdon I'll DÌE

Such clauses often have double information focus, one nucleus coming on the theme, and the other on a later (usually terminal) part of the clause.

One may thirdly distinguish examples characteristic of written English, and in which the marked theme seems to have the negative function of ensuring that end-focus falls on the most important part of the message:

> *Most of these problems* a computer could take in its stride
> *To this list* may be added ten further items of importance

Note
Some adverbials (mainly disjuncts and conjuncts) appear characteristically in initial position, and so should not be accorded thematic status at all. However, certain adjuncts, especially those which would otherwise immediately follow an intransitive or intensive verb, may be treated as 'marked theme' when placed initially. Furthermore, adjustment of end-focus may also involve the initial placing of adverbials.

Inversion
14.12
SUBJECT-VERB INVERSION

Here comes the bus (A V S)
There, at the summit, stood the castle in its medieval splendour
  (A A V S A)
In went the sun and down came the rain (A V S, A V S)
Equally inexplicable was his behaviour towards his son (C V S)
'Go away!' said one child; 'And don't come back!' growled
  another. (. . . V S, . . . V S) (*cf* 11.52)

This type of inversion (*cf* 8.28) is mainly found in clauses of Types *SVA* and *SVC* where a normally post-verbal element is so tied to the verb that when that element is 'marked' theme the verb is 'attracted' into pre-subject position. The last example illustrates a different type of inversion, with verbs of saying.

Note
Adverbial *there* in the second example is stressed, and so is distinguished from the unstressed existential *there* (14.19 *ff*), which can also appear in preverbal position.

14.13
SUBJECT-OPERATOR INVERSION

So absurd was his manner that everyone stared at him
 (11.44 Note)   [1]
Far be it from me to condemn him (7.64)   [2]
Under no circumstances must the switch be left on (7.37)   [3]
Hardly had I left before the quarrelling started (7.39)   [4]
I worked and so did the others (10.29 *ff*)   [5]
Well may he complain of the misfortunes that have
 befallen him (formal)   [6]
Throwing the hammer is champion William Anderson,
 a shepherd from the Highlands of Scotland   [7]

The inversion of [6] is decidedly literary in tone, and unlike the preceding examples, is optional. Normal subject-verb order, with the adverb following the auxiliary, would usually be preferred. Example [7] is a journalistic type of inversion, in which the predication is fronted in order to bring end-focus on a complex subject.

14.14
Theme in subordinate clauses
In subordinate clauses, the usual items occurring as theme are subordinators, *wh*-elements, and the relative pronoun *that*. Other items occur as theme only in idiomatic or literary constructions of minor importance:

Should you change your plan ... (11.25 Note *d*)
Keen though I am ...
Say what you will of him ... } (11.26 Note)

The first example is a conditional clause, and the others are conditional-concessive clauses.

Cleft and pseudo-cleft sentences
14.15
CLEFT SENTENCES
A special construction which gives both thematic and focal prominence to a particular element of the clause is the cleft sentence, so called because it divides a single clause into two separate sections, each with its own verb.

Most cleft sentence statements begin with the pronoun *it* followed by the verb *be,* which in turn is followed by the element on which the focus falls. From a single clause such as *John wore his best suit to the dance last night,* it is possible to derive four cleft sentences, each highlighting a particular element of the clause:

S as focus:

It was JÒHN who/that wore his best suit to the DÁNCE last night

O_d as focus:

It was his best SÙIT (that) John wore to the DÁNCE last night

A_{time} as focus:

It was last NÌGHT (that) John wore his best suit to the DÁNCE

A_{place} as focus:

It was to the DÀNCE that John wore his best SÚIT last night

The cleft sentence unambiguously marks the focus of information in written English, where intonation is absent. The highlighted element has the full implication of contrastive focus: the rest of the clause is taken as given, and a contrast is inferred with other items which might have filled the focal position in the sentence. Thus each of the above sentences has an implied negative, which can be made explicit, as in the following examples:

It wasn't Jim, but John, who/that ...
It wasn't to the theatre, but (to) the dance ...

Apart from S, O_d, and A, the two less common clause elements O_i and C_o can marginally act as the focal element of a cleft sentence:

O_i as focus:

It was *John* (that) he gave the book
(but *It was John (that) he gave the book to,* or *It was to John
(that) he gave the book,* with focus on *John* as prepositional
complement, is more likely)

C_o as focus:

It's *dark green* that we've painted the kitchen

V does not occur at all as focus, but the restriction is sometimes circumvented by using the verb in a non-finite form and substituting *do* for it in the second part of the sentence:

?It's teach(ing) that he does for a living

Note
The introductory part of a cleft sentence is largely restricted to *It is* or *It was* though
other forms of *be* occur:

It *must have been* his brother that you saw

14.16
THE 'RELATIVE CLAUSE' IN CLEFT SENTENCES
The final part of the clause, after the focal element, is obviously close in
structure to a restrictive relative clause: pronouns used in relative clauses
(*who*, *that*, 'zero' pronoun) are also used to introduce cleft sentences, and
they can be fronted, even from a position in a prepositional phrase:

It's *the girl* that I was complaining about (not the boy)

There are differences, however, from relative clauses, in that the *wh*-
forms are rare in comparison with *that* and zero. Characteristic intonation
is also different:

It was the DÒG I gave the WÁTER to (*dog* is focus in cleft sentence)
It was the dog I gave the WÀTER to (*dog* is head of postmodified
   noun phrase)

A further difference is that the focal element in cleft sentences may be
an adverbial:

It was *because he was ill* (that) we decided to return
It was *in September* (that) I first noticed it

A *wh*-pronoun cannot be used at all in cleft sentences where the focal element is an adverbial.

Note
[*a*] The cleft sentence structure can be used in questions, exclamations, and subordinate clauses:

Was it for this that we suffered and toiled?
Who was it who interviewed you?
What a glorious bonfire it was you made!
He told me that it was because he was ill that they decided to return

[*b*] The focusing function of the cleft sentence may be compared with that of the additive and restrictive adverbs *too*, *only*, etc (8.8 *ff*).

14.17
PSEUDO-CLEFT SENTENCES
Like the cleft sentence proper, the pseudo-cleft sentence makes explicit
the division between given and new parts of the communication. It is an
SVC sentence with a *wh*-relative nominal clause as subject or complement.
The following are virtually synonymous:

$$\begin{cases} \text{It's a good rest that you need most} \\ \text{A good rest is what you need most} \end{cases}$$

The pseudo-cleft sentence occurs more often, however, with the *wh*-clause as subject:

What you need most is a good rest

And it is less restricted than the cleft sentence in that, through use of *do* as pro-form (10.29), it permits marked focus to fall on the verb or predication:

What he's done is (to) spoil the whole thing
What John did to his suit was (to) ruin it

The complement or 'focus' of these sentences is normally in the form of an infinitival clause (with or without *to*).

Progressive or perfective aspect in the original sentence is regularly represented in the *wh*-clause of the pseudo-cleft sentence. With the progressive, the aspect is equally reflected in the non-finite clause and this is quite often the case also with the perfective:

They are ruining the economy
  → What they *are doing* is *ruining* the economy
They have ruined the economy
  → What they *have done* is *ruined* the economy

In other respects, the pseudo-cleft sentence is more limited than the cleft sentence. Only with *what*-clauses does it freely commute with the cleft sentence construction. Clauses with *who*, *where*, and *when* are sometimes acceptable, but mainly when the *wh*-clause is subject-complement:

The police chief was *who I meant*
Here is *where the accident took place*

But *whose*, *why*, and *how*, for example, do not easily enter into the pseudo-cleft sentence construction.

14.18
Sentences of the pattern *She's a pleasure to teach*
There is a type of construction that gives the emphasis of thematic position in the main clause to the object or prepositional object of a nominal clause. The item so fronted replaces anticipatory *it* as subject of the main clause (cf 14.24 ff):

To teach her is a pleasure → It's a pleasure to teach her
                              → She's a pleasure to teach
It's fun for us to be with Margaret → Margaret is fun for us to be with

There is a similar construction for *be sure* and *be certain*, *seem* and *appear*, *be said*, *be known*, etc (*cf* 12.13). In these cases, however, the corresponding construction with anticipatory *it* requires a *that*-clause, and it is the subject of the nominal clause that is fronted:

> It seems that you've made a mistake
> → You seem to have made a mistake

Existential sentences
14.19

Existential sentences are principally those beginning with the unstressed word *there*, and are so called because when unstressed *there* is followed by a form of the verb *be*, the clause expresses the notion of existence:

> There is nothing healthier than a cold shower
> ('Nothing healthier exists than a cold shower')

There is a regular relation of equivalence between existential clauses with *there* + *be* and clauses of the standard types (7.2). The equivalence applies, however, only if the clause of the normal pattern has (1) an indefinite subject, and (2) a form of the verb *be* in its verb phrase. We may derive existential clauses from regular clauses by means of a general rule:

> subject + (auxiliaries) + *be* + predication
> → *there* + (auxiliaries) + *be* + subject + predication

The subject of the original clause may be called the 'notional' subject of the *there*-sentence, so as to distinguish it from *there* itself, which for most purposes is the 'grammatical' subject (14.20).

Existential *there* is a device for leaving the subject position vacant of content; *there* may be regarded as an empty 'slot-filler'. As we have seen (14.10) the subject of a clause is thematic in typically conveying given information. But when the subject is an indefinite noun phrase, it introduces new information (4.20). Hence, in sentences like *A book is in the cupboard* there is a certain awkwardness, which may be avoided by introducing *there* and postponing the indefinite noun phrase to a non-thematic position: *There is a book in the cupboard.*

Examples of the seven clause types (7.2) are:

> *SVC:* Something must be wrong → There must be something
>   wrong
> *SVA:* Was anyone around? → Was there anyone around?
>   *SV:* No one was waiting → There was no one waiting
> *SVO:* Plenty of people are getting promotion → There are
>   plenty of people getting promotion

$SVOC:$ Two bulldozers have been knocking the place flat → There have been two bulldozers knocking the place flat

$SVOA:$ A girl is putting the kettle on → There's a girl putting the kettle on

$SVOO:$ Something is causing her distress → There's something causing her distress

Passive versions also occur:

$SV_{pass}:$ A whole box has been stolen → There has been a whole box stolen

$SV_{pass}C:$ No shops will be left open → There'll be no shops left open

Note

[a] The 'bare existential' sentence simply postulates the existence of some entity or entities. It has a simple clause structure *there + be +* indefinite noun phrase:

Undoubtedly, there is a God ('God exists')
There have always been wars ('Wars have always existed/taken place')

[b] The rule that existential sentences should have an indefinite noun phrase as 'notional subject' prevents the derivation of sentences like **There's the money in the box* from *The money is in the box*. This limitation can be waived, however, in answers to existential questions (actual or implied):

A: Is there anyone coming to dinner?
B: Yes, there's Harry and there's also Mrs Jones

Also acceptable is the indefinite exclamatory *the* followed by the superlative as in:

There's the oddest-looking man standing at the front door!

[c] Existential *there* occurs widely in dependent clauses:

Let me know if there's anyone waiting

It is also fronted as subject in a type of sentence discussed in 14.18:

There appears to be something wrong with the engine

14.20
Existential *there* as subject

The *there* of existential sentences differs from *there* as an introductory adverb both in lacking stress, and in behaving in most ways like the subject of the clause:

(a) It often determines concord, governing a singular form of the verb (especially in declarative sentences) even when the following 'notional subject' is plural (see 7.18 Note *a*):

There's two patients in the waiting room (informal)

occurs alongside:

There are two patients in the waiting room

(b) It can act as subject in *yes-no* and tag questions:

> *Is there* any more soup?
> There's nothing wrong, *is there?*

(c) It can act as subject in infinitive and *-ing* clauses:

> I don't want *there to be any misunderstanding*
> He was disappointed at *there being so little to do*

14.21
Existential sentences with 'relative clauses'

There is an important additional type of existential sentence which consists of *there* + *be* + noun phrase + clause resembling a postmodifying clause (*cf* 14.16). Such sentences can be related to sentences of basic clause types without the two restrictions mentioned in 14.19: the verb need not be a form of the verb *be*, and although there must be an indefinite element, it need not be subject:

> Something keeps upsetting him
> → There's something (that) keeps upsetting him
> I'd like you to meet some people
> → There's some people (that) I'd like you to meet

It is interesting that the pronoun *that* can be omitted even when it is subject of the 'relative clause', something not permissible according to the rule for normal relative clause formation.

There is also a common existential sentence pattern *there* + *be* + noun phrase + *to*-infinitive clause:

> There was no one for us to talk to
> There's (always) plenty of housework to do

Such infinitive clauses are also allied to relative clauses (*cf* 13.16), as we see on comparing

> At last there was something to write home about

with the stiffly formal construction

> At last there was something about which to write home

This type of existential sentence sometimes has a definite noun phrase as notional subject:

> There's the man next door to consider

Note
Also there is a restricted idiomatic construction consisting of *there* + *be* + negative + participial *-ing* clause:

> There's no telling what he'll do

14.22

Existential sentences with verbs other than *be*

We have finally to consider a less common, more literary type of existential clause in which *there* is followed by a verb other than *be:*

> There exist similar medieval crosses in different parts of the country
> There may come a time when Europe will be less fortunate
> Not long after this, there occurred a revolution in public taste

This construction, which may be accounted for by a simple rule $S + V \rightarrow$ *there* $+ V + S$ (where S is indefinite), is equivalent in effect and style to subject-verb inversion after an initial adverbial. One may notice that the *there* can be freely omitted in sentences of the structure $A_{place} +$ *there* $+ V + S$:

> In front of the carriage (there) rode two men in uniform

The notional subject of the sentence, again, usually has indefinite meaning, and the verb is selected from verbs of existence, position and movement (*lie, stand, come,* etc).

14.23

Existential sentences with *have*

Corresponding to the type of existential sentence discussed in 14.19 (*there* $+ be + S +$ predication) there is a type in which the thematic position is not 'empty', but is filled by a noun phrase subject preceding the verb *have* (or especially in BrE, *have got*):

> He has several friends in China
>
> > (*cf* There are several friends (of his) in China; Several friends (of his) are in China – Type *SVA*)
>
> I have two buttons missing (on my jacket)
>
> > (*cf* There are two buttons missing . . .; Two buttons are missing . . . – Type *SV*)
>
> They had a few supporters helping them
>
> > (*cf* There were a few supporters helping them; A few supporters were helping them – Type *SVO*)

The subject of *have* refers to a person, thing, etc, indirectly involved in the existential proposition. Often the subject's role is that of 'recipient' (7.11); but the nature of the 'recipient's' involvement in the sentence can be very vague, and the more specific meanings of *have* (*eg* possession) are not necessarily implied. A sentence such as *My friend had his watch stolen*, in fact, indicates not possession, but lack of possession. The relation of the subject to the rest of the clause can often be expressed by other means, *eg* by a genitive:

> He has a brother in the navy
>> (= There is a brother of his in the navy; A brother of his is in
>> the navy)

Unlike the *there*-existential clause, the *have*-existential clause can have a 'notional subject' with definite meaning:

> He has his eldest son in a boarding school
> The car had its roof damaged
>> (*cf* *There was its roof damaged)

Furthermore, sentences with an underlying clause structure *SVA* often have a pronoun prepositional complement which refers back to the subject of *have:*

> He had his wife working for *him*
>> (*cf* His wife was working for him)
> The trees had loads of apples on *them*

Have-existential sentences can also contain relative and infinitive clauses:

> I've something I've been meaning to say to you
>> (*cf* There's something . . .)
> He has a great deal to be thankful for

The infinitive clause cannot have a subject introduced by *for* in this construction, as its semantic function has already been appropriated by the subject of *have;* contrast:

> There's a great deal *for him* to be thankful for

Note

[a] In the passive, the verb is generally actional rather than statal (*cf* 12.15 Note *b*):
My friend had his watch stolen implies 'Someone stole my friend's watch' rather
than 'My friend was without a watch because it was stolen'.

[b] In a further use of this construction (especially, but not necessarily, with the passive) the subject of *have* gives up its 'recipient' role for one of indirect agency: *He
had all his enemies imprisoned* is most likely to mean 'He caused all his enemies to be
imprisoned'.

Postponement
Extraposition
14.24

There are devices that have the effect of removing an element from its normal position, and placing it towards or at the end of the sentence.

These devices of postponement serve the two principles of end-focus (14.2) and end-weight (14.8).

We use the term EXTRAPOSITION for postponement which involves the replacement of the postponed element (especially a nominal clause) by a substitute form.

14.25

EXTRAPOSITION OF A CLAUSAL SUBJECT

A clausal subject is often placed at the end of the sentence, and the subject position is filled by the anticipatory pronoun *it*. The resulting sentence thus contains two subjects, which we may identify as the postponed subject (the clause which is notionally the subject of the sentence) and the anticipatory subject (*it*). A simple rule for deriving a sentence with subject extraposition from one of more regular ordering is:

subject + predicate → *it* + predicate + subject

But it is worth emphasizing that for clausal subjects, extraposition is more usual than the basic position before the verb:

SVC: It's a pity *to make a fool of yourself*
      (*cf: To make a fool of yourself is a pity*)
SVA: It's on the cards *that income tax will be abolished*
  SV: It doesn't matter *what you do*
SVO: It surprised me *to hear him say that*
SVOC: It makes her happy *to see others enjoying themselves*
SV_{pass}: It is said *that she slipped arsenic into his tea*
$SV_{pass}C$: It was considered impossible *for anyone to escape*

14.26

EXTRAPOSITION OF PARTICIPLE AND OTHER CLAUSES

Most kinds of nominal clause may be extraposed. A notable exception is the nominal relative clause; thus *Whoever said that was wrong* cannot be rendered **It was wrong whoever said that*. Extraposition of a participle clause is possible:

It was easy *getting the equipment loaded*
  (*cf* Getting the equipment loaded was easy)

but is not very common outside informal speech. Informal examples frequently involve negative + *use/good:*

It's no use *telling him that*
It wouldn't be any good *trying to catch the bus*

Note

[a] For certain constructions (*cf* 14.18, 12.19 Note *b*) which have all the appearance of clausal extraposition (*It seems/appears/happened/chanced/*etc), the corresponding

non-extraposed version does not occur. For example, there is no sentence *That everything is fine seems* to correspond with *It seems that everything is fine*. In such cases, we may say that the extraposition is obligatory.

[*b*] Clauses with extraposed subject must be distinguished from superficially similar clauses in which *it* is a personal pronoun or empty 'prop' subject: *It's good to eat* (*eg* 'This fish is good to eat'); *It's lovely weather to go fishing*.

14.27
EXTRAPOSITION OF A CLAUSAL OBJECT
In *SVOC* and *SVOA* clause types, nominal clauses can or must undergo extraposition from the position of object:

$SVOC$
$\begin{cases}$ I find *it* exciting *working here* \\ (*cf* I find working here exciting: Working here is exciting) \\ He made *it* his business *to settle the matter* $\end{cases}$

$SVOA$
$\begin{cases}$ I owe *it* to you *that the jury acquitted me* \\ (*cf* I owe my acquittal to you) \\ Something put *it* into his head *that she was a spy* $\end{cases}$

14.28
Postponement of object in *SVOC* and *SVOA* clauses
When the object is a long and complex phrase, final placement for end-focus or end-weight is often preferred in *SVOC* and *SVOA* clause-types, but there is no substitution by *it:*

[A] Shift from S V O_d C_o order to S V C_o O_d order:
　　They pronounced guilty every one of the accused except the
　　　man who had raised the alarm

[B] Shift from S V O_d A to S V A O_d:

　　I confessed to him the difficulties I had found myself in
　　We heard from his own lips the story of how he had been
　　　stranded for days without food

14.29
Order of direct objects, indirect objects, and particles
There is a free interchange, provided there are no pronouns involved, between the two orderings

(a) $O_i + O_d \leftrightarrow O_d$ + prepositional phrase (7.6)
(b) particle + $O_d \leftrightarrow O_d$ + particle (12.3)

The choice between the two is generally determined by the principles of end-focus and end-weight:

(a) $\begin{cases} \text{The twins told mother all their sècrets} \\ \text{The twins told all their secrets to mòther} \end{cases}$

(b) $\begin{cases} \text{He gave all his heirlooms awÀy} \\ \text{He gave away all his hèirlooms} \end{cases}$

14.30
Discontinuous noun phrases
Sometimes only part of an element is postponed. The most commonly affected part is the postmodification of a noun phrase, the postponement resulting in a discontinuous noun phrase (13.42):

A rumour circulated *that he was secretly engaged to the Marchioness*
  (*cf* A rumour that ... circulated)
The time had come *to decorate the house for Christmas*

The noun phrase can be a complement or object, as well as subject:

What business is it *of yours?* (*cf* What business of yours is it?)
We heard *the story* from his own lips *of how he was stranded for days without food*

Discontinuity often results, too, from the postponement of postmodifying phrases of exception (6.40):

All of us were frightened *except the captain*

14.31
Pronouns in apposition
In many cases, the postponed elements undergo postponement no doubt because their length and complexity would otherwise lead to an awkwardly unbalanced sentence. With another type of noun phrase, however, it is clearly to give end-focus rather than end-weight that the postponement takes place. This is the noun phrase with an emphatic reflexive pronoun (*himself*, etc) in apposition:

He himsèlf told me → He told me himsèlf
Did you yoursélf paint the portrait? → Did you paint the portrait yoursélf?

As the emphatic reflexive pronoun frequently bears nuclear stress, the postponement is necessary here if the sentence is to have end-focus. The postponement is possible, however, only if the noun phrase in apposition with the pronoun is the subject:

I showed Ian the letter *myself*
*I showed *Ian* the letter *himself*
  (*but cf* I showed *Ian himself* the letter)

Note

With some other cases of pronominal apposition, it is customary to postpone the
second appositive to a position immediately following the operator rather than to the
end of the sentence:

> *They're none of them* experts
> *They* don't *either of them* eat enough
> *We've all* made up our minds

Similarly *both* and *each* (*cf* 9.42).

14.32
Other discontinuities

Comparative constructions of various types are frequently discontinuous.
If we think of a comparative clause functionally as forming the postmodification of the comp-element (11.37 *ff*), then the demands of end-focus or
end-weight often result in its separation from the head:

> He showed less pity to his victims than any other blackmailer in
>   the history of crime (*cf* 5.5)

The equivalent sentence without postponement would be extremely awkward: ?**He showed less pity than any other blackmailer in the history of
crime to his victims*. In other cases, the comparative clause, unless postponed, would anticipate the parallel structure in the main clause, making
ellipsis virtually impossible:

> *More people* own houses *than used to years ago*

(rather than ?**More people than used to years ago own houses*). Final
position for comparative clauses following *too*, *so*, and *enough* is normal,
and therefore discontinuity is bound to arise whenever the comp-element
is not in final position:

> I was *so thrilled* by the present *that I forgot to thank you*

Other adjective phrases are occasionally discontinuous:

> I was *afraid* after that $\begin{Bmatrix} \text{to leave} \\ \text{of leaving} \end{Bmatrix}$ *the children alone*

14.33
Structural compensation

As part of the principle of end-weight in English, there is a feeling that the
predicate of a clause should where possible be longer than the subject,
thus a principle of structural compensation comes into force. With the
SV pattern, one-word predicates are rare, and there is a preference for
expressing simple present or past actions or states by some other, circum-
locutory means. For example, the verb *sang* is very rarely used as a predicate in itself, although semantically complete. We may easily say *He sang
well* or *He was singing*, but would rarely say simply *He sang*.

A common means of 'stretching' the predicate into a multi-word structure is the progressive aspect, as we have just seen. Another is the construction consisting of a verb of general meaning (*have, take, give,* etc) followed by an 'effected object'. The curt *He ate, He smoked,* or *He swam* can be replaced by *He had a meal, He had a smoke, He had a swim* (*cf* 7.15). Similarly, the habitual use of the present or past in *He smokes* and *He smoked* can be expressed by an *SVC* structure: *He is/was a smoker.*

Emotive emphasis
14.34
Apart from the emphasis given by information focus and theme, the language provides means of giving a unit purely emotive emphasis. We have noted in various chapters a number of features of this type. They include exclamations (7.63), the persuasive *do* in commands (7.58 *ff*), interjections, expletives, and intensifiers (5.14, 5.23 *ff*, 8.12 *ff*), including the general clause emphasizers such as *actually, really,* and *indeed.* A thorough study of emotive expressions would take us into the realms of figures of speech such as simile, hyperbole, and irony. Here we confine ourselves to two devices which fall squarely within the province of grammar.

14.35
Stress on operators
If an auxiliary is stressed or given nuclear prominence, the effect is often to add exclamatory emphasis to the whole sentence:

  ·That wÌLL be nice!   What ÁRE you DÒING?   We HÀVE enjoyed
                                                    ourselves!

Auxiliary *do* is introduced where there would otherwise be no operator to bear the emphatic stress:

  You DÒ look a wreck.   He ¹does look PÅLE.   You ¹did give me
                                                    a FRÌGHT.

This device is distinct from that of placing information focus on the operator (14.6). In the first place, emotive emphasis on the operator is not necessarily signalled by pitch prominence: ordinary sentence stress can have a similar effect. Secondly, emotive emphasis has no contrastive meaning; by saying *That wÌLL be nice,* for example, we do not imply that now or in the past things have been the opposite of nice. Further intensification, if desired, can be achieved by placing an emphasizer such as *really* or *certainly* in front of the operator: *It really does taste nice.*

14.36

Non-correlative *so* and *such*

In familiar speech, and especially perhaps in the speech of older women, stress is also applied to the determiner *such* and to the adverb *so*, to give exclamatory force to a statement, question, or command:

> He's sùch a nice man!
> Why are you ˈsuch a bàby?
> Don't upsèt yourself ˈso!

Again, for extra emphasis, the exclamatory word *so* or *such* may be given nuclear prominence: *I'm sò pléased. So* and *such* in statements are almost equivalent to *how* and *what* in exclamations (7.63):

> They're ‖such delightful children!
> What delightful children they are!

Note
Other words of strong emotive import may take a nuclear tone for special emotive force:

> I wìsh you'd lìsten!   I'm tèrribly sórry!

Reinforcement

14.37

Reinforcement by repetition and pronouns

Reinforcement is a feature of colloquial style whereby some item is repeated (either completely or by pronoun substitution) for purposes of emphasis, focus, or thematic arrangement. Its simplest form is merely the reiteration of a word or phrase for emphasis or clarity:

> It's *far, far* too expensive (*cf* 5.33)
> I agree with *every word* you've said – *every single word*

A reinforcing pronoun is sometimes inserted, in informal speech, within a clause where it substitutes for an initial noun phrase (*cf* 9.52 Note *b*):

> This man I was telling you about – he used to live next door to me

The speaker may insert the pronoun because the initial phrase is too long and unwieldy to form the subject of the sentence without awkwardness or danger of confusion or because he cannot in the act of speaking think of any way of continuing without restructuring the sentence and therefore decides to make a fresh start.

14.38

Noun phrase tags

The opposite case arises when a noun phrase tag (*cf* 9.52 Note *a*) is added to the end of a sentence in informal speech, clarifying the meaning of a pronoun within it:

They're all the sÀme, these politícians

The tag generally occurs in a separate tone unit, with a rising tone. It can be inserted parenthetically, as well as placed finally:

He's got a good future, your brother, if he perseveres

An operator is added to the noun phrase for greater explicitness in some dialects. We have therefore a tag statement rather than a tag noun phrase:

That was a lark, *that was!*
He likes a drink now and then, *Jim does*

Bibliographical note
Theme, focus, emphasis, and related matters are treated in Firbas (1966); Halliday (1967–8) and (1970); Huddleston (1971), Chapter 8; Lees (1960b); Rosenbaum (1967); Svartvik (1966).

APPENDIX I
WORD-FORMATION

I.1

A form to which a rule of word-formation is applied is called a BASE (as distinct from STEM: see Note below), and the chief processes of English word-formation by which the base may be modified are:

(1) AFFIXATION
- (a) adding a prefix to the base, with or without a change of word-class (*eg: author → co-author*) (App I.12 *ff*)
- (b) adding a suffix to the base, with or without a change of word-class (*eg: drive → driver*) (App I.13 *ff*)

(2) CONVERSION, *ie* assigning the base to a different word-class without changing its form ('zero affixation', *eg: drive* v → *drive* n) (App I.23 *ff*)

(3) COMPOUNDING, *ie* adding one base to another (*eg: tea+pot → teapot*) (App I.33 *ff*)

Once a base has undergone a rule of word-formation, the derived word itself may become the base for another derivation; and so, by reapplication, it is possible to derive words of considerable morphological and semantic complexity. A moderately complex example is the word *unfriendliness*, the derivation of which we set out as follows:

(1) *friend* — NOUN
(2) *friend-ly* — NOUN → ADJECTIVE
(3) *un-[(friend)-ly]* — ADJECTIVE → ADJECTIVE
(4) *{un-[(friend)-li]}-ness* — ADJECTIVE → NOUN

There are possibilities for mixing processes of derivation in the same word; for instance, compounding and affixation are both found in *colour-blindness*, a word derived from the compound adjective *colour-blind* by the same rule which derives *happiness* from *happy*.

Apart from these major word-formation processes, English calls upon a number of minor devices – reduplication, clipping, blending, and acronymy (App I.43 *ff*) – as means of forming new words on the basis of old.

Note
We distinguish the base of a derived word from the stem, which is the part of the word remaining after every affix has been removed: *friend* in the above example. In a word which has only one affix, such as *friendly*, the stem (*friend*) is also the base; *friendly* is the base, but not the stem, of *unfriendly*.

Prefixation
I.2
Prefixes do not generally alter the word-class of the base. Productive prefixes normally have a light stress on their first (or only) syllable, the main stress of the word coming on the base: ˌpreˈfabricated. This stress pattern will be assumed in the examples in the following tables, unless words are marked to the contrary.

I.3
Negative prefixes

	meaning	*added to:*	*examples*
UN- (*cf* App I.4)	'the opposite of' 'not'	adjectives participles	*unfair* *unassuming* *unexpected*
NON-	'not'	various classes	*non-smoker* *non-drip* (*paint*)
IN-	(as for *un-*)	adjectives	*insane*
DIS- (*cf* App I.4)	(as for *un-*)	adjectives verbs abstract nouns	*disloyal* *dislike* *disfavour*
A-	'lacking in'	adjectives nouns	*amoral* *asymmetry*

Note
[a] *Non-* can normally be regarded as corresponding to clause negation: non-smoker = *one who does not smoke*. It frequently contrasts with *un-* in expressing binary (non-gradable) contrast, rather than the opposite end of a scale: *eg: non-scientific* vs *un-scientific*.
[b] *In-* is realized as *il-* before /l/, *eg: illogical*, *im-* before bilabials, *eg: improper*, and *ir-* before /r/, *eg: irrelevant*.

I.4
Reversative or privative prefixes

	meaning	*added to:*	*examples*
UN-	'to reverse action' 'to deprive of'	verbs	*untie* *unhorse*
DE-	'to reverse action'	verbs abstract nouns	*defrost* *deforestation*
DIS-	(as for *un-*)	verbs participles nouns	*disconnect* *discoloured* *discontent*

I.5
Pejorative prefixes

	meaning	*added to:*	*examples*
MIS-	'wrongly' 'astray'	verbs abstract nouns participles	*misinform* *misconduct* *misleading*
MAL-	'bad(ly)'	verbs abstract nouns participles adjectives	*maltreat* *malfunction* *malformed* *malodorous*
PSEUDO-	'false, imitation'	nouns adjectives	*pseudo-intellectual* (n or adj)

Note
For other prefixes with pejorative overtones, see ARCH-, OVER-, UNDER-, and HYPER- (App I.6). Like *pseudo-* is QUASI-.

I.6
Prefixes of degree or size

	meaning	*added to:*	*examples*
ARCH-	'highest, worst'	nouns (mainly human)	*archduke,* *arch-enemy*
SUPER- (*cf* App I.8)	'above, more than, better'	nouns adjectives	ˈ*super*ˌ*man,* ˈ*super*ˌ*market* *supernatural*
OUT-	'to do something faster, longer, etc than . . .'	verbs (mainly intrans)	*outrun,* *outlive*

	meaning	*added to:*	*examples*
SUR-	'over and above'	nouns	ˈ*surtax*
SUB- (*cf* App I.8)	'lower than, less than'	adjectives	*subhuman,* *substandard*
OVER-	'too much'	verbs participles adjectives	*overeat* *overdressed* *overconfident*
UNDER-	'too little'	verbs participles	*undercook* *underprivileged*
HYPER-	'extremely'	adjectives	*hypercritical*
ULTRA-	'extremely, beyond'	adjectives	*ultra-violet,* *ultra-modern*
MINI-	'little'	nouns	ˈ*mini*ˌ*skirt*

Note

Mini- is often used for humorous coinages. The contrasting prefixes *maxi-* ('large',
'long') and *midi-* ('medium') are less common, *eg: maxi-skirt.*

I.7
Prefixes of attitude

	meaning	*added to:*	*examples*
CO-	'with, joint'	verbs nouns	*cooperate* *co-pilot*
COUNTER-	'in opposition to'	verbs abstract nouns	ˈ*counteract* (also *counter*ˈ*act*) *counter-revolution*
ANTI-	'against'	nouns denominal adjectives adverbs	*anti-missile* (attrib- utive) *anti-social* *anti-clockwise*
PRO-	'on the side of'	nouns denominal adjectives	*pro-Common Market* (attrib) *pro-communist*

Note

Anti- suggests simply an attitude of opposition, while *counter-* suggests action in opposition to or in response to a previous action.

I.8
Locative prefixes

	meaning	added to:	examples
SUPER-	'over'	nouns	¹super₁structure
SUB-	'beneath, lesser in rank'	nouns adjectives verbs	¹sub₁way subconscious sublet
INTER-	'between, among'	denominal adjectives verbs nouns	international intermarry interaction
TRANS-	'across, from one place to another'	denominal adjectives verbs	transatlantic transplant

I.9
Prefixes of time and order

	meaning	added to:	examples
FORE-	'before'	mainly verbs abstract nouns	foretell foreknowledge
PRE-	'before'	nouns adjectives	pre-war (attributive) pre-marital
POST-	'after'	nouns adjectives	post-war (attrib) post-classical
EX-	'former'	human nouns	ex-husband
RE-	'again, back'	verbs abstract nouns	rebuild, re-evaluate resettlement

Note

As an exception to the statement in App I.2, *pre-* and *post-* normally involve conversion from noun to adjective.

I.10
Number prefixes

	meaning	examples
UNI-, MONO-	'one'	unilateral, monotheism
BI-, DI-	'two'	bilingual, dipole
TRI-	'three'	tripartite
MULTI-, POLY-	'many'	multi-racial, polysyllabic

Note

Bimonthly is notoriously ambiguous, in that it can mean either 'every two months' or 'twice every month'. *Biweekly* has the same ambiguity. *Biennial* normally has only the meaning 'every two years' (in contrast with *biannual* 'twice a year'), but many speakers find it as ambiguous as *bimonthly*.

I.11
Other prefixes

	meaning	examples
AUTO-	'self'	*autobiography*
NEO-	'new, revived'	*neo-Gothic*
PAN-	'all, world-wide'	*pan-African*
PROTO-	'first, original'	ˈproto͵type
SEMI-	'half'	ˈsemi͵circle
VICE-	'deputy'	*vice-president*

I.12
Conversion prefixes

	added to → to form	examples
BE-	(a) nouns → participial adjectives	(a) *bewigged* *bespectacled*
	(b) { verbs, adjectives, nouns } → { transitive verbs }	(b) *bedazzle* *becalm* *bewitch*
EN-	nouns → verbs	*enslave*
A-	verbs → predicative adjectives	*afloat*

Suffixation
I.13
Classification of suffixes

Unlike prefixes, suffixes frequently alter the word-class of the base; for example, the adjective *kind*, by the addition of the suffix *-ness*, is changed into an abstract noun *kindness*.

We shall group suffixes not only by the class of word they form (as noun suffixes, verb suffixes, etc) but also by the class of base they are typically added to (DENOMINAL, *ie* from nouns, DEADJECTIVAL, DEVERBAL suffixes, etc). More usefully, we may extend this latter terminology, where convenient, to the derived words themselves, and talk of *worker* as a DEVERBAL noun, *hopeful* as a DENOMINAL adjective, etc.

On stress with suffixation, see App II.2.

Note

[a] Inflectional suffixes, if any, always follow derivational suffixes: *workers.*

[b] Deverbal nouns do not include the 'gerund' class of nouns ending in *-ing* (*waiting*, etc) which are designated VERBAL NOUNS (13.23). Because of the complete productivity of the verbal noun category, the relation between verbal nouns and the corresponding verbs is considered to be purely grammatical rather than derivational. Another class of words having arguably the same status of full productivity is that of AGENTIAL NOUNS (App I.16): *worker*, etc. Notice that although not all verbs have a corresponding institutionalized (or 'permanent') agential noun (*trick* ~ **tricker, flout* ~ **flouter*), it is always possible to create an *ad hoc* or 'temporary' agential noun in a frame such as *a (regular) . . . -er of N:*

John regularly flouts authority ~ *John is a flouter
                                      John is a regular flouter of authority

I.14
Noun → noun suffixes

	added to → to form	meaning	examples
[A] *occupational*			
-STER, -EER	nouns → personal nouns	'person engaged in an occupation or activity'	*gangster,* *engineer*
-ER (*cf* App I.16)	nouns → nouns	varied meanings, *eg* 'inhabitant of X'	*teenager,* *Londoner*
[B] *diminutive or feminine*			
-LET	count nouns → count nouns	'small, unimportant'	*booklet,* *piglet*
-'ETTE	nouns → nouns	(a) 'small, compact'	*kitche'nette* *statu'lette*
		(b) 'imitation' (material)	*flanne'llette*
		(c) 'female'	*ushe'rette*
-ESS	animate nouns → animate nouns	'female'	*waitress*
-Y, -IE	nouns → nouns		*daddy, auntie*

	added to → to form	meaning	examples
[C] *status, domain*			
-HOOD	nouns → abstract nouns	'status'	*boyhood*
-SHIP	(as for *-hood*)	'status, condition'	*friendship, dictatorship*
-DOM	(as for *-hood*)	'domain, condition'	*kingdom, stardom*
-ˈOCRACY	(as for *-hood*)	'system of government'	*deˈmocracy*
-(E)RY	chiefly nouns → (a) abstract nouns (b) concrete count 　　nouns (c) non-count nouns	(a) 'behaviour' (b) 'place of acti- 　　vity or abode' (c) 'collectivity'	(a) *slavery* (b) *refinery, 　　nunnery* (c) *machinery*
[D] *Other*			
-ING	count nouns → non-count nouns	'the substance of which N is composed'	*panelling*
-FUL	count nouns → count nouns	'the amount which N contains'	*mouthful*

Note

[a] The diminutive suffix *-ling* is added to various word-classes, usually with a mildly contemptuous flavour: *princeling, underling.*

[b] The suffix *-y/-ie* largely restricted to familiar contexts, indicates endearment or familiarity. It is frequently added to a clipped form of the base *eg: movies* (esp AmE: 'moving pictures').

I.15
Noun/adjective → noun/adjective suffixes

	added to → to form	meaning	examples
-ITE	nouns (chiefly names) → personal nouns	'member of com- munity. faction/type'	*Israelite socialite*
-(I)AN	nouns (chiefly proper) → personal nouns, non-gradable adjectives	'pertaining to . . .'	*Indoˈnesian, reˈpublican*
-ˈESE	(as for *-(i)an*)	'nationality'	*Chiˈnese*

	added to → to form	meaning	examples
-IST	nouns/adjectives → personal nouns/adjectives	'member of a party, occupation'	*socialist violinist*
-ISM	nouns/adjectives → abstract nouns	'attitude, political movement'	*idealism, communism*

Note

Many nouns in *-ism* correspond to a noun in *-ist* which denotes an adherent of the principle, etc involved: *communist/communism*.

I.16
Verb → noun suffixes

	added to → to form	meaning	examples
-ER, -OR	verbs (mainly dynamic) → nouns (mainly personal)	agentive and instrumental	*driver receiver actor*
-ANT	verbs → nouns	agentive and instrumental	*inhabitant, disinfectant*
-EE	verbs → personal nouns	passive	*employee*
-ATION	verbs → (a) abstract nouns (b) collective nouns	(a) 'state, action' (b) 'institution'	(a) *explo¹ration* (b) *organi¹zation*
-MENT	verbs → nouns (chiefly abstract)	'state, action'	*amazement*
-AL	verbs → nouns (chiefly count abstract)	'action'	*refusal, dismissal*
-ING	verbs → (a) abstract nouns (b) concrete nouns	(a) 'activity' (b) 'result of activity'	(a) *driving* (b) *building*
-AGE	verbs → non-count abstract nouns	'activity, result of activity'	*drainage*

I.17
Adjective → noun suffixes

	added to → to form	meaning	examples
-NESS	adjectives → abstract nouns	'state, quality'	*happiness*
-ITY	(as for -*ness*)	'state, quality'	*sanity*

I.18
Verb suffixes

	added to → to form	meaning	examples
-IFY	nouns, adjectives → verbs (chiefly transitive)	causative	*simplify*
-IZE (BrE: also -*ise*)	(as for -*ify*)	causative	*popularize*
-EN	adjectives → verbs (a) transitive (b) intransitive	(a) causative (b) 'become X'	(a) *deafen* (b) *sadden*

I.19
Noun → adjective suffixes

	added to → to form	meaning	examples
-FUL	nouns (chiefly abstract) → gradable adjectives	'having . . ., giving . . .'	*useful* *helpful*
-LESS	nouns → adjectives	'without . . .'	*childless*
-LY	nouns (chiefly concrete) → gradable adjectives	'having the qualities of . . .'	*cowardly*
-LIKE	(as for -*ly*)	'having the qualities of'	*childlike*
-Y	nouns (chiefly concrete non-count) → gradable adjectives	'like . . ., covered with . . .'	*creamy,* *hairy*

	added to → to form	meaning	examples
-ISH	nouns (chiefly proper and count) → adjectives		
	(a) non-gradable	(a) 'belonging to . . .'	(a) *Turkish*
	(b) gradable	(b) 'having the character of . . .'	(b) *foolish*
-IAN	nouns (chiefly proper) → adjectives	'in the tradition of . . .'	*Dar'winian*

I.20
Some adjective suffixes common in borrowed and neo-classical words

suffix	used to form:	examples
-AL (also -ial, -ical)	primarily non-gradable adjectives	*criminal, edi'torial, musical*
-IC	gradable or non-gradable adjectives	*he'roic*
-IVE (also -ative, -itive)	gradable or non-gradable adjectives	*attractive, affirmative, sensitive*
-OUS (also -eous, -ious)	primarily gradable adjectives	*virtuous, courteous, vivacious*

Note

[a] In some adjectives, -*ic* alternates with -*ical*, with a difference of meaning:
  an *economic* miracle ~ the car is *economical* to run
    ('in the economy')   ('money-saving')
  a *historic* building ~ *historical* research
    ('with a history')   ('pertaining to history')

[b] There are several less common neo-classical affixes, among which -*ary*, -*ate* and -*ory* are particularly notable: *revolutionary, affectionate, obligatory*. Adjectives in -*ory* alternate (with or without stress shift) with nouns in -*tion*: *o'bligatory ~ oblig'ation, satis'factory ~ satis'faction*.

I.21
Other adjective suffixes

	added to → to form	meaning	examples
-ABLE, -IBLE	verbs (chiefly transitive) → adjectives	'able/worthy to be V-*ed*'	*readable, forcible*
-ISH	gradable adjectives → gradable adjectives	'somewhat . . .'	*youngish*
-ED	nouns or noun phrases → adjectives	'having . . .', etc	*balconied*

I.22
Adverb suffixes

	added to → to form	meaning	examples
-LY	adjectives → adverbs of manner, viewpoint, etc	'in a . . . manner', etc	*happily, strangely*
-WARD(S)	adverbs, nouns → adverbs of manner/ direction	manner/direction	*backward(s)*
-WISE	nouns → (a) adverbs of manner	(a) 'in the manner of . . .'	(a) *crabwise*
	(b) viewpoint adverbs	(b) 'as far as . . . is concerned'	(b) *weather-wise*

Note
Also -STYLE and -FASHION ('in the manner/style of') are sometimes used as adverbial suffixes: They ate *American-style* (*cf* 8.20).

Conversion
I.23
Conversion and suffixation
Conversion is the derivational process whereby an item changes its word-class without the addition of an affix. For example, the verb *release* (as in *They released him*) corresponds to a noun *release* (as in *They ordered his release*), and this relationship may be seen as parallel to that between the verb *acquit* and the noun *acquittal*.

I.24
Verb → noun
    [A] 'State' (from stative verbs to nouns): *doubt, love*
    [B] 'Event/activity' (from dynamic verbs): *laugh, walk*
    [C] 'Object of V': *answer* ('that which is answered'), *catch*
    [D] 'Subject of V': *bore* ('someone who bores/is boring), *cheat*
    [E] 'Instrument of V': *cover* ('something that covers things'), *wrap*
    [F] 'Manner of V-*ing*': *throw, walk*
    [G] 'Place of V': *retreat, turn*

I.25
Adjective → noun
Miscellaneous examples are *daily* ('daily newspaper'), *comic* ('comic actor') (*young*) *marrieds* ('young married people'; informal). The

adjective → noun conversion can usually be explained in terms of a well-established adjective+noun phrase from which the noun has been ellipted.

I.26
Noun → verb

[A] 'To put in/on N': *bottle, corner*

[B] 'To give N, to provide with N': *coat* ('give a coat [of paint, etc] to'), *mask*

[C] 'To deprive of N': *peel* ('remove the peel from'), *skin*

[D] 'To ... with N as instrument': *brake, knife* ('stab with a knife')

[E] 'To be/act as N with respect to ...': *nurse, referee*

[F] 'To make/change ... into N': *cash, cripple*

[G] 'To (a) send/(b) go by N': (a) *mail, ship;* (b) *bicycle, motor*

I.27
Adjective → verb

[A] (transitive verbs) 'to make (more) adj': *calm, dirty*

[B] (intransitive verbs) 'to become adj' (generally adjectives in Type A can also have this function): *dry, empty*

Sometimes a phrasal verb is derived from an adjective by the addition of a particle: *calm down* ('to become calm').

This category of conversion competes with *-en* suffixation (App I.18), and sometimes both derivations are available for the same adjective:

He blacked/blackened his face with soot

I.28
Minor categories of conversion

[I] *Conversion from closed-system words to nouns:*

This book is a *must* for the student of aerodynamics

[II] *Conversion from phrases to nouns:*

Whenever I gamble, my horse is one of the *also-rans*
(*ie* one of the horses which 'also ran' but was not among the winners)

[III] *Conversion from phrases to adjectives:*

an *under-the-weather* feeling ~ I feel very *under-the-weather*
(*ie* indisposed)

[IV] *Conversion from affixes to nouns:*

Patriotism, and any other *isms* you'd like to name

I.29
Change of secondary word-class: nouns

(a) *Non-count → count*

    (i) 'A unit of N': two *coffees* ('cups of coffee')

    (ii) 'A kind of N': Some *paints* are more lasting than others

    (iii) 'An instance of N' (with abstract nouns): a *difficulty*

(b) *Count → non-count*

    'N viewed in terms of a measurable extent' (normally only after expressions of amount): a few square feet of *floor*

(c) *Proper → common* (initial capital usually retained)

    (i) 'A member of the class typified by N': a *Jeremiah* ('a gloomy prophet')

    (ii) 'A person, place, etc called N': There are several *Cambridges* ('places called Cambridge') in the world

    (iii) 'A product of N or a sample or collection of N's work': a *Rolls Royce* ('a car manufactured by Rolls Royce'), a *Renoir*, a (complete) *Shakespeare*

    (iv) 'Something associated with N': *wellingtons*, a *sandwich*

(d) *Stative → dynamic*

    He's being a *fool* ('He's behaving like a fool')

I.30
Change of secondary word-class: verbs

(a) *Intransitive → transitive*
    'Cause to V': *run* the water

(b) *Transitive → intransitive*

    (i) 'Can be V-*ed*' (often followed by an adverb such as *well* or *badly*): Your book *reads* well

    (ii) 'To V oneself': Have you *washed* yet? ('washed yourself')

    (iii) 'To V someone/something/etc': We have *eaten* already

    (iv) 'To be V-*ed*': The door *opened*

(c) *Intransitive → intensive*

    (i) Current meaning: He *lay* flat

    (ii) Resulting meaning: He *fell* flat

(d) *Intensive → intransitive*

    The milk *turned* (*ie* 'turned sour')

(e) *Monotransitive → complex transitive*

    (i) Current meaning: We *catch* them young

    (ii) Resulting meaning: I *wiped* it clean.

I.31
Change of secondary word-class: adjectives
   (a) *Non-gradable → gradable*

   > I have a very *legal* turn of mind

   (b) *Stative → dynamic*

   > He's just being *friendly* ('acting in a friendly manner')

I.32
Approximate conversion: voicing and stress shift
In some cases, conversion is approximate rather than complete: that is, a word, in the course of changing its grammatical function, may undergo a slight change of pronunciation or spelling. The most important kinds of alteration are (1) voicing of final consonants, and (2) shift of stress.

   (1) *Voicing of final consonants* (noun → verb)
   advice → advise, thief → thieve, sheath → sheathe, and (not shown in spelling) *house → house*

   (2) *Shift of stress* (see App II.2)

   > When verbs of two syllables are converted into nouns, the stress is sometimes shifted from the second to the first syllable:

   > *conduct, conflict, contrast, convert, convict, export, extract, import, insult, permit, present, produce, rebel, record*

Occasionally, a word of more than two syllables varies in this way: *over'flow* (v) → *'overflow* (n). There are many examples of disyllabic noun-verb pairs which do not differ in stress; for example, *'contact* (v), *'contact* (n), and *de'bate* (v), *de'bate* (n).

Compounds
I.33
A compound is a unit consisting of two or more bases (App I.1). There is no one formal criterion that can be used for a general definition of compounds in English (*cf* 13.34 *f*); on stress *cf* App II.3.

   We concentrate on the productive or creative types of compounding, and indicate the syntactic relations of the compounding elements by paraphrases. For example, the two compounds *playboy* and *call-girl* are superficially similar, consisting of verb + noun. Yet the relations of their elements are different:

   playboy ~ *the boy plays, ie* verb + subject
   call-girl ~ *X calls the girl, ie* verb + object

Noun compounds
I.34
SUBJECT AND VERB COMPOUNDS

SUNRISE ~ *the sun rises*	bee-sting
noun + deverbal noun	earthquake
Very productive type	headache
RATTLESNAKE ~ *the snake rattles*	flashlight
verb + noun	hangman
DANCING GIRL ~ *the girl dances*	firing squad
verbal noun + noun	washing machine

I.35
VERB AND OBJECT COMPOUNDS

SIGHTSEEING ~ *X sees sights* (*cf* App I.39)		air-conditioning
noun + verbal noun		brainwashing
(Number is neutralized)		dressmaking
Very productive type		story-telling
TAXPAYER ~ *X pays taxes*		gamekeeper
noun + agentive or instrumental noun		record-player
(Number is neutralized)		songwriter
Very productive type		window-cleaner
BLOODTEST ~ *X tests blood*	*count nouns*	*non-count nouns*
noun + deverbal noun	book review	birth-control
	haircut	self-control
CALL-GIRL ~ *X calls the girl*		knitwear
verb + noun		
CHEWING GUM ~ *X chews gum*		cooking apple
verbal noun + noun		spending money

I.36
VERB AND ADVERBIAL COMPOUNDS

SWIMMING POOL ~ *X swims in the pool*	typing paper
verbal noun + noun	adding machine
Very productive type	walking stick
DAYDREAMING (*cf* App I.40)	sun-bathing
~ *X dreams during the day*	sleepwalking
noun + verbal noun	handwriting

BABY-SITTER ~ *X sits with the baby*	factory-worker
noun + agentive noun	sun-bather
	daydreamer

HOMEWORK ~ *X works at home*	boat-ride
noun + deverbal noun	daydream
Most examples are count	gunfight

| SEARCHLIGHT ~ *X searches with a light* | dance hall |
| verb + noun | plaything |

I.37
VERBLESS COMPOUNDS

| WINDMILL ~ *the wind [powers] the mill* | hydrogen bomb |
| noun + noun | motorcycle |

| TOY FACTORY ~ *the factory [produces] toys* | oil well |
| noun + noun | tear gas |

| BLOODSTAIN ~ *the blood [produces] stains* | hay fever |
| noun + noun | sawdust |

DOORKNOB ~ *the door [has] a knob*	shirt-sleeves
noun + noun	table leg
Very productive type	television screen

| GIRL-FRIEND ~ *the friend [is] a girl* | oak tree |
| noun + noun | tape measure |

| DARKROOM ~ *the room [is] dark* | hardboard |
| adjective + noun | madman |

FROGMAN ~ *the man [is] like a frog*	goldfish
noun + noun	kettledrum
Very productive type	tissue paper

| SNOWFLAKE ~ *the flake [consists] of snow* | bread-crumb |
| noun + noun | sand dune |

ASHTRAY ~ *the tray [is] for ash*	coffee time
noun + noun	facecloth
Very productive type	fire engine

Note

The difference between *teacup* (~ 'cup for tea') and *cup of tea* (~ 'cup containing tea') can be paralleled with *matchbox, winebottle, soup plate*, etc.

I.38
BAHUVRIHI COMPOUNDS

PAPERBACK	noun + noun	adjective + noun
~ [the book has] a paper back	blockhead	fathead
A 'bahuvrihi compound'	hunchback	loudmouth
names an entire thing by	pot-belly	paleface
specifying some feature		

Adjective compounds
I.39
VERB AND OBJECT COMPOUNDS

MAN-EATING ~ X eats men (cf App I.35)	breath-taking
noun + -ing participle	heart-breaking

I.40
VERB AND ADVERBIAL COMPOUNDS

OCEAN-GOING ~ X goes across oceans (cf App I.36)	law-abiding
noun + -ing participle	mouth-watering
HEARTFELT ~ X feels it in the heart	handmade
noun + -ed participle	self-employed
HARD-WORKING ~ X works hard	easy-going
adjective/adverb + -ing participle	good-looking
QUICK-FROZEN ~ X is frozen quickly	far-fetched
adjective/adverb + -ed participle	new-laid

I.41
VERBLESS COMPOUNDS

CLASS-CONSCIOUS ~ X is conscious with respect to class	duty-free
noun + adjective	homesick
GRASS-GREEN ~ X is green like grass	brick red
noun + adjective	sea-green
BRITISH-AMERICAN (initiative) ~ the British and the Americans jointly (made an initiative) adjective + adjective (coordination compound)	bitter-sweet deaf-mute

Note
The first element of coordination compounds frequently ends in -o and is not itself an independent word, eg: psycholinguistics, Anglo-American.

I.42
Verb compounds

SIGHTSEE ~ *X sees sights* noun + verb	house-hunt lip-read
SPRING-CLEAN ~ *X cleans in the spring* noun + verb	baby-sit sleep-walk

Note

These examples are 'back-formations' from such nouns as *sightseeing* (App I.35) and *spring cleaning* (App I.36), and from a historical viewpoint cannot be described as noun + verb compounds.

I.43
Reduplicatives

Some compounds have two or more elements which are either identical or only slightly different; *eg: goody-goody* ('affectedly good', informal). The difference between the two elements may be in the initial consonants, as in *walkie-talkie*, or in the medial vowels, *eg: criss-cross*. Most of the reduplicatives are highly informal or familiar, and many derive from the nursery, *eg: din-din* ('dinner'). The most common uses of reduplicatives are

- (a) to imitate sounds, *eg: tick-tock* (of clock)
- (b) to suggest alternating movements, *eg: seesaw*
- (c) to disparage by suggesting instability, nonsense, insincerity, vacillation, etc, *eg: higgledy-piggledy, wishy-washy*
- (d) to intensify, *eg: tip-top*

I.44
Clipping

The term 'clipping' denotes the subtraction of one or more syllables from a word. The shortening may occur at

- (a) the beginning of the word: *phone ~ telephone*
- (b) the end of the word (more commonly): *photo ~ photograph*
- (c) at both ends of the word (rare): *flu ~ influenza*

The clipped form tends to be used especially in informal style.

I.45
Blends

In a blend at least one of the elements is fragmentary when compared with its corresponding uncompounded word form. For example *brunch* (esp AmE, 'a meal subsuming breakfast and lunch') is derived from *br(eakfast) + (l)unch*. Many blends have only a short life and are very informal, but some have become more or less fully accepted in the language, *eg: motel* from *motor + hotel, smog* from *smoke + fog, transistor* from *transfer + resistor*.

I.46
Acronyms
Acronyms are words formed from the initial letters (or larger parts) of words. New acronyms are freely produced, particularly for names of organizations.

> (1) Acronyms pronounced as sequences of letters can be called 'alphabetisms':
>
>> (a) The letters represent full words: *C.O.D.* ~ *cash on delivery, UN* ~ *the United Nations*
>> (b) The letters represent elements in a compound or just parts of a word: *TV* ~ *television, GHQ* ~ *General Headquarters*
>
> (2) Many acronyms are pronounced as words, *eg: radar* (from 'radio detecting and ranging').

Bibliographical note
Marchand (1969) is the most comprehensive reference work on English word-formation, but *cf* also Adams (1973). For bibliography, see Stein (1973).

APPENDIX II
STRESS, RHYTHM, AND INTONATION

II.1

Stress, rhythm, and intonation are all concerned with the perception of relative PROMINENCE. We speak of STRESS when we are considering the prominence with which one part of a word or of a longer utterance is distinguished from other parts. Thus we say that *indignant* has stress on the second syllable or that the word *like* is stressed in 'Does he like it?':

In'dignant   Does he 'like it?

We speak of RHYTHM when we are considering the pattern formed by the stresses perceived as peaks of prominence or beats, occurring at somewhat regular intervals of time, the recurring beats being regarded as completing a cycle or 'measure'. Thus, as a language with a tendency for 'stress-timed' rhythm, English often shows an identity of rhythm in sentences like the following, provided that the number of syllables does not vary too widely:

'John's at 'home   to'night
'John's   'here   'now
The pro'fessor's in 'London this 'evening

We speak of INTONATION when we associate relative prominence with PITCH, the aspect of sound which we perceive in terms of 'high' or 'low'; thus we can say that the 'intonation nucleus' in the following sentence has a 'falling tone' (App II.7):

The 'man has GÒNE.

II.2
Stress within the word

There is a binary opposition – stress versus no stress – though it is often relevant to distinguish an intermediate or secondary stress. We mark stress with a high vertical stroke before the syllable carrying the stress, leaving lack of stress unmarked. When a stronger stress needs to be indicated, a double vertical mark is used, and where it is desirable to indicate secondary stress, there is a low vertical stroke before the syllable concerned. For example:

ˈseveral ˈpretty ǁwomen
ˌcontriˈbution

Native words and early French adoptions tend to have the main stress on the root syllable and to keep it there, regardless of the affixes that word-formation may add:

ˈkingly	ˈstand(ing)	ˈpassion
ˈkingliness	underˈstand(ing)	ˈpassionately
unˈkingliness	misunderˈstand(ing)	disˈpassionate

By contrast, with the more recent adoptions and coinages, especially those based on words from the classical languages, the place of the stress varies according to the affixation:

	antepenultimate	*penultimate*
ˈtelegraph	teˈlegraphy	teleˈgraphic
	teˈlepathy	teleˈpathic
ˈphoto(graph)	phoˈtography	photoˈgraphic
ˈtransport	transˈportable	transporˈtation
ˈargument	arguˈmentative	argumenˈtation

The last two items exemplify an important generalization: all abstract nouns ending in *-ion* are stressed on the syllable preceding this ending.

Similar *penultimate* examples with adjectival *-ic* (App I.20):

ˈphoneme ~ phoˈnemic	ˈemblem ~ embleˈmatic
eˈconomy ~ ecoˈnomic	ˈsympathy ~ sympaˈthetic

and *antepenultimate* with nominal *-ity* and nominal or adjectival *-ian:*

uˈnanimous ~ unaˈnimity	ˈcurious ~ curiˈosity
ˈlibrary ~ libˈrarian	uˈtility ~ utiliˈtarian
ˈgrammar ~ gramˈmarian	ˈCromwell ~ Cromˈwellian

By contrast, *-ite* leaves the place of the accent unchanged:

ˈTrotsky ~ ˈTrotskyite	ˈJefferson ~ ˈJeffersonite

A fairly numerous set of words that can operate without affixal change as noun or adjective on the one hand, and as verb on the other, have an accentual difference in the two functions (App I.32); for example:

noun or adjective: ˈconduct, ˈcontrast, ˈattribute, ˈpresent, etc
verb: conˈduct, conˈtrast, atˈtribute, preˈsent, etc

In one of these (*contrast*) and in several of the other examples that might have been cited (*eg: export*), there is a tendency to discontinue a separate verb form and to use in all functions the form as stressed for the noun.

II.3
Compounds

In contrast to noun phrases like *a ˌblack ˈbird*, corresponding compound nouns (App I.34 *ff*) are generally stressed on the first element but with a strong secondary stress on the second element:

ˈblackˌbird	ˈblackˌboard	ˈgreenˌfly
ˈearthˌquake	ˈwaitingˌroom	ˈfire-exˌtinguisher

When such a compound is made part of another compound, the stress and secondary stress are re-distributed to give the same rhythm: ˈlight-ˌhouse but ˈlighthouse-ˌkeeper.

A somewhat smaller number of compounds have phrasal stress pattern:

ˌappleˈsauce   ˌfirstˈrate

Such compounds are often not nouns, but verbs (ˌback-ˈfire), adverbs (ˌhenceˈforth), and especially adjectives (ˌknee-ˈdeep, ˌflat-ˈfooted). Some examples are variable:

ˌfield ˈmarshal *or* ˈfield ˌmarshal; ˌoverˈseas *or* ˈoverˌseas

In any case, the stress often shifts from second component to first when the compound is being used attributively in a noun phrase:

The room is ˌdownˈstairs   *but*   A ˈdownˌstairs ˈroom
His work is ˌfirstˈclass   *but*   His ˈfirstˌclass ˈwork

Note
In AmE there is a strong tendency to give initial stress to compounds and in normal AmE use we have. for example ˈappleˌsauce. ˈlawnˌtennis, ˈbackˌfire. This stress distribution occurs quite often in BrE also.

II.4
Stress in phrases and other syntactic units

Stress distribution provides a firm basis for distinguishing between different underlying relations:

A ˈtoy ˌfactory *produces toys;* a ˌtoy ˈfactory *is a toy*
A ˈbullˌfight *involves bulls;* a ˌbull ˈcalf *is a young bull*
A ˈFrench ˌteacher *teaches French;* a ˌFrench ˈteacher *is French*
A ˈslate ˌquarry *yields slate;* a ˌslate ˈroof *is made of slate*

A heavier stress (though usually realized as an intonation nucleus: App II.7) marks the head of a lengthy premodified noun phrase, the final item of a heavily postmodified noun phrase, the last lexical item of a clause, and similar points of grammatical importance:

A reaǁlistic ˌlittle ˌtoy ǁfactory
The ˌtoy ˈfactory he ˈgot for his ǁbirthday
ˈThat's the adˈdress he ˈsent the ǁletter ˌto

II.5
Contrastive stress

We can interfere with normal accentuation to highlight any word we please by means of contrastive stress, again often realized by means of intonation. In this way, for example, the closed-system words like *and*, *of*, *have* (which normally have /ə/ and often consonant loss as well) are pronounced with the vowel and consonant values that these words have in isolation:

A: ˈJohn and ˈMary ǁwent   /ən/
B: ˈReally! ˈJohn ǁand ˈMary?   /and/

Contrastive stress is not limited to sequences longer than the word: the normal accentuation within the word can also be distorted at the speaker's will if he wants to make a contrastive point. Thus instead of *unˈhappy* one might say *ˈunhappy* in a context such as

A: She was looking ˈhappy tonight
B: You thought so? She seemed ˈunhappy to me

Note

Contrastive stress can also override the distinctions made in App II.4: in *I ˈsaid she was a "French ˌteacher, not a "fresh ˌteacher*, we could be referring to nationality.

II.6
Rhythm

Broadly speaking, and in the absence of contrastive stress, English connected speech has stresses on the (stressed syllables of) open-class items, and absence of stress upon the closed-system words accompanying them:

He ˈtold his ǁmother
He ˈsent it to his ǁmother
That's the adˈdress he ˈsent the ǁletter ˌto
She was ǁlooking ǁhappy toˈnight

The natural rhythm of English, when unaffected by other factors such as hesitation which may slow down the speaker or excitement which may speed him up, provides roughly equal intervals of time between the stresses (*cf* App II.1).

But absolute regularity of rhythm is the exception rather than the rule. When the intervals between stresses achieve something like equality, the stylistic effect is oppressive. One exception is in counting: when we have to count a fairly large number of items, we tend to adopt quite naturally a strictly regular rhythm:

> ¹one ¹two ¹three ¹four . . . ¹seventeen ¹eighteen ¹nineteen . . .
> seventy-¹four seventy-¹five seventy-¹six . . . a hundred-and-¹three
> a hundred-and-¹four . . .

So too when we are compiling an inventory, giving a list of names, or the like. Insistent regularity may also be introduced in religious discourse, in reading poetry, or for emphasis. In ordinary discourse, it is common when one is implying repetition of something which ought to be accepted without argument, and especially again perhaps when the speaker is expressing irritation or sarcasm:

> You should ¹never ¹move the ¹papers ¹on my ¹¹desk

Intonation
II.7
Tone unit, nucleus, and the falling tone

Intonation is normally realized in tone units consisting of a sequence of stressed and unstressed syllables but on occasion the unit may consist of a single pitch-prominent syllable. The peak of greatest prominence is called the NUCLEUS of the tone unit and it is indicated in this book by being printed in small capitals. The first prominent syllable in a tone unit is the ONSET, and it is commonly preceded by one or more syllables with light stress and on a low pitch. Its position can be indicated by a preceding thin vertical (|) and the end of the tone unit by a thick vertical (|). Some of the earlier examples are now given, with stresses reinterpreted where relevant:

(a) He |told his MOTHer|
(b) That's the ad|dress he ¹sent the LETter ₁to|
(c) She was |looking HAPpy to¹night|
(d) You |THOUGHT ¹so|
(e) She |seemed UNhappy to ME|

Pitch prominence is usually associated with pitch change, and the commonest change is a FALL. We would expect a fall on the nuclear syllable in (a) and (b) above, as in most sentences of English. We expect a fall also in questions beginning with a *wh*-word, as in (f) and (h), on one-word

answers to questions, and on words or names or even letters uttered in
isolation, as in (g) and (i):

   (f) |What's his NÀME|
   (g) Phy|LÀKtis|
   (h) |What's the first LÈTter|
   (i) |P̀|

II.8
The rising tone

The next commonest tone is the RISE, used when we wish to indicate that
our utterance is non-final or that we are leaving it open and inconclusive.
This may be because we are counting or listing and have not come to the
last item; or because another clause is going to follow; or because we seek
a response from someone (but not by means of a *wh*-question):

   ... |TWÉLVE| |THÍRteen| |FÓÚRteen| |FÍFteen|
   There are |fifTÈÈN|
   |When he CÁME| I |GRÈÈTed him|
   I |saw him this MÓRNing| and in|vited him to DÌNner|
   You're |going alRÉADY| |MÚST you|

Some of the examples in App II.7 might well have a rising nucleus,
especially (c) perhaps, not so much in order to make it a question as to
suggest politely that a (confirmatory) comment would be welcome. Alternatively, one might add a tag question (7.48 *f*), with a falling nucleus:

   She was |looking HÁPpy to|night| |WÀsn't she|

Since a rise lacks dogmatic finality, it enables us to make an imperative
gentle and persuasive:

   |Don't be unPLÉAsant|

Other nuclear tones
II.9

There are no nuclear tones anything like so common as the fall and the
rise, but four other tone contours are nevertheless important. The FALL-
RISE occurs in many 'contingency' environments (for example as the
nucleus of a conditional clause), but it is perhaps especially common with
initial adverbials (8.3):

   I'll |see him if he CǑMES|
   |FǏNally| we de|cided not to GÒ|

The converse of this, the RISE-FALL, must be sharply distinguished from
it since it is really a rather persuasive variant of the falling tone, used to

express a genuine or sarcastic warmth or on the other hand a feeling of
surprise or shock:

|That's wôNderful|
He's a com|plete FôOL|

Rarest of all is the LEVEL tone. This is perhaps a variant of the rise, and
it is used to suggest (often somewhat pompously) the exact predictability
of what is to follow:

He |DRĀNK| he |STŌLE| he was |soon desPĪSED|

II.10
The remaining tone pattern, FALL-PLUS-RISE, is probably used more
often than any other except fall and rise, but we have left it till the end because, unlike the others, this pattern has two nuclei. Especially in BrE, it
would be expected in example (e) of App II.7:

She |seemed ÙNhappy to MÉ|

The nucleus is always a peak of 'information' content in the tone unit;
with the fall-plus-rise we have two such peaks of information interest,
and they are related, the first being superordinate. When we first introduced this example (App II.5), it was in order to illustrate 'contrastive
stress'. Now contrastive stress often involves moving a tonal nucleus from
its normal, unmarked position onto the contrasted item. But this need not
entail removing all nuclear prominence from elsewhere in the sentence.
The fall-plus-rise allows the speaker to express a double contrast, and in
the present example he in effect says (a) 'She seems *un*happy rather than
happy', and (b) 'This is *my* view as opposed to yours'.

The fall-plus-rise is commonly used with marked focus (*cf* 14.2 *ff*), with
the fall placed on the displaced and focused item, the rise on the final
lexical item in the tone unit. For example:

It's his |wÌFE that I don't LÍKE| = The |one that I don't LÍKE| is
his |wÌFE|
It's his |wÌFE that's always NÁsty|

beside the unmarked

I |don't like his wÌFE| His |wife is always NÀsty|

II.11
Prosodic marking compared with punctuation
In so brief a sketch we must ignore other features of oral English such as
pitch height, pitch range, tempo. Even so, we now have a system of conventions capable of expressing on paper for spoken English what the sys-

tem of punctuation marks does for written English. There are numerous respects in which conventional punctuation is inadequate, but we need mention here only one or two such points to show how our prosodic notation both explains and transcends the difficulty.

For example, although in rather informal punctuation we can indicate emphasis (usually by means of italics), we cannot distinguish emphases of radically different sound and value:

(a) You shouldn't give her *any* flowers
    (= You must give her no flowers at all)
(b) You shouldn't give her *any* flowers
    (= You must give her only certain flowers)

But prosodic notation adequately represents the difference we hear:

(a) You |shouldn't give her ÀNY flowers|
(b) You |shouldn't give her ᴀ̆NY flowers|

Consider now the prosodic realizations which give sharply different meanings to the various members within each of the following sets of sentences; in each case we begin with the 'unmarked' and most neutral form the sentence might have:

(1) I should |GÒ|
    I should |GÓ| (Is that your advice?)
    |Ì should go| (Not you!)
    I |SHÒULD go| (And I defy you to deny it)
    I |SHŎULD go| (But I don't think I will)

(2) |Somebody must have TÀKEN it|
    |Somebody MÙST have ᶦtaken it| (It's no use your arguing)
    |SŎMEbody must have ᶦtaken it| (Even if you didn't)

(3) You |said he would CÒME|
    |You said he would CÒME| (I was personally doubtful)
    You |said HĔ would come| (You didn't say that his wife was coming as well)
    You |SĂID he would come| (But that doesn't mean he really will)
    You |SÀID he would CÓME| (And, my goodness, there he is!)

Bibliographical note

A detailed account of all prosodic systems is given in Crystal (1969), especially Chapters 4 *ff*, and these are related to style in Crystal and Davy (1969). On stress, see Gimson (1970), especially Part III; Halle and Keyser (1971), Chapter 1. On rhythm, see Abercrombie (1967), Chapter 6; Leech (1969b), Chapter 7. On AmE intonation, see Pike (1945).

APPENDIX III
PUNCTUATION

III.1
Punctuation serves two main functions:

(1) SEPARATION of
- (a) *successive units* (such as sentences by periods, or items in a list by commas)
- (b) *included units* (as when parentheses mark off an interpolated phrase or clause)

(2) SPECIFICATION of language function (as when an apostrophe indicates that an inflection is genitive).

Successive units
III.2
Successive units form a hierarchy as follows:

- (a) the individual letters within a word;
- (b) the parts of a word independent enough to be separated by a hyphen;
- (c) the individual words separated by a space;
- (d) the dependent units in sentence structure (usually phrases or clauses) separated by a comma;
- (e) the non-parenthetic appositive units (*cf* 9.47) separated by a colon;
- (f) the independent units (usually clauses) separated by a semicolon;
- (g) the sentences separated by a period and a following capital;
- (h) the paragraphs separated by switching to a new line of writing, often indented.

There are of course still larger units in the hierarchy, such as chapters, but in this brief sketch we must ignore all points except (b) and (d) above.

III.3
The hyphen
There are two principal uses of the hyphen:

(1) Word division at the end of a line. Natural breaks (orthographic, syllabic, morphological) are observed; thus *establish-ment* not **establis-hment*. BrE practice tends to favour morphological breaks (*struct-ure*), AmE syllabic (*struc-ture*).

(2) The division, especially in BrE, of words not regarded as wholly established units (*anti-war*, *flower-power*) and the junction of phrasal units used as premodifiers (*a vase of the fourth century* but *a fourth-century vase: cf* 13.38 *f*).

III.4
The comma

The comma separates items in lists; coordinate clauses (especially those with *but*); adverbial clauses and phrases, especially initial ones, from superordinate clauses; a vocative from the rest of the sentence. To illustrate each in turn:

> The farmer owned sheep, cattle, pigs(,) and poultry.
> The lecture was good, but few people were present.
> When she saw him, she burst out laughing.
> John, do you know Mary's address?

A comma cannot separate subject from predicate or verb from object:

> *A man of his great abilities, would always be successful.
> *John thought, that the weather would improve.

Note
[a] With initial conjuncts and disjuncts, a comma is virtually obligatory, but it is often optional after adjuncts: *Incidentally, he sings* . . .; *Frankly, he cheated* . . .; *Frequently* (,) *he works* . . .; *cf* 8.2.
[b] A restrictive relative clause cannot be separated by a comma from its antecedent in the noun phrase, while a non-restrictive clause is regularly so separated (13.3):

> You should have asked the man who left yesterday
> You should have asked Mary, who left yesterday.

III.5
Included units

The two commonest types of included unit are (1) parenthetic or subordinate matter, and (2) quotation or other reference to a different linguistic sphere. The punctuation marking such included units must be correlative, one occurrence indicating the beginning of the inclusion, a second occurrence indicating its completion.

(1) Parenthetic matter may be adverbial, appositive, or structurally unrelated. The punctuation marks are commas, parentheses ('brackets', BrE), or dashes:

The other man, David Johnson, refused to leave.
John (or perhaps his wife) will collect the parcel.
David Johnson – I don't know why – refused to leave.

As the above examples suggest, parentheses subordinate more definitely than commas, and dashes are particularly suitable for informal 'asides'.

(2) Direct speech is enclosed in single or double quotation marks (in BrE called also 'inverted commas'; they are usually single, especially in print); quotation within quotation uses both to mark the distinction:

'I heard "Keep out" being shouted,' he explained.

Reference outside the variety of English being used is similarly marked:

A carafe of 'plonk' accompanied the meal.

III.6
Specification

The functions most commonly specified by punctuation signs are questions, exclamations, genitives, contractions, and abbreviations.

John has gone already?
Isn't she beautiful!

In these examples, the specification signs are especially relevant since the grammatical form would otherwise suggest that the first is a statement and the second a question. The exclamation mark is, however, sparingly used in English and it does not occur with epistolary formulae or (normally) with vocatives or imperatives.

The apostrophe is used in writing the genitive singular and plural (thus marking the difference between *dogs*, *dog's*, and *dogs'*) and the informal contractions, especially of the negative particle and of auxiliaries with pronoun subjects: *John didn't; he'll; I've.*

Abbreviations by initials are indicated by capitals with or without periods (*P.T.O.*, *PTO*), or by lower case letters where the absence of periods is less common (*i.e.*, *e.g.*). Shortened forms of words normally have a period (*Prof.*), though this need not be so if the abbreviation ends with the last letter (*Dr*).

Note

[a] After the initial greeting in a letter, there is either a comma (BrE, informal AmE) or a colon (AmE), the first sentence then beginning on the next line with a capital:

Dear Mr Johnson,
    Several weeks have passed since . . .

[b] Italics are sometimes used to specify an emphasized word:

It was not so much anger as *self-reproach* that made him agitated

Italics are also used (with initial capitals for open-class words) in quoting titles of books, etc:

His next play was *Peace in the Dark.*

BIBLIOGRAPHY

AARTS, F. G. A. M. (1971) 'On the Distribution of Noun-Phrase Types in English Clause-Structure', *Lingua* 26, 281–93

ABERCROMBIE, D. (1967) *Elements of General Phonetics*, Edinburgh

ADAMS, V. (1973) *Introduction to Modern English Word-Formation*, London

AIJMER, K. (1972) *Some Aspects of Psychological Predicates in English*, Stockholm

AKSENENKO, B. N. (1956) *Predlogi Angliiskogo Yazyka*, Moscow

ALLEN, R. L. (1966) *The Verb System of Present-Day American English*, The Hague

ANDERSON, J. (1971) *The Grammar of Case*, Cambridge

BACH, E. (1968) 'Nouns and Noun Phrases', in Bach and Harms (1968)

BACH, E. and HARMS, R. T. (1968) (edd) *Universals in Linguistic Theory*, New York

BALD, W-D. (1972) *Studien zu den kopulativen Verben des Englischen*, Munich

BOLINGER, D. L. (1957) *Interrogative Structures of American English*, Birmingham, Alabama

   (1967a) 'The Imperative in English', *To Honor Roman Jakobson* Vol I, The Hague, 335–63

   (1967b) 'Adjectives in English: Attribution and Predication', *Lingua* 18, 1–34

   (1971) *The Phrasal Verb in English*, Cambridge, Mass

   (1972) *Degree Words*, The Hague

BOURQUIN, G. (1964) *Le Groupement nominal en anglais écrit,* Publications Linguistiques de la Faculté des Lettres 3, Nancy

CHOMSKY, N. (1957) *Syntactic Structures*, The Hague

   (1965) *Aspects of the Theory of Syntax*, Cambridge, Mass

CHRISTOPHERSEN, P. (1939) *The Articles: A Study of their Theory and Use in English*, Copenhagen

CLOSE, R. A. (1962) *English as a Foreign Language*, London

CRYMES, R. (1968) *Some Systems of Substitution Correlations in Modern American English*, The Hague

CRYSTAL, D. (1969) *Prosodic Systems and Intonation in English*, Cambridge

CRYSTAL, D. and DAVY, D. (1969) *Investigating English Style*, London

FILLMORE, C. (1968) 'The Case for Case', in Bach and Harms (1968)

FILLMORE, C. and LANGENDOEN, D. T. (1971) (edd) *Studies in Linguistic Semantics*, New York

FIRBAS, J. (1966) 'Non-Thematic Subjects in Contemporary English', *Travaux Linguistiques de Prague* 2, 239–56

FRIES, P. (1970) *Tagmeme Sequences in the English Noun Phrase*, Norman, Okla

GIMSON, A. C. (1970) *An Introduction to the Pronunciation of English*, 2nd edn, London

GLEITMAN, L. R. (1965) 'Coordinating Conjunctions in English', *Language* 41, 260–93

GREENBAUM, S. (1969) *Studies in English Adverbial Usage*, London
(1970) *Verb-Intensifier Collocations in English: An Experimental Approach*, The Hague

HALLE, M. and KEYSER, S. J. (1971) *English Stress*, New York

HALLIDAY, M. A. K. (1967–68) 'Notes on Transitivity and Theme in English' *Journal of Linguistics* 3, 37–81, 199–244; 4, 179–215
(1970) 'Functional Diversity in Language as seen from a Consideration of Modality and Mood in English', *Foundations of Language* 6, 322–61

HUDDLESTON, R. D. (1971) *The Sentence in Written English: A Syntactic Study Based on an Analysis of Scientific Texts*, Cambridge

HUDSON, R. A. (1970) 'On Clauses Containing Conjoined and Plural Noun-Phrases in English', *Lingua* 24, 205–53
(1971) *English Complex Sentences*, Amsterdam

JACOBS, R. A. and ROSENBAUM, P. S. (1970) (edd) *Readings in English Transformational Grammar*, Waltham, Mass

JACOBSON, S. (1964) *Adverbial Positions in English*, Stockholm

JACOBSSON, B. (1970) 'English Pronouns and Feature Analysis', *Moderna Språk* 64, 346–59

JESPERSEN, O. (1909–49) *A Modern English Grammar on Historical Principles* I–VII, London and Copenhagen

KARLSEN, R. (1959) *Studies in the Connection of Clauses in Current English: Zero Ellipsis and Explicit Forms*, Bergen

KLIMA, E. S. (1964) 'Negation in English', in *The Structure of Language: Readings in the Philosophy of Language*, edd J. A. Fodor and J. J. Katz, Englewood Cliffs, NJ, 246–323

KRUISINGA, E. (1931–32) *A Handbook of Present-Day English*, Groningen

LAKOFF, R. (1971) 'If's, and's and but's about Conjunction', in Fillmore and Langendoen (1971)

LEECH, G. N. (1969a) *Towards a Semantic Description of English*, London
(1969b) *A Linguistic Guide to English Poetry*, London
(1971) *Meaning and the English Verb*, London

LEES, R. B. (1960a) *The Grammar of English Nominalizations*, Indiana University Research Center in Anthropology, Folklore and Linguistics 12, Bloomington, Indiana
(1960b) 'A Multiply Ambiguous Adjectival Construction in English', *Language* 36, 207–21

LYONS, J. (1968) *Introduction to Theoretical Linguistics*, Cambridge
(1977) *Semantics*, Cambridge

MACHÁČEK, J. (1965) *Complementation of the English Verb by the Accusative-with-Infinitive and the Content Clause*, Prague

MALONE, J. H. (1967) 'A Transformational Re-examination of English Questions', *Language* 43, 686–702

MARCHAND, H. (1969) *The Categories and Types of Present-Day English Word-Formation*, 2nd edn. Munich

MCDAVID, R. I. Jr (1963) (ed) *The American Language by H. L. Mencken*, New York

PALMER, F. R. (1974) *The English Verb*, London

PIKE, K. L. (1945) *The Intonation of American English*, Ann Arbor

POLDAUF, I. (1972) 'Factive, Implicative, Evaluative Predicates', *Philologica Pragensia* 15, 65–92

POUTSMA, H. (1926–29) *A Grammar of Late Modern English*, Groningen

QUIRK, R. (1968) *Essays on the English Language: Medieval and Modern*, London

(1972) *The English Language and Images of Matter*, London

QUIRK, R., GREENBAUM, S., LEECH, G., and SVARTVIK, J. (1972) *A Grammar of Contemporary English*, London and New York

REIBEL, D. A. and SCHANE, S. A. (1969) (edd) *Modern Studies in English*, Englewood Cliffs, NJ

ROBBINS, B. L. (1968) *The Definite Article in English Transformations*, The Hague

ROSENBAUM, P. S. (1967) *The Grammar of English Predicate Complement Constructions*, Cambridge, Mass

SCHEURWEGHS, G. (1963–68) *Analytical Bibliography of Writings on Modern English Morphology and Syntax, 1877–1960*, Louvain

SCHOPF, A. (1969) *Untersuchungen zur Wechselbeziehung zwischen Grammatik und Lexik im Englischen*, Berlin

SØRENSEN, H. S. (1958) *Word-Classes in Modern English with Special Reference to Proper Names, with an Introductory Theory of Grammar, Meaning and Reference*, Copenhagen

STEIN, G. (1973) *English Word-Formation over Two Centuries*, Tübingen

STOCKWELL, R. P., SCHACHTER, P., and PARTEE, B. H. (1973) *The Major Syntactic Structures of English*, New York

SVARTVIK, J. (1966) *On Voice in the English Verb*, The Hague

THORNE, J. P. (1969) 'English Imperative Sentences', *Journal of Linguistics* 5, 205–14

TURNER, G. W. (1973) *Stylistics*, Harmondsworth

VAN EK, J. A. (1966) *Four Complementary Structures of Predication in Contemporary British English*, Groningen

VENDLER, Z. (1968) *Adjectives and Nominalizations*, The Hague

INDEX